IDEOLOGY and
the IMAGE

IDEOLOGY and the IMAGE

Social Representation in the Cinema and Other Media

BILL NICHOLS

INDIANA UNIVERSITY PRESS
BLOOMINGTON

Dedicated to my mother,
Nellie Mae (Register) Nichols

Library of Congress Cataloging in Publication Data

Nichols, Bill.
Ideology and the image.

Includes bibliographical references and index.
1.Moving-picture plays—Criticism and interpretation. 2.Moving-pictures—Psychological
aspects. I.Title.
PN1995.N48   791.43′01′41   80–7684
ISBN 0–253–18287–5
ISBN 0–253–20256–6 (pbk.)   3 4 5 85 84

Contents

Contents

Preface

Contradictions reveal, among other things, the passing of time. We change our minds. Our interests shift. Old assumptions are carried over to new situations; often they are no longer appropriate, and yet their incongruity may not be apparent. A sense of unity is more important to us than an absolutely rigorous logic, and a sense of unity with our own past seems of particular importance. We want our lives and thoughts to make sense, to add up; yet vexing but inescapable contradictions penetrate the very heart of this devoutly wished-for unity like marbling through a stone.

Such is no doubt the case here, as in most books, and all myth. I have eliminated those inconsistencies and contradictions apparent to me, but I have no doubt that others persist, cloaked beneath assumptions too obvious, too automatic for me to see.

Some may be due to logical inconsistency and are the most easily corrected—once seen: but they are not always easy to spot. Others are due to basic assumptions and their gradual shifting through time and are much harder to correct, requiring a vigorous ironing out of perceptual categories and evaluative priorities onto a single Procrustean bed of logic. My suspicion is that we are only capable of such rigor in narrow domains and for limited periods of time. Scholarship attempts to isolate such domains and to capitalize upon discrete bursts of rigorously logical thought. Yet even here biases, assumptions, and the attendant rationalizations that work to resolve, or appear to resolve, contradiction crop up, inevitably. They show themselves wherever we exhibit purposeful or goal-seeking behavior. Such behavior requires premises, semi-conscious or unconscious assumptions or codes, and these premises do not correspond to a fixed goal and clear-cut rules out there but to a process that relies upon approximation far more than certainty. Our purposes, like the goal-seeking activity of other organisms, are not tied once-and-for-all to the stake of some Absolute Knowledge or Goal. Purpose is constant but not its ends. Goals change. Determinations of class, sex, race—social and personal history—enter in, and alter with time. We want to see things add up. We want our way of seeing and acting to be clear, clean, and whole. But it seldom is. Undertows and shifting tides of purpose and cross-purpose create rhythms of their own.

The material brought together here does not add up perfectly— partly, no doubt, because of the lack of absolute rigor, partly because of the presence of more than one purpose. This book grew through time: the chapters on *Blonde Venus* and on still images took shape around lectures given in 1975–76; the chapters on perception and on *The Birds* and most of the chapter on narrative were written in 1976– 77; the chapter on Frederick Wiseman, the introduction, the conclusion, Appendixes A and B, and the current, revised version of the chapter on documentary, in 1977–78; and the chapter on ethnographic film and the final part of the narrative chapter, on paradox, in 1979. At all these times what remained foremost in my mind was what the patterns I found in films and other images had to do with the rest of life. What does a society make of images—especially in relation to its need to reproduce the existing relations of production? Why do certain patterns in the selection and arrangement of images afford pleasure? Is that pleasure innocent or does it (and all the questions of aesthetics raised thereby) bear some necessary, but variable, relation to ideology? I want to understand the relation between the cinema and other images and the exploitation at the heart of our economic system. I want to comprehend how our consent to this exploitation is elicited, how images are used to mask or attenuate the experience of oppression in all its forms. And I want to do these things so that we might better continue a prolonged struggle to change this system and the exploitation it requires in order to persist. No doubt it will, if left alone, eventually destroy itself (by destroying its environment, all it defines as "other"), but in doing so it may well destroy most of us as well. Active, continual struggle remains as essential today as it was a century or more ago.

Within this context, there are several things this book does not attempt. Except in passing it does not examine the use of images in relation to direct mobilization around specific issues. To a very large degree it does not attempt to situate the production and circulation of images within a precise historical moment or to spell out those mediations between image production as an aspect of culture and its times. The former is something I have considered previously in relation to the Left film-making group, Newsreel. The latter is something I hope to explore at another time. What receives the greatest consideration here is the relation of images to aesthetics and ideology at a fairly global level. What gives this area of consideration more concrete focus is the attempt to isolate specific strategies (or signifying practices) at work in the fabrication of images and the aesthetic and ideological implications they bear. This focus also tends to center on narrative and documentary film. It clearly profits from a long tradition of Marxist cultural criticism but also looks to work in structuralism, semiology, psychoanalysis, communications theory, the psychology of perception, and the philosophy of science in order to both consolidate and advance debate about the relations between art, broadly put, and ideology.

What has shifted through time is the exact nature of this focus. The earliest material, especially the chapter on *Blonde Venus*, sought to extend the concern for centrality of visual style which I first defended in the article, "Style, Grammar, and the Movies" (*Film Quarterly* 28, 3 [Spring 1975], reprinted in *Movies and Methods*). The chapter on perception sought to understand how ideology takes root in the same soil as our visual perception of the world around us, where style matters less than habit or code, our way of seeing and its possible linkage with the realms of imaginary and symbolic relationships. The chapters on documentary and Frederick Wiseman's films sought to inaugurate a theory of the expository film and to consider its affiliations with narrative. Again, style seemed of subordinate importance to questions of structure. The chapters on narrative and *The Birds* continued this exploration in terms of narrative structure and narrative work—those procedures leading to the fabrication of a "finished" film that bear analogy to Freud's concept of dream-work. Finally, the last section, on paradox, in the narrative chapter and the chapter on ethnographic film take up the question of affect, or the position we occupy as viewers; these parts of the book acknowledge psychoanalytic concepts, but attempt to account for affect and position primarily in terms of communication theory (logical typing, contradiction, and paradox). Naturally, I believe these different concerns are aspects of a single problem which can be broadly put as the relations between images, on the one hand, and aesthetics and ideology, on the other. The resolution of paradox, for example, appears to rely frequently on the procedures of narrative-work, and these procedures can often be read by attending to structure and style. I have no illusion, though, that the concepts advanced here offer any definitive solution, not only because of the kinds of internal contradiction I suspect exist, but also because such a thing as a "solution" to the nature of social relations is an impossibility. At best, we offer explanations. And explanations are always based on shifting foundation of purpose in such a way that their adequacy cannot be measured against a master answer key but only in relation to the purposes informing them. I hope, in those terms, that this study may make some modest contribution to the continuing struggle to change our lives and those systems of social relationship that work to alienate and exploit us.

* * *

I owe large debts of gratitude to a number of individuals and institutions who helped make this work possible. Maaret Koskinen has provided absolutely invaluable aid as my research assistant for the past year, attending to innumerable details and offering salient criticism of the work as a whole during its evolution. Sophie Bissonnette filled a similar role in 1976–77. Between them, they have helped me avoid a great many errors and have made it possible to organize the book in its present form—around the use of numerous photographic reproductions. Without their help this strategy would have presented insurmountable obstacles in terms of the time and energy required for its execution. Seaton MacLean, Judy Krupansky, Blaine Allan, Peter Steven, and Jayne Loader also made valuable contributions to this strategy which I gratefully acknowledge.

I must also thank Jim Kitses for encouraging me to first explore some of these ideas in a series of departmental seminars in 1975–76; I also wish to thank my other colleagues—Nicholas Kendall, Joyce Nelson, Peter Baxter, and Peter Morris—for the support, stimulation, and insights they have provided. Working at Queen's University has been a continuing pleasure largely because of the congenial, spirited qualities of these colleagues. Joyce Nelson, Nick Kendall, and Peter Baxter also made a vital contribution by successively co-teaching with me our first-year course, Introduction to Film Form, where many of the ideas expressed here first took shape. The many students who have taken this first-year course also have my gratitude for their patience with my somewhat obscure sense of pattern and for the brilliant work they have sometimes done almost despite my limitations and in response to what they and I, in rare moments, see as the figure in the carpet, the perspective that imposes meaning where it had not existed before. From their responses to what I have done, I have learned a great deal. Teaching is not always recognized as the two-way process it is. Those I have taught have also taught me, even if they do not know it, and for that vital act, I am thankful.

Many individuals have also helped me develop these ideas in their capacity as tutors for this course; and among them, Pat Douglas-Murray, Robin Lee, Chris Copp, Leslie Anderson, Chris Whynot, Sophie Bissonnette, Mike MacMillan, Seaton MacLean, Jan Platt, Robin Russell, and Maaret Koskinen deserve far more thanks than I can specify here for the comments, support, and, not least of all, the enthusiasm they brought to this course and its goals. Without them, shaping thoughts that began with this course into publishable form would have been a very lonely project indeed.

Additional support and insight came from the students in my fourth-year Film Theory seminar and a fourth-year seminar in Ethnographic Film in 1979. Leslie Anderson, Mike Callich, and Chris Copp, in particular, introduced thoughts into the ethnographic seminar that I have further elaborated here.

Janey Place, at U.C. Santa Cruz, and Bob Rosen, at the UCLA Film Archive, provided much-needed assistance in the task of making frame enlargements for *Blonde Venus*. This is the only film for which I had access to a 35 mm print, and the combination of Janey Place's frame-copying equipment and Bob Rosen's administrative assistance have produced results I can only wish were possible in the other chapters, too. Chick Callenbach at the University of California Press has offered continual encouragement over the years, in the form of constructive criticism regarding this manuscript as well as in the exercise of his editorial skills at *Film Quarterly*. Gerald O'Grady, James Blue, and Brian Henderson arranged for a talk at the Center for Media Studies at SUNY-Buffalo which was of great value in the development of the chapter on ethnographic film; I also benefited greatly from informal discussions with Bill Rothman at Harvard University on this topic of the ethnographic film. To them I offer my sincerest thanks.

Finally, Dr. Susan J. Lederman at Queen's University helped introduce me to some of the current literature in the psychology of perception, and subsequently she and I together wrote what appears here as Appendix A, a discussion of the perception of apparent notion in film. She also oversaw the development of a device to demonstrate visual flicker and the phi phenomenon. I have successfully used this device in my introductory course several times, and I owe her my deepest thanks for the contribution she has made to my understanding of visual perception and its implications for film criticism.

The Advisory Research Council of Queen's University provided financial assistance for exploratory work in the production of frame enlargements, and the Social Sciences and Humanities Research Council of Canada provided a substantial research grant, which allowed this work to be carried to completion.

My appreciation also goes to Helen Phelan, for typing several drafts of the manuscript, and to Jill Spettigue, who has served as administrative assistant at the Department of Film Studies during the time this book evolved and who, as much as anyone, created a congenial, supportive climate in which to work. For their contribution to a climate conducive to one's best efforts in teaching and research I must also thank the Dean and Associate Dean of my Faculty, Duncan G. Sinclair and W.C. Lougheed.

Earlier versions of some of the material here have been published previously: chapter 5 as "An Analysis of Visual Style in *The Birds*," *Film Reader* No. 4 (1979); chapter 6 as "Documentary Theory and Practice," *Screen* 17, 4 (Winter 1976–77); chapter 7 as "Frederick Wiseman's Documentaries: Theory and Structure," *Film Quarterly* 31, 3 (Spring 1978); a small portion of chapter 8 as a review of *The Hunters* in *American Anthropologist* 82, 1 (March 1980); and Appendix A as a paper in *The Cinematic Apparatus* (London: Macmillan), an anthology, edited by Teresa de Lauretis and Stephen Heath, of papers presented at a conference of the same name at the Center for Twentieth Century Studies, University of Wisconsin-Milwaukee, February 1978.

The frame enlargements from films printed here have been made from film prints by means of a Duplikin II copier attached to a Pentax Spotmatic (except for the *Blonde Venus* stills, as previously noted). The prints for *The Birds* derive from color transparencies made for lecture purposes. In this and in other cases the quality is less than optimal, due to improper choices of film stock or to the condition of the print copied. In many cases the frame enlargements were redone several times and in several instances they were printed on two or three different occasions in an attempt to achieve optimal quality, but, finally, constraints of time and budget required compromise. The entire process of making frame enlargements in support of specific critical analyses is enormously time-consuming and, despite the compromises, I am pleased simply to have succeeded in venturing as far as I have into this still underdeveloped means of communicating a critical analysis of film.

Throughout the book I have attempted to use he/she or him/her rather than allow the masculine pronoun to "speak for" both sexes. In a few instances the resulting construction proved highly awkward, and I reverted to the masculine form only. I hope the time will come when it will be as natural to rely on the female pronoun as the one to represent us all.

Kingston, Ontario
January 1980

Acknowledgments

Illustrations are reprinted by permission of the following sources:

Allied Artists Picture Corp. for still from *Gun Crazy* (2.15b). Copyright ©
Allied Artists Picture Corp.

American Psychological Association for subjective contour patterns (1.3)
from *Psychological Review* 79 (1972). Copyright © American Psychological
Association.

Association pour la diffusion des arts graphiques et plastiques for reproduction of Magritte paintings: *L'usage de la parole* (1.20, 2.2), *La condition
humaine* (2.1), *Les promenades d'Euclide* (1.13), *Le soir qui tombe* (2.5).
Copyright © A.D.A.G.P.

The British Psychological Society for the impossible triangle (1.8) from the
British Journal of Psychology 49 (1958). Copyright © British Psychological
Society.

Deutsche Fotothek Dresden for "Svet Georgij Pobedonisica" (St. George,
the Bringer of Victory) (2.4), from Konrad Onasch, *Icons*. Copyright ©
Deutsche Fotothek Dresden.

Escher Foundation for reproduction of M.C. Escher's *Day and Night* (1.4)
and *Belvedere* (1.5). Copyright © Escher Foundation—Haags Gemeente-
museum—The Hague.

Film Study Center, Harvard University for reproduction of frames from *The
Nuer* (8.1–47). Copyright © Film Study Center.

W.H. Freeman and Co. for illustration 1.9, from J.B. Deregowski, "Pictorial
Perception and Culture," *Scientific American*, November 1972, pp. 82–88.
Copyright © 1972 by Scientific American, Inc. All rights reserved.

Harvard University Press for Thematic Apperception Test illustration (2.10).
Copyright © 1943 by the President and Fellows of Harvard College;
copyright © 1971 by Henry A. Murray.

The Institute for Intercultural Studies, Inc., for stills (8.48–8.55) from *First
Days in the Life of a New Guinea Baby* and *Childhood Rivalry in Bali and
New Guinea*, photographed by Gregory Bateson, distributed by New York
University Film Library. Copyright © The Institute for Intercultural Studies,
Inc.

Ligne française de l'enseignement et de l'education permanente for the rum ad (2.17) and the illustration of Lenin (1.24–28).

The Metropolitan Museum of Art, Fletcher Fund, 1929, for Suzuki Harunobu's *Girl with Lantern on a Balcony at Night*. All rights reserved. The Metropolitan Museum of Art.

Museo del Prado for Velasquez's *Las Meninas (The Maids of Honor)*. Copyright © Museo del Prado, Madrid. All rights reserved.

The National Gallery for Van Eyck's *Wedding Portrait of Giovanni Arnolfini* (2.6). Reproduced by courtesy of the Trustees, The National Gallery, London. Copyright © The National Gallery.

Oslo Kommunes Kunstsamlinger, Munch-Museet, for Edvard Munch's *The Scream* (1.15). Copyright © Oslo Kommunes Kunstsamlinger.

Prentice-Hall, Inc., for the moiré pattern "Disturbance of Security" (p. 43) from Durelli, Parks, *Moire Analysis of Strain*. Copyright © 1970. Reprinted by permission of Prentice-Hall, Inc., Englewood Cliffs, New Jersey.

The Psychonomic Society, Inc., and W. Richards for "The Corridor Illusion" (1.10) from W. Richards and J.F. Miller, Jr., "The Corridor Illusion," *Perception and Psychophysics* 9 (1971). Copyright © The Psychonomic Society, 1971.

San Diego Museum of Art for Arthur Dove's *Formation I* (2.3). Reproduced by permission of the Curator of Painting. All rights reserved.

The Tate Gallery, London, for Picasso's *Nude* (1910) (2.9). Copyright © S.P.A.D.E.M., London. All rights reserved.

Universal Pictures. All frame enlargements from the motion pictures *Blonde Venus, The Birds, All that Heaven Allows*, and *Touch of Evil* made available through the courtesy of Universal Pictures. Copyright © Universal Pictures.

The Viking Press for permission to quote 3 lines from Walt Whitman's "Song of Myself," printed in *Leaves of Grass*, Viking Press, 1959. Copyright © The Viking Press, 1959. All rights reserved.

John Wiley and Sons, Inc., for the Critical Fusion Frequency graph in Appendix A (p. 295), modified from Richard H. Schiffman's *Sensation and Perception: An Integrated Approach*.

Zipporah Films, Inc. All frame enlargements from *Hospital* (chapter 7) made available through the courtesy of Zipporah Films, Inc. Copyright © Zipporah Films, Inc.

"I quite agree with you," said the Duchess; "and the moral of that is—'Be what you would seem to be'—or, if you'd like it put more simply—'Never imagine yourself not to be otherwise than what it might appear to others that what you were or might have been was not otherwise than what you had been would have appeared to them to be otherwise.'"

"I think I should understand that better," Alice said very politely, "if I had it written down: but I can't quite follow it as you say it."

—LEWIS CARROLL

Do I contradict myself?
Very well then. . . . I contradict myself;
I am large. . . . I contain multitudes.

—WALT WHITMAN

Adam Smith's contradictions are of significance because they contain problems which it is true he does not resolve, but which he reveals by contradicting himself.

—KARL MARX

IDEOLOGY and
the IMAGE

Introduction:
Picking Up the Trail

IMAGES SURROUND US. There are those we fabricate ourselves, perceptually; there are those fabricated for us, artistically or commercially. Images are things that represent (re-present) something else. *Represent:* to stand for or in place of something else, to bring clearly before the mind (OED). To represent with images is to symbolize, and symbolization is basic to intercommunication. By means of symbols we can enter into processes of communication and exchange with one another. Symbols (we will refer primarily to images or signs in this study) represent us in these processes. They act as delegates, standing for, or in place of, that to which we refer. They even stand for us; symbols are our own representatives: You and I share "I" in direct verbal encounter; in person or in a photograph my body-image represents me for others, even represents me to myself.

Ideology arises in association with processes of communication and exchange. Ideology involves the reproduction of the existing relations of production (those activities by which a society guarantees its own survival). Ideology operates as a constraint, limiting us to certain places or positions within these processes of communication and exchange. Ideology is how the existing ensemble of social relations represents itself to individuals; it is the image a society gives of itself in order to perpetuate itself. These representations serve to constrain us (necessarily); they establish fixed places for us to occupy that work to guarantee coherent social actions over time. Ideology uses the fabrication of images and the processes of representation to persuade us that how things are is how they ought to be and that the place provided for us is the place we ought to have.

Such a definition stresses the interconnection of base and superstructure or of social existence and consciousness. If we abstract ideology into a system of beliefs or ideas justifying a dominant class's position, we may begin to assume that social existence or

1

the economic base lacks an ideational dimension, that it is devoid of meaning or value and therefore "produces" them as a separate realm of consciousness or superstructure in order to justify itself. When we then attempt to link the one realm to the other, we find we are connecting phantoms, idealist reifications of an ongoing, systemic process. Communication and exchange are always signifying acts and part of what they signify or represent is our own place within the processes of communication and exchange, be they base or superstructure. Language, especially when it is conceived of semiotically as including all forms of communication based upon signs, whether they are words, clothes, gestures, or moving pictures, belongs to neither base nor superstructure but is a necessary element of all material social practice. Language organizes differences into information that, as coded process, conveys meaning. All human activity that involves communication and exchange, whether it is the economic production of an automobile or the artistic production of a painting, produces meaning. The elements of this production that represent the needs of the dominant class order are ideological elements.

We need to be able to identify these ideological elements, to discover the aspects of representation that embody them, to understand the place set out for us within such processes. One crucial aspect of this place is that it proposes a way of seeing invested with meanings that naturalize themselves as timeless, objective, obvious. What remains hidden is the process of representation itself, the investment of meanings as a material social process.

Ideology appears to produce not itself, but the world. It proposes obviousnesses, a sense of "the way things are," within which our sense of place and self emerges as an equally self-evident proposition.

In those terms ideology is clearly not coercive, nor is it reducible to specific, articulated systems of belief (populist or racist ideology, for example). Such systems may constitute specific ideologies, but they rest upon a more general process of representation through which individuals are recruited into a social order. This general process must be desired by those it recruits: no society could long endure if it had to constantly force its members, from cradle to grave, to assume their places within its relations of communication and exchange. (Who, for example, could force those who force others to assume those places to assume their place?) The places or positions represented and the sense of self represented by the dominant social order must appear desirable; we must want to be recognized in that place, in that image we take to be our-selves.

In our society, this recognition exacts a toll. We assume certain positions prepared for us and assume that they are natural and obvi-

IDEOLOGY AND THE IMAGE

ous despite their fabrication, supported in the certainty of our belief by the relatively fixed habits and codes that underpin our consciousness. We do not see things for what they are. But the most damaging part of this is not the mistaken assumptions per se, but rather the means by which value is extracted from the overall process of communication and exchange, from the relations of production specifically. Considered in terms of economics, this value is the surplus-value extracted from labor-power in a system that allows for the accumulation of capital in the hands of a few. Considered more generally, this value involves that range of possibilities extending beyond the constraints ideology works to uphold. It is the potential value of all those underrepresented selves we might otherwise become.

Later we will consider ideology in terms of an imaginary (as opposed to symbolic) relationship to the material processes of communication and exchange. *Imaginary* here does not mean unreal, existing only in the imagination, but rather pertains to views, images, fictions, or representations that contribute to our sense of who we are and to our everyday engagement with the world around us. These images are the signs of social representation, the markers or bearers of ideology; we will examine at length the manifestations of ideology in the cinema and, briefly, its manifestations in other visual media. We will want to know how various institutions of representation like the cinema relate to the needs of a dominant class, how we can counter or expose the ideological dimension that limits human possibility according to the needs of a dominant class order, how it becomes possible to represent and recognize ourselves within those processes of communication and exchange that inevitably bear an ideological dimension and yet are not exhausted by that dimension. I take it as a given that we are more than what ideology makes of us. It is that realm at the horizon of ideology that makes wisdom and change possible; and if our goal is to change the world, access to that realm—on the borders of the obvious, the natural, the self-evident—becomes essential. I also take it as given that the only ultimate criterion of evaluation for change is whether a given change is likely to lead to the long-range survival of the system, the ecosystem, of which we as specimens and as a species are a part, and which is being destroyed by the present relations of dominance and exploitation. Wisdom means finding our collective way toward such survival. Criticism will be the act of distinguishing signs that may help guide us from those that circumscribe us within ideology. It will be directed mostly toward the cinema as a major institution of social representation but will also touch on a number of other, related areas including perception and representation in still images.

Tracking all the signs of the cinema requires an expeditionary force of some size if thoroughness is the primary goal. The goal of this book is to scout the territory. The information we bring back will, it is hoped, fill in some of the blanks on our present maps and enable future expeditions to set forth better equipped. That we will ever have an exhaustive map for this terrain remains extremely unlikely—it may well prove impossible. For now beginnings, exploratory forays, are as much as we can hope for.

The signs we seek to track are multiple, the result of several different kinds of activity. There are first the literal signs of the cinema—"Bijou," "Roxy," "Double Feature Tonight," "Winner of 4 Academy Awards," "A Different Kind of Jaws," and so on. These signs announce how the cinema as institution (or apparatus) for the production and consumption of moving images represents itself. They send us on a trail overgrown with the illusion that the cinema simply provides us with what we want. What these signs never announce is what they are most fundamentally—the signifiers of ideology, rhetorical practices in the art of courtship with which the cinematic institution merchandises "product." Tracking down the history and function of these signs is no small task, but it will have to await the formation of a more extensively equipped expedition that the present one.

Second, there are the signs of the cinema left by other institutions or apparatuses. Signs of things to come. Photography has earned considerable attention for this reason, as have the various devices (the thaumotrope, phenakistiscope, stroboscope, or zoetrope) that simulated movement before the invention of the motion picture projector. These signs are tracked here—not to discover the "origins" of the cinema but to gauge the degree of overlap between the use of certain signs in film and their use elsewhere. Considerations of lighting, composition, color, and linear perspective, for example, are common to many forms of visual representation, with a history going back thousands of years before their usage in the cinema. These signs are closely linked to the codes governing human perception itself, and so this foray takes us through some of the workings of visual perception onto the fields of photography, painting, advertising, and photojournalism.

Finally, there are the signs of the cinema proper, those signs that together make up the codes we find in film. Tracking their spoor will lead us to cinematic and extracinematic codes (montage and narrative, for example) and how they merge into the distinctive sign systems of film texts. This is the heart of the country: here we hope to cut some well-marked trails through the undergrowth of more than eighty years of film production.

4

This work of this expedition does not end with the compilation of some survey maps, however. It is also after somewhat bigger game, namely, the ways in which the signs of the cinema set traps for the unwary. At the moment when we believe we are safely stalking signs, we may suddenly discover that we ourselves are being stalked, our tracks leading in a circle toward an imaginary and reciprocal capture by what we seek, by the very things we desire (to have or know). The big game is ideology and what it does to us. Some define ideology as "views that serve to rationalize the vested interests of some group."[1] These views are usually thought of as arguments or stated beliefs, but they may also be, literally, views. After all, seeing is believing, and how we see ourselves and the world around us is often how we believe ourselves and the world to be. Images generally present views; films present particular kinds of views. These views are ideological, and how we see them has everything to do with how we see ourselves, what we take our-selves to be, and what we want our-selves to become. The projects we set for ourselves are often projections of the views we receive. If these views secure the interests of groups from which we are excluded, then our investments in our "own" projects are investments in servitude. The cinema, like other art forms and the institutions of the superstructure generally, is an arena for ideological contestation. The dominant ideology, representing the ideas of the dominant class in order to perpetuate its dominance through the psychic and material investments we are led to make as signs of acquiescence, has the upper hand. Our expedition will seek to discover how it keeps that advantage, what investments it promotes that pay dividends back to itself as well as to the investor. By learning to spot the trace of ideology in the signs of the cinema we may better learn how to outflank it or at least expose it when it attempts to cover its trail with "natural" signs like illusionism or realism—appearances that seem to say "this is the way it really is."

Learning to see signs where there appears to be only natural and obvious meaning is difficult. We need tools to help us do so. There are several: narratology, semiotics, structuralism, psychoanalysis, formalism—plus the motivating force of Marxism to use these tools to safeguard ourselves and our environment from exploitation by the few. I have defined these approaches and put together examples of their use in *Movies and Methods*. Here I should like to stress the importance of a formal aspect common to all these methods. They all operate on films as texts, as sites of signifying activity. They all regard texts as systems of signs. In some instances these approaches are more concerned with *how* texts signify than with *what* they signify or with the even more remote question of *how well* they signify. Indeed it seems reasonable to presume that an aesthetics of film must remain provisional at best until we have come to understand more fully how films signify at all. It is the formal aspect of these methods that has contributed heavily to such an understanding in the last ten years.

Yet the question of *how* is not purely formal. Signifying practices are social practices and the value and meaning they hold varies with time and place. When a discrete unit of signification like a text enters into exchange, as with an audience, its value comes to it from outside, from its function within a system founded upon a higher level of organization. But this value must attach to something. Generally it attaches to the systems of signs, the codes and their interrelationship, that characterize the text. Hence as a strategic priority a formal emphasis seems to be an appropriate first step. We must, however, bear in mind the need eventually to address a larger context. As a first *and* last step, formal analyses lead to a normative idealism. Brecht put it succinctly: "*Formally he is right.* That means that actually he is not right. . . ."[2]

As a matter of strategic priority this means that the present study will tend to underemphasize certain aspects of context. It takes time and space to do anything, and there is simply not enough to do everything. Placing signs in an historical context or discussing them in national, institutional, or economic terms will seldom be done in this book. Fortunately, a number of other studies have contributed to our understanding of film in those terms, but few book-length studies yet exist that emphasize a semiotic-Marxist approach. (I will sometimes use semiotics as an umbrella term for narratology, structuralism, psychoanalysis, and linguistics, inasmuch as they all are concerned with the processes of signification.)

Finally, the rigor provided by the formal component of the various methods used here adresses itself to those codes least specific to the cinema. Again it is a matter of priorities. Other writers, perhaps Christian Metz most notably,[3] have attempted to determine what is most specific to the cinema. This is obviously an essential activity. The very success it achieves in marking off the cinema from related semiotic activities, however, may be inversely proportional to the attention it gives principles supporting communication in a range of allied media. I take the opposite tack here, on the assumption that our understanding of cinematic communication may be facilitated if the points of contact between cinema and related fields are used to gain entry to the cinematic as such. It can even be argued that the most important codes in cinema are often those least specific to the medium:

If the analysis takes into account not just the primary object of semiology (the study of cinematic language), but its secondary object as well (the study of films as systems), it is possible to argue that the specific codes are not necessarily the most important codes of a film system. The non-specific codes also play a role in the establishment of that system, and the question then is whether this role is not perhaps always the primary one.[4]

Whether always primary or not, knowing how to read the nonspecific codes obviously yields carry-over value. Indeed it is hard to imagine that anything definitive can be said about how cinematic codes operate on their own until we have an adequate understanding of how they fit within a larger frame of reference and interact with the nonspecific codes that figure into the filmic text. Since the dominant ideology of a period attempts to dominate everywhere, it is also likely that the nonspecific codes will be very significant bearers of ideology. By emphasizing the less specific codes, we will be able to explore some of the major ideological implications of the cinema as well as take advantage of our previous acquaintance with these codes in other signifying systems.

One consequence of this choice is that experimental film receives less consideration here than narrative and documentary film. Experimental film, as a predominantly poetic mode, depends heavily upon the specific cinematic codes. Many films of this type in fact elevate such codes to pride of place; their themes become focus, the moving film strip, flicker, the zoom or tracking shot, and so on. Work of this kind is an invaluable aid in understanding how film signifies; it is also clearly valuable in its own right as a kind of liberating renewal of possibilities foreclosed by dominant or conventional procedures. It is this very quality, however, that marks off the experimental film as more completely idiosyncratic than those films that rely heavily upon narrative or expository codes. The latter films not only rely upon nonspecific codes of narrative or exposition but also tend to remain more obediently within the parameters of illusionism or realism, thus linking them with an extensive range of texts in other media. Once again, as a matter of priority, narrative and documentary receive the bulk of the attention here. This carries no implication about the ultimate status or significance of the experimental film but rather testifies to the need for compatibility between the object of study and critical approach.

The signs of the cinema are manifold. We will need all the methodological help we can muster in tracking them. Only a few of the trails these signs have left can be pursued here. Other trackers, using different mixes of methodologies, have already followed some of the others. Yet others remain to be pursued or perhaps even discovered. The pleasure of stepping into the brisk, clean air of critical inquiry makes this work exhilarating. The possibility that we will bring back knowledge of value to how we live, and control, our lives makes the journey not only exhilarating but essential. As long as signs are produced, we will be obliged to make the effort to understand them. This is a matter of nothing less than survival.

1.

Art and the Perceptual Process

Signs of Communication in Film and Reality

Assumptions are a good place to begin: all communication depends on a relationship between communicators. A relationship is a social phenomenon, and since communication affects the relationships it creates or rests upon, communication is not only social but political: it works for or against, within or beyond, any particular organization of social relationships. Even disavowals of political intent are political communications when they occur inside (as they inevitably do) an already political milieu whose persistence is thereby facilitated. Communication is a necessary form of social exchange that invariably interacts with the environment supporting it. This pragmatic concern with how communication affects relationships and the behavior issuing from them will be the central concern of this study.

The cinema is a kind of communication overlapping numerous other categories: art, entertainment, essay, myth, propaganda, and advertising. Defining the precise boundaries and specific properties of the cinema is less important than developing a perspective to account for its effect upon human beings. This perspective is itself explicitly political. Its goal is not understanding for the sake of understanding but understanding as a tool in the struggle to determine our own lives and shape our own society. Its goal is to render possible changes in our ways of seeing that will help unveil the political implications of acts we have either taken for granted or excised from the realm of the "really" political, such as, perhaps, perception itself or our relationship to visual images in general or films in particular. Some statements necessarily remain valid until the situation prompting them alters. Karl Marx's Eleventh Thesis on Feuerbach is such a statement and can be taken as the guiding principle of this study: "The philosophers have only *interpreted* the world, in various ways; the point is to *change* it."

Some further assumptions: Narrative, documentary, and experimental films are particular kinds of communication. As with other kinds of communication—still photographs, architecture, clothing, novels, traffic signals, plays, or food—their intelligibility depends on languages or codes shared by communicators. In film these codes include verbal language (English, French, Chinese . . .) but also many other codes (color, fashion, lighting, editing, spatial proximity [the science of proxemics], and etiquette, for example). The communications themselves are particular realizations of these codes: They are texts. To be understood they must be read, that is, referred to the codes of which they are a particular manifestation. (This referral is not to a place or thing since the codes are abstractions or concepts, constructs to insure intelligibility.)

Communication, always political, is realized in texts that have to be read in relation to the codes organizing them. The principal focus of this study will be searching for and reading the signs of the cinema. It will attempt to develop an apparatus for the prehension of such signs (*prehension* to stress the root meaning in *comprehension:* "seizure, taking hold of, an active process of making things mean"). A beginning will be to consider how the signs of the world around us are perceived. Since the cinema so often seems to reproduce these signs, we may well begin by asking by what means they are com-prehended.

Such a beginning has its justification on two levels. Traditionally film critics and theorists have made much of the relationship of film to reality. The cinema is a strongly representational art: it presents us with recognizable figures or objects whose lifelikeness is sometimes uncanny. Its ability to re-present the surfaces of reality has even been erected into an aesthetic, most notably by André Bazin and Siegfried Kracauer. Likewise, critics often call special attention to styles that depart from representational realism by adopting it as an explicit or implicit standard. For example, Fred Camper, in describing Frank Borzage's visual style writes, "One feels that all things, not only the people, exist only as two-dimensional areas of light and texture."[1] But of course images are always two-dimensional displays of light and texture. By what process do we consider them otherwise, and how can the result of this process be naturalized into an aesthetic? One way of beginning to provide an answer is to consider how things, and people, are perceived in the physical world. We may then ask what correlation exists between this process and the perception of the film.

A second justification for exploring the relationship between film and reality is somewhat more theoretical. If films are texts and texts presuppose codes, we will want to know what the basic characteristics of the codes organizing the signs of the cinema are. Again representation rears its head. Many of the perceptual codes at work in cinema seem to refer us to the conditions of perception at work in everyday reality. This similarity is sometimes described as the mechanical reproduction of reality (by the cinematic apparatus: camera, lens, projector, screen, etc.). But the similarity of a text to reality does not just happen: it involves the work of codes. A photographic image, for example, bears a relationship of resemblance to its referent, the thing photographed. If we call that image a sign, then it must be distinguished from the arbitrary signs of verbal language, which seldom resemble what they refer to. (*Chair* looks in no way like a chair; *love*, though only a word, is already too concrete, too tangible to resemble the quality it refers to.) When a sign resembles what it refers to—as a picture of a chair does a physical chair or a portrait of a couple embracing tenderly does love—the sign is motivated, analogical, or iconic. More specifically, if a sign enjoys an existential bond to its referent such that the referent determines its appearance in some way, the sign is called indexical. This is like the template coding of DNA and RNA. The referent may not produce a facsimile of itself (DNA governs the production of an array of proteins, not just more DNA) but the sign produced will necessarily exhibit a characteristic linkage with the referent. The point-for-point correspondence of light intensity between referent and photographic image testifies to an indexical aspect in the photographic sign, for example. By contrast, the word *chair* is called an unmotivated, arbitrary, or digital sign since it bears no resemblance to the appearance of an actual chair. Hence the apparent act of duplication of mechanical reproduction of everyday reality in the cinema depends upon the work of specific codes characterized by iconic and indexical signs. It is not reality up there on the silver screen but iconic signs that re-present reality.

The utilization of iconic representation in film would justify by itself examining how our perception of film and reality correspond. Clearly the process of recognizing a face in a film must bear some resemblance to the process of recognizing a living face. But there is an even more precise resemblance than the simple fact that film utilizes codes characterized by iconic signs based, as they are, on referents in the physical world. Our perception of the physical world is also based on codes involving iconic signs. The world does not enter our mind nor does it deposit a picture of itself there spontaneously. Perception depends on coding the world into iconic signs that can re-present it within our mind. The force of the apparent identity is enormous, however. We think that it is the world itself we see in our "mind's eye," rather than a coded picture of it, even more certainly than we believe that "real" people and objects populate the silver screen of a movie theater. Hence both cinema and perception itself share a common coding process involving iconic signs. How this process operates in everyday perception therefore makes a logical place to begin.

Everyday Perception of the Physical World

To be comprehended, the physical world must first be mediated and translated. Light waves, like sound waves, mediate between a distal object and a proximal stimulus. (The focus here will be on visual perception although aural perception shares many of the same general characteristics.) The brain provides the translation service, organizing sensory impressions into patterns and then conferring meaning upon various kinds of patterns in order to construct a familiar, recognizable world. In time this world becomes so instantly recognizable that it seems as though it must have been always already meaningful. A useful habit formed by our brains must not be mistaken for an essential attribute of reality. Just as we must learn to read an image, we must learn to read the physical world. Once we have developed this skill (which we do very early in life), it is very easy to mistake it for an automatic or unlearned process, just as we may mistake our particular way of reading, or seeing, for a natural, ahistorical, and noncultural given.

What enters the eye then, and provides material for translation, is not the physical world itself but an array of sensory impressions to which the retina is sensitive. These sensory impressions are variations in light (brightness or intensity, hue, saturation) that correspond to, or establish a correlation with, the physical arrangement of three-dimensional space. Their display upon the retina is in some ways similar to the display of light from a projector or cathode ray tube upon a screen. These impressions are the stuff from which meaning is made but they are not meaningful in and of themselves.

An awareness of this distinction can be achieved with a simple experiment. Gaze blankly at the space in front of you. Avoid "fixing" the space into objects and spaces between objects; instead, try to see it as a continuum of impressions. If the necessary degree of purposeless gazing is achieved, the space will lose its familiar properties. Instead of receding in depth, it will seem to float dimensionless from the bottom to the top of the field of vision. A rectangular book, instead of lying flat on a table, will be a trapezoidal patch of a certain color and texture rising vertically in this flattened field. Some of the differences

IDEOLOGY AND THE IMAGE

between "bracketed perception" and normal perception can be summarized as follows:

Bracketed Perception	Normal Perception
a bounded visual space, oval, approximately 180° laterally, 150° vertically	unbounded visual space
clarity of focus at only one point with a gradient of increasing vagueness toward the margin (clarity of focus corresponds to the space whose light falls upon the fovea)	clarity of focus throughout
parallel lines appear to converge: the lateral sides of a rectangular surface extending away from the viewer appear to converge	parallel lines extend without converging: the sides of a rectangular surface extending away from the viewer remain parallel
if the head is moved, the shapes of objects appear to be deformed	if the head is moved, shapes remain constant
the visual space appears to lack depth	visual space is never wholly depthless
a world of patterns and sensation, of surfaces, edges and gradients,	a world of familiar objects, of signs, signals and symbols,
information	meaning

Normal perception becomes so dominant over the course of time that many people have great difficulty achieving bracketed perception. And yet the qualities of normal perception are not inherent; they are provided by the brain's translation service. This process of organizing sensory impressions into patterns and conferring meaning upon these patterns to which we attend has been studied by psychologists for a considerable time. Gestalt psychology, for example, has enumerated many of the cues or criteria by which impressions are organized. (These criteria appear to remain valid for human beings generally, except for certain cross-cultural variations, especially in responding to two-dimensional, pictorial representations of reality. Gestalt theories of how the brain actually works in order to make use of these criteria, however, have been largely discredited.) Of the various perceptual processes involved, those pertaining to the discrimination

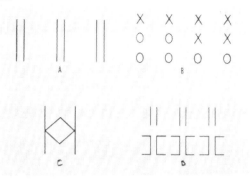

1.1. A: The first pair of lines is considered figure rather than, say, the second and third lines: preference for small regions as figure. B: X's and O's tend to be grouped separately: preference for proximity and similarity. C: A diamond wedged between parallel lines is preferred to two M's, one atop the other: preference for closed contours and small area (the diamond), and good continuation (few breaks or disruptions in the boundaries). D: Lower set of lines are grouped as rectangles or pairs of brackets instead of sets of parallel lines vertically and horizontally: preference for closed contours, symmetrical regions, and good continuation.

of figure/ground relationships and to the perception of depth seem most relevant to a consideration of film.

Certain kinds of sensory impression arrays are more likely to be organized as figures than others (1.1). These figures can be animate or inanimate, but in either case they are distinguished from their surroundings by a boundary. In a sense this can be regarded as an elementary form of digitalization: the carving out of discrete units from an experiential continuum. (The term *digitalization* comes from computer science. Digital computers rely on yes/no, on/off forms of information. Either/or choices of this kind are of vast importance in logic, where the ability to form oppositions like A/not A represents a similar process of digitalization.) These units, or figures, can be regarded as signs of the visual language constituted by this very act of digitalizing.

When movement is involved, preference is given to figures moving in the same direction against a stationary ground or a ground of random movement or general movement in another direction. (This principle is known as "common fate" and has been well exploited by directors acknowledged for their ability to handle crowd scenes— Sergei Eisenstein, Ernst Lubitsch, King Vidor).

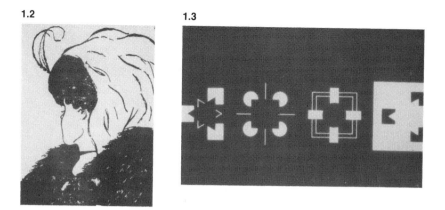

1.2. The drawing presents an ambiguous figure; depending on how the viewer attends to it, either a young woman or a very old woman can be seen. This effect is similar to that of Escher's work (see 1.4 and 1.5).

1.3. The white triangle, the black circle, the black square, and the black triangle (from right to left) are all subjective: their outlines are imaginary. It is easier for the viewer to supply the missing outline, however, than to organize the data without it. In the second example, the "presence" of a black circle allows the viewer to imagine that it is superimposed on two intersecting white bars. Conferring subjective contours conforms with the laws of simplicity.

In general these Gestalt principles, sometimes incorrectly called "laws," favor simplicity—the form of organization that will account for the sensory data most economically. When images are constructed, as they are in the visual arts generally, these principles can be played with in a variety of ways—from striving to make figure/ground discrimination as easy as possible (caricature) to deliberately confounding perception by violating the Gestalt principles (camouflage). This is possible precisely because the principles are not laws: perception is an active process. The figure/ground relationships are a function of the punctuation we provide; the boundary between figure and ground does not belong to either. It belongs to a different level of organization—indeed, it is not *in* reality at all but *in* our perception, our punctuation of it. It therefore remains entirely possible for the visual artist to play with our expectations of where a boundary should emerge, or of which side of a boundary will be figure (1.2–7).

The illustrations from the work of Escher and von Sternberg elaborate another point as well: even when figure and ground are located on the same plane, as in an image, the perceptual process tends to raise the figure or bring it closer to the viewer. The imaginary boundary between figure/ground not only isolates discrete units but pries them away from the surrounding, and connecting surface. Hence the discrimination of figure/ground relationships leads directly

1.4, 1.6   **1.5**

1.4–5. Escher's work confounds figure/ground and depth relationships. In 1.5, the conventions of linear perspective are deliberately manipulated in an unorthodox fashion to create a complex rendition of the "impossible triangle" (see 1.8) just as the relation of figure/ground between bird and earth are subtly inverted from left to right in 1.4 to create a paradoxical kind of pictorial space. These paradoxical displays of space are made possible by the distinction between two-dimensional representations and their three-dimensional counterparts. A representation is both a two-dimensional plane and an allusion to a three-dimensional depth: by inconsistently applying the rules governing the representation of the latter by the former, Escher is able to create an "impossible" kind of space.

1.6. This figure from *Blonde Venus* illustrates the principles of camouflage. The two characters are almost indistinguishable from the surrounding space.

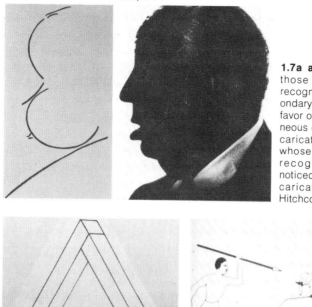

1.7a and b. In caricature only those features necessary for recognition are provided. Secondary features are eliminated in favor of clean lines and homogeneous color. 1.7a is a line-drawn caricature of Alfred Hitchcock whose stylization to facilitate recognition can be readily noticed by comparing it with a caricature-like photograph of Hitchcock's profile, 1.7b.

1.8. It is impossible to follow one side of the triangle around without altering its spatial relationship to the other sides. An ambiguous push/pull effect results that cannot be resolved—at least not in the single place of the representational image.

1.9. This illustration summarizes those monocular depth cues associated with figures—i.e., location relative to the horizon (the elephant is more distant), overlap (the hill behind the antelope is closer than the one below the elephant; the man is nearer than the rise behind him), relative size (if constancy is assumed and the comparative sizes of elephants and antelopes are known, then the elephant can be assumed more distant). When images are used to represent depth cues, it should be remembered that skill must be acquired in learning to read the image itself. This particular illustration is often used to measure such skill among members of cultures with little experience of images by asking them which animal the hunter is preparing to spear.

Art and the Perceptual Process

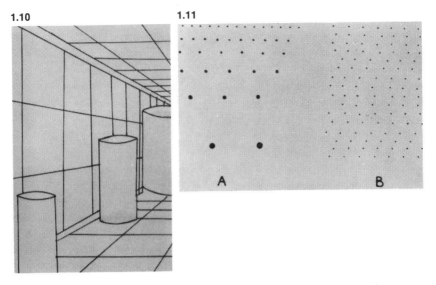

1.10. The cylinders are all exactly equal in size. Since in everyday perception we expect objects of the same size to appear smaller at a distance (size constancy), then depicting them the same size in an illustration will make the apparently more distant cylinders appear larger.

1.11. A texture gradient is an analogical function that usually forms a ground for figures. The gradient itself—the diminution of intervals between recurrent elements of the texture with distance—is a powerful clue to depth. Holding this book upside down will invert the depth perspective in A (from a floor to a ceiling, for example) but not diminish its effect. Film stocks are normally designed to minimize their own grain, allowing the texture gradient of the scene recorded to emerge clearly. Excess grain in the film stock acts like the dots in panel B: they stress the monoplanar nature of the image and obscure the illusion of depth.

to consideration of depth perception and also indicates another variable with which the artist or image-maker can play—the association of figure with greater proximity than ground. (Generally, this relief effect is accentuated by caricature and lessened by camouflage.) See 1.8.

Many cues for depth perception are related to figure/ground perception although there are some cues that are independent of this form of digitalization. Binocular depth cues, for example, are simply a function of the fact that we see with two eyes: the amount of difference in the registration of the same object by each eye decreases in proportion to the distance of the object from the observer. Other cues are monocular since they only require one eye. And since the lens of a camera registers a scene upon a celluloid emulsion in a manner similar to the way the lens of one eye registers light impressions on the

IDEOLOGY AND THE IMAGE

1.12. The converging parallel lines indicate depth by linear perspective. This illustration also depicts the effect of a texture gradient, which yields the impression of depth by relying on the decreasing clarity of those sensory perceptions characterizing the texture of a surface as distance from an observer increases.

1.13. The appearance of horizontal depth to the street versus the limited depth of the tower fixed in vertical space is achieved by an admixture of the cues discussed above plus a final one, illumination generally and its subcategory of aerial perspective (the increasingly bluish quality of light near the horizon).

retina, these monocular depth cues are available to our perception of photographic images as well as of the physical world (1.9). The graphic depiction of a room illustrates linear perspective (1.10). Linear perspective corresponds to bracketed perception (parallel lines appear to converge), but serves as an approximation of normal perception and the appearance of depth. The artistic elaboration of uses of this cue during the Renaissance was a fundamental aspect of the heightened ability of paintings to evoke a unified sense of depth.

In fact, we can say that representational images organized around a single coherent system of linear perspective belong to the distinct subcategory of illusionistic images. Their use of linear perspective conveys the impression or illusion of depth most forcefully; the ability of the camera lens to form iconic images characterized by linear perspective virtually identical to the perspective generated by our own perceptual mechanism places most cinematic images within the realm of illusionism as well. (Maximum illusionism occurs with ''normal'' lenses—about 50 mm in focal length for 35 mm photography; telephoto

Art and the Perceptual Process

19

and wide-angle lenses depart from the conditions of normal perception and introduce apparent distortions, distortions relative to our normal perception of depth, that is.)

Illustrations 1.11–13 refer to depth cues not dependent upon figures as such.

The Perception of the Representational Image

Since we have been using two-dimensional illustrations to represent the depth cues operating in our perception of three-dimensional physical space, it will be useful to summarize the differences between normal perception and the photographic image:

photograph	normal perception (as distinct from bracketed perception)
clarity throughout a limited depth of field, the extent being proportional to the lens angle and f-stop (wide-angle lenses and high f-stops—small apertures—yield the greatest depth of field)	clarity of focus throughout
perspective varies with lens angle (wide-angle lens gives heightened sense of perspective, telephoto the converse)	invariable perspective
depthless, conveying the appearance of depth	never wholly depthless
bounded by physical limitations, a frame	unbounded
parallel lines converge, lateral sides of a rectangular surface converge (These phenomena, however, are taken as cues to depth—linear perspective)	parallel lines extend without converging lateral sides of a rectangular surface extend parallel in depth
An image made up of chemical or physical variations of surfaces, edges and gradients, information taken to be a world of familiar objects or signs	a world of familiar objects, of signs and signals, and meaning

IDEOLOGY AND THE IMAGE

Although the photographic image, strictly speaking, is closer in characteristics to bracketed perception than normal perception, we often perceive images as though they were analogous to normal perception. Depthlessness is converted to depth, converging parallel lines to lines extending in depth and so on. The brain's translation service tends to read these differences as cues to an approximation of normal perception even though we can also readily recognize the differences. In fact most people can recognize the depthless quality of a photograph more easily than they can switch from normal to bracketed perception of the everyday world.

As with figure/ground relationships, depth cues are subject to artistic manipulation. Variations of lens angle and f-stop are familiar avenues for departure from an obedient approximation of normal perception in photography and film. Violations of scale, size, constancy, and color expectations and the introduction of multiple perspectives—all these strategies and many others go to make up an artist's style, his or her distinctive way of seeing and re-presenting the world (1.14–19).

Since images bear an analogous or iconic relationship to their referent (a relationship of resemblance), it is easy to confuse the realms of the image and the physical world by treating the image as a transparent window (especially the photographic image), or by treating the physical world idealistically by assuming that something like its essence has been transferred or reproduced in the image. Many films employing realist styles encourage such a confusion, and yet it is essential to remember that a film is not reality any more than an image is what it re-presents. We may recognize many of the same signs, organize them within the same sign-systems or codes, draw upon the same or similar cues to figure/ground and depth relationships; but the overall matrix or context is decidedly different. The emergence of a sign-system, even an iconic one, forces us to step aside from the immediacy of brute presence. We need to recognize a signifying of presence-through-absence, the adoption of referentiality by communication. We seldom mistake a menu for a meal or a map for a territory; to confuse an image with its referent or a film with reality is to commit precisely this kind of error, an error that many realist narratives and documentaries seem to explicitly invite (1.20).

Further, whereas in the perception of the physical world meaning is conferred in the passage from bracketed perception to normal perception, with an image we are dealing with a source of sensory impressions upon which meaning has already been conferred. That is to say, the image has been organized by another human being—this is obvious to us when the image is a painting but it is also true of a photograph, at least in the choice of subject, lens type, camera posi-

1.14. Configurations like the Necker cube and the vase/profile drawing illustrate the potential ambiguities of perception. Depth is not *in* a picture any more than a boundary belongs to a figure. Both are constructs of the perceiving mind as it tries to com-prehend the image. When there are conflicting cues, as in the Escher drawings, or the impossible triangle, perception may remain inherently ambiguous, putting on display, as it were, our active project of conferring the meanings we usually assume to be already there.

1.15. Munch's expressionism strays from the conventions of a realism which guide the construction of images bearing maximum resemblance to normal, everyday perception (i.e., maximum illusionism). Such images are no less stylized or constructed though some theorists attack, or defend, realist styles for the artist's apparent self-effacement before an already meaningful reality since their objective is to approximate our perception of a comparable scene in the everyday world.

1.16. This Japanese painting, like "The Scream," places a figure next to a railing, but conveys much less sense of depth than Munch's "The Scream": there is no vanishing point nor any hint of a texture gradient. Although far from expressionistic, this painting illustrates another form of departure from maximal resemblance to everyday perception.

IDEOLOGY AND THE IMAGE

Ceci n'est pas une pipe.

1.17. Hitchcock frequently disregards size constancy in favor of depicting objects relative to their emotional importance. The enormous mock-up of Marion's glasses reflects an image of her own murder by Bruno (Robert Walker) in *Strangers on the Train.*

1.18. In *The Birds* depth of focus is used to locate characters in a spatial relationship that echoes their psychological involvements. Mitch's mother dominates the foreground and the relationship between Mitch and Melanie, who are divided to either side of her in the background.

1.19. In *Performance,* depth of focus, proximity to the camera (close-up), and a wide-angle lens are all used to give the sense of menace and dominance by the foreground character, Harry Flowers, whose gaze is directed at the off-screen protagonist, Chas. That Flowers's gaze (as well as that of the other character, Joey) almost falls on the camera places us as viewers very close to Chas's position and implicates us more strongly in the emotional tension structured by the shot.

1.20. Not only does the painting not contain an actual pipe, neither does the statement, "This is not a pipe." This is usually more obvious with verbal language and its arbitrary signs, but is no less true of the painting. This painting, in fact, can be taken as a master paradigm for one of the central themes of this book: images and series of images (films, for example) constitute a special language, one that we must learn to read like any other, just as we once learned to read the physical world around us.

Art and the Perceptual Process

tion, or framing. More simply, an image belongs to culture, not nature, as do other social products.

Images in this sense are part of the mind-affected world where meanings, values, and purposes are realized or made manifest. Some—houses, cars, or food, for example—are usually called commodities. Others—posters, magazines, or movies—are called signs or systems of signs. The difference, though, depends on whether we wish to emphasize their economic production or their social exchange. If our concern is exchange, then we can regard commodities as also functioning like signs; their transfer occurs within systems of exchange that are socially defined as codes—free enterprise, gift-giving, barter, and so on. If our concern is production, then we see that signs, like commodities, bear traces of the activity or labor that produced them; they carry coded information about their production that makes them recognizable products of human activity if we know the code (cars and mass production or realist photographs and perception, for example). Unlike the physical world (in its natural state) the image is, to some degree, already meaningful; it bears, in the variation of the sensory impressions across its surface, the trace of a previous activity, a process of work—just as this page bears into the future the trace of an activity initiated at 9:15 A.M. on May 30, 1978.

Nonetheless, we do not passively absorb a ready-made meaning; another process of work is demanded before meaning can arise from the trace, even with the seemingly transparent meaning of a photograph. And since representational images imply a dual or bivalent nature, these traces can be read either as a set of two-dimensional relations or as cues to three-dimensional relations. The possible simultaneity of both these readings adds yet another element of play, and ambiguity, to the image, and opens up the need for formal analysis (by which I will mean the prehension of meaning from relations between the terms of a language, code, or system of codes with minimal reference to context or environment). We might even say, metaphorically, that realist images are an objectification, or projection, of the normal perceptual process. What our nervous system initially encountered as unorganized sensory input is now encountered as the organized or signifying output of these objectifications or images. If we know the codes that governed this organization of the image, we can then read the image as we can read other utterances or communications such as stories or plays, even though most illusionist images give us the impression that we are being read to (often by the physical world itself). Recognizing traces of an overall consistency or pattern to an image, or any other text, suggests that the traces are the mark of a distinctive combination of the codes governing them. This distinctiveness, a unique combination of codes peculiar to an individ-

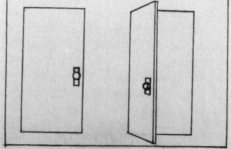

1.21–22. These two shots suggest one of the stylistic features of *Performance:* the use of complementary compositions between shots. Chas (1.21), seen from a low angle, is neatly caught by the wedgelike door frame, whereas Joey (1.22), seen from a high angle, is similarly trapped by the lampshades on either side of him.

1.23. In bracketed perception we would register two different shapes: a rectangle and a trapezoid. In normal perception we tend to register one object, a door, in two different positions. This is partly a matter of economy—the simplest way of organizing information—but it is also a survival mechanism—maintaining a meaningful relationship to significant objects like doors even when their actual, visual appearance changes.

ual or group, constitutes the textual system, which is also known as style (1.21, 22).

To summarize, in normal perception an array of sensory impressions bearing a correspondence to the physical world enters the eye and stimulates nervous impulses to the brain. A translation service, the perceptual process, organizes this array into a pattern or patterns, yielding information that is made meaningful by matching information to the codes governing its disposition. We translate sensory impressions into information and process this information in relation to codes in order to sustain a meaningful dialogue or relationship between ourselves and our environment (1.23).

Art and the Perceptual Process   25

Once we have conducted this process for a period of time in a given cultural context, a certain constancy of perception emerges. The variability of the everyday world becomes translated by reference to less variable codes. The environment becomes a text to be read like any other text. To not know the perceptual codes maintained by a given culture is tantamount to being an illiterate infant wandering through an unintelligible world. (An example would be the utter inability of most members of non-Eskimo cultures to distinguish the dozens of different kinds of snow for which the Eskimo has separate words.)

Representational images, like other texts, also rely upon culturally determined codes. The learning we undertook that enables us to perceive the world in a predictable way lies behind images as a given, a presupposition that becomes the image-maker's point of departure as he or she more or less reverses the perceptual translation process to fabricate images subsequently perceivable by others. His or her way of seeing the world is communicated by texts (images that seem to be already meaningful not because they re-present a naturally meaningful world but because they re-present work), work which prompts us to rely on the same or similar perceptual codes first learned in our encounters with the physical world.

Perception and the Unconscious

Our sensory systems provide the navigational information necessary for us to chart a course through the world around us. To hold ourselves on course requires that this information be interpreted in a consistent manner. This consistency extends beyond the invariant properties of the sensory impressions initially received (the fixed relation between wave length and color value for light, for example). It is also greater than the invariant properties of bracketed perception (where a certain figure may remain recognizable as a figure but undergo geometric transformations that could be interpreted either as different figures or the same figure in different positions—see the open and closed door of illustration 1.23, for example). This consistency emerges with the acquisition of codes that guide normal perception.

A meaningful relationship between ourselves and our environment, then, requires a greater degree of constancy than our sensory systems initially provide. Although the answer may seem obvious, we should probably specify why a consistent relationship to our environment is important: such a relationship offers survival value. It allows for goal-seeking activity to be carried out in relation to the environment whether it be natural or cultural. Perception can be purposeful because it is consistent. Perception is consistent so that purposefulness can be realized. Purposeful perception is necessary to a purposeful organism.

Exactly how perception, or the translation service catering to it, works is not yet clearly understood, but what is important here is the general principle by which it operates. The translation from sensory impressions to bracketed perception to normal perception flows so smoothly we are normally not even aware of its operation: we think of the world as already meaningful. And yet we have seen that there is indeed a process of work that we must learn to carry out if our sense of self-in-relation-to-the-physical-world is to have consistency—the sense of a historical self with past and future encountering familiar objects and people persisting through time, changing according to rhythms not necessarily identical with changes in the reception of sensory impressions of light.

A learned but basically unconscious process customarily involves a component of skill and can be called a habit. That is, there are relatively invariant rules or procedures governing perceptual habits that change so little compared with the constant flux of sensory impressions that they can sink down into the unconscious. These rules can be called the code(s) of perception (they will vary, within limits, between individuals and even more between cultures).

The benefit of an unconscious program or code can be gauged by the enormous economy of effort effected: every visual encounter need not be consciously decoded, a process that would swamp our conscious circuits and virtually destroy the possibility of immediate reaction to changes in stimuli. Imagine trying to drive a car, play tennis, or, in a more evolutionary context, hunt or fight off an enemy if we consciously had to work out our spatial co-ordinates at every moment and constantly redetermine the relationships between figure and ground as objects change their apparent shape in relation to our position. Subscribing to the translation service of the perception code has obvious survival value. It reduces a virtual infinity of possible meanings—alternative punctuations of a continuum of sensory experience—to a consistent meaning, a consistent or habitual way of seeing both ourselves and the world around us that allows us to drive, play, hunt, or kill with enough efficiency to guarantee survival—of the species if not the individual (provided this way of seeing does not obliterate its own environment).

Analysis of skilled sequential behaviors (whether they be maze learning, skilled motor acts like typing or piano-playing, or language production and perception) all suggest the existence of guiding structures:

of "expectations," "cognitive maps," or "deep structure." From such cognitive structures [called codes here—BN] quite different specific detailed response sequences may be generated, all of which are equivalent only in that they produce the same end result. . . . I add here only that most or all visual perception also involves highly skilled sequential purposive behaviors, and that some large component of the perceptual process in the adult is best understood in terms of the "expectations" and "maps" (or codes) that underlie these skilled behaviors.[2]

The perceptual "habit" we develop can be called, after John Berger, our way of seeing. If change is an awareness of difference achieved over time, then habit is an awareness of order sustained through time. An image-maker's, or to use a more traditional term, an artist's, style is also a way of seeing, since it is an objectification, or message, displaying order and skill and the unconscious codes that always accompany skill. The artist himself may not be able to say what this way of seeing is or means because the governing code has sunk into his unconscious. (The more skilled he is, the more inaccessible these rules of the game are likely to be.) What is important to the artist is not that he or she is able to say how or why she structures her messages, or art, in a particular way but that she is able to do so. (Likewise at a comparable level of performance we need not know *how* but *what* we see.)

Analytically speaking, codes are a construct of the analyst (the perceptual psychologist or art critic or semiotician); functionally speaking, codes are the algorithms of the unconscious (precise, logical rules of procedure in contrast to the popular notion of the unconscious as a murky hotbed of destructive impulses).

A functional code, then, may be an analytic construct on the one hand (when a linguist suggests rules governing speech, for example), but on the other hand it is also built in to the least accessible parts of the mind (for individuals competent in the speech acts studied by the linguist, for example). In this sense codes are internalizations of learned procedures to which we adhere quite strictly. Our difficulty in "seeing" bracketed perception exemplifies the constraining power of these constructs, codes. The code itself, being unconscious, doesn't give a fig about the specific objectives we may assign ourselves—to drive to the store, type a letter, stalk a particular wild boar; its concern is with the invariable aspects of these tasks—the relationship between the gas pedal and acceleration, between the individual characters of the typewriter keyboard, or between distance and the velocity of a dispatched arrow. In this sense they are like algebraic functions where what is significant is not a particular value of x but a fixed relationship between variables (such as $x = y^2 + 5y + 6$, or that

IDEOLOGY AND THE IMAGE

doubling the pressure on the gas pedal increases the car's speed by a certain percentage). Hence codes differ considerably in character from the messages or behavior they govern. Gregory Bateson elaborates this point succinctly:

> Consciousness talks about things or persons, and attaches predicates to the specific things or persons which have been mentioned. In primary process [the "site" of codes—BN] the things or persons are usually not identified, and the focus of the discourse is upon the *relationships* which are asserted to obtain between them. This is really only another way of saying that this discourse of primary process is metaphoric. A metaphor retains unchanged the relationship which it "illustrates" while substituting other things or people for the relata. . . . In primary process (as in art) there are no markers to indicate to the conscious mind that the message material is metaphoric.[3]

The Perception of Self

Bateson's point is significant from a contextual or political viewpoint as well as a textual or formal one. An individual learns to read the world, or images, develops skill in this activity and hence forms a habit or way of seeing. This is a half-truth insofar as learning is a social process and can also be called, especially at such fundamental levels as perception or language skill, socialization. Socialization in this sense involves those procedures through which human contact is patterned according to codes or conventions held desirable or necessary by society.

Now if a code retains the constancies that mark a relationship between shifting relata, one of the most important constancies in our social relationships, if not the most important, is our-self. Our sense of self as a subject, ego, or consciousness—as a constancy or persisting constellation of attributes—can itself be attributed to those codes that in the aggregate hold such a self in place. This attribution can be made even for what seem to be the most personal and spontaneous aspects of our-selves, such as deep-felt emotions. Peter Berger argues, for example, that "it is not so much the emotion of love that creates a certain kind of relation, but that carefully predefined and often planned relationships eventually generate the desired emotion."[4] It is not surprising that so crucial a constancy in relationships as the self should be determined (or over-determined) by many codes, of which the perceptual code is but one (others would include codes governing verbal language use, role-playing, body language, etc.).

If describing the self in such a way seems to empty it of some of its customary or assumed solidity and to propose instead a self fixed into a more or less constant place by the contingencies of intersecting codes, this is not accidental. The self-as-subject is a social construct whose place will vary according to the construction process. It is not a fixed-for-eternity entity but a term in a relationship; and *how* we are termed as selves can therefore be defined as an ideological question, a matter of the position we occupy or believe we occupy within a social and cultural order.

Without our own consent we could never be brought into social captivity. The dynamics of this socializing process have long been the subject of scrutiny and speculation and recent theories or models, such as Jacques Lacan's, discussed below, belong to a large body of thought. This body has been thoroughly anatomized in two texts, *Invitation to Sociology* by Peter Berger and *The Social Construction of Reality* by Peter Berger and Thomas Luckmann. Various approaches stress different aspects, but all agree upon the social nature of self, its function as a locus within a social system.

Society depends upon the fact that its members grant its founding fictions, myths, or codes a taken-for-granted status. Constant reflection upon first principles would be as paralyzing for a society as for an individual. We can no more afford to stop and ponder out anew an appropriate greeting ritual at each encounter than to relearn the guiding codes of driving, typing, or even perceiving. Roles, conventions, attitudes, language—to varying degrees these are internalized in order to be repeated, and through the constancies of repetition a consistent locus gradually emerges: the self. Although never fully determined by these internalizations, the self would be entirely undetermined without them. The self and our sense of self is bestowed upon us, maintained, and altered by a continual series of social encounters. "The social self is simply any idea, or system of ideas, drawn from communicative life, that the mind cherishes [or learns to cherish—BN] as its own."[5] for:

> Each to each a looking glass
> Reflects the other that doth pass.

A French psychoanalyst, Jacques Lacan, suggests a particularly provocative role for perception in this setting into place of the self. Since we have begun this study in the domain of visual perception it can serve as a useful model for the bridge between an individual psychology of perception and an encompassing sociology of perception. In a seminal paper, "The Mirror-Phase as Formative of the Function of the I,"[6] Lacan proposed that the young child between six and eighteen months old, before acquiring speech, establishes a distinctive relationship with the visual image of the other (in most cases, the

IDEOLOGY AND THE IMAGE

mother). Compared to the incomplete control of its own body, the image of the other appears whole, complete, full, a plenum of realized potential. Likewise, the child's own image represents an ideal to which the child aspires. It is internalized as an ego-ideal or superego to serve as the armature upon which the ego, or subject, constitutes itself.

The consequences of this are vast. The self-as-subject or ego will be precisely a term in a relationship; the subject comes to define itself in a relationship of opposition to, and identity with, the other. (We speak of our own identity but forget to ask identical with what—for Lacan, our identity is identity with the other, the image of perfection apparently denied us.)

This puts the seeming autonomy of the ego on slippery footing. Even after the founding moment of the mirror-phase, that part of the self which we will call the subject or ego remains dependent upon the other for its very identity. The ego's articulations of desire always pivot around this moment of formation: the goal of desire is recognition by the other; the very sense of an autonomous ego depends on acknowledgment by the other. Only by being the object of an other's desire can the ego be the subject of the self's desire. Desire reduces, ultimately, to the desire for desire itself, the only (impossible) object that replicates the (impossible) situation of establishing an autonomous identity by means of identity with an other. These descriptive statements are not easy to grasp; and if their meaning is not immediately clear, at least the reason why it isn't should be: the formation of the ego or subject, according to Lacan, rests upon a basically paradoxical relationship between self and other.

The prime meridian of the ego's sphere of activity is this boundary between self and other represented by the mirror-phase; the other is an imaginary wholeness with which the ego identifies itself in order to define itself as subject, as distinct from the environment around it. Because of the central metaphor of the mirror—the image of the other or the self as an other—Lacan calls this relationship from which the ego emerges the Imaginary realm (henceforth referred to as "the imaginary"). This realm fixes the ego in place, but in the fundamentally split place between subject and other. For this reason the ego is often called a paranoid construct and we can refer to this constitution of the subject in the imaginary as a paranoid fixation, a stabilizing or fixing into place that remains inherently unstable.

Lacan goes on to speak of another realm, the symbolic, in which the child is able to dis-place himself from the imaginary, from the confusion of identity (of the total self) with the paranoid identity of the ego. For Lacan, the symbolic is the realm of verbal language, the world of arbitrary signs, and in gaining mastery of this realm the child is able to enter into a locus of relationships in which signs like "I," "me," or "you" are exchanged between individuals to uphold a constancy of relationship more than of entities (like the ego, which sees its self, its "I," only in the eye of the beholder, preventing the kind of "free play" that characterizes symbolic exchange where the "I" is a floating signifier upholding a stable relationship). The imaginary is pre-occupied with place, the place of the ego, the other, the tug of war waged by desire between identity and opposition, the desire to take or be the place of the other.

This tug of war is paradigmatically acted out in the child's passage through what Freud called the Oedipus complex. The male child, for example, seeks to take over the place of the father, a place expressly prohibited even though intensely desired as a consequence of his imaginary identification with the mother. The symbolic realm involves a displacement away from this imaginary fix, a de-centering of the ego's place as the center of the self, to relationships, not of possession but of exchange, which can only succeed if the tokens exchanged (the words, for example) are not hoarded or incorporated. In classic psychoanalysis the symbolic realm harbingers the resolution of the Oedipus complex, for now the child can substitute for his desire for the place of the father desire for the place of the Father (the symbolic function of fatherhood), a place which is no more than a locus of relationship, represented by a sign which, like "I", must be exchanged between different entities, different individuals, if the essential constancies of relationship and meaning are to be preserved.

In other words, the symbolic realm is concerned with sustaining relationships (between self and other, between the conscious and unconscious self), the imaginary with defining entities (the self-as-subject autonomous from, yet ultimately dependent on, the other). The imaginary compels us as subjects to seek positive identification with, or antagonistic opposition to, the other. We are what we possess. In our culture reified substitutes or equivalents for the other are often taken as a measure of effective possession—money as a general equivalent of exchange facilitates this process to an exceptional degree: we are what our money can buy. In this case of imaginary exchange the exchange is directed to shoring up the identity of the self-as-subject or ego; *in imaginary exchange, exchange becomes emblematic of an entity*. Imaginary exchange is digital in form and function, in it information is reduced to an equivalent of matter-energy. It involves a reification of the construction of meaning.

Symbolic exchange is also digital in form but is analogue in function, for the information refers more to relationships than relata, thereby avoiding reification.

The symbolic realm lies beyond the imaginary. Passage through the mirror-phase is a necessary precondition for symbolic exchange in the realm of language since it constitutes the subject or ego who speaks. Symbolic exchange acts like a negative feedback loop to check paradoxical oscillation between either/or choices in the imaginary. The symbolic introduces a realm of both/and where the self is both subject, or ego, and not-subject, other and not-other. What remains constant is the inclusiveness of relationships founded upon difference and maintained by the circulation or exchange of difference (i.e., information such as words or other signs). In symbolic exchange, the emphasis is upon the maintenance of the system to which parts, terms, or entities belong; *in symbolic exchange, exchange becomes emblematic of a relationship.* (In nature this system can be considered as the eco-system. Darwinian notions of "survival of the fittest" applied to individuals in society are a clear example of a reduction of the symbolic to the imaginary: entities, individuals take precedence over the systems to which they belong. The errors of this epistemology are becoming increasingly visible all around us. Symbolic exchange in nature concerns the survival of the eco-system, not the individual specimens or even species within it.)

If the imaginary sharpens difference into opposition and identity to form an ego-centric universe, the symbolic preserves differences in a system of circulation or exchange. For example, the kula trade described in Malinowski's *Argonauts of the Western Pacific* cannot be reduced to any general equivalent of exchange. The system of exchange maintains a range of social relationships: the exchange itself establishes values that are only meaningful in context and that generate the individuals' desire to participate. The symbolic realm testifies to man's profoundly ex-centric nature within which the self-as-subject or ego is circumscribed.

Even this brief summary carries us a long way from the basics of a psychology of perception, but it gives an indication of the kind of basic questions motivating this study. Perception is indeed purposive and serves larger social purposes than individual survival. It helps mold the very image we have of ourselves as subjects. It helps obscure that larger sense of self beyond the conscious self that harbors the rules-of-the-game, the codes that, among other things, weave the web in which the ego is centered. Bateson puts it well:

> If . . . the total mind is an integrated network . . . and if the content of consciousness is only a sampling of different parts and localities in this network; then, inevitably, the conscious view of the network as a whole is a monstrous denial of the integration of that whole.[7]

Although the word takes on a slightly different meaning, George H. Mead's description of the profoundly social nature of mind substantiates the assertion that the ego or subject's imaginary view of itself (as a discretely bounded entity fashioned in the image of an other) cuts across the grain of a basic pattern of relationship:

> If mind is socially constituted, then the field or locus of any given individual mind must extend as far as the social activity or apparatus of social relations which constitutes it extends; and hence that field cannot be bounded by the skin of the individual organism to which it belongs.[8]

The Politics of Perception

This can also be put in more political terms by asking more specifically about the social functions of this consciousness, or ego. Extrapolations of Lacan's work by the Marxist theoretician Louis Althusser propose that the constitution of the self-as-subject is very clearly a socializing function carried out by the various institutions characterizing the modern capitalist state (or any other society, for that matter). The setting into place of the subject becomes the principal act in guaranteeing the reproduction of the relations of production (namely, class relations) and is an over-determined act practiced by all institutions from the family to the educational, religious, and legal systems.

In each case the individual is called into being as a subject by the other; his or her identity hinges upon the other by whom she is objectified and to whom she is subjected. The solidity of his identity as subject is dependent upon the solidity of the other as generalized Other, or Subject, an imaginary center to position individuals dead center on their consciousness of self-as-subject. The Subject used to be God and the ambiguity of the subject as a free individual yet made in the image of God, objectified as a discrete, named, and naming subject/object by Him, was part of the explicit (and explicitly paradoxical) credos of the Jewish and Christian faiths. The individual was a free subject whose freedom was a consequence of his subjection to, and objectification of, the Other (God).

The Subject now fluctuates more fluidly around the idealistic Absolutes proposed by various institutions: Knowledge in schools, Justice in the courts, Law in politics, Facts in journalism, Truth and Beauty in art, and the Father in the patriarchal family.[9] These Absolutes hide more relative, socially determined values; they obscure the fact that, as Marx put it, the material conditions of existence determine men's consciousness and not the other way around. Althusser, in fact, defines this process of the setting into place of the self-as-subject as the ideology of ideology, the transhistorical first principles of socialization. More specifically, he defines ideology as an imaginary relationship (based on the identity and opposition between subject and Subject). That is, the realm of imaginary exchange in society at large is the arena within which ideology functions to call forth the self-as-subject subjected to a set of Others which obscure the symbolic realm of relationship and the material base of consciousness itself in the relations of production. The imaginary does not then pass away after the mirror-phase and the emergence of the symbolic realm; it continues to reappear in new guises, often infiltrating the symbolic to reduce it to the imaginary, most notably through the workings of ideology.

Our point of departure in a psychology of perception is only one of many possible departure points, but it is so clearly a nodal point that choosing it almost immediately unveils a densely reticulated network of psychological, aesthetic, political, and psychoanalytical interdependencies, among others. We have discussed how perception com-prehends the physical world in a habitual manner that can be called a way of seeing. We have discussed how the constancy of the self as subject is socially constructed in the imaginary as the fundamental act of ideology. Since we perceive the world as parading past this fixed viewpoint—the balcony of the ego or subject—we can speak of our way of seeing as a function of ideology as well. The codes of perception guarantee a constancy of relationship between subject and world on which an imaginary relationship can be founded.

And, to go one final step further, we have spoken of the construction of images as a re-presentation of a way of seeing as well. Photographic images or films that reproduce many of the perceptual cues used in encountering the physical world, or correlates of them—images within the vast stream of styles known as realism—place before us an objectified token or trace of the very categories of meaning we initially constructed. Now these categories appear to be doubly "already there": the habitual or coded nature of perception obscures our own active role in perception and that obscuring is now compounded by the object-status of the image. Meaning has been fixed onto film for all to see, and know. The camera, like a magician, appears to read our mind, and our own act of reading, our necessary act of collaboration in this deceit, goes unnoticed and unnoted. Photographic realism, then, works to naturalize com-prehension; it hides the work of perceiving meaning behind the mask of a "naturally, obviously" meaningful image. The world truly appears to have been made in our image, for we can know it effortlessly. The ego is reinforced. It finds itself already there in the other, in a relationship of

1.24   **1.25**

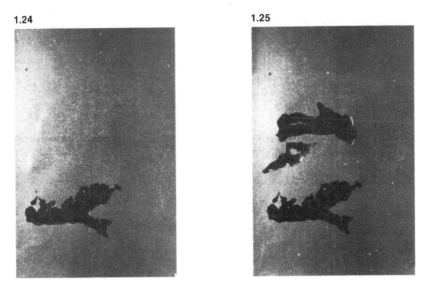

1.24–28. On the succeeding pages are additional images in this series. What do you see? At what point, in which image, do you see more than a figure/ground relationship? What name do you give to the figure? Recognition in this context may remind you of the subjective contours exemplified by illustration 1.3.

identity and opposition which the realistic image invites the ego to enjoy with it (self).

This reinforcement is an ideological function insofar as the ego or subject is the individual anchorage point for imaginary social relations. It is also ideological in its implication that the surfaces of things are already meaningful, that this meaning is an objective given rather than a social construct. Our acquiescence in this process confirms our way of seeing and the ideology supporting it. Our sense of self-as-subject is given to us by an already meaningful world that subjects us to an imaginary Other whose authority we freely accept in exchange for the pleasure of recognizing the image of ourselves in the world around us (or on the screen before us).

The Aesthetics and Politics of Recognition

A final question about our "confirmation" by photographic realism, and its basis in normal perception, needs to be asked. We have seen that perception offers survival value in a dual sense: as a necessary economy ensuring the possibility of skilled, sequential behavior and as a necessary, partial support for the ideological constructs of society (namely, the construction of the self-as-subject).

Being necessary, our way of seeing and our sense of self-as-subject function as givens so obvious that we seldom question them. But we can question them and ask, for example, what indicates, fixes, or marks this obviousness. In a word the answer would be recognition, but it is a word in need of more extended consideration.

By means of recognition we are able to establish meaningful units (signs, figures, symbols) in the physical world and then maintain them despite changes in the array of sensory impressions our mind encounters. Variations in this array will lead to variations in information that are anchored to a consistent meaning. (Illustration 1.23 demonstrates this difference between variable information and consistent meaning: instead of perceiving different figures we take the rectangular shape of a door as a constant, then interpret the variations as changes in position.)

In other words the phenomenon of recognition indicates the maintenance of consistent relationships by marking their reappearance. We confirm this maintenance service of our perceptual program or code by saying, "Yes, I re-cognize this; I perceive it as identical to something previously known despite alterations in appearance."

Recognition stands upon a tautological principle. It reconfirms our way of seeing, it validates our habit. It allows us to be released upon our own recognizance in a world of potentially unlimited flux. Recognition has the force of a mold shaping new information to expected meanings. Recognition of the familiar in the realist image, discussed above, belongs to this pattern of confirmation. Inasmuch as photographic realism is constructed in accordance with codes analogous to our own codes of perception, we are invited to recognize a

Art and the Perceptual Process　　　　　　　　　　　　37

familiar world, one already and naturally meaningful. Meaning appears to be already there as it does in the everyday world. Our perceptual habit, our way of seeing is confirmed. When we say, "I see (what the image means)" this act simultaneously installs us in a place of knowledge and slips us into place as subject to this meaning. The place seems given, ready-made, available due to the image's recourse to the codes of realism. Instead of seeing the activity of our own perception and the construction of an image's meaning, we see through our perceptual habit and the image's construction to an already meaningful world (without, in this case, "seeing through" the deception that is involved, the actual production or fabrication of meaning).

All the viewer need do is fall into place as subject, an easy step yielding the pleasure of recognition as identity is once again confirmed. In this case it is identity with a way of seeing peculiar to a camera lens, but so closely approximating the human eye's that it unfurls a landscape that might have been peeled, like a film, from our own retina. In the case of many films, including the most familiar narrative ones, it may also be identity with the image of the other fixed into place as character and/or star, that seemingly complete, perfectly unified, anthropomorphic constancy of flickering light with which we can fix ourselves in a rush of recognition/identification.

Even a realist film, however, need not enforce a process of recognition at every moment to collude in the confirmation of the subject, its paradoxical identification with an absence presented as image. Film, and certainly narrative generally, can play with recognition on a variety of levels, sometimes establishing conventions as cues for certain expectations that are only partially realized or are delayed, as in various forms of narrative suspense or the promise of most documentaries to provide knowledge. Other cues related to formal self-reflexive processes or explicit reference to actual historical events or processes can also initiate forms of play whose significance is considered in later chapters. For now we can note that even realist films depend upon a dynamic balance between the familiar and the unfamiliar. Art generally depends on both confirmation and transgression of expectations, an oscillation between credulity and skepticism or recognition and deception through which the artwork plays itself out.

In fact, failure to recognize the familiar in the new need not detract from the subject's incorporation or confirmation at all. We lack any base of certitude or truth that can be the final measure of experience—our perception is a way of punctuating a continuum of sensory impressions so as to create meaning. Every situation is encountered purposively, in search of consistencies. If recognition is only sporadic, there is still no reason to abandon our perceptual map or code; the search for meaning simply continues, the trial-and-error quality perhaps being rationalized as "life's like that," since there is no absolute grammar, no Esperanto of punctuation that will unleash the force of recognition in every new situation (and what a horror if there were!). As Bateson points out, "The premises of purpose are simply not of the same logical type as the material facts of life, and therefore cannot easily be contradicted by them."[10]

Recognition can be seen as a triumph over time and flux, a means of holding our view of the world and ourselves together. It enhances our ability to act, by replacing the unfamiliar with the familiar. Recognition aids making, forming sense of what we see. It allows us to say "I see" and mean "I understand, I see the point, I recognize what's before me." The very naturalness of this process is what Louis Althusser takes not as a sign of a neutral "human nature" or a "naturally" meaningful world, but as the key to the general function of ideology:

> It is indeed a peculiarity of ideology that it imposes . . . obviousnesses as obviousnesses, which we cannot *fail to recognize* and before which we have the inevitable and natural reaction of crying out (aloud or in that "still, small voice of conscience"): "That's obvious! That's right! That's true!"[11]

What guarantees that we cannot fail to recognize? What makes the recognition of Lenin's portrait in patches of grey and black color (1.28) so natural that, once it has occurred, it seems so obvious as to have been foreordained? The answer itself seems obvious: something happens at the moment of recognition. Things change. In illustration

1.29. What do you see? Do you recognize a familiar object?

1.29, the field of black and white patches can be comprehended on several levels—as a graphic depiction or image, as a random array of black and white, or as a particular image in which a familiar figure/ ground relationship can be recognized.

When the depiction is recognized at the last level, our relationship to it changes. We experience a click of recognition. A sense of relief, and pleasure, surges up as a new meaning appears (and this meaning will appear to have always been there, though just discovered by us, rather than the result of active com-prehension). This click corresponds to a shift of levels (like the click when a car gear locks into place). It is akin to the click of recognition when we "discover" the solution of a riddle—whether banal like "What is black and white and red (read) all over?" or complex like Kekule's search for the structure of benzene—and to the burst of laughter that accompanies perception, and comprehension, of a joke or gag. Through the act of recognition the maintenance service of the perceptual code substitutes a more abstract, more organized, and more meaningful concept for a less abstract, less organized, and less meaningful sensory impression. To recognize a figure is to recognize persistent principles or characteristics of organization of that figure. Recognition allows attention to be directed toward the persistence of familiar figures, units, or contexts through time (especially, once again, the persistence of our-selves), rather than to the full range of fluctuation in sensory impressions themselves. Recognition is like the border guard who guarantees the integrity of a boundary through time so that a consistent way of seeing can be maintained. Recognition achieves the paradoxical intersection of the present plane of temporal unfolding (diachronics, metonymy) with a parallel plane of mental recall (synchronics, metaphor), to "bend" a geometric metaphor—itself perfectly apt for what is involved. Recognition joins what it seems could not be joined: here and now with there and then. Recognition is like the support columns of a building joining one floor to another, except that the floors themselves seem to buckle toward each other at these anchor points where identity is established.

Pleasure-in-recognition is especially forceful when what we recognize is a figure or unit highly charged with meaning, such as ourselves, and that alone can provide a tremendous inducement to preserve our habitual "fix" on ourselves and our way of seeing. If breaking the habit of normal perception to "see" bracketed perception was hard, imagine how much harder it is to not recognize our self-as-subject, our self as ego. The pleasurable reflux of self-recognition helps guarantee the obviousness of ideology, its disappearance behind the inevitable, for who in the midst of pleasure would seek to disrupt it by analyzing its source or consequences?

What analysis there has been points precisely to the fundamental importance of such pleasure-in-recognition. Freud drew a basic connection with our pleasure in jokes: "This rediscovery of what is familiar is pleasurable, and once more it is not difficult for us to recognize this pleasure as a pleasure in economy and to relate it to economy in psychical expenditure."[12] He also went on to remind us, quoting Groos, that "Aristotle regarded joy in recognition as the basis for the enjoyment of art . . ."[13]; and that joy (although both Groos and Freud qualify it) remains a basic component of the aesthetic experience. Art, in fact, appears to yield up this pleasure in a distinctive state, relatively detached from the purposive function of recognition in the physical world. The pleasure of recognition, among other things, marked off from the necessity for action, may provide at least one point of entry in an attempt to explain the aesthetic experience, a line of thought pursued quite often in traditional aesthetics, which will be replaced here by a greater emphasis upon the ideological implications of aesthetic experience. Recognition of the place of the spectator as subject, whether associated with action or not, seems to be precisely that kind of ideological consideration in need of further investigation.

One goal of this study is to conduct such an investigation. The stakes are high. Large categories of art risk being dismissed as little more than an ideological conspiracy. All Hollywood cinema, for example, may be dismissed as mindless stultification foisted upon Us by Them (who say They give Us what We want). Much smaller areas of art that reflect on this risk—in a political manner or a purely formal one—may be posed as the only acceptable solution, a posing which leaves much to be desired, mainly because such a solution ignores the majority in favor of an elite of the already convinced or aesthetically sophisticated. The intersection of ideology and art needs to be carefully specified, for it is my belief that the specificities of style and structure in a text, a work of art, militate against generalizations intended as rules common, say, to all representational art or illusionistic film.

Yet it is possible that such "militance" occurs within a context subject to generalization, a possibility that has governed the structure of this opening chapter. Any particular film, say, may go against the grain of its context in a distinctive manner. These distinctions have to be examined lest we flatten all art into categories of art on which we paste various aesthetic or political labels. Individual members of a category or class operate under constraints imposed by that category, but how they operate in detail can no more be predicted than how various individuals will respond to the same general problem. Hence the close studies of Josef von Sternberg's *Blonde Venus,* Alfred Hitchcock's *The Birds,* Frederick Wiseman's documentaries, and a number of ethnographic films act as counterbalances to the risks of over-generalization or generalizations left to stand as necessary and sufficient explanations.

Nonetheless, the general principles of perception, recognition, and pleasure are extremely crucial; they threaten to center the self-as-subject in an act of fundamental mis-recognition when they serve an ideological function. Mis-recognition traps us within an imaginary realm of identity and opposition governed by desire to be what we are not and to possess what cannot be "had." This is the realm that fixes us in an imaginary (paranoid) relationship to the real conditions of existence (versus a symbolic relationship), a relationship doomed to an inescapable, and paradoxical, oscillation. As Kojève puts it, "To desire the desire of an other is thus, in the last analysis, to desire that the value that I am or that I 'represent' be the value desired by that other . . . In other words, every human, anthropogenic, desire . . . is . . . a function of the desire of 'recognition'."[14]

The grand deceit of ideology in this context is that it employs recognition and desire to convince us of our own freedom, subject to no one. We believe our-selves free in order to freely subject ourselves to the rule of ideology. We assume we are free to act upon our own recognizance. We work all by ourselves. The unasked questions, though, remain re-cognizance in relation to whom; "all by ourselves" in relation to whom; free with our "own" identity, but identical with what or whom, obscuring or denying what, to what end; boundaries maintained by whom, at what price—in short, where do we draw the line, who draws it, and for what purpose?

1.29 represents a dalmatian dog.

2.

The Analysis of Representational Images

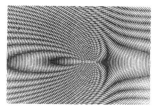

Signs and Referents

IN DISCUSSING NORMAL perception and the perception of visual images the difference between a sign and its referent came to our attention several times. An image is not what it represents, for in making its referent present again it does so despite the referent's absence, its actual location elsewhere. The zone between sign and referent marks the boundary between two different logical levels, or realms, much as the boundary between a growl and a bark, that between a baring of teeth and a snarl, and that between a nip and a bite can all mark the boundary between play and combat. Recognizing the difference is essential to understanding the kind of activity engaged in, the language or code employed. Some forms of communication insist quite boldly on making this difference apparent (most experimental films, for example); some communication obscures the difference (most realist films). The difference between sign and referent, however, remains. It is as Bateson would say, a difference that makes a difference, for it signals a shift in the code(s) or frame of reference needed to understand what the message is about (2.1).

The risk of creating short circuits between sign and referent in representational styles is great, and the very vocabulary employed in film criticism often increases this risk. We often speak of films as though they were indeed a decal of the reality they represent and as though the line of critical march naturally and inevitably follows the arc of a short-circuit confusion of realms: we say, John Wayne is in *The Searchers,* rather than his image or his image as star; we say, the violence of *Starsky and Hutch* is reprehensible, rather than the image or representation of violence. Such phrasings reify: they represent a

2.1. Magritte's painting plays with the dangers of confusing sign and referent. The painted landscape appears to stand in for the real one (itself, of course, painted); it stands like a window onto the world, and yet it is not the world. Looking through or beyond it like a transparency means misrecognizing the background landscape for the painting's referent in the physical world, if there was one. This points to a fundamental characteristic of sign systems: signs refer primarily to each other, to other signs within a chain of signification. To break this chain and equate it or parts of it with its referent is equivalent to creating a short-circuit in an electrical system.

false concreteness, confusing an object or quality with its representation and masking our active comprehension of meaning in favor of meanings already there, waiting to be absorbed. Such phrasings inevitably occur here as well since their avoidance is more cumbersome than their use as a convention. The weight of all that has been said so far, however, is meant to serve as a context constraining the impulse toward hazardous shorts.

The Nature of the Iconic Sign

But so far in semiological terms we have only distinguished between sign and referent. A further splitting of the sign is necessary, this time between signifier and signified. Since Ferdinand de Saussure first proposed this split, it is appropriate to refer to his original definition: "I propose to retain the word sign (*signe*) to designate the whole and to replace *concept* and *sound-image* respectively by *signified* and *signifier;* the last two terms have the advantage of indicating the opposition that separates them from each other and from the whole of which they are parts."[1] Saussure initially aimed his distinction at arbitrary signs like words: the sounds *boat* and *ride* are signifiers to which the listener, if he knows the code, attaches the appropriate concept. The signifier arrives at the mind's doorstep via our sensory receptors; we then supply the appropriate (we hope) signified from our storehouse of memory traces, thereby recognizing the familiar in the new. That we do so actively is immediately evident

2.2. The signifier of "pipe" is the depiction as a whole, which can be broken down into lesser tributaries: the oval, modelled in depth and light, that stands as signifier for the top of the pipe bowl, for example. The signified, "pipe" or "pipe bowl," however, is not in the painting but conferred upon it by the viewer, a point emphasized by illustrations 1.28 and 1.29 (Lenin and dog). Until the mind confers with this array of sensory impressions in order to assign meaning, there is only noise, i.e., patterns or information not yet decoded.

when we hear an unfamiliar word: *plock*, for example, sounds like noise, non-information until we learn that it means, say, "to listen inattentively," whereupon we pin a concept, a mental image to this bit of newly acquired information.

This distinction holds true for motivated signs like images as well. To begin with we learn to distinguish figure from ground. And even though the figures of motivated, or iconic, signs bear a resemblance to their referents, we must learn to read, or decode, them just as we learn, at a very early age, to read their referents, figure/ground relationships in the physical world.

The signifier/signified splitting, like figure/ground or sign/referent (and self/other), refers to the fixation of meaning upon persistent objects or qualities even when sensory impressions or social encounters vary (over a limited range). The bar, or boundary—represented by a slash (/)—marks a division of realms. Fundamentally a methodological division, an act of punctuation within a continuum of process, of symbolic exchange, the bar has considerable usefulness. In an iconic, or motivated, image the signifiers blend into one another or refer primarily one to another as the signifieds do for the perceiver (2.2). In effect there are two chains of signification—one composed of signifiers, one composed of signifieds—each located in a different place or locus. In decoding a message made up of such signs, signifieds must be pinned to signifiers to yield meaning, comprehension, coherence. That this pinning down of meaning can vary in accordance with different answer keys—codes or ways of seeing—is demonstrated by illustration 2.10. The effect of this pinning down is like that of recognition: the parallel planes of signifiers and signifieds intersect at nodal points, stapling the one to the other, the message to the code. (And as with the setting into place, or pinning down of the self-as-subject, in a complex message like a text these nodal points can be determined by a number of codes, or overdetermined. In the psychoanalysis of dreams, for example, the formation of nodal points is known as condensation.)

This stapling, like the entomologist's pinning of insects into fixed positions of mutual relationship, secures meaning, subjection to the code(s) or rules of the game. A constancy of relationship is upheld among shifting, or sliding, relata (signifiers and signifieds). The intersection of parallel planes at nodal points becomes the guarantor of a fixation of meaning. The recurrence of these nodal points, their maintenance, depends once more upon recognition and even so modest a feat as the recognition of the bivalent or reversible meaning of the old/young woman image (1.2) has its modest accompaniment of pleasure. Such pleasure makes habits or ways of seeing comfortable as well as useful or harmful, and makes it all the more difficult to change habits (the task of detoxification) even when we feel such change is necessary.

The chain of signifiers within an image or set of images enjoys two kinds of relationships between its units and their sovereign code: syntagmatic/paradigmatic, diachronic/synchronic, metonymic/metaphoric, or displacement/condensation. Although these pairs are not entirely synonymous, the first term in each pair involves a temporal axis of consecutiveness—what follows what—the second term refers to an axis of simultaneity—how one signifier may stand for or represent other signifiers. In the gastronomic code, for example, an entrée of filet of sole syntagmatically follows the appetizer, say tomato juice, while the selection of tomato juice paradigmatically stands for or represents a specific choice among possible appetizers. This play between message and code, text and codes, necessitates a game of hide-and-seek, a methodological apparatus capable of engaging in the study of presences and absences (the constraints of what has been said upon what will be said, or metonymy; and the surplus of meaning referring to what is not said by what is said, or metaphor).[2] This play along axes, involving expectations and associations is a basic quality of the relationship between message and code, and it remains at the disposal (often unconscious) of an artist (or, more generally, a communicator).

Locating this play among motivated signifiers can be more difficult than among arbitrary signifiers like the phonemes and monemes of verbal language. Codes involving motivated signs lack discrete units like the phonome and the phenomenon of the double articulation (the combination of a small number of bits of information, phonemes, to yield a vast number of units of meaning, monemes: $p+t+a\rightarrow$ "pat," "tap," and "apt," for example). Codes of motivated signs involve graded relationships where one signifier shades into another with no on/off intervening gap of non-sense. Borrowing from computer terminology, such codes can be called analog in contrast with digital codes like spoken language where gaps (nonsense sounds) clearly exist.

Isolating discrete units whose meaning can be pinned down becomes a forbidding task. Figure/ground perception and recognition may prompt identifying a certain array of sensory impressions as "dog" or "gun" but even so, no base-line meaning like the denotation of words can be established. Images are always particularized representations, a way of seeing is built in (since a way of seeing built them) and hence connotation is built in. The distinction between denotation and connotation found in digital codes like written language becomes indistinguishable. For methodological purposes we may try to single out the more from the less expressive aspects of an image but there is no ultimately binding rationale, no court of appeal, to uphold the choice.[3]

The graded quality of analog codes may make them rich in meaning but it also renders them somewhat impoverished in syntactical complexity or semantic precision. By contrast the discrete units of digital codes may be somewhat impoverished in meaning but capable of much greater complexity or semantic signification. The full but ineffable experience of a work of art compared to the complex but relatively impoverished experience of a critical analysis of that work illustrates this difference. The two are not in opposition to each other; neither is better. Each yields different kinds of results, which should not be confused or pitted in antagonistic combat. This rich poverty, as it were, of analog codes leads to problems, for it is often difficult to say what they mean (since the richness is precisely the richness of the continuum, which is lost in digitalization, the demarcation of discrete units becomes burdened then with the task of referring to what they are not nor can hope to be).

The Critical Analysis of Iconic Signs

As a consequence of this difference between analog and digital codes we are often in the position of using the complex instrument of language to speak about the rich meanings of art where a proliferation of words can never match the gradations of meaning to which the words allude. (Perhaps the closest approximation comes when we double or treble the verbal chain through metaphorical figures, but this is still clearly an approximation.) Often we are put in the position of describing gradations of meaning with obviously crude instruments such as the distinctions background/foreground, diagonal/vertical, black/white, close-up/medium shot/long shot. The distinctions can be further qualified (extreme close-up, medium close-up, etc.) but much of the "stuff" of meaning will nonetheless pour straight through our analytical grid.[4] There is no remedy for this other than to speak as precisely as possible, while recognizing that this very precision is fundamentally alien to the analog codes to which it is sometimes applied.

In film study, and most art study generally, the text is the privileged unit of study. It marks a distinctive coalescence of codes (in the manner of an idiolect) whose interference with and reinforcement of one another set up a *moiré* pattern* known as the textual system, or style. (The text is customarily a single finished entity but could be a body of closely associated works—the oeuvre of an auteur, a genre, a stylistic school, and so on.)

In the case of film, where so many different codes can coalesce, their interrelationships and patterns of dominance, reinforcement or counterpoint, and overdetermination become central. This holds true regardless of whether a given code is cinematic (specific to the cinema, like montage) or extracinematic (shared with other means of expression, like codes of gesture and *mise-en-scène* taken from the theater). These interrelationships and patterns therefore provide a primary focus for critical investigation. Likewise, critical analysis in film may focus on the codes themselves in isolation rather than the text in which they coalesce. In this case the specificity of a code becomes one large area of concern. Specificity involves questions of whether a code is cinematic or extracinematic and to what degree; many cinematic codes, montage, for example, are in fact shared with

---

*A *moiré* pattern is the appearance of a new pattern created from the combination of two others. Two half-tone screens superimposed at an acute angle will usually produce a new pattern not in either of the first two just as beats are heard at a certain frequency when two sounds of different frequencies are combined.

The moiré pattern shown at the beginning of this chapter (p. 43) was created by displacing two elliptical gratings along an axis; this particular pattern is known as "Disturbance of Security."

IDEOLOGY AND THE IMAGE

television. Another concern is generality (the range of texts within a medium where the code appears; the considerable generality of spoken English, for example, compared to the limited appearance of Swahili, or to be more precise (in Hollywood films at least), pidgin Swahili). Similarly, code-centered studies may seek to differentiate subcodes (various editing or lighting systems, for example).

All these are important activities in need of considerable attention in the cinema. Activity here can be further supported by contextual study that crosses the ''bar'' or boundary between logically distinct levels to ask how codes in the environment or context constrain the actual coalescence of codes within a part of the environment, the text. How, for example, did Paramount Studios exert constraints upon the films of Josef von Sternberg or how did shifts in the American economy after World War II establish new constraints on the textual organization of westerns?

These different emphases upon code, text, and context are mutually compatible but require considerable space for their individual development. The emphasis in this study is upon textual analysis, relying upon the results of codical analysis (especially in semiology and cybernetics), and serving as a preparatory moment for contextual analysis. This is, however, clearly a matter of emphasis rather than exclusion/inclusion; and part of the work of this study is precisely to formulate questions about codes and context in relation to texts that further investigations may pursue.

In turning to an analysis of texts we will begin with the still image. This focus does not lead step-by-step to the motion picture since there is a radical break between the two sign systems, but the still image is a realm both important in its own right and instructive for its utilization of codes also found in films (particularly extracinematic codes specific to visual representation). We should note that images can be broken down into various categories of a concentric nature according to the relationship between sign and referent. These categories can be represented diagramatically:

Non-representational images lack recognizable lifelike figures or objects (ideograms, perhaps, or abstract and minimalist art [2.3]). Representational images present recognizable lifelike figures or objects in all styles, from Japanese landscape paintings, cubism, or cave paintings to photography (2.4). Within representational styles we can iso-

2.3

2.3. A non-representational image.

late as illusionist those styles using a system of central perspective converging at a vanishing point to create the illusion of depth, such as Renaissance painting, surrealism, or photography (2.5). Within illusionist styles we can isolate as realist those styles using central perspective within specific limits to maximi:e their similarity to our perception of the everyday world (2.6). We normally recognize realist styles as styles but frequently believe they have somehow captured or transferred to the text intact essential qualities of the everyday world, or reality itself, sometimes as a result of an indexical or template-like relationship to the referent. Realist styles might embrace the European art genres of landscape painting and portraiture, the Italian post–World War II films known as neo-realist, and most news photography.

Non-representational styles extend over a far greater range than can be considered here and seem to invoke a different sort of perceptual experience and perhaps ideological effect. The weight of the present consideration will be placed upon the analysis of representational texts, and, due to their preponderance in styles dependent upon

2.4. A representational image with "impossible" spatial relationships according to the codes of normal perception. Once these codes were effectively simulated in painting, illusionist and realist styles began to evolve.

2.5. An illusionistic image utilizing the conventions of linear perspective and a singular witness point which we, as viewers, are invited to assume. Magritte pushes representation beyond the norms of everyday perception into a zone of heightened sur-realism (most evident perhaps in his treatment of color).

2.4, 2.6   **2.5, 2.7**

2.6. A realist image. This painting attempts to approximate what we would ourselves perceive if we were positioned at the painter's vantage point. (Compared with Magritte's, van Eyck's treatment of color is also much closer to everyday perception).

2.7. Religious icons marked a place of meaning precisely and singularly. If they were moved, their meaning could no longer be the same. These integral relationships between signifier, geography, and meaning (or signified) have been totally altered by the camera and the reproducible image. Duplicating images pries meaning loose from a necessary link to geography, place. The signifier becomes potentially free-floating, unpinned, ready for exchange within (in our society) a cash nexus that determines new meaning. In fact, cash value, together with the pinning into place of the self-as-subject, becomes the principal signified of the reproducible photographic image in many instances.

2.8. The process described in the caption for 2.7 is itself put on display in this extraordinary work by Velasquez. The point of origin is inscribed into the canvas, Velasquez himself, and at the vanishing point is the mirror image of his subject, The King and Queen of Spain, occupying the place of origin yet being represented in the painting. This construction seems to exclude or bar the viewer from his place at the same time as it displays that place, an effect likened to point-of-view editing in film by some recent writers.[6]

the camera, most of this weight will fall upon the two smallest circles—illusionist and realist styles.

The Renaissance Painting and the Photographic Image

By cracking the code of linear perspective (see illustrations 1.9–13 and 2.8), Renaissance painters fabricated textual systems approximating the cues relating to normal perception better than any other strategy until the emergence of photography. The ease with which the viewer recognizes a lifelike world of people and objects modeled in depth coincides, in John Berger's view, with the common function of oil painting since the Renaissance: to display the wealth and mastery of the owner of the painting.[5] Objects shimmer in lustrous, flattering light; intricate textures parade the full glory of their richness; individuals in portraits loom magisterially, the purified whiteness of their faces boasting eyes that survey the landscape and the viewers brought before them to announce a quietly determined dominance, if the sitter is a man, and a sensually fabricated availability, if a woman.

This display of wealth and mastery, of objects and others, was firmly connected with a sense of place. The globules of carefully applied oil pigment condensed into a limited frame the wealth more diffusely but immediately surrounding them. They spoke metaphorically of a relationship between men (sic) and their world as, in a similar fashion, the religious icon marked the precise place of meaning in

IDEOLOGY AND THE IMAGE

humankind's relationship to God (2.6). But the signifiers of illusionistic oil painting served another, equally important place-marking function: the unitary signified of the viewer's presence, his place not only of meaning but as the meaning incorporated by the subject.[7] We being the signified that constitutes the consciousness that comprehends the painting, the one thing we normally do not comprehend is this very constitution, a self-awareness of our own construction as subjects.

The compelling illusionism of this kind of painting rests heavily upon the dual pivots of linear perspective: the vanishing point toward which the image itself recedes and the point of origin, before the canvas, from which this perspective arose. The plane of the canvas corresponds to the conjunction of two pyramids brought together at their bases. The pinnacle of one pyramid corresponds to the imaginary vanishing point, the other to the imaginary subject whose place we propose to fill, a place we are nominated to assume.

The Renaissance painting allows us to think that what it displays is the riches of its owner (even spiritual riches) while this display simultaneously puts us in our place, fixing us there in a dialectic of appropriations, in a display of imaginary capture. The painting stands in for the world it represents as we stand in for the singular but imaginary point of origin; we recognize the identification marks of the world re-presented while this very identification marks our position, our capture and appropriation. The possibilities of symbolic exchange to which art often testifies become at least partially arrested by this placement in the realm of the imaginary. The centering of and upon the subject or ego in Renaissance painting coincides with the first signs of a growing emphasis upon the individual rather than a chain of being, an emphasis that flourished with the emergence of entrepreneurial capitalism. A false solidity rushes toward the reciprocal vanishing point of the painting as this complex fixation, this fixation complex, plays itself out across the boundary of signifier/ signified— the sign of objects and our-selves present in the places from which they are absent (2.8).

This entire process culminates in the yet-more-perfect replication of normal perceptual codes possible with the camera and its photographs or films. The most global signified of the photographic image is that fixture of meaning, ourselves as subjects, which first achieved solidity at the beginning of the emergence of capitalism in the Renaissance. This signified resembles the denotative level of words in its act of naming or designating a thing, that "thing" (ourselves as subject) being as distinguishable severally as the diverse meanings of different words. If it is possible to speak of a denotative level to the illusionist image at all, it is in terms of the constitution of the self-as-subject, I believe, that it must be posed.

2.9. This cubist painting by Picasso violently upsets the coherence of Renaissance perspective. Cubism signaled a major shift within the conventions of representation when it first appeared, but it no longer poses a revolutionary challenge. Such formal challenges tend to have historical parameters and tend, with time, to become absorbed into the general progression or flow ascribed to art by many critics.

2.10. The Thematic Apperception Test depends upon ambiguous still images as an indicator of the subject's personality. The assumption is that the subject, in charting a course through the sea of possible meanings for this unanchored image, will reveal aspects of his own way of seeing, and personality, to the psychologist. TAT images can be seen as one extreme along an axis of ambiguity; at the other end we find the advertising image.

Parenthetically, at this point, it might be noted that this work of the image in addressing us, in/to an imaginary "fix," can, and must, itself be the focus of political and/or formal contestation. Fracturing the solidity of the image's condensation toward a vanishing point fractures the solidity of that other place reciprocally constituted. Much of modern art and many film makers, especially experimental film makers, have moved in this direction along a road of avant-garde experimentation (Paul Sharits, George Landow, Ernie Gehr, Hollis Frampton, Stan Brakhage, Michael Snow, David Rimmer, Joyce Wieland, and, interestingly enough, many of the studio cartoonists of the thirties and forties, like Chuck Jones, Bob Clampett, and others). What they commonly lack from a political perspective is an historical specificity to the reflexive or self-reflexive operations of their art so that the risks or consequences of being called forth as a subject within

2.11. This image, though immediately m⌐aningful, is also, like Escher's paintings, profoundly ambiguous. The less context provided within an image for its most significant aspects such as a face, generally the more ambiguous it will be. The intense impact of close-ups in film usually depends on a context of surrounding images or shots that help pin down or anchor the range of possible meanings. At the same time, recognition of a particular meaning involves the mis-recognition of alternative meanings. Guaranteeing or playing with this reciprocal mis-recognition is important to the advertiser and the artist, respectively.

2.12. In this scene from *Dr. Strangelove* (Stanley Kubrick, 1963) mis-recognition arises from the use of deep-focus composition. General Turgidson (George C. Scott) commands the foreground as he discusses the developing crisis with the President. In the background, immediately to the left of Turgidson's face, is Dr. Strangelove. We do not hear him at this point and scarcely see him, but he becomes the dominant signifier for the kind of insane rationality that pushes the world over the brink of nuclear annihilation.

2.13–14. The image of Henry Fonda (2.13) from *Young Mr. Lincoln* (John Ford: 1939) contrasts sharply with the image of Richard Widmark (2.14) from *Night and the City* (Jules Dassin: 1950). Choices of camera position, composition, lens, and lighting all contribute to the expressive quality of the images, as do less specifically photographic codes of dress, gesture, and expression (how each actor marshals troops of facial muscles into signifying formations). In *Letter to Jane* (1972), Jean-Luc Godard and Jean-Pierre Gorin argue that Henry Fonda displays the expression of an expression:—"I think, therefore I am"—which they see as a classic liberal response to social conflict. It embodies the detachment of a pained intellect disconnected from a program for action and has a long history in the Hollywood film. It even, they argue, infiltrates Jane Fonda's response to the Vietnamese on her tour of North Vietnam, as though life were imitating art. By contrast Widmark appears to display an expression more directly: "I fear."

2.15a, c, e,   **2.15b, d**

2.15a-e. These images of pistols illustrate how even similar but ambiguous images vary in their meanings. Each is a close-up that announces, "Here is a gun." But they are not so neutral. They are particular guns lit and positioned in particular ways. Each says something like, "A gun is being pointed menacingly (towards me/towards an intended victim/towards the point of origin, the camera).[8] The degree to which various aspects of this utterance are emphasized depends heavily upon the interplay of the analog codes constituting it (as image) and our codes of perception. Were there a perceptual Esperanto, a master code to unevil the fixed meaning of the physical world, such play, and ambiguity, would not be so easily possible.

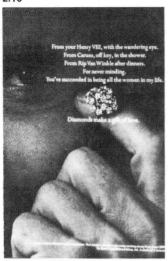

From your Henry VIII, with the wandering eye.
From Caruso, off key, in the shower.
From Rip Van Winkle after dinners.
For never minding.
You've necceeded in being all the women in my life.

Diamonds make a gift of love.

2.16. This advertising image seeks to convey a single, overwhelming meaning: the value of purchasing the commodity it represents. Ambiguity is strenuously avoided so that the full force of the ad may be enlisted in this campaign. This is not to say that the full meaning is necessarily obvious or immediately accessible to our perception. Many such ads rely on subliminal techniques to establish unconscious associations. Frequently these involve camouflaged or embedded images of genital organs, sex-role reversals, and, in liquor and cigarette ads, grotesque or death-related images—all hidden from immediate view. Apparently these subliminal devices have enhanced the effectiveness of advertisements and hence contribute significantly, in ways that are yet to be specified, to the overt meaning of the text. Likewise, ads frequently resort to suggestive innuendo at an overt level. This is clearly intended and carefully communicated, however it is not the same as the ambiguity of a TAT picture.

an imaginary realm go unexamined in relation to existing social conditions. This leaves their challenges to an illusionistic tradition easily re-incorporated within an avant-garde tradition of formal innovation unlike the more materially, historically rooted reflexiveness of a Bertolt Brecht or the later work of Jean-Luc Godard and the Dziga-Vertov group (2.9).

The Meaning of Images

The photographic image, however, does more than place the viewer; and these other functions, no less fraught with ideological implications, also need examination. A still image, for example, is a remarkably mute object testifying perhaps only to a "having been there" of the image's referent at that single instant in time of its capture. Meaning, though rich, may be profoundly imprecise, ambiguous, even deceiving. A large component of the work undertaken in the construction and reading of images becomes directed toward a distillation of that ambiguity of meaning into a more refined, and limited, concentrate. Possible meanings are scattered to the periphery of a solid charge of determined, or overdetermined, meaning pinned down by those nodal points of intersection between signifiers and signifieds, the shadowy trace of a complex *moiré* pattern. The strategies available to the image maker to anchor or secure meaning are numerous and have been frequently catalogued in introductory film texts and in the work of theoretical writers like Rudolf Arnheim or Bela Balazs.

The Analysis of Representational Images   57

2.17

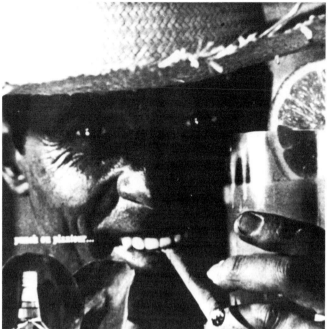

Rather than repeat them here, it should be more profitable to trace their application in a number of concrete instances (2.10–17).

We readily recognize illustration 2.17 as a member of the genus *advertising image*. No one cue provides the warranty for identification, but some of the cues intersecting at this point of meaning are (1) the carefully balanced and focused composition, (2) the camera's unprovocative proximity—the privilege accorded it of approaching a man who has receded behind his function as signifier of warmth and pleasure, (3) the finely rendered texture with its attendant spill of gentle light, (4) the preeminence of these two additional signifiers of warmth and pleasure—the man's drink and the top of a liquor bottle whose status as commercial merchandise is naturalized by the broad tropical leaves ringing it like a bouquet of floral petals, and (5) the corporate imprimatur (*"punch au planteur . . ."*) authorizing the image but incorporated within it, arising from it almost as though (as though!) these very words of authorization had been put into the man's mouth in order to be passed on to us, unmediated by a business world, from one friend to another. . . .

We can go further and tease out those points at which potentially floating signifiers are pinned to the specific signifieds of warmth and

IDEOLOGY AND THE IMAGE

pleasure, the dominant association invited between image and product and assured by the image as product, the image as a site readied for and prepared by production, the work of codes. One level of work involves the paradigmatic or metaphoric level: the choice of a specific figure or feature from a repertoire of possibilities, similar to the choice of a specific item from a list of appetizers during a meal. Each choice carries with it a certain meaning—implications or associations that accrue to it on the basis of its difference from other possible choices. Again, this snaring of meaning is overdetermined but would include: (1) the clean (not dirty), frayed-edged (relaxed, not formal) straw hat; (2) the rich brown skin tones (sun-warmed, not etiolated or charred); (3) the white (not stained), regular (not unpleasant) teeth; (4) the slim cigar (neither cigarette—placid and non-aromatic—nor stogy— coarse, acrid); and (5) the flecks of stippled light radiating, improbably, from the man's shaded eyes, rendering them lively (not dull).

Other choices of features could also be identified paradigmatically (in terms of the significance of the actual choice from among possible choices), but it is useful to dwell further on one of the compositional nodal points of the image: the man's mouth. Here the level of work is at a syntagmatic or metonymic level: the actual arrangement of figures or features chosen from a larger repertoire. Our concern is with the spatial (and in film, temporal) relationships between those figures that are present rather than the relationship of figures present to figures absent. The man's mouth is one such figure and its syntagmatic relationships are what might be more traditionally discussed in terms of style.

The mouth occupies a privileged position—centered, one third of the way up from the bottom edge. It is further centered by the shadows deemphasizing the eyes, nose, and chin, by its location midway between beverage and bottle, by the loosely curled fingers aimed toward it, the cigar extending from it, and, of course, by the words that seem to have poured from it. This carefully orchestrated center of attention, although consigned to a deeper plane than either drink or bottle, boasts possession of the one object bridging this spatial chasm—the cigar. The cigar, lit but not smoking, provides, like a straw, a bridge from (inflamed) oral cavity to (cool) refreshing drink. Our friend, gazing at us, is drawn via this hypertrophied and tubular tongue into a foreground zone of liquid pleasure. This zone, midway between the two pyramid apexes of vanishing point and camera/viewer, stands ready to sheer or buckle in two directions like a sheet of paper tossed into a fire: the curl of his fingers waits to draw the refreshing drink inwards toward him; the curve of the leaves wait to escort the bottle outwards toward us. Between friends a source of warmth and pleasure is to be exchanged. (Need we add, " . . . for a price"?)

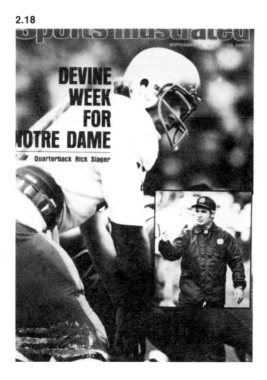

Images in Combination

The potential ambiguity of the single photographic image can be pinned down by the work of codes internal to that image with or against each other. But, commonly, an image's environment enters into the production of meaning. In film this environment includes the succession of one image, and shot, by another along a diachronic axis and the accompanying sound effects, music, speech, or written words organized in tandem with the image track. With still images combinations of the same possibilities arise (comic books and slide shows, for example), although without the impression of movement peculiar to motion pictures and television. In most instances image-image and images-written-word combinations have the greatest importance. These combinations can be regarded as relationships of context/text or syntagmatic aspects of a text, depending on our point of view and the specifics of the situation. A magazine cover may provide a contextual frame for those images displayed inside the magazine, for example, whereas combination of images used to produce the cover itself may be more easily seen as a syntagmatic aspect of one text. The emphasis here will once again be on textual analysis and hence syntagmatics.

This image (2.18) announces its class (advertising image), genus (magazine cover), and species (*Sports Illustrated* cover) quite readily, if we know the codes of magazine merchandising and football. Its combination of images and words is clear testimony to the funneling of meaning, the reduction of ambiguity, made possible by the interplay of codes. Even though meaning is pinned down, it may not be paraded forthrightly, especially since the relationship of codes such as word to image need not and cannot be one of pure redundancy, guaranteeing already apparent meaning. Much of the meaning continues to originate from the matrix of analog codes that we are hard put to recognize as codes and whose messages are often received at less conscious levels despite being precisely formulated. With this proviso in mind, we can begin an analysis of this cover by noting the complementary relationship between the inset of the coach and the quarterback in the center of attention. This relationship involves (1) the approximation of an eyeline match (the imaginary meeting of their gazes); (2) the reciprocal pinning down of the quarterback's expression and the coach's gesture from a larger repertoire of possibilities to "What should I do" and "Let me help you"; (3) the mutual color bond of the quarterback's badge of bloodstains and the red border of the inset, which sublimates the brutality of combat from the coach to his frame, to the boundary between brawn and brain; (4) the contrast of scale (looming brawn, diminished brain) rendered ironic by the placement of lettering of the quarterback's jersey (where his own name should be emblazoned, but where the coach's reigns both benevolently—"divine," guiding—and oppressively—on his back). This unspoken bond invokes much of the lure football holds for the armchair quarterback—the formulation of strategy, the crossing of the boundary between brain/brawn—and its very invocation upon the magazine's cover carries with it a promise of revelation: within the issue's interior, mysteries of strategy and relationship will be unveiled.

The play on words (Devine/divine), far from diffusing meaning, buttons it still more closely. The coach, Dan Devine, has just come to Notre Dame from the professional ranks: two forms of supremacy (of spiritual being and professional sport) coagulate in the red-framed, free-floating portrait of the coach alongside his team. This meaning, like many others employed in advertising topical commodities like a sports magazine, requires a pre-existing familiarity with current events, with the kind of events the magazine would have covered in a previous issue, for example. Punning here signifies not only the relationship of Devine to Notre Dame and his previous job but also the *au courant* status of the issue itself and its placement in an ongoing series of updates.

2.19–21. The increments of meaning added to the highly ambiguous image of a woman's face by combination with another image and by yoking both images to a single caption pin down a range of possible interpretations to a far more limited set. This pinning also proposes conceptual constraints around the topic of divorce that are clearly ideological, i.e., sexist.

2.22

RETOUR DE HANOI

Jane Fonda interrogeant des habitants de Hanoi
sur les bombardements américains.

Images and Ideology

The function of words in relation to images has often been singled out as a factor of singular importance in holding meaning in check. The great precision of a digital code like written language allows a dense mass of meaning to be packed into a relatively small surface area to which the eye is almost inevitably attracted and from which meanings are discharged like a shower of needle points to pin down the ambiguity of images (2.19–21). In analyzing a widely disseminated photograph of Jane Fonda in North Vietnam (2.22), Godard and Gorin have this to say about the caption originally printed in *L'Express* (this image forms the basis of their film *Letter to Jane,* 1972).

. . . The text doesn't mention the Vietnamese people in the photo-graph. For example, the text doesn't tell us that the Vietnamese who cannot be seen in the background is one of the least known and least moderate of the Vietnamese people. This photograph, like any photo-graph, is physically mute. It talks through the mouth of the text writ-ten beneath it. This text does not emphasize, does not repeat, because a photograph speaks and says things in its own way. The fact that the militant is in the foreground, and Vietnam is in the background. The texts says that Jane Fonda is questioning the people of Hanoi. But the magazine does not publish the questions asked, nor the answers given by the representatives of the North Vietnamese people in this photo-graph. In fact, the text should not describe the photograph as Jane

Fonda questioning but as Jane Fonda listening. This much is obvious and perhaps the moment only lasted 1/250th of a second but that is the 1/250th that has been recorded and sent throughout the western world.[9]

Words can indeed lie, and they can lie about images as well as anything else, though the very ambiguity of an image seems to soften these possible lies to helpful notes of emphasis. The play between word and image remains a site for disintegration as well as integration, of non-cooperation as well as incorporation. The interplay of codes constituting the image, like those constituting the self-as-subject, forms an ideological arena and an arena for ideological contestation. Frequently this contestation never escapes the arena informing it; the reflexiveness of formal play, as in illustrations 2.23a-g, succumbs to the sovereignty of the system with which and in which it plays.

The recent emphasis in film theory upon treating films as texts composed of codes or sign-systems has also led to a strong interest in those texts that emphasize their own textuality, the signs of their own production. Such an emphasis has characterized a great deal of twentieth-century art, where the stress has fallen on qualities of the signifying material (paint, celluloid, print, etc.) rather than the qualities of a more distant referent (reality itself or an imaginary, fictional world). This shift in emphasis is a central feature of modernism generally and seems to represent an increased concern with such basic phenomena as reading or viewing rather than their absorption into a second-order experience of some kind.

Insofar as modernism represents an occlusion of traditional ways of reading or seeing, it intensifies our awareness of the activity required to make texts mean. In a cultural landscape where the dominant forms of mass communication return to pre-modernist models of untroubled passage between meaning and viewer (both already there), a strong impulse may arise to consider any modernist text as a politically progressive act, breaking down as it does some of the hidden assumptions at work in our culture. The informing ideology may indeed be put on display, but this may only involve a sophisticated game of displacing it from one level only to reinsert it at another (as the "Babs and Joey" text does).

Distinctions must be made. For the purposes of this study figures like Bertolt Brecht remain informative guides for the process of gauging the pragmatic or political efficacy of art and of increasingly sophisticated reflexive operations in modernist art. Brecht's concern lay rooted in a realism that ran deeper than verisimilitude. It involved

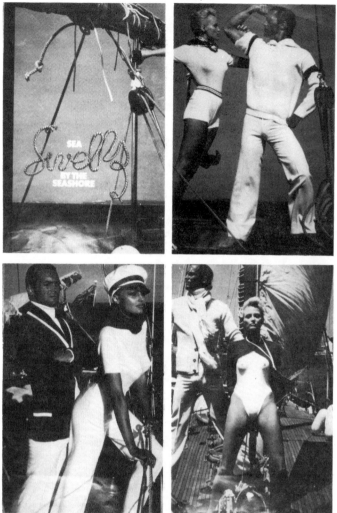

2.23a-g. This set of photographs feigns a parody of fashion photography. They exaggerate qualities and physical assets frequently exploited in a more muted form and yet nonetheless propose to sell the same kind of fashion commodity by means of this exaggeration. Parody, or "reflexive art," like this where signifiers refer to other previous signifiers in a formal game of inter-textuality has no necessary relationship to radical innovation at either a formal, avant-garde level or a political, vanguard level. Like many Hollywood cartoons or advertisements that include allusions to the reader's knowledge that he/she is not being taken in, these photographs demonstrate that reflexive or formal innovations have no universal signified; their ultimate significance must be determined in relation to specific texts and specific historical periods.

The Analysis of Representational Images   65

2.23e, f, g

They're setting off for lunch onshore, above, wearing mostly white with some hot touches of red. It's the kind of disciplined style they love you for in St.-Jean-Cap-Ferrat, so maybe they'll pick up some new friends while they play with their bouillabaisse and sip Pouilly-Fuissé from chilled glasses. He's in those tight Jacques Bellini pants again ($85), an investment he'll get a lot of mileage from, with a red-and-blue sweater ($50) from Cerruti CXIII and a slicked-back haircut that sets off a handsome profile. Her ultraclassic white wool gabardine suit ($550) is tailored by Jacques Bellini and is guaranteed to stay in style for years, because, like the color white itself, it can never really go out of style. Her red sweater is from Pringle, her scarf ($6) is from Echo, and her neat blond hair curls around a perky hat by john david rinaldi.

Below: Joey's fisherman jersey was first worn in the Twenties by Gerald and Sara Murphy, pals of the Fitzgeralds at Cap d'Antibes. It looks swell under a conservative blue blazer ($100) by Yves Saint Laurent Men's Clothing with white gabardine trousers ($38) by Arthur Richards. Babs's passionate purple sweater is from Halston, the red is from Pringle. Her lush 13-button blue-velvet sailor pants ($70) are by Victor Joris for V & J Design.

SWELL STUFF

In your January fashion pictorial *Sea Swells by the Seashore,* Babs's boobs appear to be so swollen by silicone that I'm surprised she doesn't keel over. Obviously, none of the sweaters affect either of her rock-hard assets. Speaking of rock-hard, what does Babs's friend Joey have stuffed in his pants from his crotch to his waist? Perhaps he's found a new place to store the spinnaker.

Barbara Fischer
Miami, Florida

Babs and Joey's only reaction to your comments, Barbara, is to repeat the oft-heard-but-never-so-well-illustrated statement: If you've got it, flaunt it.

66   IDEOLOGY AND THE IMAGE

2.24

Keep It Simple

Strike three.
Get your hand off my knee.
You're overdrawn.
Your horse won.
Yes.
No.
You have the account.
Walk.
Don't walk.
Mother's dead.
Basic events
require simple language.
Idiosyncratically euphuistic
eccentricities are the
promulgators of
triturable obfuscation.
What did you do last night?
Enter into a meaningful
romantic involvement
or
fall in love?
What did you have for
breakfast this morning?
The upper part of a hog's
hind leg with two oval
bodies encased in a shell
laid by a female bird
or
ham and eggs?
David Belasco, the great
American theatrical producer,
once said, "If you can't
write your idea on the
back of my calling
card,
you don't have a clear idea."

(United Technology)

2.24. The ideology of clarity masks the clarity of ideology. Things are not always what they seem. "Clearing up" apparently clear images of things and what things mean may sometimes be difficult. Patience may be necessary, obfuscation never.

discovering the causal complexes of society/unmasking the prevailing view of things as the view of those who rule it/writing from the standpoint of the class which offers the broadest solutions for the pressing difficulties in which human society is caught/emphasizing the element of development/making possible the concrete, and making possible abstraction from it.[10]

Clearly much formal innovation, including the reflexive parody of "Babs and Joey," fails to fulfill these criteria. Brecht insists upon the final judgment being a contextual judgment, an informing judgment where art is measured against the real conditions of existence within which it is produced. As Dana Polan argues,

The Analysis of Representational Images 67

Like the Lacanian theories of the subject, Brecht's theory depends upon a notion of positioning. The attitudinal position of the viewing subject springs from an attitudinal position in the work—the political artwork embodies a distance between the way things are and the way they can be.[11]

The codes governing a text change as the codes governing society change (not necessarily in lock-stop fashion). The political text displays change as a human possibility and not simply as the play of formally evolving codes. Such texts are rare. More common are texts displaying less total breaks with ideology (like *Salt of the Earth* on the one hand and *Wavelength* on the other). The studies of particular works in later chapters explore the possibilities and limits of art that is not fully realist in Brecht's sense. Nonetheless, Brecht's position remains a valuable guide and direction, one which informs the general goals of this book.

3.

The Cinema: Movement, Narrative, and Paradox

Motion Pictures: The Making of a Text

THE APPEARANCE OF movement pries film away from the world it re-presents at the very moment it deploys codes similar to those presiding over our perception of the physical world. Apparent movement organizes a medium of communication similar to but clearly distinct from the still photograph.* There is a metonymic relationship between the two based on the codes of iconic representation; the single photographic image stands as part to cinematic whole. But this metonymic relationship is not as powerful a bond as it might at first appear. The impression of movement kicks the image chain into a wholly different trajectory from that of the still photograph (itself clearly at a remove from the world it re-presents). The cinema takes on an organizational coherence as a distinct system of signs and codes. As such, its metonymic links are not with another system (photography, say, or painting) but internal to the image chain. Images succeed one another syntagmatically, metonymically, and also enjoy paradigmatic, or metaphoric, relationships to other possible but not chosen images. The metonymic relationship to the still photograph fades into the distance as we achieve "lift-off." The two media take full possession of their own metonymic and metaphoric axes like other language-systems. Once we are within the orbit of film, the relationship to the still photograph, previously privileged for methodological reasons, becomes no more privileged than film's relationship to graphics, spoken language, or music.

*The psychological basis for the appearance of movement in film and its implications for debate about the ideology of the cinematic apparatus are discussed in Appendix A.

The appearance of movement brings the graded signifiers of analog codes into play along a diachronic or temporal axis as well as the synchronic or spatial axis of the still photograph. Time is of the essence. The movement of people and things—actions, gestures, expressions—takes priority over that almost instantaneous slice of time captured by the single photograph. In the film *Ways of Seeing*, part I, John Berger describes a "corridor" through time that connects the here and now of the viewer with the there and then of the painter. This temporal identity of two disparate moments is like the impossible triangle: as we proceed along the pathway it marks out we discover that we are compelled to be in two places at the same time. This impossibility, the sense of a magical *voici*, figures heavily in the experience of the still photograph or painting as a precise and awesome stillness, a brute immediacy. With film, the *voici* subsumes temporality rather than arresting it: images appear to move, in time, again, as their referents did once before.

Cinematic movement, or time, becomes organized by a series of codes like montage, kinesics, or verbal discourse itself (speech, like motion, takes time). The constellation of codes organizing a film text yields a positional and propositional fix (the relationship of viewer to text, the significance of the text). Normally, this fixing depends upon reference points comparable to Polaris, the North Star, of which in film, as in the other temporal arts, there are basically three: narrative, exposition, and poetics.

A member of this triumvirate usually serves as a global dominant that guides our sighting of successive images into a singular, and reciprocal, fix. Our sightings register the interplay of codes with and against each other. They spot the nodal points of intersection, which glitter more brightly than their surround. Our sightings map out the *moiré* pattern constituting a textual system as a concept distinct from its constituents since it is not the mechanical sum of its parts but the dynamic product of their mutual interaction and their relationship to us as viewers. As Christian Metz has argued:

> [Codes] are not regrouped, added to one another, or juxtaposed in just any manner; they are organized, articulated in terms of one another in accordance with a certain order, they contract unilateral hierarchies. . . . Thus a veritable *system of intercodical relations* is generated which is itself, in some sort, another code, and which . . . represents what is most specific in each language system (*langage* [or textual system—BN]).[1]

In film these codes do not even share the same size units as they join together. Among visual images alone (excluding sound and

IDEOLOGY AND THE IMAGE

graphics) there are enormous variations: the relatively small, and few, pertinent features that allow a face to be recognized; the small gradations of movement that characterize a simple gesture; the much larger patterns of alternating shots that signify temporal simultaneity; the weave of color in clothing and decor that might contribute a motif. If the conjuncture of these codes yields something like the braid of a rope, it is not the even braid of everyday rope but more like what would result from braiding a variety of sausage links together: short, thin breakfast sausage, longer but thin hot dogs; pepperoni, short but thicker bratwurst, thicker and longer bologna. The undulating diameter of the result would be further varied by the braids' interaction as some strands dissolve together into more compact units, others mix and foment and still others prove intermittent, starting and stopping at different points (a color motif, for example). In such a system gaps will arise within and between specific codes, but the overall textual system continues over such gaps, bridging them more or less overtly (from the smooth elision of the projection of intermittent images into a continuous flow to, say, the highly irregular and usually well-marked appearance of flashbacks in narratives).[2]

The textual system, then, is by definition primarily self-referential (being the difference between the codes founding it and the constellation of mutual relationships in which these codes are fixed, a difference measured metaphorically and metonymically at each moment). Rather than attesting to some fixed truth, a textual system attests to its own truth or way of seeing; it pinpoints coordinates of meaning and plots them not against some master template of absolute value but in relation to each other, in the relative value of difference. (This does not, of course, deny the possibility for reference to coordinates of meaning outside the film itself, especially since so many of the codes constituting it are themselves recruited from the con-text. Basically, though, the textual system describes the surplus-value produced by the work of, and the work on, the text, that something extra that is present at the conclusion, which is never boldly announced since no one code can bear its meaning, its cantilevering work of difference. This "places" the textual system both everywhere and nowhere; it is an ordering principle, an algorithm, not an entity we can point to.

Two further points need to be made about the idea of a textual system. First, when codes are regrouped into a particular text, they may still be on the same level of generality in relation to each other. One does not necessarily assume a hierarchical position of dominance relative to the other. For example, in a given text codes of verbal discourse may gain dominance over codes of editing, restricting their range so that complete utterances are presented with synchronous sound and image, for the most part. But the verbal codes are not more general than the editing codes (they do not automatically subsume editing codes as a subcategory), and this relation of dominance could be readily reversed by another text. When we consider the "other" code constituted by the textual system as a totality, however, we must necessarily consider an irreversible hierarchical relation.

Second, the notion of the textual system as an ordering principle involves us in the theory of logical types. Most simply, this theory states that there is a qualitative difference between items of information of different logical types that, if ignored, leads to serious confusion. Logical types involve levels of generalization. We inevitably confront the difference between the general and the particular, between an animal poking its head in a box and the concept of "exploration," for example. "A class cannot be a member of itself" and "a map is not the territory" refer to differences of logical type like the differences between a particular swan, a photograph of a swan, and the zoological classification to which swans belong, "swan" (members of the genus *Cygnus* or subfamily Cygninae of the family Anatidae). Codes, messages of a higher logical type ("This book is in English," for example), are of a less complex level of organization than the messages of lower logical type for which the codes establish the controlling context. (The sentences in this book have a more complex pattern of organization than any classification or taxonomy of them possibly could, since the very goal of classification is simplicity.)

Logical typing becomes a way of understanding how a context (of a higher logical type) controls or constrains communication and behavior within its domain (of a lower logical type). We cannot transfer understanding from one level to the other directly. The success or failure of a particular attempt at exploration by an animal or deception by a human will have no necessary bearing on "exploration" or "deception" as a category of behavior, just as the success or failure of a particular film will not necessarily modify "narrative," say, as a category of perception and expectation.[3] The principles of narrative belong to a higher logical type than the actions of a particular narrative and cannot be easily contradicted by them. In all likelihood, a text that "disobeys" the constraints of narrative will not alter the category of narrative but will instead see its own status as narrative called into question. (The reverse operation also remains possible and a potential source of significant innovation. Such "Gestalt switches" are relatively infrequent, though, since they require a basic alteration in our way of seeing.)

As with the codes of perception themselves—our way of seeing—once patterns of a higher logical type are learned, i.e., once

IDEOLOGY AND THE IMAGE

habits are formed about how a continuum of experience is to be punctuated, they are both hard to falsify and difficult to change. Understanding this frame necessarily involves a different level of abstraction, whether it be in terms of the textual system vis-à-vis particular codes within the text or narrative in general vis-à-vis particular narratives.

These differences of logical type are of considerable importance to the overall effect of narrative.[4] Though logic demands that strict separation be maintained between levels, most communication, including narrative, fails to keep them separate. In face-to-face encounter such violations of logical typing or inability to discriminate types (to tell what kind of message a message is) can lead to schizophrenia;[5] in narrative and exposition confusion of logical types appears to be a central facet of their aesthetic effect and is related to recognition. It raises questions of paradox, pleasure, and ideology in ways we will examine later in this chapter and in chapter 8.

The Narrative Text and Desire

Narrative, exposition, and poetics—these global dominants are the triadic linchpins of literary expression and roughly correspond to the cinematic divisions of fiction, documentary, and experimental film. Narrative is of the greatest concern here, largely for the historical reason that it has been the most nearly omnipresent of the three in the cinema's overall development. This is not to accord narrative any absolute privilege but, as in this study generally, to begin with the broadest and, to an extent, most accessible avenues of approach to the area of film study.

"Two men set out across the valley." This single sentence, even in isolation, announces itself as the harbinger of narrative. The trace of narrative can probably be best isolated in the sentence's evocation of a promise, namely, the promise to continue or develop its premise. The sentence seems partial, semi-hollow; it promises to splay itself forward in time, to display temporal development, to displace this deflated instance of inauguration with a future moment of plenitude, a rounding-up into fullness, completion.

"Two men set out across the valley, had many adventures, and returned safely." This single sentence announces itself as an embryonic narrative, too stunted to be considered art-ful yet somehow registering as a member of the genus *Narrative*. The premise (of departure, quest) has been developed and clothed with a conclusion, however scantily. The beginning has realized the end it already announced/promised and has positioned, interstitially, a middle. A beginning, a middle, and an end; and even, unlike some modern narratives, in that precise order! As a result we achieve a temporal orientation, even in this meager example, positioned by an *élan* extending between beginning and end: "our present becomes charged with a memory and a hope."[6]

Generally, a narrative is a closed system, a form of discourse presenting a sequence or series of events within a distinct milieu. Frequently the beginning is marked by a lack, on any number of levels, that motivates the course of events: a lack of work (*Bicycle Thief*); a lack of information, or information in the form of a puzzle (*Kiss Me Deadly, Citizen Kane*); a lack of knowledge (*Nosferatu, The Man with the X-Ray Eyes*); the lack of an object, possession, or goal (*The Man Who Would Be King, The Locket, The Graduate*). This form of beginning easily proposes an ending in which this lack will be resolved in one way or another. It compounds the mystery or enigmatic quality of any beginning (What kind of world am I entering; what kind of address is proposed to/for me?) with more specific ones: how can something perceived or felt as absent, wanting, be restored; what will these characters do; what qualities will they reveal? A door opens, and ahead of us lies a long corridor whose other end remains hidden from view. The appearance of this passageway depends heavily on how this initial door opens—how much light it admits, how many and what kind of questions it proposes. The passageway itself, the middle, is what most distinguishes a full-grown narrative from its embryonic counterparts: it receives far more elaborate development.

The middle forms the bulk of the narrative and provides the stretch of time during which the process of remedying the initial lack takes place. The elaboration of the middle holds considerable interest, being on the one hand redundant (the beginning announces and calls for an end; what intervenes only delays this already implicit resolution) and on the other hand indispensable to a fully developed narrative (delay is not "only" procrastination but integral to the overall pattern). Not only does narrative stretch time out; it also uses this stretch of time to flesh itself out. What supports delay over a stretch of time as cables support a suspension bridge over water is our investment of desire. Narrative dangles a lure before us; it promises to unfold in time, yet not run down or dissipate; to take form, to in-form. Desire—the desire to recognize a return, a closure, to enjoy pleasure as the subject-who-knows when we recognize the repetition/transformation of the beginning in the ending—snares us in these unraveling coils of events loosely called the story. Delay teases and tantalizes, like foreplay, with its promise of things to come. The beginning negotiates a contract toward us, with us: desire will be gratified, there will be a return, pleasure waits to be had.

If we take the lure, we yield to the tale, sacrificing the partiality of the present for the enriched future at the other end. We suspend belief across a stretch of time, suspend our own present across the unfolding present of the tale. It carries us, transports us into a fictional world (the diegesis) where the desire invoked will be satisfied. If we recognize the overall structure of the narrative, we will have our gratification: the events will add up, resolve themselves. Their fabrication—both as system and as feints, deceptions that defer the moment of reckoning—will bring us back satisfied, pleased. We will be released and relieved. The elaborations of the textual system mark a deferment of pleasure. They suspend in their trace the moment of desire; their trace marks the movement of desire toward its own gratification.

Pleasure is not wholly deferred, by any means. The fabrication of the textual system sees to that. Various puzzles, little enigmas are continually posed, deferred, and resolved; partially resolved; repressed or forgotten, replaced by new enigmas. We engage the text in its unfolding; what has gone before does not lie inert but changes like the colors of a chameleon's skin. Our re-collection of past events depends on how our present intentionality is negotiated, in a manner similar to Freud's concept of *nachträglichkeit* or, in systems theory, the feedback loop. The past does not exist outside of the selectivity, the purposefulness of our recall; this selectivity receives its guidance, in large part, from the present unfolding of the narrative into the future. Narrative plays upon a retrospective or retroactive principle in which the partiality of the moment is suspended only to be engaged by a later influx of supplemental significance. This continual basting of the tale in its own flow provides an added lure to desire, making the familiar strange, the strange familiar, creating a shadow-play of which we seldom tire.

This basting, like the working through of initial questions, occurs in the middle of the narrative. This seemingly redundant "fill" takes on more and more importance, not the least of which is its relationship to change. Things change. Yet the end refers us to the beginning. The middle gives us an account of this change. But it is more than simply a chronicle, an accounting of this, then this. Narratives are also a way of accounting *for* change; that is, they are a form of explanation and the great bulk of explanation takes place in the middle of a narrative.

Historical explanation, concerned as it is with accounting for change, frequently takes the form of narrative, and in this differs from science, which explains deductively, by recourse to general laws or principles. Thomas S. Kuhn likens the historian to a child with a picture puzzle. Like the child who assembles a picture of "recognizable objects plausibly juxtaposed," the historian selects and assembles from an array of data "a plausible narrative involving recognizable motives and behavior." Constraints obtain in the construction of the narrative, but they do not determine its particular shape or outcome. The basic criterion is our recognition that the pieces fit to form a familiar, if previously unseen, pattern. This activity of "fitting," the primitive recognition of pattern or similarity, also functions in science at a level of modeling subsequent solutions on previously successful ones "without at all knowing what characteristics of the original must be preserved to legitimate the process." But in history this broad but obscure relationship of recognizable pattern, Kuhn argues, "carries virtually the entire burden of connecting fact. If history is explanatory, that is not because its narratives are covered by general laws [unlike, say, physics — BN]. Rather it is because the reader who says, 'Now I know what happened,' is simultaneously saying, 'Now it makes sense; now I understand; what was for me previously a mere list of facts has fallen into a recognizable pattern.' I urge that the experience he reports be taken seriously."[7]

Cinematic narrative, though, approaches closer to myth than history: it seeks to resolve contradictions and provide models for action in the present, not the past, though it may use the past to do so. From this stems its relationship to ideology and social change. Narrative may explain away real contradictions or explain how real contradictions might be overcome. To a very great extent, it does so through its form. The premises governing the arrangement of events "amount to an explanation of the events, in the sense that they provide reasons why the final events follow from, are the result of, the earlier events."[8]

This entire process is tautological in that explanation follows from initial premises, adding nothing new. These premises determine what events will be represented, how they will be observed and described. The explanation, accounting for change between initial and final events, is necessarily confined to those events represented and not others. A narrative may explain nothing else, directly, but it inevitably explains itself. We take it as an explanatory model, though, because we discover a recognizable pattern, one that builds upon our sense of an ordered and meaningful world, a sense fraught with ideological risks but one also essential, as we saw in chapter 1: our way of seeing, our habitual ways of punctuating experience and attributing meaning to phenomena "out there" are a necessary economy with great survival value. Furthermore, most cinematic narratives, certainly most of those within a realist tradition, represent recognizable social situations and character types with plausible motives and behavior, even when they are clearly extrapolations rather than facsimiles as in science fiction or the western. This links cinematic

IDEOLOGY AND THE IMAGE

narrative with myth in creating "a conceptual model of important social types of people located in a complete social situation and taking significant social actions, actions that create social relationships. It is in this sense that a myth *explains* social interaction."[9]

For example, *The Birds* (examined in detail in chapter 5) begins by showing us a self-confident, alluring female, Melanie Daniels. In our initial view of her at a San Francisco streetcorner, a flock of birds circles in the far background, unthreateningly, though Miss Daniels responds to a "bird whistle" from an unseen admirer (exhibiting a smug, pleased-with-herself look momentarily). At the end of the film Melanie Daniels is virtually catatonic and has to be helped to a waiting car by two other characters. Her response, to actual bird sounds this time, is one of fear: she draws back, trying to cover her face with her hands. Birds surround her menacingly (see 5.17–26 for illustrations of this transformation).

The middle of the film operates to account for this change and, in that sense, explain it. The film as a whole represents a recognizable world of situations, types, and social relationships. That its account of change also accounts for change allows it, like myth, to explain social interaction, tautologically but not innocently, in a self-contained form, but one that also draws upon and answers to social representations circulating within our society at large.

The self-containment of narrative returns us to our investment of desire. What we desire is the coherence of a unity, the unity of coherence. Narrative explanation provides such unity and coherence; without it, it would not be an explanation. (One of the criteria for an explanation is that it satisfy our curiosity, our desire to know. See chapter 8, pp. 264-75, for additional discussion of explanation.) Gregory Bateson, in an essay on primitive art, argues that "art is part of man's quest for grace; sometimes his ecstasy in partial success, sometimes his rage and agony at failure," that grace "is fundamentally a problem of integration and that what is to be integrated is the diverse parts of the mind,"[10] and, finally, that mind "is not limited by the skin. . . . The individual mind is immanent but not only in the body. It is immanent also in pathways and messages outside the body; and there is a larger mind of which the individual mind is only a subsystem. This larger mind is comparable to God and is perhaps what some people mean by 'God,' but it is still immanent in the total interconnected social system and planetary ecology."[11] And Reynolds Price, in introducing a set of his own translations from the Bible, says of Jacob (in *Genesis* 32), "No other narrator, except Abraham, has succeeded longer or deeper in the first—and final—aim of narrative: compulsion of belief in an ordered world."[12]

The sense of an immanent god, of mind as messages-in-circuit, of an ordered world is, I believe, a necessary and correct sense of how the world is. Narrative, with the perfection afforded by the force of its tautological explanations, testifies powerfully to such a sense of the world. It affords an instructive pleasure. But not an innocent one. The unity and coherence of narrative is played out, displayed, in a series of images, the "body" or text of an other. "The fiction of anticipated totality,"[13] as Stephen Heath puts it, should remind us of another, very real fiction. It returns us potentially, at least initially, to that realm of the imaginary in which the self-as-subject is fixed via the image of the other, the desire for the place of the other from which we are screened, which we can only enter when it is dis-placed to the realm of the symbolic, where the self stands as a signifier of relation rather than a fixity of position. Narrative, potentially, fixes us in place; its pleasure, potentially, is the recognition of the imaginary solidity of that place with its attendant mis-recognition (its "monstrous denial") of the fluidity that place assumes in symbolic communication and exchange. The coherence of a narrative reciprocally inscribes the coherence of the subject; it frames ambiguity, it pins down a possible scattering of meaning, it holds in check the fluidity of self and centers it upon the subject. A dividend of the successful investment of desire is the recognition it guarantees.

All of which remains a matter of more or less. Just as the representational image both addresses us in/to an imaginary "fix," and can be the site of formal and/or political contestation (with/in ideology), so narrative rests upon a non-neutral ground of ideological ramifications with which we must contend. (We can choose to wage the battle, but we cannot choose a neutral site.) Complicity with ideology seems to be an analog phenomenon exhibiting gradations of more or less, rather than the binary either/or choice of the digital. Not all narrative is handmaiden to the dominant ideology; not all non-narrative liberates us from the grip of an imaginary relation to the real conditions of existence. The crucial political/formal question becomes not how to replace narrative but how to work within and against it.

Narrative (as well as exposition and poetics) shares with ideology a set of structural mechanisms serving to generate apparent unity and coherence. It proposes a sense of closure; it provides the sense of an ending. Narrative characterizes occurrences within a given domain in such a way as to make these occurrences systematic and therefore comprehensible. The unity thereby generated, however, is imaginary in the sense that it is a construct or effect of the narrative rather than a quality of "the thing itself." Yet it is a necessary unity if we are to have narrative or expository or poetic form at all. And the self-as-subject such a unity confirms is also a necessary, though imaginary and insufficient, construct. Necessary for identity: it is the self-as-subject that sees itself in the other (though it can never be the other). Necessary for language: it is the self-as-subject who speaks (though that "I" is not my self). Necessary for action: we must distinguish ourselves as subjects from the objects we act upon. Necessary, but insufficient: identity, speech, action require making distinctions that are imaginary even though we mistake them for real. Necessary and sufficient as precondition for the symbolic where it, the self-as-subject, circulates as the insufficient signifier par excellence. (The "I" who speaks is but a part of me: "I" is me in another place.)

But circulate it does. The self-as-subject is our point of entry; the imaginary provides the necessary sense of a self, a body that can enter into material processes of communication and exchange. That narrative or exposition or the poetic or Renaissance perspective or the cinematic apparatus confirms us in the position of self-as-subject does not end the story but begins it. What we learn from this position, what possibilities unfold or recede, what order becomes manifest or disorder identified, what change in ourselves or the world around us arises as an imperative if we are to realize order, or grace—these are the issues that address us as subjects in and through narrative as much as elsewhere. And it is as subjects, insufficient though that category be, that we will respond.

The notion of narrative closure and the sense of unity or coherence it effects can be likened to other forms of imaginary closure, and various critics have proposed a number of analogies in recent years. Realist narrative is like the dream-work; it is like the Oedipus conflict in its basic structuring of desire; the cinema, with its succession of images, returns us to the imaginary realm of the mirror-phase; it positions us like the inhabitants of Plato's cave; it creates in images a fetish object masking the secret lack we dare not acknowledge sexually or economically—the female's apparent lack of a penis, the commodity's (film's) apparent lack of production, its containment of the production of meaning as an "other scene" tucked behind a natural and obvious meaning; it proposes for the viewer a position at the keyhole, seeing but not seen, like the psychopathic voyeur.[14]

The difficulty with all these analogies is to assign a precise meaning to "like." Narrative, or even the cinema, may be like these other phenomena or constructs; and yet it is clearly not exactly like any of them. Analogy implies both similarity and difference, but an emphasis primarily upon likeness, allowing narrative or cinema to be subsumed within the discourse that creates the analogy (structuralism, semiotics, psychoanalysis, etc.), takes the grave risk of lapsing into reductionism. Explanatory principles pertinent to these other disciplines may be imported inadvertently or inappropriately. And, inasmuch as the analogies return us to a primal or ideal (exemplary) scene, they risk the reduction of history to repetition. They return us to first things without acknowledging the difference of return itself: we cannot see ourselves in the mirror for the first time twice. The context is necessarily different and this difference (the trace of history) must be accounted for. (The second time incorporates the first as part of its context.)

Narrative closure, and explanation, return us to an ongoing social reality. It may be like a number of other things and in this likeness may lie ideological threats (the illusory resolution of conflicts, the false consolation of the position of subject, the punishment or veneration of women as fetish objects, and so on), but in the differences lies the space for ideological contestation. We must account for both similarity and difference. As a distinct system of communication and exchange, like spoken language, the cinema can posit an "ought" or "what might be" alongside what is. It may expose the very contradictions at the base of a society that foster disorder or impede grace, even in its attempt to resolve them, since this will prove an impossible task and the evidence of that impossibility will be there, in the textual system, for us to discover. Though closure may be imaginary, as the punctuation of the analog by the digital is arbitrary, both are necessary. They rest upon certain givens or assumptions. The quality of closure or discrete units cannot be abolished for being imaginary so much as recognized for what it is. Reducing either to a series of likenesses should hold less priority than assessing purpose—the use to which a fabricated unity is put—against the need for a higher unity of genuine wisdom, a symbolic unity of one and all.

Narrative Time

The temporality of cinema suits all three of the possible linchpins of discourse—narrative, exposition, poetics—yet each disposes of time in potentially different ways (again a matter of more or less since any combination of them can inhabit the same textual system). Briefly, we might characterize the poetic as a predominantly metaphorical, paradigmatic mode that deflates the metonymic and syntagmatic aspects. Stress falls upon the present moment; in film dominated by this mode, as in music, temporal structure often coincides with running or screentime (the actual duration of the film). The textual system may incorporate considerations of time and its disposition as in Michael Snow's *Wavelength* or David Rimmer's *Surfacing on the Thames,* but these considerations do not require the fabrication of a secondary temporal ordering, unlike the other two modes of literary discourse.

Exposition, stemming from rhetoric, enjoins time to support an argument or description, which is typically presented to the viewer in direct address (by characters or narrators speaking directly to the viewer).[15] Stress falls on the sequential ordering of a logic that requires a certain duration (running time) for its presentation but may refer to or fabricate an imaginary time of quite different dimensions. (*The Battle of San Pietro* [John Huston, 1945] describes in thirty minutes a battle lasting several days; *Letter to Jane* [Jean-Luc Godard and Jean-Pierre Gorin, 1972] takes forty-five minutes to analyze the brief moment represented by a photograph of Jane Fonda in Hanoi.)

Narrative, finally, customarily fabricates an imaginary time that only rarely, in its totality, or sporadically, in its parts, coincides with running time. (*Cleo from 5 to 7* and *Rope* exhibit the former congruity whereas the opening shot of *Touch of Evil*—an uninterrupted long take, lasting several minutes—exhibits the latter.) Narrative inhabits a time and space of its own making, at one remove from the duration of the flow of images themselves, thereby twice removed from our everyday perception of time and space, and yet analogous in many ways to our customary way of seeing.[16] Narrative time runs along the woof and warp of its own design, collapsing and expanding events beyond the dimensions of their occurrence in the everyday. This secondary spatio-temporal realm, which can be called the diegesis,[17] transports us beyond the realm of running time or real duration.

Temporal relationships in narrative (usually revolving around editing patterns) thus primarily support the diegesis, the roadbed of a bridge, suspended outside "real" time, across which desire moves and characters play. Three forms of support can be enumerated: relationships primarily signifying an aesthetic dimension (recurrences of shape, color, movement, and so on, which need not enter into a buttress for character motivation, as many beginning texts make out, but can enjoy a relatively autonomous play of their own); a logical dimension (usually, but again not necessarily, pivoting around the fulcrum of characters and their moves—psychological plausibility, for example); and a more strictly temporal dimension proper (the woof and warp itself, how the narrative is laced up into an apparent or plausible continuum distinct from running time). This last form of support constitutes the temporal aspect of the diegesis and is where Christian Metz locates his *grande syntagmatique*,[18] a taxonomy of possible syntagms according to their temporal significance. Interestingly, in sum, these three forms of support mark a concentric recapitulation of the three kinds of discursive linchpin (poetic/aesthetic, exposition/logic, narrative/diegetic temporalities) within the sphere of narrative itself. This does not privilege narrative, however, since similar recapitulations can be located within the other two spheres as well.

The *grande syntagmatique*, outlined in Appendix B, has received considerable attention; a number of films have been analyzed in relation to it, as Fred Wiseman's *Hospital* is to a limited extent in chapter 7. This taxonomy seeks to classify image sequences (it excludes sound) in classical narrative (1933–65 or so) primarily. It breaks into a series of successive dichotomies (chronological syntagms or sequences, for example, dividing into descriptive and narrative syntagms; narrative dividing into alternative and linear; linear into scene and "sequence proper," and so on).

The categories proposed by Metz are a useful shorthand for discussing the organization of temporal relationships in narratives. This discussion, though, leaves several difficulties that need additional consideration. Many of Metz's syntagms will appear in expository or poetic films—anywhere, in fact, where temporal relationships are signaled by recourse to this classical system of editing. Some kinds of temporal signification, moreover, fall outside the taxonomy, especially in the modern cinema. (Metz himself admits that the flight of Ferdinand and Marianne from her apartment in *Pierrot le Fou* [Godard, 1965] cannot be classified in the *grande syntagmatique*.) Although designed to enumerate types of sequences temporally, the *grande syntagmatique* still leaves us at some remove from an understanding of what propels a narrative forward: the invocation of desire in association with actions and enigmas (discussed further below). Before taking up this point we should first examine the diegesis itself in further detail.

The Narrative Diegesis

As the roadbed for the narrative's advance, the diegesis marks the coalescence of numerous codes, such as lighting, costume, decor, camera angle, camera height, composition (framing), camera movement (reframing), *mise-en-scène* (movement or staging within the frame), editing, graphics, music, sound effects, and aspects of verbal sound. More strictly speaking, the diegesis is the locus of *apparent* coalescence for these codes, since the diegesis is a realm of imaginary space and time. They are actually embedded in what we can call the narrative discourse or text, which corresponds to screen or running time, and the two-dimensional space of the actual image. In classical narrative the discourse is usually constructed not to be noticed so that this host of codes may seem to belong simply and naturally to the diegesis and its characters. The textuality of the film, its discourse, the actual mechanism by and through which the fiction is told becomes hidden. The fiction or diegesis appears to unfold by itself, naturally, in compliance with our desire to know and to see. Once again meaning seems to be there already, its pleasure—to please. Understanding, or attempting to understand, how this pleasure takes shape with apparent naturalness is one of the principal tasks of this study, so that we may in turn better understand the implications of the pleasures we attend to.

In order to do so we must acknowledge the diegesis as a necessary fabrication, somewhat like the self-as-subject. Its presence helps distinguish narrative from other forms of discourse. Our recognition of it (our sense of being transported to an imaginary realm) sets the stage for the distinctive pleasures narrative affords. We are only partially deceived into believing this realm in any way re-presents the real, yet part of our pleasure comes from allowing ourselves to imagine that it does. We are duped and know we are being duped. We suspend disbelief and yet know it is not the real we face but a fabrication.

This play of awareness seems to be written into the contract we negotiate with narrative, and the diegesis is essential to it. It relates to the particular fascination of the cinema—moving iconic representations (sound and images) that seem to reproduce the full reality of another time and place, a reproduction compounded by the indexical nature of the cinematic sign under certain conditions so that we have not a likeness of the referent, as we would with a painting or caricature, but an image existentially bound to its referent (a photochemical imprint, a light impression, a visual fingerprint of that which is represented). (This indexical aspect of the sign figures most prominently in documentary and receives further discussion in chapter 8.)

Consequently, the diegesis does not present an illusory veil to be pulled aside so that we might gaze into the true heart of narrative, the machine-works that produce this fabrication. The diegesis lies squarely at the heart of the matter, as does the seemingtly redundant middle of a narrative. It is an essential surface, a necessary illusion. Although we can distinguish between the fabricating and the fabricated (the saying and the said, the *énonciation* and the *énoncé*, the production of meaning and the meaning) we insist on one or the other of these categories to the exclusion of its complement at the risk of making narrative into something simpler, in a reductive sense, than it is. Methodologically, such distinctions are invaluable, but we need to remember that we are dividing up a single complex of experience in order to understand that complexity better. Our only avenue back to that "other scene" of the fabricating process is by means of that which is fabricated, just as our only access to the dream-work is the dream.

Somewhat impressionistically, the diegesis can be defined as all that contributes to the look and feel of the imaginary world of the narrative. In that kind of film sometimes called classical narrative, one of the most distinctive attributes of the diegesis is its apparent unity or coherence. Classical narrative marks out a form of realism largely by this means and also bears, emblematically, the brunt of political critiques against the ideology of illusionism and/or narrative. Although such films embrace a form of realism, sometimes referred to as psychological realism because of the coherence and plausibility of the characters, their world and their motivations, these films cannot be equated with all the various styles of realism that have flourished in cinema. Indeed, André Bazin and others carefully distinguished types or modes of realism within the classical narrative cinema. Recent criticisms sometimes associate Bazin with one of those types, psychological realism—which he actually opposed—and then indirectly dismiss Bazin by attacking the ideological implications of the type. This has led to a certain reductionism in discussions of Bazin and classical narrative both. Neither is quite so monolithic as some recent accounts would have us believe. (The debate between Daniel Dayan and William Rothman provides a valuable insight into what is at issue here.)[19]

Not all classical narrative films are equally complicitous with either psychological realism or the dominant ideology of their time, a point made manifest by the extended body of criticism that has emerged around the classic John Ford film, *Young Mr. Lincoln*.[20] Nor is it only classical narrative films that embrace classic realism (psychological realism) in whole or in part; nor are they the only films to imply, sometimes, an obviously direct relationship with the dominant ideology. These seemingly obvious provisos must be added because of the tendency to ignore them in recent semiotic theories of film. These theories tend to drift back toward the elitist, anti-mass art—popular culture viewpoint of the Marxist-oriented Frankfurt school on the one hand (Theodore Adorno, Max Horkheimer, Herbert Marcuse, and others for whom all movies were little more than a stultifying opiate) and the conservative Great Tradition critics on the other (T.S. Eliot, Ortega y Gasset, F.R. Leavis, who favored refined or sophisticated art, "Culture" instead of "culture"). Differentiating styles of realism, the precise boundaries of classical narrative and the possible forms of ideological complicity within its bounds, belongs more properly to the province of a film history than the present study. These provisos, however, will provide a major impetus, and rationale, for the textual analyses that follow, insofar as these analyses attempt to locate general formal principles and ideological affiliations within the precise yet idiosyncratic workings of particular texts.

General characteristics of the diegesis in classical narrative to be noted are these: it normally presents itself as singular (unfragmented, an arrangement of space and time organized in terms of continuity), closed (a beginning, a middle, and an end—in that order), transparent (illusionistic, minimizing its own status as text, discourse, or signifying system in favor of unmediated representation, a decal, or duplication of everyday appearances); it affords pleasure (recognition, a rounding-up of meaning) and allows identification (of ourselves as subjects, of characters as alter-subjects[21]).

Often the diegesis takes on thematic resonance through specific strategies such as the use of symbols and markers. These strategies lard the narrative as they pass through its fictional body and often contribute significantly to the succulence, as it were, of the narrative flow. (Their absence is one of the things that makes an embryonic narrative such as the example used earlier, "Two men set out across the valley . . ." so art-less). Symbols—signifiers already supercharged with meaning, like guns, samurai swords, satin bed sheets, or Rolls Royces—form accretions around characters and/or aspects of their milieu. Likewise, markers—signifiers with fewer specific cultural connotations, like shoes, alleyways, telephones, or idiosyncratic gestures—serve as a narrative thickening agent lending density or weight to its development. Markers (3.1) and, of course, symbols that recur and take on major thematic significance in the narrative become motifs (3.2). Other markers, less thematically laden but closely associated with continuity (a set of clothing worn by a character during a scene, for example) are referred to as match, and lapses in consistency in this level as non-match (the unexplained disappearance of a handkerchief from a character's breast pocket during a scene, for example). More globally, Raymond Durgnat suggests that symbols are favored by European film makers and markers by American (Hollywood) directors,[22] though these codes are clearly not mutually exclusive and jointly testify to the dependence of narrative effect upon extracinematic codes and their reworking within a narrative context.

Another contributor to the look and feel of classical narrative is "continuity" or continuity editing: a series of strategies for minimizing the noticeability of cuts between shots by maximizing their psychological plausibility and/or their perceptual congruence. Continuity serves to suture or patch up gaps, potential fissures in the unity of the diegesis. These fissures are the trace of the fabrication of the diegesis. Continuity, by courting the active but habitual and unconscious qualities in our way of seeing—our attention to and selection of pertinent features in the visual landscape—achieves a triple masking: of our normal perceptual activity, of its learned or coded carry-over to another signifying system, film (which can only be taken as naturally

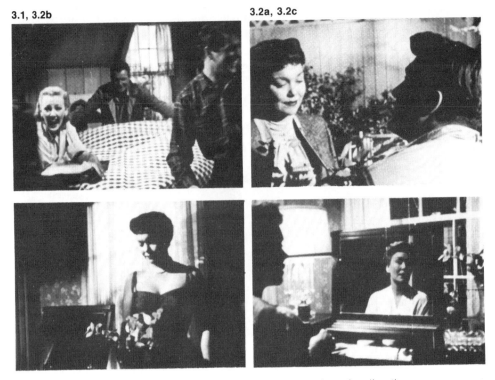

3.1. The checkered tablecloth serves as a marker, signaling the "poor but honest" milieu of Rock Hudson's friends in *All That Heaven Allows.* It contrasts sharply with the white tablecloths and more formal attire found at the country club to which the woman he loves, Jane Wyman, belongs.

3.2a-c. A motif from *All That Heaven Allows.* The branch begins as a marker, inasmuch as it is a gift from Rock Hudson to Jane Wyman. Its recurrence turns it into a motif that acquires numerous connotations: Hudson's "natural world," his absence from her life, except for this token, the gradual infiltration of his lifestyle into her world, and so on.

meaningful because of the invocation of analogs of the same codes at work in normal perception), and of its work or fabrication, precisely the work of masking. We collude in this act of fabrication, perhaps unwittingly, lured by a promise of pleasure, the desire for recognition, but at the price of other pleasures foregone, of the mis-recognition tucked into the fine print of our desire's investment negotiations.

Matches along eyeline and its corollary, point-of-view editing, offer a major avenue along which we are lured into the diegetic world of the narrative (3.3–6). Our own process of making this world meaningful becomes transferred to and identified with the attempts of characters to make their world meaningful. Continuity editing in general has the consequence of neutralizing our fabrication of meaning by naturalizing a world of always-already-meaningful fabrications. The narrative promises, in due course, to share these meanings with us. The brilliance of this conjuring up of meaning attracts us as a flame attracts moths. The shimmering lure of a tale creating itself to gratify our desire is a magical lure, a potentially ideological lure, that entices us to sit, partially contracted into an imaginary relationship, spellbound in darkness.

The Motor Codes of Narrative

If the diegesis is the imaginary arena within which the narrative advances and emerges from a confluence of cinematic and extra-cinematic codes, the narrative advance itself is a distinct phenomenon but one that is characteristic of all narrative. Structural theorists have devoted a great deal of attention to the question of how a narrative moves forward in time. The syntagmatic or metonymic aspect of all discourse (its occurrence through time) lends impetus to the need for this differentiation: what distinguishes narrative from other forms of temporal communication? And although many narrative typologies and codes have been proposed, even within the restricted range of classical narrative, perhaps the most instructive starting point lies in Roland Barthes's description of enigmas and actions as the constitutive elements of the two most basic narrative codes, the hermeneutic and the proairetic, but which we will refer to, more simply, in terms of enigmas and actions.

> Under the hermeneutic code, we list the various (formal) terms by which an enigma can be distinguished, suggested, formulated, held in suspense, and finally disclosed. . . . Actions (terms of the proairetic code) can fall into various sequences which should be indicated merely by listing them, since the proairetic sequence is never more than the result of an artifice of reading: whoever reads the text amasses certain data under some generic titles for actions (*stroll, murder,*

3.3 and 3.4. Suturing time and space. Aural continuity takes on major importance in annealing potential gaps in time: dialogue and sound effects continue without interruption despite the "cut" from shot *a* to *b* in each case. The shot/reverse-shot figure (in 3.4, the over-the-shoulder shot more specifically) also sutures up a potentially lacerated space through its skillful use of eyeline: the editing shuttles the viewer from association with the gaze of one character to the other, respecting the 180° rule and thereby achieving eyeline match. (Hudson looks screen right before and after the cuts whereas if the camera crossed the imaginary line between the two characters he would appear to look screen left after the cut, presumably at another character or object.) This form of eyeline match sometimes acts like a point-of-view figure and sometimes functions more objectively whether the second character is visible (3.4a) or not (3.3a). In both cases the editing achieves in time what Velasquez's *The Maids of Honor* (2.8) achieves in space: it reveals to us the "other scene" which the character in 3.3a and 3.4a addresses and at the same time differs from *The Maids of Honor* in that the producer of both these scenes (the cinematic apparatus) remains invisible. Also, as the narrative spills forward from one shot to the next it fails to show us the one object of our desire (ourselves) whose lack we hope will be redressed, if not in fact, at least through surrogates with whom we can identify. In passing, we may note that the production of desirable surrogates provides a primary motivation for the star system and that this system's ideological biases (in its choice of stars and star-images) accurately represent the biases by means of which an economic system extracts surplus-value (e.g., through the hierarchical relations of class, sex, and race).

3.5a, 3.6a   **3.5b, 3.6b**

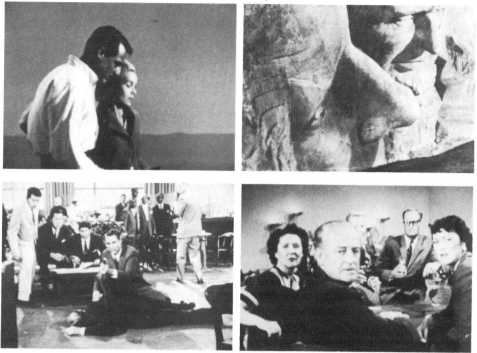

3.5. Eyeline match: point of view. Normal point-of-view shots involve a character (point of origin) looking off-screen (a cue for the cut to the next shot), the cut, and a second shot revealing what the character sees from a position at or near the character's vantage point. Numerous variations are possible; a full catalog of them is provided in Edward Brannigan's "Formal Permutations of The Point-of-View Shot," *Screen* 16, 3 (Autumn 1975):54–64.

3.6. Delayed point of view. One of the traditional forms of feedback loop or retroactive reading in classical narrative involves a reversal of the normal point-of-view figure: we first see the object being viewed but without knowing that our vantage point is also a character's; we (mis)take it for an objective shot until the second shot arrives to displace our gaze with a character's, requiring a retroactive adjustment of meaning.

Point-of-view editing sometimes serves as a key instrument in narrative play, drawing on the viewer's desire to see, the incipient voyeurism of a viewer who sees without being seen, who identifies without being identified (by characters who carry on as though he or she were not there). These kinds of strategies are central to the films of Alfred Hitchcock in particular, but they are common to classical narrative in general.

rendezvous), and this title embodies the sequence; the sequence exists when and because it can be given a name, it unfolds as this process of naming takes place, as a title is sought or confirmed; . . . its only logic is that of the "already-done" or "already-read"—whence the variety of sequences (some trivial, some melodramatic) and the variety of terms (numerous or few).[23]

Enigmas comprise these feints and delays by which desire is invoked and its gratification assured. The initial lack of many narratives often founds basic enigmas such as, "Will the lack be restored?" Individual sequences often pose smaller enigmas, sometimes under the rubric of suspense—"Will the hero escape?"—sometimes under more conceptual rubrics—"Will the hero be misled by a lie?" or "Will the hero's awareness be increased by a newly acquired fact?"

Actions normally condense around the characters who carry them out. Structurally speaking, though, a distinction can be made between narrative acts (what Vladimir Propp called functions) such as departure, interdiction, and rendezvous and the characters employed to flesh them out, to incarnate them, since many characters may perform the same action (murder, for example) and one character may perform many actions (departure, pursuit, combat, murder, return, for example). In classical narrative the main characters are usually highly individuated: many narrative acts accrue to them and their methods of accomplishing these acts mark them off, distinguish them, and thereby promote identification. This is further accomplished by another form of condensation in much classical narrative: the inhabitation of "character" by "star," a supernova in the constellation of some textual systems. More generally, cinema, like theater, allows characters to be inhabited "in the flesh" by actors, although cinema, unlike theater, is marked by the presence of the actor where he/she is absent—by the image, and the "image" (icon, idol) thereby established.[24]

Actantiality (Barthes's proairetic code) has been a primary focus of the structural study of narrative for some time. Vladimir Propp's work on the Russian folktale stands as a pioneering contribution to an understanding of actantiality as a key aspect of the narrative discourse, deserving, in fact, greater priority than typologies according to character, theme, or other qualities connoted by the diegesis. Propp argued that a large number of folktales, despite considerable surface variation, exhibited structural similarities in terms of functions and moves (the sequential arrangement of functions). Functions are equivalent to Barthes's actions—a simple (not compound) subject/predicate relationship such as "the hero defeats the villain" or "interdiction." Functions can also be descriptive attributes—for example, "The hero shows mercy to a suppliant" or "honesty." The subject of a function is thus a character: a character is the sum of the functions he assumes (the acts performed by or upon him and the attributes he gives or receives).

Propp demonstrated that these functions exhibit certain stable characteristics:

1. The functions ("lack, insufficiency," "call for help," "test of the hero," "solution of a task," "wedding," "accession to the throne") are themselves stable; they remain invariant across a range of tales.
2. The total number of functions is limited within any given type of narrative.
3. The sequence of functions remains constant (some tales may lack some functions but those present always follow one another in an invariant order). Consequently,
4. Narratives can be classified according to type on the basis of whether or not they share in a common structure established by the nature and sequence of the functions.[25]

This form of narrative analysis departs significantly from Claude Lévi-Strauss's structural study of myths, most noticeably perhaps in the intimate relationship between sequential ordering and underlying structure. Whereas Lévi-Strauss derived binary oppositions from myths irrespective of their position in the syntagmatic chain (food/not-food, autochthonous/not-autochthonous) and then examined how they were transformed or mediated, Propp examined how functions condense around characters and serve as a pivotal fulcrum between the texture of the diegesis and the logic of the discourse. Lévi-Strauss strips myths down to their structural bones; Vladimir Propp dissects the relationship between flesh and bones insofar as functions provide a "logical principle of ordering" for the temporal flow of a tale.

Other studies of narrative have pursued these questions of actantiality, temporal organization, and the relationship of diegesis to discourse in some detail. A.J. Greimas, for example, extends the notion of an initial lack eventually restored or redressed to argue that the basic operation of most narrative is one of conjunction and disjunction. Events centered around separation/union, struggle/reconciliation, or deception/recognition might organize an entire narrative as well as certain discrete passages of a narrative. The resolution of an opposition and the revelation of a similarity are therefore common acts of narrative closure. Separation/union, for example, might be considered the structuring principle to *Blonde Venus* as a whole but also to those passages of *The Birds* in which the heroine, Melanie

Daniels, is isolated during bird attacks and then rescued or rejoined by other characters.

Various forms of exchange often accompany these operations of disjunction and conjunction and provide the demarcation between one figure of actantial closure and another. Exchange can take the form of values, objects, or characters. *Winchester 73* (Anthony Mann, 1950) involves the transfer of a rifle from one individual to another until a thematic circle has been completed, whereas *North by Northwest* (Hitchcock, 1959) centers around an exchange of identity between Roger Thornhill (Cary Grant) and a fictitious George Kaplan; narrative resolution thus requires a restoration of Thornhill's rightful identity. On a more micro level single functions may also be marked by patterns of exchange: in *On the Waterfront* (Kazan, 1954) the circulation of Edie's (Eva Marie Saint's) glove between herself and Terry Malloy (Marlon Brando) signifies the beginning of an intimate relationship between them, and the exchange of money in *Night and the City* (Dassin, 1950) marks off discrete steps in the downfall of the *film noir* hero, Harry Fabian (Richard Widmark).

Most narratives also have two kinds of characters: the protagonists and the helpers, donors, or dispatchers—those agents who help navigate the hero toward his or her goal. There is a very curious fact to be noticed about these secondary characters: Their activities are often complementary to the hero's non-activity. The hero is often as much a passive creature as an active one: the hero is sent; he is challenged; he is helped; he is confronted by obstacles and so on. Heroes are very often reactive. In *My Darling Clementine*, for example, Wyatt Earp spends the bulk of the film not seeking out the men who killed his brother. It requires a considerable number of interventions by other characters before he takes up his responsibility to carry out justice. In fact, Claude Bremond identifies two basic character types on this basis: agents and patients, those who carry out actions and those to whom actions occur.[26] Roger Thornhill and Terry Malloy, for example, are clearly patients as much as, if not more than, they are agents; and much of the narrative in these cases involves maneuvering them into situations where they must respond decisively or take initiative as agents. It is also very interesting to note how a female hero can lead to a heightening of this passive aspect of the central character as social (sexist) conventions exert a tangible pressure toward reactive behaviour: Douglas Sirk's *All That Heaven Allows* (1956) and Federico Fellini's *Juliet of the Spirits* (1966) accentuate this quality in markedly different ways, for example.

Basically, then, classical narrative stores its fluid propellants of actions and enigmas in characters. This guarantees that we, too, set great store by them as we chart a course through the diegesis on the basis of our character "fix." We could say, in summary, that classical narrative is a special form of the invocation of desire and the promise of gratification in an imaginary time and space peopled by characters performing actions around whom and by whom enigmas are posed.

Pragmatics, Paradox, and Pleasure

Pragmatics, as distinguished from syntax and semantics, involves the effect of messages upon communicants or the question of how communication affects behavior.[27] The difference between establishing agreements about meaning and the effect of agreed-upon meanings is the difference between the content of a message and the relationship between communicators which this message enjoins. To modify slightly a description of this difference in *The Pragmatics of Human Communication,*

> [The semantic aspect is] . . . synonymous in human communication with the content of the message. It may be about anything that is communicable regardless of whether the particular information is true or false, valid, invalid, or undecidable. [The pragmatic aspect] on the other hand, refers to what sort of message it is to be taken as, and, therefore, ultimately to the *relationship* between communicants.[28]

The relationship, reciprocally, governs how the content of a message will be received. By means of this reciprocation relationships alter, escalating in symmetrical confrontation (ascending severity of insults, for example) or settling into grooves of complementary interaction (a pattern of submission/dominance, for example).

The authors of *The Pragmatics of Human Communication* note that the difference between semantics and pragmatics is similar to the difference between data communicated to a computer and a program of instructions about how to treat this data. The latter provides rules about what sort of message any given data is to be taken as. It is akin to a habit or code governing human behavior (like perception, greetings, driving a car, and so on). A program, like a habit or code, is of a higher logical type (more abstract, less variant, and hence less conscious) than the data, messages, or other phenomena it treats. A program is a meta-communication since it is information about information and cannot, without logical error, be reduced to the same level as the messages it organizes.

The pragmatic aspects of a message propose, in their effect, a certain kind of relation. Normally, this is the function of analog codes which, being of a higher logical type, set the context within which the transmission of information occurs. Lacking discrete units, analog codes lend themselves to considerable nuance, nuance that style and rhetoric rely on heavily. Individuals who are in socially "one-down" positions in our culture—women, gays, blacks, Third world people, workers, outcasts, and outsiders—often become particularly well-attuned to the analog nuances that indicate what kind of message a message is and produce the bulk of a message's behavioral effect. Fred Davis, in a paper called "Deviance Disavowal: The Management of Strained Interaction by the Visually Handicapped," notes that handicapped people rely heavily on such signs to gauge the attitudes of "normals" toward them: "Frequently he (the normal) will make *faux pas,* slips of the tongue, revealing gestures and inadvertent remarks which overtly betray this attitude (that the handicapped person is deviant) and place the handicapped person in an even more delicate situation."[29]

Pragmatics, the effect of messages upon communicants, therefore, cannot be gauged without recourse to the habits or codes governing the messages under consideration. In other words, pragmatics can only be understood contextually and cannot be reduced to a property of the text or message itself without logical error. (The humorous or maddening effect of a sign reading "Do Not Read This Sign," for example, results from its paradoxical status as a self-referential statement that cannot be obeyed if read or disobeyed if not read. It exemplifies the kind of logical error that occurs when information and information about information are confounded.) Pragmatics, then, is what allows for the insertion of messages into the existing relations of production, the real conditions of existence. The effect of messages upon communicants works either to reinforce the codes that support existing relations or to alter them. Learning the necessary skills to achieve desired effects in certain formalized kinds of communication is the province of style and rhetoric (and often, in this perspective, an aspect of ideology).

Because pragmatics operates on a separate (higher) plane of abstraction, it cannot be identified with, or opposed to, the meaning of messages: it constitutes a different order of meaning, one of behavior effect. For example, if a guest were to say to his host, "You've got a very impressive place here," the meaning (semantics) of the words is clear to anyone knowing English, but the pragmatics of the message are less clear and would depend on inflection, timing, gesture, previous discussion, and so on, such that the sentence might conceivably be coded to mean, your place is very impressive . . . for some one of your means, or . . . compared to your wife's subordinate place/role, or . . . which I admire greatly. What kind of information is communicated about the information in the message will act to establish a particular kind of relationship. The kind of relationship estab-

IDEOLOGY AND THE IMAGE

lished will affect the participants' behavior—not only in terms of further verbal exchange, though that is the most obvious effect, but also conceivably on other levels: the host may snub his guest thereafter or become exceptionally fond of him. They may even be provoked to fight, a perfect example of the radical difference between physical science and communicational science. In the former, an effect is directly estimable in relation to the energy provoking it; in the latter, enormous discrepancies exist—a single word can even unleash fatal amounts of violence.

Obviously, knowing how to structure meta-information to achieve a desired effect is a powerful skill. And, just as rhetoric works on opinions or commonplaces, so pragmatics preys upon habits or codes, those less conscious guides of skilled, sequential behavior: persuasiveness can be a matter of tapping the right set or frame of mind, of evoking one code and form of response over another. (The example above taps into coded behavior involving social status or sex roles, depending on the "twist" given to the semantics of the message.) This recourse of pragmatics to a realm of a different logical type helps account for the sense of powerlessness we may feel in the face of this aspect of a message: the effect can't be located. It isn't "in" the message but in the relationship between the message and the attitudinal set it preys upon. The effect cannot be countered at the level of the message since that is not the level at which it arises. (In the example above, to respond politely, "Thank you," according to the rules of etiquette that govern compliments, when the compliment is derogatory, fails to counteract the effect of the message.) To continue communication within the context of a code being manipulated to our detriment simply leaves us susceptible to skirmishes of the prey-or-be-preyed-upon variety.

Conversely, knowing how to meta-communicate about the kind of relationship established is vital to sidestepping detrimental or even pathological effects. Earlier, in chapter 1, the symbolic realm was proposed as precisely this kind of meta-communicative capability in relation to the imaginary realm epitomized by the mirror-phase. Whenever we engage or are engaged by film—narrative, documentary, or otherwise—our ability to meta-communicate about the kind of relationship proposed and its behavioral implications, becomes a necessary defense against accepting a place or placement of ideological proportions. Meta-communication, which here becomes comparable to a critical theory of film, affords us a means of "talking back," of displacement, of contestation as well as a means of "taking in," comprehending or recognizing (with its attendant pleasure), the underlying structure or play of codes existing in, but apart from, the messages proper.

Our goal here is meta-communication about the experience of narrative structure. The guiding assumption is that this experience, at least for the majority of classical narratives, bears the structural characteristics of paradox. The type of paradox narrative resembles is known as pragmatic or existential paradox. Pragmatic paradoxes involve logical contradiction issuing from valid deductions from apparently noncontradictory premises,[30] but they also only function within the temporal or historical dimension of human experience. An example is the paradox of Epimenides: "Epimenides was a Cretan who said, 'Cretans always lie'." To ask if Epimenides is telling the truth produces a temporal oscillation between an "if yes, then no" and an "if no, then yes" response as we shift from the larger to the smaller quotation as the controlling context. As Gregory Bateson suggests, a computer faced with this paradox would print out "Yes.No.Yes.No. Yes.No . . ." until some form of breakdown occurred.[31] The paradox is experienced in time. It is existential and cannot be resolved by any formal logic that discounts historical context or effect over time. As Wilden puts it, "The existential paradox differs from the purely logical paradox in that it involves subjects and is primarily dependent on communication. Moreover, it is part of an open system involving feedback and human time."[32]

The experience of paradox can be highly unsettling; its occurrence in narrative then, might provide both added impetus for resolution—narrative closure—and added pleasure at the attainment of such resolution. The desire for such pleasure, in turn, might encourage us to overlook the niceties of how such closure is achieved. The authors of *Pragmatics of Human Communication* offer another example: the barber paradox. "The barber is a soldier who is ordered by his captain to shave all the soldiers of the company who do not shave themselves, but no others." They continue: "Reichenbach (in *Elements of Symbolic Logic*), of course, arrives at the only logical conclusion 'that there is no such thing as the barber of the company, in the sense defined.' This definition is exhaustive on the one hand, but on the other leads straight into paradox if one tries to assign the barber himself to either the self-shavers or the non-self-shavers."[33]

Two different levels of logical type have been confounded and the barber's position between them cannot be finally resolved just as in Epimenides' paradox the member "Cretans always lie" defines the class "Epimenides was a Cretan who said. . . ." and the class defines the member, but paradoxically. Confusion of logical types seems to inevitably generate paradox, and, according to Gödel, any system of logic inevitably rests upon self-referential assumptions that guarantee paradox. Paranoia is one alternative; another is acceptance of the in-

IDEOLOGY AND THE IMAGE

evitable with an attempt to understand the uses to which pragmatic paradox is put.

Existentially, paradoxes like these create impossible situations. The order given to the soldier resembles the injunction contained in the sign "Do Not Read This Sign" or in the query "Is the Cretan telling the truth?" Maximum effect requires three conditions: a hierarchical relationship between the poser of the paradox and the recipient with the former superior; an injunction that can be neither obeyed nor disobeyed; constraints making it difficult or impossible for the recipient to sidestep the injunction.[34] (In the barber paradox this would amount to "insubordination"; in narrative, to the violation of "suspended disbelief.")

Not only do these conditions obtain in the relationship between viewer/reader and narrative text; they are also central to the very nature of the relationship. Even this may be too modest a claim. Arthur Koestler identifies the phenomena of "bisociation" as essential to humor, scientific discovery, and art.[35] Bisociation involves "perceiving of a situation or idea, L, in two self-consistent but habitually incompatible frames of reference,"[36] a definition strikingly similar to our definition of paradox. In the case of humor our intellect recognizes the sudden bisociation and comprehends it, but the suddenness catches our emotions unprepared: They cannot shift to the new frame of reference rapidly enough and so spill out into the gutter of laughter. In scientific discovery the "aha" moment brings fusion of incompatible frames and intellectual synthesis; in art bisociation involves the juxtaposition of, or the confrontation between, incompatible frames and an aesthetic experience. In the last case, the explosive quality of humor is dampened into something more prolonged; we yield to a cathartic reaction and a tendency "toward quietude, the 'earthing' of emotion. . . ."[37] Though I suspect not all narratives are quite so sublimely aesthetic, they do tend to share in this quality of stretching out paradox by holding contraries in juxtaposition before resolving them. The frames of reference are kept in an untenable bisociation, often throughout much of the middle of the narrative, so that the full force of the paradox creates a sustained, intense experience.

As we have seen, classical narrative exhibits a relationship to social reality; and as we might expect, so does narrative paradox to the experience of everyday life. Charles Eckert poses one version of this relationship with eloquent precision.

Two of Lévi-Strauss's insights are specially provocative: that a dilemma (or contradiction) stands at the heart of every living myth, and that this dilemma is expressed through layered pairs of opposites which are transformations of a primary pair. The impulse to construct the myth arises from the desire to resolve the dilemma; but the impossibility of resolving it leads to the crystal-like growth of the myth through which the dilemma is repeated, or conceived in new terms, or inverted—in short, subjected to intellectual operations that might resolve it or attenuate its force.[38]

This crystal-like growth of the myth occurs in the middle of narratives, where operations work toward a resolution. Their complexity often becomes an important measure of the aesthetic impact of the narrative. Their task is formidable: to resolve the unresolvable. ("The purpose of myth is to provide a logical model capable of overcoming a contradiction [an impossible achievement if, as it happens, the contradiction is real].")[39] But the similarity of this task across a variety of narratives will be more apparent if we adopt a single formulation for the articulation of paradox. In my article "Style, Grammar, and the Movies,"[40] I proposed Gregory Bateson's description of a schizophrenogenic episode as a model of multileveled communication:

A young man who had fairly well recovered from an acute schizophrenic episode was visited in the hospital by his mother. He was glad to see her and impulsively put his arm around her shoulders, whereupon she stiffened. He withdrew his arm and she asked, "Don't you love me any more?" He then blushed, and she said, "Dear, you must not be so easily embarrassed and afraid of your feelings." The patient was able to stay with her only a few minutes more and following her departure he assaulted an aide and was put in the tubs.[41]

Bateson's own summarization of the paradoxical injunction delivered here is, "If I am to keep my tie to mother, I must not show her that I love her, but if I do not show her that I love her, then I will lose her."[42]

This formulation has the basic structure of "If A, then B, but if B, then not-A." Across a wide range of classical narrative cinema we find characters who confront, and must live out, just such paradoxes, which manifest themselves in different guises during the course of the narrative.[43] A few examples:

All That Heaven Allows (Douglas Sirk, 1956)

If I am to win my children's love,
 I must marry;
But if I marry, I will lose my
 children's love.

Psycho (Alfred Hitchcock, 1960)

If I am to satisfy my mother, I must
    allow her to kill those who
    threaten our relationship;
But if I allow her to kill those
    who threaten our relationship,
    I cannot satisfy her.

The Birds (Alfred Hitchcock, 1963)

If I am to win Mitch, I must become
    part of his family,
But if I become part of his family,
    I cannot win Mitch.

Blonde Venus (Josef von Sternberg, 1932)

If I am to preserve our family, I must
    earn money,
But if I earn money, I cannot preserve
    our family.

Woman of the Dunes (Hiroshi Teshigahara, 1964)

If I am to be free, I must not accept
    these arbitrary constraints,
But if I do not accept these arbitrary
    constraints, I cannot be free.

The Palm Beach Story (Preston Sturges, 1942)

If I am to be a good wife, I must earn
    money for my husband,
But if I earn money for my husband, I
    cannot be a good wife.

The Deerhunter (Michael Cimino, 1978)

If I am to be a man, I must control
    my feelings,
But if I control my feelings, I
    cannot be a man.

Hard Core (Paul Schrader, 1979)

If I am to save my daughter, I must
    enter the world she has entered,
But If I enter the world she has
    entered, I cannot save my daughter.

The Man Who Shot Liberty Valance (John Ford, 1962)

If there is to be Law, I must take
up the gun,
But if I take up the gun, there will
be no Law.

Marked Woman (Lloyd Bacon, 1937)

If I am to have a decent life, I must
work outside the law as a prostitute
(a "nightclub hostess"),
But if I work outside the law as a
prostitute, I can't have a decent life.

These paradoxical injunctions apply to characters who struggle to
resolve them, but they also affect us insofar as we identify with these
characters. Identification and the suspension of disbelief provide the
constraints that hold us within the grip of paradox alongside characters. Attempts to resolve the paradox follow along the path of the
narrative codes (namely, those of actions and enigmas), but they receive their guidance from mechanisms specifically designed for the
resolution of contradiction and paradox—the operations identified by
Freud as the dream-work and, to a certain extent, the joke-work.[44] Of
those operations, two of the most potent are ones we've seen
before—condensation and displacement.

Earlier, these terms were used interchangeably with metaphoric
and metonymic, but one difference should be pointed out. Metaphor
and metonymy serve as the principal axes of language—the choice of
one word over suitable alternatives at any given point, the spill forward of the linguistic chain—and were consequently likened to the
paradigmatic and syntagmatic as well. This level of similarity remains
true, but condensation and displacement also serve a more specific
task: they transform repressed material so that it may be represented,
albeit in a disguised form. Condensation creates the laconic expression, the conjunction of several trains of thought in a singular representation. Displacement shifts attention away from the central point;
it redistributes emphases or values associated with repressed material. Hence these two operations, whether found in dream-work,
joke-work, or narrative-work, act at a higher level of specificity than
metaphor and metonymy; they work to overcome censorship, to re-
cast material so it can withstand the scrutiny of criticism, to attenuate
or resolve contradictions. They function in direct relation to a subject's intentionality or purposefulness rather than as a necessary
condition of discourse generally. Condensation and displacement are
a necessary feature of dream-work, not of mental-image formation

IDEOLOGY AND THE IMAGE

generally; just as they are a specific feature of narrative-work when there is paradox to be resolved, and not of verbal or visual discourse generally.

This added specificity removes these two forms of work from the province of linguistics or semiotics proper, which study general rules pertaining to sign systems. As Paul Ricoeur argues, the dream operations are infra-linguistic (lacking a *langue* or discrete set of rules) and supra-linguistic (bearing resemblance to other large unities of discourse like proverbs, folklore, or myth).[45] This makes these operations more similar to rhetoric than linguistics—or as Emile Benveniste suggests, "It is style rather than language that I would consider as a term of comparison with the properties Freud has shown to be indicative of the 'dream language'."[46] This line of approach proposes that any detailed consideration of the narrative-work will necessarily return us to that level of stylistic nuance and aesthetic effect that seems to remain beyond the reach of semiotic or structural analysis proper even though these forms of analysis have contributed much to our understanding of narrative on other levels.

In narrative, condensation and displacement work specifically to attenuate or resolve the force of a paradoxical injunction. Since the paradox itself arises from a confusion of logical types, these operations work to efface the confusion or to make it appear as though what belong to separate logical types actually belong to only one. If successful, this operation will allow the paradox to be resolved but by means of a sleight-of-hand: It will appear that there never was a contradiction, since what was of one logical type now seems to be of another. For example, in *All That Heaven Allows* the narrative-work operates upon the "I must marry" conclusion-condition. Ron Kirby (Rock Hudson) ostensibly a young, handsome gardener and an unacceptable marriage partner for an older, well-to-do widow, Carrie (Jane Wyman), turns out to have independent means (a tree farm) and a more wholesome philosophy of life than Carrie's class- and age-conscious children and friends. And to further alleviate the contradiction he suffers an accident at the end of the film that leaves him temporarily physically incapacitated (i.e., lacking immediate access to his sexual potential). As a result the opposition posed by her children, that she should marry the wealthy, middle-aged, essentially asexual Harvey, and not Ron, is resolved by making Ron take on the characteristics of a Harvey (albeit temporarily—this is part of the film's unsettling undertow, as though it were marking its own deceptions for us as a Brecht might do). Condensation thus occurs around Ron as a source of a higher truth, revealing a sage in pauper's clothes, as it were, while his sexual potency is displaced into an indeterminant future, beyond the end of the film in any case. This allows Carrie to resolve the role choice imposed by the paradox—to be a mother to her children and a wife to her love—by becoming mother to both her children and her love. If Ron had proved to be as definitely working-class and sexually active as he is young, this collapsing of different logical types could not work. Instead, Carrie would have to assert a hierarchy, valuing one above the other. But her resolution would still occur beneath the weight of the paradoxical double-bind her children impose upon her: marrying Ron would lose her their love, marrying Harvey would lose her his (Ron's).

The result is a deflection or displacement of the paradox itself like the way a ray of light is refracted when it passes from air to water. When we trace the ray's path back from water to air, we posit an imaginary trajectory for it, forgetting to take account of refraction. The object, a fish, say (or a marriage partner), that we think we see in one position in actual fact occupies another. Likewise, the contradiction we think we see resolved actually remains, hidden by what we take to be a resolution.

In fact, in each case of paradoxical injunction a confusion about the logical typing of a term is either clarified (re-establishing clear-cut, correct typing) or resolved by deception (establishing a non-problem of typing by sleight-of-hand. In each of the paradoxical formulations a word or phrase carries a double meaning which, if typed correctly—in truth or by deception, resolves the paradox. "I must marry" carries this ambiguity: I must marry . . . someone who will allow me to remain a mother; I must marry . . . someone to whom I can be a wife. In *Psycho* "to satisfy mother" has this quality: it leaves no place for Norman. He must satisfy unreasonable requests for an absolute unity; in doing so he must dissolve himself—the one responsible for satisfying these requests.

In *Marked Woman,* double meaning resides in "decent." In one frame of reference it means material security and comfort; in the other ethical or honorable action. This paradox can also be posed around "smart"—"If I'm smart . . ." or "If I know what's good for me . . ."—or in fact any term that captures in words the existential double-bind the character faces and we share over a stretch of time. (We can retroactively reduce the experience to a simple paradoxical formulation, but while the narrative represents this paradoxical injunction, it is lived, experienced through time, rather than intellectually or logically com-prehended.) The ambiguity of "decent" also mobilizes a work of displacement that is extremely common to Hollywood cinema and well analyzed by Charles Eckert in his study of *Marked Woman:* the shift of emotional emphasis from class conflict (the haves vs. the have-nots) to ethical conflict (revenge vs. informing).

Blonde Venus and *The Palm Beach Story* pose very similar paradoxes involving the need for a wife to earn money (compared to an independent Mary Dwight in *Marked Woman*). The difficulty arises from the patriarchal and sexist social order surrounding the films. It sets the frames of reference for the contradiction: a woman's sole means of earning money, as *Marked Woman* also assumes, is with her body and her sexuality. But the "laws" of marriage reserve this body and sexuality for the husband. Hence she cannot both earn money and be a good wife. *Blonde Venus* resolves this paradoxical injunction dramatically—holding the contraries in prolonged juxtaposition and finally establishing a clear-cut hierarchy favoring earning money over marriage (which was overturned by a studio-imposed ending that asserts the converse priority). *The Palm Beach Story* resolves the paradox comedically—Gerry announces she will be better for Tom as a sister and peremptorily assumes that role. Our laughter flows from the sudden clash of two different, mutually exclusive frames of reference, husband-wife/ brother-sister, and continues to occur through a series of duplicitous encounters until a resolution arrives (through considerable sleight-of-hand).

Narrative closure generally exhibits congruence with the resolution of paradox. The congruence heightens the sense of unity and coherence, while the concept of coherence, closure, is itself contradictorily coherent. Something exceeds it, is left over; paradox remains, finally, irresolvable: "And, as always, coherence in contradiction expresses the force of a desire."[47] We return once more to desire and the pleasure of recognition-discovery. The aesthetic gratification narrative affords helps attenuate the force of real contradictions; it also helps identify them. The power of this invocation of desire can be readily yoked to a reinforcement of the *status quo*, but it can also be harnessed to the possibilities of change, radical change.[48] Narrative cinema may work to reconstitute us in the position of self-as-subject, but it may also move us. We are not simply put in our place, we are also moved; and one possible direction that movement may follow is through and beyond the position of self-as-subject to the realm of symbolic exchange where grace or order (in an open-ended, non-imaginary sense) may be realized.

4.

Blonde Venus:
Playing with Performance

Critical Approaches to Narrative

MANY OF THE codes not specific to the cinema but appearing in it, as well as a few of the more specifically cinematic ones, have been examined so far in a general manner. We have seen that these codes coalesce within a single text in the imperfect manner of a *moiré* pattern, rendering the textual system itself as a trace of differences that bear ideological significance. Our place, our position becomes wrapped up in this mobilization of codical displacements marked by the textual system. Understanding that place means understanding something of the hierarchical ordering of codes and of their internal, organizing principles. It means, for most of us, beginning with an understanding of narrative as the code most frequently controlling popular cinema.

Having established this general context, a choice opens of elaborating them in greater detail, but at a still general, or theoretical, level or of developing them in more detail through their application to specific texts. I have chosen the latter course, partly because continued theoretical elaboration would demand a more technical and less accessible approach and partly because practical application is not conceived as a mechanical laying on of an answer key but as a dialectical testing out of assumptions and hypotheses. The results of such an engagement with specific texts should be continued theoretical elaboration, not according to an increasingly rarefied logic, but according to how these ideas work in practice.

Such a process is necessarily arrested when committed to print; it runs the risk of appearing reified with each of the terms set in place, the concept of dialectic cranked out as a fudge against "errors" that may have crept into the purity and truth of the theory. This risk is real but acquiescence to it is imaginary. Acquiescence allows a symbolic discourse about the realm of imaginary discourse to be taken for what it is not—imaginary, objectifying, a token of reification. This text, then, is marked by a displacement of codes, by difference, by gaps that cannot be contained except in the imaginary. It takes a critical attitude toward the ideological aspects of its own constitution while also welcoming the lack of fixity or unity informing it. This text only "fits" within a larger system of discourse, within a series of displacements activated by other texts engaged in a process of discovery. It is only in the realm of the imaginary that process becomes product. Only in the imaginary does the text receive a quotient of truth which it will have or possess from now to eternity.

The need to differentiate, to make and acknowledge differences, draws upon a political motivation in the case of this study. The questions at the end of chapter 1 regarding who draws the line refer to this motivation as do the questions we can pose here about narrative films: what differences exist amongst groups of similar films such as the classical narrative cinema, what makes criticism of texts necessary at all, what separates criticism from theory? The first question will be pursued in practice through discussion of *Blonde Venus, The Birds,* Fred Wiseman's documentaries, and the ethnographic film. The third refers to different levels of logical typing or generality about which the most directly relevant point is the lack of any simple transference of information from one level to the other: neither knowledge of texts nor textuality provides the necessary and sufficient basis for comprehension of the other; each "body" of knowledge must be developed with a certain degree of autonomy.

What makes criticism necessary at all involves a number of considerations, foremost of which are the duplicity of the text and the phenomenon of its speech through silence: although it cannot say what it means (the text is mute) it nonetheless bears meanings we acknowledge (we know to whom the film speaks). Criticism could not exist if the discourse of others were totally alien; criticism would not be necessary if such discourse were perfectly clear. The mind-affected world is the realm where "inner states find outward expression."[1] That they do so, but imperfectly, becomes a primary motivation for critical discourse, be it in the formal shape of a monograph or as informal discussion amongst friends.

The sense of being spoken to (including but not limited to calling up the self-as-subject) must be the source of our search for meaning, value, and purpose in a text. Mute, inanimate objects address us. They bear the trace of outward expression through their organization as systems of signs. They appear as nodal points, as radiant hot spots in our surround. Consciousness awakens in this act of intentionality toward an other. Consciousness is always of something, and here it is of being addressed. The consciousness directs itself toward something palpable, discrete, immediate. Through signification inner states appear incarnate, an intending made flesh.

The text embodies system or pattern. Like the unconscious, it is the locus of those processes that invoke a necessary unity. Like our sense of our own bodies, our acknowledgment of the text fluctuates between representation within ourselves and object outside ourselves.[2] The text, like the bodily symptom, points beyond itself; it stands in for an "other scene" from which its unity originates but which is only accessible through outward manifestations such as speech, symptom, or the report of a dream.

The act of representation necessarily requires mapping. Signs stand for things absent. To know in what manner, by what rules or codes this "standing for" occurs, requires an act of interpretation. The requirement is all the more necessary because the duplicity of the text refers not only to the presence-in-absence characteristic of all sign systems (the double register of signifiers referring to one another and to a more distant referent), but also to the specific process by which signs concatenate. We have seen this process operate via narrative-work in a manner similar to dream-work. We have seen how this process bears a relationship to ideology in its capacity for social (mis-) representation and to revelation in its capacity to speak to us about the necessary integration of mind. This dual possibility places us beneath the roofs of two critical schools—the school of revelation and the school of suspicion. Paul Ricoeur identifies a common element in Nietzsche, Marx, and Freud, the originators of the school of suspicion, by saying, "what all three attempted, in different ways, was to make their 'conscious' methods of deciphering coincide with the 'unconscious' *work* of ciphering which they attributed to the will to power, to social being, to the unconscious psychism. *Guile will be met by double guile*" [his emphases].[3]

Lodged within meaning, occupying the lacunae created by presence-in-absence, as it were, we find intentionality (the sense of being addressed, what we called the denotative level of the still image) and production (traces, all we ever have, of signification itself). Manifest/latent, surface/deep, literal/metaphoric—terms like these often seek to indicate this duplicity and to gauge whether it ought to have a pejorative overtone or not. These "deep" levels of the text arise from the same topographical surface, however, while being of different logical types. They do not control or govern invisibly, apart, but interact in one and the same process of communication. They are not a higher reality but part and parcel of one reality, one plane of manifestation. What Laplance and Leclaire say of the unconscious pertains as well to these levels of the text: "the unconscious stands in relation to the manifest, not as the intended meaning to the literal text, but on the same level of reality. It is what allows us to conceive a dynamic relationship between the manifest text and that which is absent from and to be interpolated in that text: it is a fragment of discourse that must regain its place within discourse."[4] The objects of immediate sensation, the signs of meaning, only acquire their full meaning for us when we associate what we experience directly with what we do not.

We seek a logic for duplicitous meaning that acknowledges the argument that two different logics cannot operate on the same level without creating an untenable position. This is precisely the untenable position of paradox, which we have already met. We part company with the rules of formal logic that decry this untenability in order to adopt the temporal, historically-open rules of a dialectical logic.[5] We couple the present to the absent; we attend to gaps, lacunae, to the guile of the unconscious psychism that speaks to us through outward manifestations. We prepare ourselves to listen for revelation; we steel ourselves to listen with suspicion. The ridge is narrow along which we walk, but there is no straighter way for us to go.

The attempt to walk on less vertiginous ground runs the risk of reductionism, not only in prescribing a predetermined fixity of meaning to the text, which assumes general rules or codes fully determine specific messages, but also in ascribing an harmonious unity to the text, the absence of gaps or symptomatic discourse in favor of a full presence of meaning. Flaws may well be cited here but they are precisely that—blemishes, regrettable lapses from an ideal—and not symptoms to be read and deciphered. This risk has been particularly prevalent amongst *auteur* and *auteur*-influenced critics. (*Auteur* critics, though, can still serve as a model for the centrality they accord style or idiolect and their insistence on testing hypotheses—the director is the *auteur,* e.g.—in actual practice.)

In discussing John Ford's film career, for example, Andrew Sarris writes, "If there is one idea above all others that has dominated what some call 'the world of his films' it is the idea of Community. It is an idea that glows through all his late films. . . ."[6] This kind of perspective collapses films into the harmonious sum of their parts, a view of film and ideology radically different from that of the editors of *Cahiers du Cinéma*[7] and, in particular, from their reading of John Ford's *Young Mr. Lincoln,* where notions like "Community" fracture under the pressure of a monstrous ideology Ford cannot contain.[8] What are we to make of this fractionation of social cohesion, particularly in the radical otherness of Lincoln himself? How are we to place the evocation of Community within an historical and ideological context, at what angle does it intersect the dominant ideology of its period? Andrew Sarris's mode of analysis does not tell us, or rather, it announces the absence of gaps or fissures as cause for celebration—stylistic/thematic unity has been revealed.

There is also the risk of reducing meaning to a stylistic dictionary. This tendency is apparent in most introductory film texts and in some forms of *auteur*-influenced criticism. Louis Gianetti in what is probably the best introductory text, *Understanding Movies,* for example, tells us that, "[High-angle camera shots] tend to reduce a subject to insignificance, suggesting vulnerability; we are superior to the subject. Low angles, on the other hand, increase a subject's importance, creating a sense of dominance over the viewer."[9] James Monaco in *How to Read a Film* seconds this notion: "It goes without saying that high-angle shots diminish the importance of the subject while low-angle shots emphasize its power."[10] Both authors neglect the larger determinations of the textual system, the sliding relationship between signifiers and signifieds and how these floating, parallel chains are stapled or pinned together at nodal points by the work of many codes. Unlike spoken language, analog communication lacks the discrete units and the instance of a denotative level that allow the compilation of a dictionary of meanings. Meaning in relation to camera angle must be pinned down in order to be registered and the fact that it is commonly pinned in the manner Giannetti and Monaco describe does not preclude alternatives (which any theory must account for). Calvin Pryluck puts the case eloquently:

> . . . the attempts to define the meaning of coding variables do not take into account some interesting counter-examples. For instance, in *Citizen Kane,* Charles Foster Kane has been defeated and humiliated in his attempt to be elected governor. The first time Kane is seen following the election, he is confronted by his oldest friend. This scene is depicted from a low angle, considerably below eye level. Kane dominates the scene in a formal sense, yet the flow of the confrontation suggests not dominance but placation.
>
> There is probably an interpretation of this scene which would make use of the idea of dominance, for instance, a giant in defeat or ironic commentary on previous dominance. But these interpretations make a muddle of any simplistic attempt at definition of coding variables.[11]

Another risk is less a matter of conceptual adequacy than stance or point of view. From the political, Marxist, point of view I have chosen, this risk can be described as turning formal analysis into an abstract game theory of interest in and of itself. Theory for theory's sake can never be acceptable (though it may be conceptually adequate, and even elegant) if we are concerned with changing the world and our place within it—the world not simply of an imaginary diegesis but of all material processes of communication and exchange. Jonathan Culler, in an article on structure and ideology in literature, defends this approach by involving the relativism of all ways of seeing: "given that there is no ultimate and absolute justification for any system or the interpretation flowing from it, one tries to value the activity of interpretation itself, or the activity of theoretical elaboration, rather than any results which might be obtained."[12] He also argues that interpretation is not a matter of "recovering" meaning but "rather an attempt to participate in and observe the play of possible meanings to which the text gives access."[13] This approach finds an echo in the concluding sentence of Kristen Thompson and David Bordwell's excellent formal analysis of Yasujiro Ozu's films: "In such working upon the narrative, Ozu's spaces demand to be read plurally, for their own sakes, challenging us to play, however vertiginously, within them."[14] Thompson and Bordwell "play" with great dexterity and considerable elegance, but fail to place their, and Ozu's, play within an ideological/political context. They do not consider "the contradictions this kind of play can induce vis-à-vis the social relations of the various audiences . . ."[15] (except for brief speculation regarding the place of the spectator).[16]

Such an approach at its worst (from which Thompson and Bordwell are far removed) extols criticism-for-criticism's-sake as the final criterion. Such a criterion functions as a convenient measure of the exchange value of criticism in the academic institution: the production of critical texts can be exchanged for appointments, salary increases, promotions, or tenure without questions of larger purpose ever being asked. This is a form of imaginary exchange and its values have little or no value at all in symbolic exchange.

Some forms of textual system may invite heightened forms of play, they may offer a carnival of delights if we learn to read them right, but the controlling questions remain: at what expense, and whose expense (self? subject?), in what place, by whose rules? To insist on asking these questions as opposed to other possible questions is a function of stance, assumptions. Logic cannot prove them necessary or correct, though I believe them to be so (without running into paradox); they are simply stated, openly, so that you may take your stance in relation to them.

Sternberg and the Critics

Blonde Venus (Josef von Sternberg, 1932) provides a useful starting point for textual analysis since it can be located within a main-stream cinema (Hollywood and classical narrative in this case) and yet stands somewhat to the side. This allows two goals to be postulated for the analysis: (1) to demonstrate that von Sternberg's visual style is not a gratuitous finish to inconsequential stories, as some have claimed, but is in fact an integral quality of the textual system, what, in a certain sense, finishes it. In more ways than are usually recognized, this visual style directly colludes in the marking of a narrative course; (2) to demonstrate that, within the dominance of a narrative structure, stylistic inflections may open up the film and even jeopardize the apparent autonomy of its diegetic universe while remaining, in Sternberg's case at least, ultimately subordinate to the control of the narrative. This may allow us to classify von Sternberg as a modernist, but is definitely not enough to classify him as a Brechtian (political) modernist.

Despite Josef von Sternberg's resurrection from the lower depths of the socially unconscious film maker in the last few decades, largely on the basis of his stylistic achievement, that style remains poorly examined. It is not so very surprising that Richard Griffith, summing up in 1948 a decade of critical consensus, said that through Sternberg's series of six Dietrich films,

> action and continuity were progressively drained away in favor of an ordered flow of a pattern of images, often lovely in themselves, sometimes floridly vulgar, but always empty of real dramatic meaning.[17]

It is more surprising that Andrew Sarris, one of the *auteur* critics responsible for our revived interest in Sternberg, would reverse Griffith's moral judgment but retain his evaluation of the relevance of style to story:

> Curiously, the fact that the plot of *Blonde Venus* lacks surface conviction gives it a certain freedom in its fantasizing, and not the least of its charms is its careless regard of Dietrich the woman trying to cope with the demands of her myth. That her nightclub numbers are utterly unmotivated in terms of the plot is the key to the extreme stylization of Dietrich's character, extreme, that is, even for Sternberg.[18]

Both these accounts are wrong. Neither one analyzes visual style sufficiently to unravel its integral relationship to the narrative, or the full complexity of Sternberg's strategies. The purpose here will be to demonstrate the careful weaving together of various codes into a singular textual system that can be loosely described as modernist rather than judged as vulgar or unmotivated.

The visual style of *Blonde Venus* deals primarily not with

pleasure—self-indulgent pleasure, as many believe—but with the control of pleasure, with the mediation of desire by style and performance—a mediation that spans the character, Helen Faraday; the star, Marlene Dietrich; the director, Josef von Sternberg; and us, the viewers. The attempt to control pleasure, marshalled through the non-immediacy of the image, the fetish, the star (the "image" of star/actor/character), leaves its trace in the nooks and crannies of the textual system where our critical reading may rediscover it.

For methodological purposes, analysis of this style can be broken down into an analysis of the various codes, some of which function to help constitute the narrative but in/against all of which Sternberg's style has left its mark.

Synopsis

Ned (Herbert Marshall) and Helen Faraday (Marlene Dietrich) meet and become married after an idyllic romance in Europe. The story resumes in America where they live with their young son, Johnny. Ned is a scientist who discovers he is seriously ill and needs $1500 to return to Europe for a risky operation. In despair he offers to sell his body to a physician to help his family. The doctor offers him some money to help him get to Europe, but Ned is too proud to accept it. At home, he and Helen put Johnny to sleep by retelling the story of their courtship as a fairy tale. Later Helen announces she will return to the stage.

Helen enters a drab, crowded agent's office and is singled out by the agent, who changes her name to Helen Jones and offers to get her work immediately. They visit O'Connor, a nightclub owner, who agrees to use her. She is billed as "The Blonde Venus," usurping the place of the former star, Taxi. In her first number, "Hot Voodoo," she moves through the audience in an ape costume, which she gradually removes on stage. Nick Townsend (Cary Grant), who had been involved with Taxi, is captivated and visits her backstage. As the scene ends he notices her photo of Johnny; the film dissolves to a close-up of a check for $300 being made out to Helen by Nick. Helen gives $300 to Ned, telling him that she has received an advance.

Helen and Johnny wish Ned bon voyage as he boards a ship for Europe; and as they leave, they meet Nick Townsend. O'Connor cannot locate Helen and becomes frantic, then Nick calls saying her stage career is over. Nick provides her with an apartment and then they agree to go away to the countryside. She realizes, however, that she must go back to Ned when he returns.

Ned, though, has returned early to an empty apartment. They

confront each other, and Helen confesses her infidelity. When Ned threatens to take Johnny from her, she flees with the boy and becomes a wanted woman followed by detectives. As she drifts southward, her plight becomes increasingly desperate: her money runs low, she washes dishes for a meal, she is arrested for vagrancy. A detective picks up her trail somewhere near Galveston, and she finally surrenders, disclosing her identity to him.

Ned arrives by train to claim his son and pays back the $1500 Helen had earned for him. Helen, at her nadir, enters a flophouse, gives away the money, and leaves, announcing that she can rise again on her own. A montage sequence leads directly to "The Helen Jones Revue" in Paris, where she is attracting large audiences. Nick Townsend, who had gone to Europe to console himself after losing her, happens to attend a performance. Helen appears in white tails as the master of a harem to do her final number. Nick visits her backstage and proposes marriage, which she rejects.

The scene cuts to a newspaper headline announcing her engagement to Nick. Their boat arrives in New York, and they go to Ned's apartment so she can see Johnny. Ned begrudgingly admits her; Johnny persuades her and Ned to enact their bedtime fairy tale; and as they do so, they appear to become reconciled. With the reunion of the family the film ends.

Editing

Although most sequences in *Blonde Venus* might fit comfortably with Christian Metz's *grande syntagmatique*, the sense of coherent plausibility normally fabricated within the diegesis of classical narrative is noticeably flawed. The synopsis itself, which may seem virtually spastic in its lurching, poorly motivated movement, is an accurate account of how the film presents itself. The "flaws" of the synopsis are repeated in the diegesis, where match cuts on movement or eyeline are infrequent. Many sequences are dominated by one shot between characters who do not look directly at each other, stressing the relationship of character to background or decor over the relationship between characters. (As a corollary, changes in decor, discussed below, take on considerable signifiicance.) The flawed or lacunaridden quality of the diegesis stands as an early sign of Sternberg's play in/against the assumptions, and codes, of classical narrative.

Composition

By composition I mean the framing of shots rather than the staging or the control of movement within the shot (*mise-en-scène*) or the control of camera movement. Composition plays two important roles, both common to film melodrama: developing characters and developing relationships between characters. Helen's character is supported compositionally in the early stages of the film—during her theatrical ascent—by shots in which black dominates the lower portion of the frame (4.1). These compositions suggest her rise, floating up from obscurity toward the radiant allure already promoted by the high-key, soft-focus lighting of her face. Later, during her fall (and flight), blackness extends across the top and bottom of the frame emphasizing her entrapment in a world not of her own choosing (4.2). A doubling of the bar—the bands of blackness—leads to a reversal of effect.

Relationships are developed by other compositional means: rear-screen projection and the placement of Nick and Helen during their pleasure-boat ride suggests their lack of connection, the artificiality of their (adulterous) vacation while Ned is in Europe (4.3). Their boat also moves laterally, flatly, across the frame in contrast with the ship bringing Ned back from Europe (or the arrival of his train in the South [4.4]), which moves forward, toward the camera/ viewer. Composition brings the sense of intrusion, and threat, onto the side of Ned, the husband, rather than to the side of Nick, the interloper, despite the imperfection of Nick's relationship with Helen. (It is just not his movement forward, toward Helen and us, that implies threat, but this movement in association with the judgmental wrath that has developed around him.)

At a later point, a wedge-like or V-shaped composition occurs in relation to the imminent meeting between Helen and a detective in New Orleans. The foreground objects or shadows that reveal only fragments of the characters' bodies within this wedge steer the meaning of the composition toward entrapment, while dialogue and a shot/ reverse-shot pattern further steer meaning toward a sense of confrontation between opposing forces (4.5–4.7).

Lighting

Lighting plays three important roles in *Blonde Venus*. High-key, soft-focus lighting is reserved for the luminous star, Marlene Dietrich (4.8). By singling her out, it reminds us of the interplay between star and character and of the possibility of discrepant diegetic realms, since high-key halo lighting belongs to a different subcode than the other lighting setups, which are generally forms of low-key lighting (4.9). This discrepancy is not without tradition; as Laura Mulvey suggests, "The presence of woman is an indispensable element of

4.1, 4.3, 4.5   **4.2, 4.4, 4.6**

114   IDEOLOGY AND THE IMAGE

spectacle in normal narrative film, yet her visual presence tends to work against the development of a story line, to freeze the flow of action in moments of erotic contemplation."[19] Sternberg's disinterest in narrative per se allows this eroticism greater rein than usual, while Helen's, embarking upon a stage career allows the narrative to partially defuse the disruptive potential of this moment of contemplation.

Lighting is also deployed in a customarily melodramatic manner either to enhance mood or to comment on characters. When Ned offers to sell his body to science, for example, the scene is lit so that the bodies of Ned and the doctor are mostly in darkness (4.10). Only their heads and the skull on the doctor's desk are well lit, by a wedge of light that renders them disembodied objects in an alienated discussion.

An even more striking example is the progressive alteration in lighting when Ned confronts Helen after his return from Europe. The shifting degree of shadow upon their faces sets up an ironic counter-

4.11a, c, e   **4.11b, d, f**

4.11a-t. These stills represent all the shots during Ned and Helen's confrontation except for one shot when she walks from the window to behind Ned's chair (4.15) (eliminated to clarify the transition, which is most evident in the close-ups). The stills are arranged in two columns to make the change in lighting more readily noticeable.

point to the coincidence of dialogue with social mores: at the very
moment Ned is socially vindicated in casting Helen out for blackening
her-his name, the lighting vindicates her and criticizes him (4.11a-t).
(His immediate recourse, when Helen flees, to the guardians of mo-
rality, the police in this case, receives further comment when he

passes behind a window whose diagonals form an X, a confirmation of this melodramatic marking by light [4.12]).

Finally, the dominant subcode of low-key lighting is often utilized—in association with other codes—to merge characters with their environment, especially Helen (4.13–15). The play of shadows

stirred up by low-key lighting, the scattered placement of irregular objects across the frame, the predominance of shallow-focus photography—all coalesce into a camouflage motif that confounds our recognition of figure/ground relationships. This confusion of figure/ground stresses the two-dimensional quality of the image as image rather than its three-dimensional quality as illusion of reality, and, as such, it becomes part of Sternberg's play with, and within, narrative space.

Decor

The use of decor involves the elaboration of at least two significant motifs (via an accretion of markers rather than symbols): the tropical motif and the motif of the slats.

The tropical decor motif begins as a theatrical backdrop for Helen's first stage number, "Hot Voodoo" (4.16). It is not found in her home life with Ned (4.17). Gradually, though, as her career rises and then plummets during her flight from Ned, the tropical motif begins to envelop her, on stage and off. What began as a stage role—a "play" with lush imagery—becomes an existential trap whose imagery pervades her entire life (4.18–19). The development of this motif corresponds closely to the development of the slat (or horizontal line) motif.

Various black or white bands cut across the frame horizontally throughout the first rise and subsequent fall in Helen's stage career. The motif is initially restricted to her stage career and is absent from the early domestic scenes (4.20–22); but after she flees with Johnny, the slat motif spills over into her personal life (4.23–25). When the motif is traced through this portion of the film, its felt presence is seen

4.12, 4.14, 4.16   **4.13, 4.15, 4.17**

4.15. Sometimes Sternberg organizes shadows to achieve camouflage effects. Note the wall shadow that lines up perfectly with the fur collar of Helen's coat and the chair shadows that fan out from Helen's mid-section, obscuring her outline.

to intensify, building to a crescendo during her visit to the flophouse, the nadir of her flight. At this point, after Ned has taken Johnny away, the slat motif achieves its resolution: as Helen strides through the hovel, the background is filled by a long row of bunk beds (dark, horizontal slabs) upon which are stretched out the defeated bodies of

Blonde Venus: *Playing with Performance*   121

4.24, 4.26, 4.28   **4.25, 4.27, 4.29**

IDEOLOGY AND THE IMAGE

broken women (4.26). The way in which the motif is pinned to character actions and at times directly composed of metaphorical signifiers turns it toward a metaphor for defeat and death. Helen has descended to the lower depths, and she is as close to losing all control over her life (her performance, her style) as she will come.

Sternberg marks this climax by doubling the motif. Not only does the slat motif dominate a very shallow background, his camera itself cuts a narrow band or swath of horizontal images from this world as he tracks, first right and then left, the full length of the flophouse (4.27–28). It is one of the few sustained camera movements in the entire film, and its significance clearly extends beyond keeping the character in view: Helen may be in danger of losing her control, but Sternberg is very far from losing his. The motif concludes at this point as Helen announces her determination to rise again and ascends the flophouse stairs.

Clothing

Clothing weaves another strand in Sternberg's idiolect; it is another code contributing to the plurality of meaning that flashes up from differing codes intermittently like glitter from the facets of a jewel. Its most evident contribution involves Helen's attire, especially her theatrical costumes. The costumes are designed to evoke the erotic, which they do with fur and cleavage (4.29). As Roland Barthes asks, "Is not the most erotic portion of a body where the garment gapes?"[20] Intermittence, the flash of skin between two folds of clothing, the game of hide-and-seek raised to an erotic level—this is what seduces. And this is what Helen's performance is meant to play upon.

Let's focus for a moment on one particular item in Helen's "Hot Voodoo" costume—the heart-shaped, fur covering that extends from waist to groin (4.30). Given the tropical eroticism, given Helen's threatening ape-like entrance, given her suggestive stance and gestures, is it possible that this displaced epaulet is what transforms her into Sternberg's version of a certain species of carnivorous plant, that this costume marks her as a Venus Fur Trap, as it were—a symptomatic manifestation of the psychodynamics of erotic contemplation.

The association of erotic attire with Helen Jones, the creation of, and fascination with, this character as a sensually alluring figure on and off stage to the men who surround her (except Ned) increases throughout the rise and fall of her first career. It is masked or absent from her second career, her triumphal return to the stage in Paris, and it is recalled but also denied at the end of the film when she rejoins

her family. This pattern seems directly related to Sternberg's interest in the control of pleasure: as long as her career is controlled by others (men) the lure of her sensuality is a threat to herself, a threat reinforced by the tropical decor and slat motifs. But the decline in control by other characters parallels an increasingly unmediated control by a different other (Sternberg and/or the viewer), a point to be elaborated further. More immediately, it appears that when she controls her own career the threat of being controlled diminishes, while the lure (her white tails) can be even more tantalizing for disclosing less, and for bringing closer to the surface the drive behind this self-control and auto-fetishism: the repression of sexual difference.[21] If we examine the concept of performance in *Blonde Venus* more specifically, it may be possible to begin linking up the points of intersection between these stylistic inflections.

Performance

In *Blonde Venus,* performance revolves around display, but dialectically: it promises pleasure in a context of presence and absence, hide and seek, offer and withdrawal which establishes a parallel between Sternberg's performance and his character's, between his spectacle and Helen's (Marlene Dietrich's).

Helen's first number, "Hot Voodoo," emphasizes this promise blatantly. It is a provocative, suggestive call to pleasure as beauty emerges from the beast to sing and sway amidst a tide of tropical eroticism (4.31–34). This stage image, this theatrical reality, however, is not under Helen's control; it is the design of others for the pleasure of others. The dialectic is weak; when all is said and done Helen's performance is an announcement of her availability (as one of her antecedents, the nude in most classical oil paintings so often announces). Nick Townsend's movement into her life is ample evidence of this.

During her flight, and fall, the aura of this kind of performance becomes a mask she cannot remove (4.35). She is hunted by means of her stage appearance, implausible perhaps but metaphorically appropriate as what had been confined to the world of stage reality permeates her everyday reality. Hence the film can be said to pivot around her struggle to gain control of her performance, control signalled by her Paris triumph in white tails (4.36).

Her initial performance, and Sternberg's, revolve around an announcement of availability, or, at Sternberg's level more specifically, around the promise of illusionism, the seamless reality of an illusion. The nightclub audience watches her display her control of their desire, believing her available; the film audience watches Sternberg display his control of their desire, believing his world real, available to the mind as a plausible unity (a diegetic universe). But Sternberg controls an image that refers to objects and events no longer present, present only as "image" (of star/actor/character). He presents, makes present, what cannot be literally seen or had "in the flesh."

It is at this level of directorial style, in Sternberg's insistence on the fragility of illusionism, that the play of hide-and-seek, presence and absence emerges full-blown. He stresses the tenuous alliance between our knowledge of the illusion and our belief in its reality. He threatens to unveil a scandal before our very eyes; he invites us to play in the gap, the wedgelike opening, his style unveils. The threat of deconstruction hovers alongside a widened space for play. Like Yasujiro Ozu, Sternberg can be read as a modernist but, like Ozu, that

decisive step toward Brecht and a political modernism is only threatened, never taken.

And just as Sternberg insists we recognize and accept this substitute present (this illusion) by stressing its fabrication, its two-dimensional quality—the better to appreciate his artistic mastery of the distinction between illusion and reality, his present to us, rather than his hewing out of an historically specific space between spectacle and spectator—so Helen and Marlene Dietrich struggle to gain control of their performance, insisting that we recognize and accept the constraint of desire, the unavailability of what is momentarily promised without recognizing the act of disavowal that founds the entire fetishizing "play."[22]

The achievement of this control is stylistically marked by the white tails. Like her earlier fur trappings, the tails hide in order to promise that absent object required by the male viewer/voyeur (4.37–38). Unlike the fur, the white tails almost turn the dynamic of

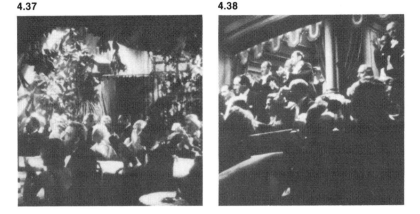

4.37–38. The audience for Helen's "Hot Voodoo" number is clearly composed of men and women, whereas in Paris (4.36) her final number in the film is directed toward an almost exclusively male audience.

the fetish into a scandal by stressing the male rather than the female gender of the promised by absent object. But as the costume closes the distance to the phallocentric origin of fetishism, it ironically *increases* the distance from the disruption of the very mechanism propelling it. The delirium that accompanies the threat of scandal triumphs as a heightened play, a compelling tease, and the "baring of the device" remains cloaked beneath a veil of fetishistic delight.

Helen's success then depends upon signifying that she seems to be something she is not, and that *she* is in control of the difference. The dynamic of the fetish remains triumphant. What is guaranteed is the delicious, tantalizing fullness of waiting for what is promised but neither revealed nor exposed. The delirium of desire has been assured its full measure of satisfaction. And Sternberg's performance has been perfectly doubled. The unavailability, the intangibility of the "image" has been suspended in a delirious gap between illusionistic seduction and materialistic reflection (in the non-Marxian sense of the film material—the projection of light upon a flat and silvered screen).

Narrative Progression

The weaving play of codes discussed in the above sections can be summarized by following Helen Faraday/Jones' narrative trajectory. When she decides to return to the stage, an agent singles her out and takes her to a nightclub owner. The transition between these two locales (4.39, 40) is mediated by a continuation of the just-introduced slat motif. The owner, O'Connor, closes a window and faces Helen

4.39–40. Her agent in his office (4.39) dissolves to the office at O'Connor's nightclub (4.40), using the slat motif to achieve a smooth graphic match.

(4.41). Outside, shut off from Helen by the manager's intervention, are two black workers. This image represents a nodal point, a point of condensation within the narrative chain overloaded with meaning. When these condensed, metaphoric meanings are teased out, the pattern of her rise and fall can be foretold in the subsequent merger of background/foreground (Helen and the blacks, stage reality and everyday reality) and in her struggle to gain mastery over what is orchestrated by others (men).

Narrative progression involves a realization that the tropical eroticism Helen originally "apes" is not a source of pleasure; it is a labyrinthian trap leading to a slab. Unlike other films that present a theatrical world (especially musicals), *Blonde Venus* does not pivot around providing access to a more "real" backstage world. Instead, the film revolves around making the illusionism of the stage become the very world which Helen, like Dietrich and Sternberg himself, must dominate in turn (see 4.31–34).

128   IDEOLOGY AND THE IMAGE

Helen extricates herself from the fly-trap world encircling her by an act of will: upon giving away all her money, she parodies her husband, saying, "If I had the time to exploit it properly, I could have made a fortune." That, however, is what she then proceeds to do—not in terms of a general equivalent of economic exchange (money), however, but in terms of a more specific and personal exchange (of self-as-image) in terms of the general equivalent of sexual exchange (the phallus).

In so doing, Helen locates herself within the imaginary realm of identity and opposition: who has the phallus and for whom does she/he bear/bare it? A signifier to be communicated or exchanged stands for a thing (to be had or possessed). Anthony Wilden suggests that

> the phallus may therefore correctly be said to represent the mediating function of the lack of object in our present psychosocial relationships. . . . If the alienated labor of men in the economic system is purchased with money, then the equally alienated labor of the housewife is presumably recompensed in the psychosexual system with some equivalent commodity. Unfortunate as it may be to recognize it, this commodity appears in part to be children, long equated with the phallus in psychoanalytical theory. Children are indeed treated in general as accumulated objects of exchange with which to achieve status and by which to mediate one's relationship with others.[23]

Much of *Blonde Venus'* narrative strategy involves turning Helen into a fetishistic object of desire and visual pleasure, which must finally be renounced for the de-eroticized but "proper" place of housewife with its corresponding recompense—the affections of Ned and little Johnny.

The actual process of exchange and advance accompanying Helen's career is only summarized by Sternberg, however. A montage sequence takes her from the funereal flophouse to the Paris stage in a matter of moments (4.42–44). Censorship unveils itself here in what it veils, but it is only a specific instance of a more general censorship in Hollywood cinema—the masking of real work (taken up and revealed so forcefully in the *Cahiers du Cinéma* editors' analysis of *Young Mr. Lincoln*).[24]

Sternberg presents not the labor process but the result: Helen's Paris triumph. Her final number contrasts sharply with her first number: venus fur trap/white tails; self as part of an erotic motif/self apart from an erotic motif (4.45–46); sensuality controlled by others/ sensuality controlled by self; a blonde Venus with her chorus/a master with his-her harem (4.47); Helen caps this performance during her backstage encounter with Nick in which she now has the upper hand.

4.42, 4.44, 4.46

4.43, 4.45, 4.47

　　　　　　　　　　　IDEOLOGY AND THE IMAGE

4.48–54. Helen and her agent bargain for a job. The agent begins to escort her out when the club manager will not agree to his terms (4.49), but his bluff works: the manager agrees. The agent puts his hat on the statue until they conclude their negotiations. Compare this with Helen's "capping" gesture in her dressing room with Nick when she turns down his marriage proposal (4.52–54).

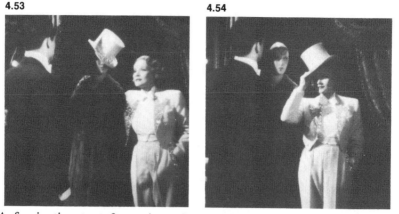

A fascinating transformation of an earlier piece of "business" cements the change—see 4.48–54.

Power and control have been transferred to Helen. She has assumed the role of he-who-controls without occupying the place of he-who-controls (by (mis)representing sexual difference). The paradox that can fuel desire perpetually has been realized—the unattainable in the guise of the attainable—compounded by its regress to the plane of Sternberg's own control over a fictional reality and the reality of fiction, a three-dimensional world and a two-dimensional image (triangulated as "image").

Sternberg would have ended the game at this level of delirious paradox, but another ending was imposed by the studio. Helen relinquishes control and reaffirms the principle of availability for the other. She is re-united with Ned and her child, and the zippered-up suggestiveness of the fur coat she wears when she arrives with Nick is abandoned for the erotic dress she displays only for Ned (and her son—a matter of some small interest in more than one sense). A new but more trivial game, one of reconciliation, of forgive and forget, attempts to gloss over the more basic game of hide-and-seek, desire and denial, performance and control, narrative and style—that complex game played by Josef von Sternberg and Marlene Dietrich alike.

To conclude—but without the marks of final closure that mask the lack of conclusive fixation within the text itself: Helen is set in place as the signifier of desire, in (the) place of the signifier of desire, the phallus, a signifier she seeks to possess and a place she seeks to capture. Her success is a sign of deeper failure, of her continued entrapment within the objectifications of a phallocentric culture, of her capture (as signifier, as "image") within the aestheticizing, or fetishizing modernist play of Josef von Sternberg. For when all is said and done, it is his career that Helen Faraday Jones'/Dietrich's performance and dis/play finally caps.

5.

For *The Birds*

5.1–3. *The Birds* centers around looking and being looked at, around the point-of-view shot, and the ambiguity of our position as viewers in relation to characters as viewers. This closed point of view (5.1–3) typifies one of the key visual dynamics of the film; its implications are examined in what follows.

Critical Assumptions

SOME ASSUMPTIONS: if textual analysis is concerned with the patterns of communication and exchange peculiar to a given text, then there are two master patterns of paramount concern: sexual communication and exchange and economic communication and exchange. These cannot be adequately described in a frame of reference limited to the text as a thing in itself; the nature of these patterns as they are negotiated with, and by, the viewer is equally crucial. Our relation to the text can then be considered in relation to the two most basic models for these patterns: the Freudian and the Marxian.

Both of these models explore the question of the relationship between self and other but from different perspectives. By delimiting these perspectives we can augment their initial overlap. We can attend to the recent revisions of Freud, which involve a translation of bio-mechanistic terminology into semiotics, and to the semio-structuralist revision of Marx, which also translates economics (and ideology) into the same semiotic terms. The result, still in need of considerable elaboration, is one model of communication and exchange based upon goal-seeking activity (which most often answers to the name of desire). An initial stage in comprehending this model involves questions about the constitution of the self-as-subject, about the maintenance and consequences of this constitution. Questions like these can be brought to bear on study of the organization of a textual system and the viewer/text interaction, as they will be here, in order to understand better the patterns of communications and exchange established in and by a text.

Psychoanalysis, for example, has traditionally used the text to speculate on the author's or his society's psychosexual disposition. Marxism has traditionally attempted to relate any art product to the economic conditions under which it is produced and of which it is, in some way, indicative. These are contextual considerations fraught, primarily, with reductionist dangers but no more or less legitimate than the focus chosen here. The intersection of sexual and ideological patterns of communication and exchange in the space between viewer and screen, reader and text, may not be the only intersection of interest; but it is assumed to be a crucial one that can, if understood, contribute to our study of these even larger, contextual questions. Indeed, it is hard to imagine being equipped to place the text within a larger context if we cannot locate our place in relation to the text. Of course, the choice of one starting point over another is a somewhat arbitrary matter since the ultimate goal is to specify the conjunction of text and context and our place within this larger zone.

Classical Narrative, Ideology, and the Imaginary

Alfred Hitchcock's *The Birds* (1963), like Sternberg's *Blonde Venus*, contributes to the characteristic profile of classical narrative, though study of the particular does not directly transfer to study of the general: the differences between Hitchcock and Sternberg make this clear while the similarities beneath differences begin to flesh out a portrait of classical narrative. Peter Wollen describes these similarities in terms of narrative transitivity, identification, transparency, single diegesis, closure, pleasure, and fiction in contrast to opposing qualities of intransivity, estrangement, foregrounding, multiple diegesis, aperture, unpleasure, and reality in his discussion of Godard's *Vent d'Est*.[1] Yet, despite similarities, classical narrative films are neither formally nor ideologically identical. In terms of the way women figure in the narrative, Laura Mulvey argues that Hitchcock's films, for example, opt for one extreme (punishment) and Sternberg's the other (over-valuation).[2] A great many others (Capra, Sturges, Minnelli, Cukor) do not fit comfortably into well-carved niches at these extremes, yet all pose questions involving sexual difference, its reconstruction into opposition within the imaginary realm, and the recruitment of this opposition for ideological ends. The general characteristics of classical narrative, though, will be of less importance than the ways in which the particular textual strategies of *The Birds* implicate us as viewers in imaginary relationships and ideological positions. These strategies are not necessarily those of other classical

IDEOLOGY AND THE IMAGE

texts. Hitchcock's films exhibit a self-awareness of cinematic effect that does not occur very frequently in the Hollywood films of the classical period. Even in comparison with von Sternberg, whose work also displays a form of self-awareness, there are clear differences, and both directors operate at some appreciable remove from the work of Michael Curtiz or Howard Hawks or the self-aware style of comic directors like Lubitsch or Sturges.

We might, for example, immediately note the more active sense of involvement of the viewer in Hitchcock's film. If Sternberg plays with the control of pleasure through fetishistic moments of erotic contemplation, Hitchcock mounts an assault on pleasure through sexual aggression with which we as viewers are implicated. The two moments of the imaginary realm's constitution of the self-as-subject, identity and opposition (the subject subject to the other, the subject's "free" subjectivity), are here articulated psychologically as identification and aggression, a battle of love and hate oscillating on a frequency tuned to the paranoid construct of the subject/ego itself.

Sighting *The Birds*

The Birds was not one of Hitchcock's greatest critical successes. Many critics scoffed at the special-effect gimmickry of mock bird attacks, at the stilted acting and the overall implausibility. *Variety*, industrial trade paper and audience bellwether, wrote it off: "A cock-and-bull story that's essentially a foul ball . . . little more than a shocker-for-shock's sake." Ardent Hitchcock admirers like Andrew Sarris praised the film as "a major work of cinematic art," but such critics were generally inclined to regard the film either as a moral test of characters or as a testimonial to Hitchcock's technical skills without much regard for their "moral" implications.[3] These approaches seem wholly inadequate. They drain off a pool of signifieds (moral themes) as though they were a cultural resource at large rather than pinned to the distinctive organization of the film, or they drain off signifiers (techniques) as though they were a non-signifying aesthetic resource employed effectively by Hitchcock. Other forms of reductionism abound, as we shall see, but any adequate reading of *The Birds*, it seems, must begin with the textual system. Only those technical and thematic qualities pinned down by the pattern of codical interaction can be seriously entertained, though how they are entertained will depend heavily upon the methodological apparatus at work.

The master enigma to *The Birds*, if there is one, might be described as, "Will Melanie Daniels get what she wants?" Posed in terms of the other central characters the question becomes, "Can a boy have his mother all to himself despite the incest prohibition?" or, alternatively, "Will a mother be abandoned by her son or will she keep him and also gain a daughter?"* Somewhat Oedipal questions, perhaps. The injunction against incest, however, is not issued by the father figure (who is absent from the film, having died). Instead a lure is offered away from the potentially incestuous relationship of mother and son by a somewhat shallow-minded but "cocky" playgirl named Melanie Daniels (Tippi Hedren). Hitchcock, like von Sternberg in *Blonde Venus,* places a woman at the center of his narrative, as hero, and one of the central concerns of both these textual analyses will be to consider carefully what kind of place that is.

Synopsis

Melanie Daniels, well-dressed and somewhat coy, arrives at a pet shop to claim a mynah bird she's ordered. Mitch Brenner (Rod Taylor) pretends to mistake her for a salesgirl and asks to see some lovebirds. They banter, Melanie accidentally lets a bird loose, and Mitch, on catching it, reveals that he knows her identity. Mitch leaves and Melanie makes a call, using the resources of her father's newspaper to discover Mitch's name and city address. She decides, on her own, to deliver the two lovebirds he wanted for his sister's birthday.

When she discovers Mitch has gone to Bodega Bay, she drives up after him and learns his address by talking to a shopkeeper and to Annie Hayworth (Suzanne Pleshette), the local schoolteacher and Mitch's former lover. Melanie surreptiously delivers the birds by hired boat, but as she is leaving the Brenner dock, Mitch spots her. He drives around the bay by car, and as he watches her approach the dock, a gull swoops down, striking her on the forehead. Mitch guides her to a nearby cafe, attends to her wound, and after introducing her to his mother, Lydia (Jessica Tandy), invites her to dinner.

Melanie returns to Annie's and arranges to stay the night. Lydia expresses apprehension about Melanie to Mitch, who reassures her while also continuing to tease Melanie about her playgirl reputation. Later that night Melanie and Annie discuss Mitch's family relationships after Mitch calls to invite Melanie to his sister, Cathy's, birthday party. As the two women prepare to retire a bird crashes into the front door, killing itself.

Mitch and Melanie talk further at the outdoor party, in part about the value of mother-love. Suddenly, birds begin attacking the children, and everyone helps bring them inside to safety. That night a mass of sparrows fly down the chimney, apparently attacking Melanie and the Brenner family. The sheriff nonchalantly dismisses the episode, but Lydia is deeply upset by the series of events. Melanie

---

*Paradoxical formulation of this dilemma has already been given from the hero's, Melanie's, perspective: "If I am to win Mitch, I must become part of his family, But if I become part of his family, I cannot win Mitch."

puts Cathy to bed and agrees to stay over another night.

In the morning Lydia visits Dan Fawcett, a nearby farmer, only to find him dead, his eyes pecked out by gulls. She flees in horror. Melanie has begun to receive more earnest affection from Mitch, and with Lydia virtually dumbstruck, she begins to assume some of Lydia's duties, volunteering, in particular, to pick up Cathy from school; while she's waiting, crows mass in the playground behind her. Upon discovering them she and Annie organize the children's escape; they run down the school road, under attack, with Melanie and Cathy taking temporary refuge in a parked car.

When Melanie reaches the town cafe she calls her father, who receives the news of the bird attacks skeptically. Debate ensues about the nature of the attacks. Mitch arrives; another attack begins; and a man under attack accidentally ignites the gasoline pumps. Melanie becomes trapped in a telephone booth from which Mitch rescues her. After they run back into the cafe, a distraught mother glares at her and blames her for the attacks, pronouncing her evil.

Mitch and Melanie go to Annie's to pick up Cathy, only to find Annie dead, having sacrificed herself to save Cathy. That evening Mitch boards up the house, and then they all gather to await another attack. It is not long in coming. Lydia begins to regain control of herself during the attack, while Melanie becomes increasingly isolated. Afterwards, as they all rest, Melanie hears a noise in the attic and goes to investigate. Birds have broken through the roof, and as she enters they attack her, knocking her to the floor before Mitch and Lydia can rescue her. Melanie continues to flail out against now imaginary birds. Her only words after this point are "No, no." As dawn arrives, Mitch escorts all of them to the car, Cathy brings the lovebirds, Lydia cares for Melanie, and they leave Bodega Bay as thousands of birds perch ominously all around them.

The Mise-en-scène of a Family Intrigue

"Hitchcock," the narrator of the tale, has left clear signs of the characters' interaction along the path of the narrative. Many of these spoor by which we can track the course of the narrative are visual signs, usually embedded in the cine-plastics of camera angle, composition, and *mise-en-scène*. In summary, the trail results from Melanie's attempt to infiltrate the Brenner family by means of Cathy in order to displace Lydia, an attempt that succeeds for a brief while before the mother regains her position and Melanie's place becomes the locus of mounting aggressivity. This section of the chapter is told primarily through frame enlargements with commentary to help clarify Melanie's progression as it is visually represented.

5.4–5. Melanie first meets Lydia, whose stern gaze disavows the image of Melanie as erotic object. The similarity of hair styles, facial features, and general appearance is most striking though the mother clearly holds the upper hand (via the difference in camera angle, which, as noted earlier, is not in itself expressive of dominance/submission, but in this context the intersection of numerous codes supports this conventional notation). When Mitch tells Lydia that Melanie has brought a pair of "birds . . . lovebirds," the mother's knowing response (identical to Annie's earlier) is, "Oh, I see."

5.4

5.6–9. A fragile relationship. The diffused light and the clothing, especially Melanie's shoes, work to distance the characters from their surroundings (5.6). The scene, composed mostly of one-shots, plays on verbal misunderstandings as Melanie attempts to dispel some of Mitch's first impressions of her. The scene's quality as unstable interlude, akin to the scene from Hitchcock's *Notorious* shown in 5.7, is underlined by the gazes directed at Mitch and Melanie by Annie (5.8) and Lydia (5.9); the bird attack on the children follows almost immediately.

5.6

5.7

5.5

5.8

5.9

5.10. The introduction of the "teacup" motif during Melanie's first invited visit to the Brenner home. Lydia serves drinks. As the film develops, who serves whom becomes a key indicator of the relationship between Lydia and Melanie. Likewise, the physical damage to teacups during the first attack (5.11o) and at the Fawcett farm (5.12a) gives evidence of the fragility of Lydia's world and its disruption by the birds.

During the first attack inside the Brenner home, the movement of the characters seems particularly significant. In essence, Melanie and Mitch take active roles: Melanie escorting Lydia and Cathy to safety, Mitch at the window trying to drive the birds out. In its aftermath Lydia rather than Melanie appears to be the one broken by the attack (5.11). Particularly important aspects are:

1. Melanie sights the birds first (5.11b, c).
2. Lydia is isolated on the sofa in the corner (5.11d), just as Melanie will be in the second attack.
3. Melanie protects Cathy (5.11d, e).
4. Lydia retreats to the same corner of the room where Melanie will cower during the second attack (5.11h).
5. Melanie is an active agent, escorting Lydia and Cathy from the room (5.11j-k).
6. Melanie appears in low-angle shots at the conclusion, whereas Lydia appears in high-angle shots as she collects broken pieces of china. We see this exchange from Melanie's point of view (5.11n,o).

5.11b

5.11c

5.11b and c. Melanie is the first to see the birds; her gaze precipitates the attack. In narrative, chronological occurrence often implies causality: what happens later is explained by what happened earlier.

5.11d

5.11e

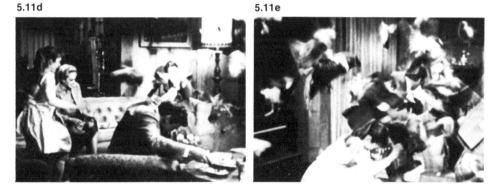

5.11d. Lydia is isolated in the same corner of the sofa where Melanie huddles during the second attack (see 5.44). Cathy turns to Melanie for protection (cf. 5.42).

5.11f

5.11g

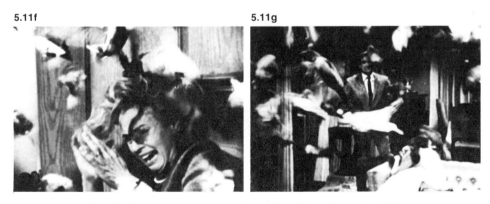

5.11g. Mitch assumes an active role fending off the birds (cf. 5.47).

For The Birds

5.11h   5.11i

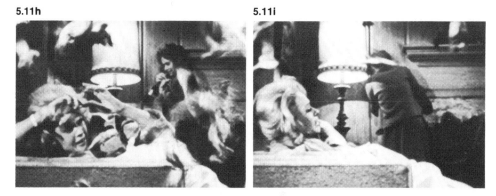

5.11h. Lydia cowers in the same corner where Melanie is later entrapped (cf. 5.45–46).

5.11j   5.11k

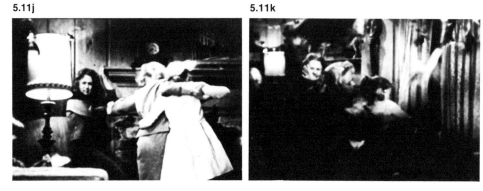

5.11j. Melanie takes an active role escorting the other women from the room, a role taken over by Mitch in the final attack.

5.11l   5.11m

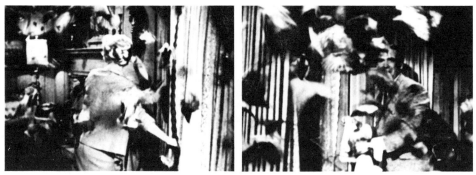

5.11n   5.11o

5.11n– o. This point-of-view figure (5.11n-o) echoes Lydia and Melanie's first meeting (5.4–5). The camera angle again gives dominance to the one standing (although now it is Melanie) and soft-focus accentuates Melanie's appearance, while Lydia's composure is sorely tested. In 5.11n Melanie gazes at Lydia (5.11o), who is picking up the pieces of her teacups/life. Shortly after this, Melanie assumes control of the teacup motif (5.18).

5.12–24. At this point, after the sparrow attack and Lydia's encounter with the mutilated body of Dan Fawcett, Melanie begins to displace Lydia successfully, Lydia even giving partial consent to Melanie's new role.

5.12a   5.12b

For The Birds   143

5.12c

5.12d

5.12e

5.12f

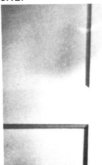

5.12g

IDEOLOGY AND THE IMAGE

5.13–18. Melanie takes control of the teacup motif, and the inversion of camera angle accorded each woman continues.

5.13

5.14

5.15

5.16

5.17

5.18

5.19, 5.21

5.20, 5.22

5.23

5.24

5.19–24. Two kitchen scenes: The relationship of proximity between Mitch and his mother during their kitchen dialogue, 5.19–22 (just before the sparrow attack), succumbs to the more intimate, ascending relationship between Mitch and Melanie, 5.23–24 (after Lydia's encounter with Dan Fawcett).

The budding relationship between Mitch and Melanie begins to turn after the attack on the children at school. At the town café it is Melanie who, marginal to the discussion about what is to be done, first notices the beginning of the next attack (compare 5.27 with 5.11b). (The series of shots pivoting at the café window occur during

IDEOLOGY AND THE IMAGE

this attack; see 5.71.) Subsequently, Melanie takes refuge in a telephone booth, where she is trapped by the birds (5.30). Hitchcock has likened this to a birdcage, but it is also a substitution for the Brenner household, where the bird attacks initially served to bring Melanie and Mitch together. Inasmuch as she is attacked in vulnerable isolation, the attack also foreshadows the final attack in the attic (compare with 5.62a and b and 5.55–57). Other events further strengthen the sense of Melanie's increasing isolation and her association with the birds' attacks (5.31–37).

5.25

5.26

5.27

5.28

5.29

5.25– 29. Mitch seeks to become the active agent, soliciting the aid of the fisherman Sebastian in an effort to "do something" about the birds (5.25). Melanie, though displaced to the side of the frame (5.26), topples this asymmetrical composition toward further aggression: her look out the window announces the next onslaught of the birds (5.29).

5.30

5.31

5.32

5.30–32. This attack on the town, instead of bringing Mitch and Melanie together, isolates her in the phone booth (5.30). We share her point of view as violence at the window takes on heightened force, leading to the death of Annie Hayworth (5.31) and the general holocaust which we see, for the first time, from a bird's-eye point of view (5.32).

5.33–36. Looks turn against Melanie as she is denounced as evil, and our point of view both attaches to and detaches from Melanie, with and against the violence at the window.

5.33

5.34

5.35

5.36

5.37. Just before the second attack on the Brenner home, Mitch says, "Hand up another one, darling," conferring on Melanie a word previously addressed to his mother, but as we have seen, the tide against their relationship has already begun to turn on the image track.

The second attack on the Brenner home confirms Melanie's failure. The movement and placement of characters echoes the *mise-en-scène* of the first attack but more as a transformation than a duplication. Mother and son sit beneath the father's portrait (5.38). All that need be done to complete the family circle is to recall Cathy (5.41–43) and absorb Melanie in a nonthreatening form (see 5.87). At this point it is Lydia who is an active agent, taking charge of the teacup motif for the first time since before the sparrows' initial attack on the house (5.39–40). When the birds attack, Melanie sits alone on the sofa where Lydia had been (compare 5.44 with 5.11d), and then retreats into the same corner of the room (compare 5.45–46 with 5.11h-j). Mitch and Lydia are the active agents (5.41–43,47), Melanie the passive one (5.48), an inversion of Lydia and Melanie's roles during the first attack. All that remains is to de-sexualize Melanie so that her relations with Mitch and Lydia can be absorbed into the original equilibrium of the Brenners' family romance (5.38–59).

5.38

5.39

5.40

5.38–40. Picking up the pieces. Lydia resumes control of the teacup motif as Melanie and Mitch, who sits under the image of his father, look on. In contrast with the corresponding scene after the first attack, the position of the camera has broken with Melanie's point of view and even tracks in a subtle arc toward Mitch and Lydia as Lydia takes the tea service into the kitchen.

5.41

5.42

5.43

5.41–43. This time Lydia assumes responsibility for Cathy, who begins the scene with Melanie but turns to her mother once the onslaught actually begins.

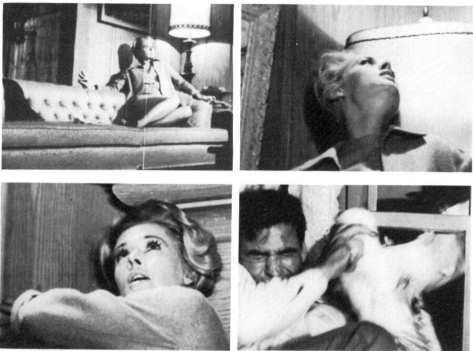

5.44–47. Melanie withdraws before the imaginary (off-screen, present but absent) birds (5.44). Her isolation and passivity or recoil throughout this scene (5.45–46) contrast with her role in the first attack and with Mitch's active battle at the window to keep the birds out (5.47).

5.48. The heavily ironic, and final, "bar" of visual imagery at the end of the attack. The low angle, Lydia's placement in the background, Melanie's insertion between Mitch and Lydia, Mitch's rugged solidity—all confound the dictionary citations of stylistic meaning found in introductory textbooks. The "heroic" low angle seems unearned by characters who can at best withstand but not control the adversity they face; Melanie's position lacks weight in the aftermath of her isolation during the attack. A retrospective reading would suggest she is being supported by Mitch and Lydia rather than wedging herself between them, a reading supported by her presence in relation to the absence of Cathy.

5.49–59. The *coup de grâce*. This is the birds' final attack on Melanie; it drives her from the Brenner house (indirectly) and pushes the theme of aggression against the (erotic) image of the other to its extreme. Although the attack has strong sexual overtones—the soft, incessant fluttering of wings, Melanie's moans and plaintive call of "Oh, Mitch" (see 5.55, 5.57, and 5.59)—it is far more than Melanie bargained for when she responded to a "bird whistle" so smugly in the opening scene (see 5.73). This aggressive discharge terminates her role as active agent and deeroticizes her image to that of a helpless, catatonic child.

5.49, 5.51, 5.53

5.50, 5.52, 5.54

For The Birds   153

This narrative progression, if read correctly, marks the film as profoundly regressive. We are transfixed at the window where violence takes place, where aggression accumulates, mounts in (the) place of difference. The textual system balks on the other side of the line between the imaginary and the symbolic: we are placed on a streetcar named desire going from here to eternity with no exit. We see what we want (lack): that "you" is "I" in an/other place. An (imaginary) line keeps "us" apart which, rather than being accepted as the necessary condition and paradox guaranteeing language and symbolic exchange generally, is taken as the pretext for violence at and against the line, the window. *The Birds* may entertain but at an extraordinary price—for Melanie, for the place of women, for us as viewers reconfirmed in the ideologically complicit message that is the hallmark of the imaginary: hell is other people.

Metaphor and Nodal Points: At the Window

If the central enigma poses a question about a family intrigue, as it were, the dominant action revolves around transgression/punishment—a series of tests or trials followed by reward or punishment in which the hero, Melanie, ends more vanquished than vanquishing. The film, in summary, is about the explosion detonated by, and against, a transgressor-hero (Melanie Daniels) who invades a fragile relationship between a son and his mother.

In these terms, the narrative of *The Birds* has the trajectory of an un-*Bildungsroman* although some critics hold out for a therapeutic ending and growth through mortification (by attempting, I would argue, to impose a ready-made answer key on Hitchcock's overall *oeuvre* despite the evident mismatch with individual films).[4] Transgression or violation is perhaps the single most important narrative action. It carries a powerful charge of aggressivity (both as an act and in the reactions it provokes) and, as such, figures throughout the film.

Transgression, in fact, takes the figure of metaphor inasmuch as there are discrete, recurrent moments/images that condense within them a surplus of transgressive and violent meaning. These nodal points from which a reading, like the codes of the film, can spin out a web of interstitial relationships, might be designated collectively by "at the window" (5.60–64).

What helps condense meaning into this nodal point is that not only the characters but also we, the viewers, are positioned "at the window," gazing into another space in a substitutive/transgressive act reciprocated here by violence instead of erotic display as in Sternberg's *Blonde Venus*. (We and characters become caught up in a

IDEOLOGY AND THE IMAGE

5.60–64. Other frames used in the analysis to follow also belong to this metaphor as well as many of the verbal comments, such as Mitch's reference to one of Melanie's pranks that resulted in a broken plate-glass window.

5.60, 5.62a, 5.63   **5.61, 5.62b, 5.64**

complex exchange of places.) Violence is directed "at the window"—directly at characters and us, at our window onto the world or more specifically, and still metaphorically, at the camera/character/viewer's eye[5] (5.65–71. See also 2.13).

5.65–70. Assault "at the window," or at the "evil eye," whether it be that of (1) an innocent victim (Dan Fawcett, the Brenners' neighbor, 5.65–67); (2) Melanie (accused of causing the bird attacks, 5.68; attacked by nonexistent birds, their place taken by the camera, 5.69); or (3) the camera itself (during the attack in the Brenner attic, 5.70) when the camera, and we, the viewers, take the place of a character.

5.65

5.66

5.67

5.68

5.69

5.70

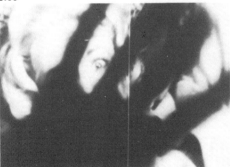

5.71a-k. During this sequence we literally pivot at the window of the town café as the camera cuts back and forth from Melanie Daniels inside the café to what she sees outside.

5.71a, c, e   **5.71b, d, f**

5.71g, i, k   **5.71h, j**

This metaphorical dimension to the violence poised at the window in part turns on the principle of central perspective basic to the photographic lens (and its precursor: linear, Renaissance perspective). The installation of the viewer as subject depends upon reserving a singular place for him or her, the reciprocal in front of the image of the vanishing point "behind" it, the point of origin from which the camera "took" its view and where we now take ours. The two-dimensional image, from the point of view of central perspective, stands in for the world it re-presents as would an ordinary window if the view beyond it could somehow be imprinted on its surface. This, incidentally, is precisely the metaphor elaborated by Leonardo da Vinci to describe how central perspective is achieved by a painter (and strikingly similar to the registration of a latent image on a film strip).

The window that admits and frames the scene confirms the camera in its ascension to the fixed position of source or origin which we, in turn, are invited to assume. To launch an assault at the window is, in turn, to assault the place of the viewer; it is an act of aggression against the eye of the beholder and the "I" of the self-as-subject insofar as that "I" originates in the realm of the imaginary. Whereas von Sternberg affords us the pleasure of erotic contemplation, Hitchcock makes us squirm in our seat as we are fully exposed to an imaginary assault.

Little wonder, then, that paranoia figures in when assault at the window only serves to confirm the fundamentally paranoid constitution of the subject (or ego). The subject's abiding fear that the image of the other appropriated as "ego" (or ego-ideal, to be more exact) will withhold recognition and turn against him/her is a real fear that easily leads to paranoid hallucination (5.72). The nodal image of aggression at the window then aptly inaugurates a central meaning of *The Birds*.

In *The Birds* the metaphor of violence "at the window" becomes, by way of central perspective generally and point-of-view editing in particular, violence primarily against Melanie Daniels and the viewer—those figures at the window from, by, and for whom the image seems to originate. Violence in the narrative turns against the visual source of the narrative. Melanie's transgressive attempt to infiltrate the Brenner household earns ample, if not excessive, punishment from the birds. Our voyeuristic relationship to her actions, as relayed by substitutive point-of-view editing, is likewise punished as a transgression, an unauthorized taking in of images. Between these moments a dynamic emerges on which the narrative can play itself out.

5.72. Mitch and Lydia coax Melanie out of the house at the end of the film. Melanie hesitates, whispering "No, no" at the sight of the masses of birds passively watching them (see 5.76).

Metonymy, Desire, and Transformation

If the ending of a narrative is recognizable as a transformation of the beginning, thereby effecting closure, we might expect this transformation to be visually apparent in a motion picture. Such is the case with *The Birds,* as 5.73–82 show. In each of these five pairs of shots, the first is from near the beginning of the film and the second from near the end of the film.

IDEOLOGY AND THE IMAGE

5.73–74. The transformations from the beginning to the end of the film often take the binary form of associating opposites and likes. In *The Birds*, opposites prevail, as in these stills where Melanie's sexual coyness turns to dreadful paranoia.

5.75–76. From paucity to plenitude—the birds.

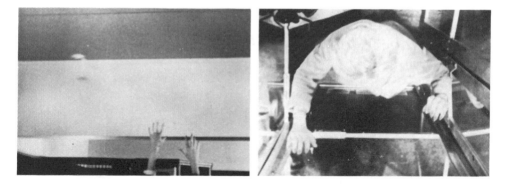

5.77–78. From a single bird, out of reach, to be returned to its cage to a single person, out of touch, caged by a mass of birds.

For The Birds

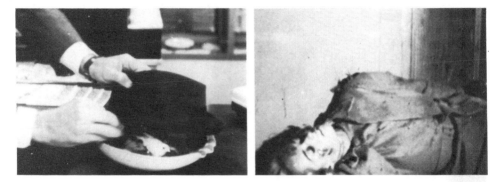

5.79–80. A single bird trapped beneath a hat to Melanie collapsed beneath the weight of waves of bird attacks.

5.81–82. The look of Melanie Daniels transformed, the hero vanquished, the erotic object unsexed, a playgirl's empty talk stopped by silence.

The movement of the narrative, the middle between beginning and end, hinges on Melanie Daniels's quest to restore a lack, initially posed by the lovebirds Mitch Brenner wants to give his sister, more succinctly posed, later, by Annie Hayworth as the one thing Lydia cannot give Mitch—love (taken to mean sexual love). Two transgressions are implicit here: the potentially incestuous bond between a son and his mother and the sexual union between Mitch and Melanie that threatens to displace it. Melanie, like most female heroes in classical narrative, occupies the place of hero in an equivocal fashion: she becomes the agent of narrative progression by being the object of erotic contemplation. It is significant that, of all the characters, she is the only one photographed in a soft-focus style (5.83–86), signifying an object available for erotic contemplation, something that when looked at becomes a source of pleasure.

5.83–86. In each pairing the second shot directly follows the first in the film itself. In each case it is only Melanie Daniels who is somewhat abstracted from the three-dimensional texture of the diegesis by soft-focus photography.

But the character Melanie Daniels is not solely an erotic object available to the gaze of others, an essentially passive role; she is also an active agent. Her own aggressiveness and ability to get her own way (in large measure, by exploiting her femininity) are stressed early in the film. The successive ventures of taking the birds to Mitch Brenner's city apartment, to Bodega Bay, and, finally, into the Brenner home strongly indicate her capacity to act. In this regard, the presentation of her as an erotic object in soft focus is somewhat disruptive to the narrative: its temporal progression is arrested in a moment of prolonged contemplation before an icon of "beauty," a moment when desire discovers its object rather than defers discovery for a moment further along the narrative chain. This arrest abstracts Melanie from active agent to passive object (as a subject subjecting her "looks" to the look of others). The narrative must overcome this threat to its own flow.

For The Birds

In many films the problem is surmounted by making the female hero a showgirl—as in *Blonde Venus, Gentlemen Prefer Blondes* (Howard Hawks, 1953), *Cover Girl* (Charles Vidor, 1944), *River of No Return* (Otto Preminger, 1954), or *The Revolt of Mamie Stover* (Raoul Walsh, 1956). *The Birds* poses an alternative solution. Essentially, the narrative progression, signalized by the transformations linking beginning and end, works to de-eroticize Melanie, to make a spectacle of her-self that also strips her of her erotic image. The aggressivity of the narrative, objectified in the birds, is mounted against (and in the final attack, mounts) the place of erotic contemplation. It takes the place of erotic contemplation. To be an erotic object is to be subject to the gaze of the other which, in *The Birds*, is not held in check but topples toward aggression, vindicating, in the process, the relationship of mother-son Melanie attempts to displace. Lydia does indeed gain a daughter (5.87).

5.87

IDEOLOGY AND THE IMAGE

A brilliant economy reveals itself here as the narrative recoups the very moment threatening to disrupt it by pivoting precisely around looks, gazes, violence at the window. Needless to say, this economy comes at a considerable price, one which taxes the female hero to the utmost limit. A powerful current of misogynist energy in-forms the narrative, baring the violence of a phallocentric culture and of the imaginary realm, the other side of the coil of identity and identification: opposition and aggression. "If looks could kill" becomes more than a loose analogy for what the birds do to the hero proposed by the narrative.

If violence begins with a discrete target, however, it clearly exceeds its mark. Narrative closure is imperfect, asymmetrical. If beginning and end rejoin like the bivalve closure of a giant clam, there is an uncontained excess that spills out. It leaves the final frames marked by an unchecked threat of violence swelling larger and larger. The temptation to link this to the paranoid fixation of the subject/ego is strong: the imbalance registers the asymmetry of an "I" constituted elsewhere; the frozen speech and glazed eyes of Melanie Daniels block her passage to the symbolic realm of language. The tyranny of the gaze prevails and the paranoia of its complex fixation spills over the frame/window we share with the watchful birds. That we share this place, at the window, also serves to confirm our paranoia. Like so much of popular culture disseminated under the sign of the dominant ideology (in two words: phallus, money), *The Birds* preys upon our fears of the other not so much to help overcome them as to confirm them. Beneath the surface veneer, for Hitchcock as for Conrad's Kurtz, lies a heart of darkness—we are powerless and defenseless—a perfect moral for an economic structure fed by exploitation and oppression.

But this temptation to treat the film as a palimpsest in which we read the secret workings of the imaginary realm needs to be checked in turn, lest it spill over into an uncritical endorsement of Freud and Lacan's "compulsion to repeat." The very excess can also be read as the product of the social manipulation of this childhood moment before the mirror, the surplus charged to the account of an ideology preying upon insecurity in its strategies of divide-and-conquer-for-profit, what Marcuse termed "surplus-repression."

To project this excess back to a repetition of origins is, in fact, to repeat in the act of criticism the paranoia we have attributed to the film itself and to ignore the transformational differences between a founding moment of schism and the uses to which it is put in a given social order, especially the reification of economic exchange by a general equivalent, money. Like the phallus, money, when it serves as the measure of all things, situates us squarely within the realm of imaginary communication and exchange. We are faced here less with the question of a "compulsion to repeat" than with the question of material practices of repetition—those social conditions, those relations of production, that ensure the renewal of a given system and structure by means of repeatedly preying upon its constituents' most vulnerable moments. If we are concerned with the violence against the woman in the window, then its association with the paranoid aspect of the mirror-phase is, at best, a metaphor for a paranoia repeated and nourished many times over in a fundamentally phallocentric culture.

Psychoanalysis Aside

Polemically, this little addendum could be punctuated, "Psychoanalysis, aside!" But this is not the place for a pitched battle against the defenders of the primal scene, and a more modest aside is all that is intended. Having introduced and deployed a certain number of psychoanalytic concepts here, it is important to stipulate that this is not meant as a blanket endorsement of the numerous psychoanalytic readings of film recently undertaken nor of the assumptions that often accompany these readings. Since, for example, we have ended our discussion of *The Birds* by referring to the blockage set up between the imaginary and symbolic, we may begin by considering what passage between these realms ought to entail.

The symbolic affords escape from the either/or oscillations of the imaginary through, for example, the acquisition of language as an ex-centric locus where the subject can be represented (by "I" and other shifters) but not located. (There is a fundamental disparity between "I" and the subject it represents.) The symbolic realm provides escape from the self/other oscillations of the imaginary when we relinquish the impulse to appropriate or abolish the other and instead accept the slide of difference represented by the linguistic signifier. The question shifts from a battle of the possessed and dispossessed to an exchange of differences in which the necessary precondition is that no one possess, retain, or hoard the word. "I" must circulate if the symbolic is to emerge from the imaginary; the Word in this sense is the sign of a relationship, not a thing.

Classical narrative generally raises questions about whether the "I," or the eye, circulates in this sense. One line of reasoning holds that the "I," the viewer as subject, is pinned down and doubly so: by the illusionism of central perspective and by the strategies of classical narrative, which incorporate this perspective and the subject it fixes into the fabrication of the diegesis itself (notably by continuity editing and point-of-view editing in particular). A number of writers have championed this approach in the pages of journals like *Communications, Cahiers du Cinéma,* and *Screen.* Some writers trace this effect back to the basic technological apparatus. Others isolate it within "tutor-codes" at work in classical narrative. In this perspective, classical narrative serves a general ideological function—fixing the self-as-subject within the fluctuating identities and oppositions of the imaginary.

There is no doubt truth to this line of reasoning. The constant danger, however, has been overgeneralization about this ideological dimension to the point where a lapse into a kind of essentialism takes place and all narrative or all illusionism becomes regarded as inherently ideological. Distinctions must be made, and as to *The Birds,* distinctions must be made about what motivates and sustains the film's assault "at the window"—the place shared by character, camera, and viewer.

We may recall that, in classical narrative, point-of-view editing yields compound interest on the screen-as-window by making it a relay station within the diegesis. Point-of-view editing establishes a pattern of imbricated or overlapping gazes between characters and what they see that are tucked into the folds of the narrative and what it sees. The gaze becomes fundamental to the identification of, and with, characters. We are positioned along the seam of this imaginary world with the transfer of gazes acting like the sutures of a surgeon to hold us in place, to bridge the potential gap between one shot and another. When the second shot falls into place, that place has already been partially reserved by the gaze that originated in the first shot. The second shot replaces the off-screen space into which a character gazed. We are stitched into the delicate peritoneum of the screen/window: the impossible place where who we are turns upon who we are not, where what we see is never what we want most of all to see (our-self), where the object of desire is always wanting. The gaze of characters and viewers continually affirms the paradox of identity founded on what we want (lack). Desire, above all, the desire for recognition, guarantees our paradoxical encounter with this imaginary realm.

An "exchange of views" becomes a serious game pivoting around identity and opposition, identification and aggression. That it may turn to violence seen emanating from the other quite possibly begins, as Freud suggested, in the primal threat posed by the other, most powerfully in the threat of castration proposed to the son by the father or "confirmed" for the daughter by the mother's apparent "wound" and re-posed by the image of women, whose imaginary lack must be countered either by the denial implicit in fetishism or by the aggressivity explicit in voyeurism or sado-masochism, where the "guilty" one is punished, or forgiven, or punished and then forgiven.

We must remember, though, that this notorious "lack" borne by women is an imaginary one (it only exists in the imaginary) and can only be a threat in any case to those who fear they have something to lose—namely, men. Women have nothing to lose because they "have" no thing but instead represent difference. There is nothing lacking in the real, there are no oppositions and identities that oscillate around "having" or "possessing." There are only differences. There are no lacks other than those instituted by desire; they can only be naturalized as "real" from within the arena of a phallocentric or sexist ideology, an arena large enough to enclose a great many psychoanalytic readings, regrettably enough.

We must not make the grave mistake of reducing all aggressivity to this traumatic origin and ignoring the extent to which this initial and initiating fear of others is perpetuated and manipulated in society at large, for then we may reduce sexism in general, or Hitchcock's in particular, to an ungetoverable phase in the passage through the imaginary to the symbolic. This kind of reductionism fails to consider the degree to which the symbolic exchange of difference in our culture is constantly subordinated to the imaginary exchange of images/views and the potentially paranoid oscillation of identity and opposition that imaginary exchange guarantees. It is an unfortunate malady of those entrapped within the imaginary to be unable to recognize a difference when they see one; instead they force it onto the either/or categories of identity and opposition, seeing in the other only what is wanting in the self, a lack to be appropriated or abolished.

The application of semiotic-psychoanalytic concepts to the study of film (especially to the relationship between viewer and screen) has begun to bear considerable fruit; but constant vigilance must be maintained against the kind of reductionism that describes virtually all social phenomena in terms of the re-enactment of a childhood scenario. We cannot recognize ourselves as subjects in the image of the other for the first time twice. Any tendency toward repetition must be considered in terms of the feedback characteristics of the system in which we live, in particular, of the dominant ideology that sustains us in an imaginary relationship to the material processes of communication and exchange.

These social practices of repetition that reproduce the relations of production may take shape under the pressure of desire, but they are not reducible to that founding moment when desire began its passage from the imaginary to the symbolic. Assault in *The Birds* may remind us of Freud's primal scene with its image of a woman who intervenes in a family intrigue; it may involve the sadistic side of voyeurism in its

IDEOLOGY AND THE IMAGE

attempt to punish a woman for what she lacks (in the imaginary) or wants to take, but it is precisely not assault against a child but against an adult, Melanie Daniels. It is an assault that flows, in large part, along the channels established for such aggression within a given social order (the jibes about Melanie's promiscuous behavior, for example).

The film, like other forms of aesthetic experience, is a prospective representation more than a regressive one, that points us, not back toward infancy (though it may well build upon dynamics established there) so much as outward toward the material practices sustaining an ensemble of social relations at a given historical moment. Its attempts to resolve paradox using the signs and symbols, the oppositions and contradictions (such as the ones involving sexual difference), of an historical moment are not merely the superficial trappings in which a profound compulsion to repeat cloaks itself. These social practices channel relationships into specific patterns. They propose a place for women in society that is not simply a triumphal return to a more elementary scene but that also sustains ongoing social relationships, and, in our culture, the sexism, among other things, that attends them. We ignore the surface of things and the *bricoleur*'s principles that fabricate this surface at our own peril, for it is here that the material fabric of ideology, if not its founding moment in the play of desire, is located. Psychoanalysis is a powerful tool helping us to understand the dynamics of desire, but any attempt to reduce the social to the personal or the psychoanalytic risks reducing ideology and the ongoing material practices of a given society to an essentialism of origins. As with most tools, the value of psychoanalysis depends heavily on how we use it.

6.

The Documentary Film and Principles of Exposition

The Non-Narrative Realm: Critical Approaches

IN CHAPTER 3 WE identified three primary linchpins not unique to film but commonly present in films as structuring principles. Of these, narrative has received the greatest amount of attention because of its central role in the history of the cinema and the ideological questions this role raises. Recently, though, theoretical interests have begun to swing away from narrative and toward non-narrative film, more specifically, the experimental film. There is a logic here in that both theoretical inquiry and the experimental film are often concerned with the nature of the medium itself and with self-reflexive textual mechanisms (for example, the emphasis in Stan Brakhage's films upon the perception of the qualities of light, the concern in Paul Sharits's films with the mechanical and psychological aspects of the projection and perception of the film strip itself).

This interest in the experimental, or poetic, film has its risks, though, in terms of a political perspective. The long history of socially conscious film criticism only dimly aware of the formal properties of the medium has often provoked a polemical defense of formalist studies that confuse concern for the film material with Marxist materialism. Ever since the Russian formalists, this confusion has involved championing rigorously delimited formal studies in order to provide tools, ultimately, for more effective political usages of a medium. This is the division of syntax from pragmatics—the formal disposition of a system of communication considered apart from its actual impact upon communicators.

Although methodologically productive, this division erects a wall across the very zone that is of greatest concern to a politically motivated (Marxist) theorist—all those questions involving the place of the viewer/reader/receiver as a function of structure. Lacking a political perspective of their own, formalist studies can be adapted to serve any goal; and adapted they will be, for communication, like perception, is always purposive. It is not surprising, for instance, that Bell Laboratories supports some of the best research in perception or that commercial television advertising derives many of its technical strategies from the work of experimental film makers like Stan Brakhage. What is somewhat more surprising is that formally oriented film study endorses a division that leaves these pragmatic applications unexamined, sometimes beneath a moralistic rubric championing the purity of the noncommercial artist, sometimes in the guise of a more romantic doting on the creative artist as genius, sometimes in the mistaken notion that only by such a division is scientific study possible—this being a self-fulfilling prophecy dependent upon the kind of model chosen to exemplify science.

A concern with formal questions and even with the poetic uses of a medium need not lead into a labyrinth of self-imposed isolation from context or pragmatics. It is all a matter of where we draw the line, and for our present purposes it is more important to consider the relation between syntactics and pragmatics than to consider either in isolation. Beyond the sovereign domain of narrative, examination of either expository or poetic principles is equally valid, although the emphasis here will be on the expository simply because it has been and continues to be the most neglected of the three principles, at least at a theoretical level.

This neglect is not accidental. It stems in part from the ideological smokescreen thrown up by apologists for documentary, many of them leftist in their politics, which has clouded formal or structural issues in order to cover the advance of arguments about the social purpose of film or its privileged relation to reality compared to the other arts. John Grierson's exhortations to shun aesthetic niceties, for example, helped place documentary film making outside formal or aesthetic debate where, to a large extent, it remains today. The quest for social relevance palatable to government sponsors meant, as Grierson admitted in an interview with Elizabeth Sussex, that the documentary film "ceased exploring into the poetic use of the documentary approach with us in the 30's."[1]

More recent apologies for the documentary seem to stand in a linear relationship to Grierson's admission. Consider, for example, Henry Breitrose's comment: "Craft and style are useful and important, but the excitement exists just as much when one looks at the uncut workprint, or the unstructured archival materials. It is an aesthetic of content that drives the documentarian, and the rule that for the audience a documentary is as good as its content is interesting is difficult to falsify."[2] There is no need to belabor the naive acceptance of ideology at work here—it should be obvious by now, and a brief quotation should be sufficient to evoke the necessary criticism: "The first thing people do is deny the existence of the screen: it opens like a *window*; it is transparent. This illusion is the very substance of the specific ideology secreted by the cinema."[3] What can be added is the simple comment that it is odd that so much theoretical attention should go to those areas where the film itself (narrative, and now experimental film) at least calls attention to the fact of its being an illusion and so very little to documentary where the challenge of meeting this illusionism head on is greatest. It is only by examining *how* a series of sounds and images signify that we can begin to rescue documentary from the anti-theoretical, ideologically complicit argument that documentary-equals-reality, and that the screen is a window rather than a reflecting surface.

We need, then, to examine the formal structure of documentary film, the codes and units that are involved, in order to re-see documentary, not as a kind of reality-frozen-in-the-amber-of-the-photographic-image, à la Bazin, but as a semiotic system that generates meaning by the succession of choices between differences, the continuous selection of pertinent features from amongst the various codes and their intersection. Despite the denunciation of various cinematic "realisms," this work has scarcely begun with documentary, and yet what better place is there to confront the challenge of realism than here?

The Expository Form

The very notion of documentary is theoretically ill-defined. Christian Metz, for example, excludes documentary from theoretical priority, at least in his early work. He writes:

> It is by no means certain that an independent semiotics of the non-narrative genres is possible other than in the form of a series of discontinuous remarks on the points of difference between these films and "ordinary" films. . . . It was precisely to the extent that the cinema confronted the problem of narration . . . [that] it came to produce a body of specific signifying procedures.[4]

Thus, for Metz, documentary (which he treats as a non-narrative genre) could not possibly devise specific signifying procedures of its own. On the contrary, I believe the cinema's encounter with the structuring principles of narrative, exposition, and poetics leads, in each case, to specific signifying procedures. These procedures are not exclusionary: many forms of overlap or cross-breeding are possible.

IDEOLOGY AND THE IMAGE

Amongst them certain regulatory features of an expository dominant should be discernible.

But the problems are great, beginning with definitions. The imprecise character of standard definitions is well indicated, though inadvertently, by William Sloan: "The term documentary is used in its broadest sense to refer to films that possess truth and project reality, and are intended primarily for non-theatrical use."[5] Truth as reified possession, reality as something that can be mechanically reproduced upon a screen, and a noncommercial purpose: one lame stab at intentions and two gross epistemological naiveties scarcely constitute an adequate model. Yet Richard Meran Barsam's *Non-Fiction Film*, a book which devotes a whole chapter to definitions, only repeats these concepts at greater length, compounding them with a quantitative absurdity: for a documentary the "typical running time is thirty minutes" (p. 4). If nothing more could be said, Metz's contention would be beyond dispute.

A more adequate definition of documentary might begin by declaring it the principal domain of exposition divisible, like narrative, into several categories, among them:

1. overlapping, thematic genre(s) (the city film, biography, war reportage, propaganda—each deploying conventions, iconographic or otherwise, and invoking audience expectations);
2. directional oeuvre (Robert Flaherty, Joris Ivens, Fred Wiseman, Allan King);
3. periods or waves (the British documentary in the thirties, the NFB of Canada in the fifties, American cinéma vérité in the sixties);
4. national cinemas.

Our present concern lies less with these possible subcategories than with the structural characteristics of the domain as a whole—the qualities of exposition generally and their cinematic manifestation specifically.

In this regard it is important to stress that the division between narrative and non-narrative employed by some critics is not useful. Exposition and narrative—and poetics—are not exclusive; all three can figure into the textual system of a given film. The "crisis structure" of some cinéma vérité films relates closely to the sequential arrangement of functions in Propp's study of narrative, for example; and some experimental films like Kenneth Anger's *Scorpio Rising* incorporate narrative and documentary principles into their structure. Many documentaries, though, whether or not they borrow from the other two domains, are organized predominantly around the codes of exposition.

Exposition is traditionally the province of rhetoric, although classic rhetoric can no more account for the specificities of the documentary film than critical notions of the theater or novel can for the fiction film. Rhetoric, though, does provide a starting point. A survey of some of its chief concerns will generate a context in which remarks about the documentary film in particular can be placed.

Rhetoric divides into five departments—invention, arrangement, style, memory, and delivery. The last two concern presentation (mnemonic devices, "how to" maxims) and are of slight concern here. Description of the general contours of style lies beyond the scope of this book, whose treatment is limited to style as a textual system, a specific interplay of codes. Arrangement, or *dispositio,* will be referred to from time to time, especially in regard to the apparent lack of a necessary sequential arrangement of expository parts, unlike the narrative functions or actions, which exhibit certain regularities of ordering. (Definition need not be followed by comparison and contrast, for example, whereas the hero's departure is usually followed by his return.) Hence, by elimination, invention, or *inventio,* will be our primary concern.

Invention is the discovery of sources of argument to support any particular case. Aristotle originally categorized these inventions or proofs as inartistic (dependent on factual material available to the speaker—witnesses, contracts, confessions) and artistic (dependent upon the speaker's own invention). The second category divides into three proofs:

1. ethical—dependent upon the audience's estimation of the speaker's moral character or credibility as a function of the exposition;
2. emotional—dependent upon the speaker's appeal to the audience's emotions to produce a certain disposition;
3. demonstrative—dependent upon the exposition's recourse to real or apparent demonstration.[6]

All three forms of artistic proof figure heavily in most exposition. Television news illustrates the point. The CBS Evening News, for example, relies heavily on the persona of its anchor person for ethical proof: in the minds of many, Walter Cronkite is one of the most trustworthy public figures in America, certainly more so than many of the personalities who parade through each night's news items. Cronkite has the ability to command belief and thereby gain credibility for reportage to which we might otherwise attend with much less suspension of disbelief (6.1–2).

In television news emotional proof operates in a reverse fashion:

IDEOLOGY AND THE IMAGE

the structure of the program works to quiet, not arouse, the emotions, to win assent for the proposition that what happens "out there" need not perturb. The unfolding of history becomes encapsulated within 30-minute dramatizations of a highly mediated nature: anchor person, reporter in the field, actual event.

The mediating levels provide attenuation and closure so that ongoing processes are reduced to two- or three-minute "stories." The base level of reality, the diegetic reference point, is no longer the pro-filmic event but the anchor person, Walter Cronkite or his substitute. He becomes our point of access, navigating us through a flood of events to which order has accrued without noticeable difficulty or effort. "Leave the driving to us" goes an advertising slogan; and Cronkite's famous sign-off, "And that's the way it is," proposes a similar form of reassurance that in his hands the world will remain safe, and ultimately knowable.

The only deviation from this pattern involves a fourth level of mediation in the evening news program, a level that is literally and figuratively uncalled for. Cronkite will conclude a story looking directly into the camera. We cut 90° to a new angle in which we now see Cronkite in profile as though what is about to follow is not at his behest (in contrast to news stories whose appearance is cued by an off-screen glance from Cronkite, establishing the conceit that what follows is what Cronkite, from his anchorage, can see and beckon forth (6.3–4). What follows is a commercial advertisement. Here emotional involvement is called for.

> If we were asked to look but remain passive before, here we are asked to look and become active. We're asked to do something, to change, indeed to improve something. But what we're asked to improve is not the world but our own private situations or selves. And this improvement does not demand spiritual striving or political struggle, it simply requires the purchase of commodities.

The Documentary Film and Principles of Exposition

6.3. The 90° angle used before a commercial "break" in the news.

6.4. Cronkite's off-screen glance is traditionally the cue signaling a point-of-view shot. What follows in the news is a story from the field, told by a reporter.

6.5. The "direct address" of a CBS reporter, in this case, Leslie Stahl.

A displacement of values occurs. The news which refers to what should be our real conditions of existence becomes something almost imaginary, something highly mediated and punctuated by closure. The commercial message, which is indeed an imaginary message, becomes posited as the real, as an integral part of our lives, the part we can control and change. If the news says, Look but don't care, commercials say, Look and care.[7]

The confusion of realms woven into the fabric(ation) of the news truly staggers the mind.

Finally, television news frequently resorts to demonstrative proof—real or apparent demonstration. This is partly directed toward the specifics of a given story and partly to the authority of the news program as a whole. The latter effort joins up with ethical and emotional proof to produce our overall disposition toward what we see and hear. To a considerable extent demonstrative proof in this case works in relation to the mediating levels that originate with the anchor point of meaning, Walter Cronkite. Normally, he will sketch out the basic details of a story, then call upon a reporter for substantiation.

IDEOLOGY AND THE IMAGE

6.6 and 6.9 are from the CBS News, 6.7–8 from the Canadian Broadcasting Corporation's (CBC) National. They all illustrate the slight angle that keeps the interviewee from addressing us directly.

The device operates as if to say, I have told you about this event (as a newspaper might) but lest you doubt, I will show you. We then cut to a reporter in the field who occupies the foreground. Behind him or her is an icon signifying his or her "on the spot" presence (the White House, UN flags, the oil fields of Iran, a sign reading "Wall Street," etc.). Whereas with Cronkite we see images representing a distant event projected behind him (6.2), with reporters we see signifiers of their own immediate proximity to the event. (Strictly speaking, with Cronkite we see the image of an image representing a given story and with reporters we see an image that represents their physical relation to that story: we are at one less remove from the pro-filmic event but also at one remove from our own point of reference, the anchor person.)

Reporters may then call on witnesses to give testimony (the interview), simply report to the camera themselves (given the point-of-view figure inaugurating their report, they speak to Cronkite whose place we share, 6.3), or talk voice-over while we see images of

The Documentary Film and Principles of Exposition   177

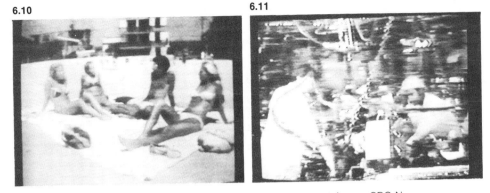

6.10 is from a CBS News story on radiation, and **6.11** from a CBC News story on the Canadian economy.

illustration. The degree to which individuals appropriated for purposes of illustration (interviewees) and reporters approach the zero-degree eyeline between camera and subject (zero degrees occurs when the subject looks directly into the camera, 90° when the subject is in profile), subsequently becomes another form of demonstrative proof. Briefly, like Cronkite himself, reporters are authorized to look directly into the camera (6.5), interviewees come within a few degrees of zero but seldom closer (6.6–9), and those who neither address us nor address those who address us (through interviews) are the truly dispossessed: they seldom approach closer than 30° except through accident or confrontation (6.10–11).[8] Controlled access to the camera as demonstrative proof, appears, like emotional proof, to run in a reverse direction from what we might expect: the closer to the unmediated activity and real social actors we go, the less an individual's access to the eye of the camera and hence to our own becomes. Seeing is believing, but not all sights are equal in the eye of the camera, or of television news.

The phrase "real or apparent demonstration" is crucial, since rhetoric is not identical with logic and the demonstration of truth. Rhetoric is concerned with pragmatic questions, with how an argument can be made persuasively; it leaves decisions about its ultimate truth to other disciplines. As Kenneth Burke puts it, " . . . the basic function of rhetoric [is] the use of words by human agents to form attitudes or induce actions in other human agents. . . ."[9] As such, rhetoric in the broadest sense, serves as a vehicle of socialization, a mediation between self and other.

A logical extension of this placement of rhetoric demands our recognition of it as a signifier of ideology. This position, adopted in the general domain of rhetoric and carried into the specific area of

IDEOLOGY AND THE IMAGE

documentary film denies the possibility of "proving" objective truths rhetorically; our acceptance of ("real or apparent") demonstrations of truth will depend upon the interaction between the demonstrator's rhetorical skill and our own assumptions rather than procedures of a necessary and sufficient logic.

Real or apparent demonstration rests upon certain shared assumptions. These constitute the topics, or commonplaces, of Aristotle, which are both commonplaces, i.e., widely held and frequently expressed opinions, and common places, i.e., abstract or analytical categories applicable to any subject. We might say that the foundation of rhetorical demonstration depends on dressing topics, places common to demonstration whatever its subject-matter or medium, in the garb of commonplaces, shared assumptions or opinions. A metaphor (one of the topics) likening government policies enacted in order to conserve energy to a war plan might seek to persuade by conveying a sense of high moral purpose, clear identification of an external enemy, and the need to marshal resources and put aside differences in the face of a mutual foe—i.e., by eliciting a set of opinions associated with crises and the prerequisites for victory whether they constitute an adequate or appropriate response to the actual situation or not. Here again we see the practical bias of rhetoric, its lack of an obligatory movement toward transcendence of opinion. Topics parade past in the fashions of opinion: "If, in the opinion of a given audience, a certain kind of conduct is admirable, then a speaker might persuade the audience by using ideas and images that identify his cause with that kind of conduct."[10]

Kenneth Burke's succinct phrase "ideas and images" embraces the broad range of possible topics. Such topics as definition, enumeration, classification, cause and effect, negation, or syllogistic progression (if P, then Q) lend themselves more readily to the more literal logic of ideas than do others, such as comparison or symbolizing, where imagery often prevails. Ever since Aristotle, various authors have created taxonomies of these topics which, if comprehensive, serve as a rhetorical *syntagmatique*, a catalogue of elements supporting the argument or demonstration.

This does not lead, however, to rules for the sequential ordering of topics. Like classical narrative, exposition displays a customary arrangement (*dispositio*) of sections equivalent to a beginning, a middle, and an end, in that order; but the arrangement of parts (topics) within a section is left unspecified. Some topics may often be followed by others, definition by example, for instance, but this is not binding.

If we recall Christian Metz's *grande syntagmatique* for the arrangement of the temporal dimension of a narrative, we may simply note that the topics do not provide an expository analogy to his syntagmas for several reasons. First, since expository, and poetic, discourse sometimes organizes time into an imaginary coherence like the diegesis of narrative, elements of Metz's syntagmatique may themselves figure into an exposition, as we shall see in chapter 7. In other words, an equivalent *syntagmatique* is not as likely as borrowings from the same one whenever a singular, unified ordering of cinematic time and space is required.

Second, even though speculation suggests that a table of "logical" parts* (e.g., the topics) should exist in exposition comparable to Metz's table of temporal parts in narrative, this, too, proves deceptive. The topics do not yield to a clearly bifurcating declension so that one and only one topic is available for a given logical effect, whereas one and only one syntagma is available for the successive representation of simultaneity—the descriptive syntagma. In exposition a given logical effect may be produced by any one of several topics: definition can be accomplished by definition in the usual sense, by example, by comparison/contrast, or by negation, among others.

But not only do the topics resist classification according to a scheme of successive dichotomies, they are not specific to any particular medium of communication. This also contrasts with Metz's *syntagmatique,* which designates a code specific to the cinema, the differences between syntagmas being a (cinematic) matter of editing or montage choices. Whereas other media use different strategies based upon their own properties to organize time descriptively, all media share the commonplace or topic of description, in different forms, to advance an argument. Description, say, in the cinema generally, does not have a singular form like the descriptive syntagma. There may be only one way in classical cinematic narrative to organize time descriptively, but in expository film there are many ways to organize an argument descriptively (for example, only verbally, verbally with visual support, only visually, with written titles, etc.)—all of which may borrow a temporal underpinning from Metz's *syntagmatique* without being reducible to it.

So far as any catalogue of topics is exhaustive, it will comprise a paradigm, or *syntagmatique,* of all the possible strategies by which an argument can be made. This paradigm will differ considerably from the one proposed by Metz for the reasons cited above. In fact, it may more closely resemble Propp's list of functions or Barthes's notion of a code of actions as a paradigm or *syntagmatique* characteristic of all exposition, whatever the medium. The possibility of constructing a

---

Logical is in quotes because of the previous comments about the basis of rhetoric in opinion. Rhetoric, or exposition generally, often has the force of logical argument without its overall form.

paradigm corresponding to Metz's *grande syntagmatique* for expository cinema as such is further lessened by the fact that the need to fabricate a singular diegesis—a necessary but scarcely-mentioned presupposition to Metz's taxonomy—is greatly attenuated in expository cinema.* Reciprocally, perhaps Metz's *syntagmatique* is less crucial to an understanding of the structure of narrative than are concepts like the codes of actions or enigmas, which bear a certain similarity to topics—namely in their applicability to different media, i.e., a generality coterminous with the phenomenon they characterize—narrative or exposition, respectively. We hope that some day we will be able to describe not only the general structural principles of exposition or narrative but also the expository or narrative procedures distinctive to a given medium during a given historical period. In the present stage of preliminary research regarding the cinema generally and documentary particularly, that day remains very distant.

The Pragmatics of Exposition

Earlier, we saw that the pragmatic thrust of rhetoric toward persuasion placed it inside an ideological arena. To put it differently, any paradigm of topics, or set of rules about arrangement (*dispositio*), is in furtherance of pragmatics (Aristotle's proofs) more than semantics. The problems of particular and specific meanings are bypassed (or left for the criteria of the various arts and sciences to determine) in favor of general tactics for the achievement of diverse effects upon the recipients of a message. These effects do not occur in isolation from semantics but, as anyone who has attended to recent political campaigns knows, the "message" has less to do with the literal meaning of statements—to which few politicians feel bound—than with the kind of attitude elicited in the audience toward the speaker—the ties that bind. But pragmatics always come clothed in semantics, just as topics come clothed in opinions, or a code in messages. No separation or opposition is possible, because the terms designate different levels of abstraction. Codes, topics, and pragmatics are all conceptual categories, choices of punctuation either proposed by analysts or already weighted with the palpable facticity of social convention (and ideology—the invocation, for example, of "personal freedom" or "human rights" as code words for capitalist democracy in contrast with communist tyranny).

We give consent or not on the basis of the success of such rhetorical proofs, not on the basis of rigorous logical proof. This process is

---

*This point is further developed on pp. 185 and 205–6.

most glaringly obvious in propaganda but underlies virtually all expository discourse (including the discourse of science—see pp. 243–50). Communicators desire persuasiveness; they have recourse to mechanisms like those of dream-work, which we have examined in relation to narrative and which could be extended to exposition. These mechanisms allow for the manifest treatment of what has been repressed from consciousness and for the attenuation or resolution of contradictions in the face of inevitable paradox. Benveniste, in fact, explicitly likens these mechanisms of the unconscious to style and rhetoric (ch. 3, n. 46), while rhetoric itself provides specific strategies to enhance expository persuasiveness to move the reader or listener in certain ways or directions. The qualities we found in narrative discourse—a duplicity in the text and the consciousness of being addressed—appear in exposition as well. How we are addressed, the kind of relationship proposed, is a crucial matter. It returns us to the question of where we draw the line, a line that cannot not be drawn, just as we cannot not communicate, even by silence.

To put it somewhat differently, messages always come addressed. They propose an address for us to which they are delivered by the very act of addressing themselves to this place. We are free to accept or reject this address, but as we have seen, this freedom is strongly circumscribed by our desire for recognition (the recognition of our self—and of those codes, programs, or habits that help fix the self in place). Never to be addressed by others would be a profound disconfirmation of self, a kind of communicational murder. To answer to an address where we do not fully live or live fully (the place of the self-as-subject, for example) is a profound distortion of self, a kind of schizophrenia. We cannot avoid the problems of address any more than those of pragmatics: they are inherent in the very act of communication. We may begin to confront the question of address in exposition by considering it in relation to formal organization in the documentary.

Modes of Address

There are two basic modes of address in documentary (i.e., patterns of sound/image relationship that specify somewhat different "places" or attitudes for the viewer): direct address or indirect address, depending on whether the viewer is explicitly acknowledged as the subject to whom the film is addressed. Each of these modes can then be subdivided according to whether the viewer is addressed by characters (individuals representing their social roles outside the film) or by narrators (individuals representing the point of view of the documentary itself, surrogate figures, usually, for the film maker's own interpretation) and whether the narration is synchronized with the images. Diagrammatically:

direct address (expository cinema)

	sync	*non-sync*
narrators	voice of authority	voice of God
		images of illustration
characters	interview	voice of witness
		images of illustration

indirect address (observational cinema)

	sync	*non-sync*
narrators		
characters	cinéma vérité	
	(voice and image	voice of social actors
	of social actors)	images of illustration

Historically, most documentaries have used the mode of direct address, and it is still preferred by television documentary, political films, and most sponsored or commercial films. This mode also lends itself more readily to the terms of the current discussion than indirect address, which returns us to some of the characteristics of narrative discourse. Indirect address invites risks of incomprehensibility (lacking the guiding hand of a narrator) and, for political film makers, empiricism (a risk well confirmed by much cinéma vérité, where pre-existing "facts" are dutifully recorded by an "objective" observer.[11] Conversely, the adoption of direct address has run the perennial risk of dogmatism, using the voice of a commentator to authoritatively, if not authoritarianly, assert what is, and what is not, the case; although direct address also offers the advantage of analytic precision.

Indirect address is also the principal mode of narrative and is a prime contributor to the creation of the diegesis, the fictional plane of reality, because it is a self-enclosed mode, not rupturing the internal plane of reality we are invited to observe by directly addressing us. It is also a mode at the disposal of the documentary film maker. When indirect address is used in documentary, however, it is not necessarily joined to a narrative but may instead support an exposition.

Consequently, the diegesis is no longer a spatio-temporal universe plausibly maintained in its autonomy, but rather a conceptual universe, the domain of the exposition. The diegesis (*diegesis* originally meant "narrative" in Greek) may reappear but usually sporadically—as one component of an argument no longer constituted by it. Instead the text enlists the diegesis as one strategy among many. This, however, removes diegesis from its close association, in Metz's writings for example, with the image track and the projection of an illusionistic universe; it makes diegesis a notion more closely linked with the sound track, primarily with speech and the logical universe of its ordering. In other words, exposition does not require the fabrication of an imaginary spatio-temporal universe so much as the fabrication of an imaginary rhetorical universe where demonstration, apparent or real, takes place. Such a radical shift in meaning may more properly call for a new word rather than an extension of the meaning of *diegesis,* which easily lends itself to the erroneous definition of documentary as somehow capturing or projecting reality. Meanwhile, in this chapter I shall use "diegesis" in quotation marks to refer to the plane of rhetorical ordering that supports exposition and diegesis without quotation marks to refer to the spatio-temporal continuity comparable to that in fiction.*

This distinction can also be examined in relation to narrators and characters. These very terms, however, may seem problematic, especially since we expect characters to appear in narrative but not in documentary. The narrator, first of all, stands in a direct relation to the exposition, seldom causing any confusion with narrative modes. Whereas the appearance of a narrator speaking in direct address almost invariably ruptures the diegesis of fictional narrative, it can *constitute* the "diegesis" of documentary exposition. Hence, the "diegesis" cannot be ruptured by the narrator's presence, although it sometimes can be by his absence, by the lack of a logical principle ordering the whole which the narrator usually makes manifest. If commentary stands outside the narrative sequence and intrudes upon it or marks it off, commentary can found the expository sequence and with it the principles of organizing such parts into a whole different in its structure from a narrative whole but no less complete or complex, despite Metz's original assertion to the contrary.

Characters, though, stand in an indirect relation to the exposition and are presumed to enjoy a certain autonomy from it (they begin as real people—social actors, not film actors—who then contribute to an exposition, rather than beginning as a function of the exposition subsequently embodied by a real person, the narrator). They thus enjoy an extra-textual autonomy as characters that the narrator does not enjoy as a narrator. This autonomy, however, either depends on

*One possible term to convey the sense of rhetorical ordering discussed here might be "rhetorical fiction."

6.12–13. These two sequential shots from *The Battle of San Pietro* illustrate the use of continuity editing (match on action) to fabricate a single event from shots recorded at different times. In this case the diegetic plane offers itself as transparent to the real but also as subordinate to the commentary. Like the use of eyeline in television news (proximity to zero degrees or eyeline match), the apparent continuity is a demonstrative proof of the authenticity of what is said: We can see what the battle was like and that what John Huston, the commentator, says is true.

our general knowledge (we know a documentary about the Rolling Stones is about real, living people) or upon the cues provided by the textual system—often either direct statements or various cues implying the ongoing, autonomous existence of characters. This last technique bears resemblance to a function of the diegesis in fiction—to give characters an imaginary autonomy.

Two distinctions should be pointed out. First, as a spatio-temporal continuum the diegesis is often intermittent in the documentary of direct address (for example, *Controlling Interest,* San Francisco Newsreel, 1977) rather than continuous as in fiction, though it may be continuous in indirect address documentaries like *A Time for Burning* (William Jersey, 1966). Typically, the diegetic realm of characters depends in part upon commentary for its evocation and may be summarily sketched in only to be abandoned for another locale needed by the commentary. (*Calcutta,* Louis Malle, 1968, and *In The Year of the Pig,* Emile de Antonio, 1969, provide further examples of this intermittent quality.) Second, the diegetic plane is located outside the film (it is in fact equated with reality itself in many instances—see 6.12–13). Characters are ceded a real-life autonomy rather than the imaginary one of a narrative's diegesis. The film marks, indexes, or refers to this location without ever fully inscribing it. Such a location proposes less the notion of fictional closure than that of open access to the real, a shift that still allows for the intersection of documentary with the illusionistic strategies of fiction. Many of the principles discussed so far are vividly illustrated by *The Battle of San Pietro,* a classic direct-address documentary (6.14–66).

The Documentary Film and Principles of Exposition   185

6.14. *The Battle of San Pietro* opens with General Mark Clark (6.14) presenting the official military view of the battle. He says, "San Pietro, in the 5th sector, was the key to the Liri Valley. We knew it and the enemy knew it. We had to take it even though the immediate cost would be high. We took it, and the cost in relation to the later advance was not excessive."

6.15–17. But John Huston, director and narrator, had a different impression and one major function of his commentary is to undercut the assertion that the cost was "not excessive." The word itself recurs once, during this sequence depicting the efforts of the Italian allies against fortified mountain positions. The commentary is reproduced above the shots (each represented by a still) over which it was originally spoken.

6.14

6.15. "The Italians were all but annihilated.

6.16. In view of their excessive losses, further operations against Mount

6.17. Lungo's strategic heights were abandoned.

6.18–48. Huston continues to undercut Clark's cost assessment through an intricate visual motif that grows out of the shots selected to illustrate portions of the commentary. Basically, this involves a traditional narrative pattern at least as old as Griffith and highly prevalent in the westerns of John Ford: long shots to convey the epic sweep of historic events, close-ups to individuate those characters whose destiny we will follow. But here visually individuated characters appear only to be subsequently lost to death (the only other time we see individuals in close-up). The pattern becomes individuated in life, de-personalized in death. We never see an American soldier's face in death (at most we see profiles). It is their lives that are precious. In contrast, we do not see living enemy soldiers in close-up at all (except for a few prisoners), but we do see their faces as well as their bodies in death. Tact matters less for lives that matter little. The loss of precious lives then becomes a major visual motif of the film, which receives very little commentative elaboration but works extremely effectively to re-insert dimensions of war that Clark's bland assessment would disavow. The stills and captions (a transcription of the voice-over narration) for 6.15–48 illustrate this motif.

6.18. Of the original force

6.19. to establish the beachhead at Salerno,

6.20. the hundred-and-forty-third had

6.21. since spent all but a fortnight in action,

6.22. under extremely bitter weather conditions.

6.23. At Salerno,

The Documentary Film and Principles of Exposition   187

6.24. at the Valterno crossing,

6.25. it had taken mortal punishment.

6.26. The task ahead promised no less bloodshed,

6.27. yet it was undertaken in good spirits and high confidence.

6.28. The toll of enemy dead mounted with each new attempt."

6.29. [music only]

6.30. [music only]

6.31. [music only]

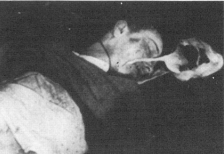

6.32. [music only]

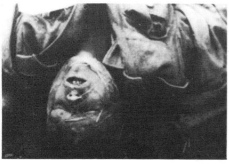

6.33. [Following other descriptions of bloody assaults by different Allied units] "But (the First Battalion) had paid for ground gained

6.34. at the rate of a man a yard

6.35. and did not have the strength to

The Documentary Film and Principles of Exposition 189

6.36. carry the fight any further forward."

6.37–48. [Following description of the successful capture of the town, Huston sums up its toll, over images of soldiers entering the town] "The second and third battalions, less than a rifle company in strength, weary to death, who were alive [sic], stumbled forward past San Pietro to consolidate gains and re-establish contact with the enemy now taking up new positions some five kilometers beyond. That is the broad shape of the battle of San Pietro . . .

6.37. which was but the first of many battles in the Liri Valley. It was a very costly

6.38. battle. After the battle, the 143rd Infantry regiment alone required 1100 replacements."

6.39. [music only]

6.40. "The lives lost were precious lives,

IDEOLOGY AND THE IMAGE

6.41. to their country, to their loved ones,

6.42. and to the men themselves.

6.43. For the living of the 143rd Infantry regiment, more than one hundred decorations for acts of valor above and beyond

6.44. the call of duty. Many among these you see alive here have since joined the ranks of their brothers in arms who fell at San Pietro. For ahead lay San Batoy and the Rapido River, and

6.45. Cassino. And beyond Cassino, more rivers,

6.46. and more mountains, and more towns;

The Documentary Film and Principles of Exposition   191

6.47. more San Pietros, greater or lesser.

6.48. A thousand more."

6.49–66. John Huston's commentary in *The Battle of San Pietro* follows the tradition of stoic understatement that Hemingway brought to Joris Iven's *The Spanish Earth* (for example, Hemingway's even-toned observation, "This is the moment which all the rest of war prepares for, when six men go forward into death, to walk across a a stretch of land, and by their presence on it prove this land is ours"). Huston departs from the more highly poetic narration of Pare Lorentz's films like *The River* and refrains from the exhortative tone of most World War II documentaries such as the *Why We Fight* series narrated by his father, Walter Huston.

In this opening sequence, Huston evokes that which is tangibly absent from these shots of agrarian countryside but which has visual signs or correlations: the war itself. We see no soldiers nor any instruments of war, but we do see signs of its general pervasiveness. Huston alludes to these signs but does not treat them as symptomatic of war explicitly. His highly laconic remarks about the terrain imply that a cycle of natural hardships has befallen the region, while his traveloguelike comments about the architecture reverberate with an irony that makes the effects of war all the more intensely felt.

6.49. "The Liri Valley lies in the Italian Midland,

6.50. some sixty miles northwest of Naples to some forty miles southeast of Rome—

IDEOLOGY AND THE IMAGE

6.51. a wide, flat corridor, enclosed between four walls of mountains.

6.52. In winter, the highest peaks of the Liri range ascend into the snows.

6.53. To the valley floor with its olive groves and ancient vines; its crops of wheat and corn is green the year around.

6.54. That is, in normal times.

6.55. Last year was a bad year for grapes and olives.

6.56. And the fall planting was late.

The Documentary Film and Principles of Exposition   193

6.57. Many fields lay fallow.

6.58. There are two ways from the south end of the valley: one a narrow pass,

6.59. the other a high, scenic road over the mountains.

6.60. They converge before the site of the ancient village of San Pietro,

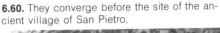

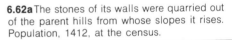

6.61. which for 700 years has stood at the threshold of Liri Valley, welcoming the traveler.

6.62a The stones of its walls were quarried out of the parent hills from whose slopes it rises. Population, 1412, at the census.

IDEOLOGY AND THE IMAGE

6.62b

6.63. A farming community.

6.64. Patron, St. Peter.

6.65. Point of Interest, St. Peter's, 1438.

6.66a and b (pan). Note—interesting treatment of chancel."

The Documentary Film and Principles of Exposition

195

The Expository Sequence

Another comparison between exposition and narrative can be made vis-à-vis the question of the sequence. The sequence is part of the problem of an overall theory of part/whole relations within the textual system. Since the whole in exposition is different from the whole in narrative, it would seem to follow that the sequence too is differently constructed.

The sequence has long remained ill-defined in the theory and criticism of the narrative film itself. As Henderson has indicated, both Eisenstein and Bazin constructed theories of the sequence as though it were identical to, or at least need not be distinguished from, the whole film.[12] No clear-cut definition of the sequence can be found in either theorist. Christian Metz, in developing his *grande syntagmatique*, offers a definition of the sequence as a syntagm, or unit of narrative autonomy: a sequence is "a coherent syntagm within which the 'shots' react (semantically) to each other."[13]

This definition provides a useful starting point although it must be pried loose from Metz's *syntagmatique* as a paradigm of narrative choices. If we begin by thinking in terms of rhetorical topics, the general notion of a coherent syntagm remains viable even though we will expect a greater range of signifying procedures for any one topic than the singular procedures Metz isolates for each of his eight syntagmatic categories. Equally significantly, the sequences (and any *syntagmatique* of them) will no longer be categories of the image track primarily, as they are for Metz. This corresponds to the shift in the meaning of diegesis and requires locating the sequence in relation to the verbal sound track. In fact, Metz's own evolution approximates such a shift; his comment about sequences in *Language and Cinema* needs only slight modification, in particular the replacement of 'images' by 'sound/image relationships,' to apply to expository sequences as well:

> The distinctive element in such a code (that of the *grande syntagmatique*) is not the sequence itself, . . . but only the logical principle of ordering which animates it and which assures it cohesion, permitting the images to form a sequence instead of remaining isolated views.[14]

At least since the early days of sound this logical principle of ordering has derived from classical rhetoric. Direct-address commentary in the British documentary of the 1930s and the American films of Pare Lorentz established a pattern elaborated on by the *March of Time*, the *Why We Fight* series (1942–45), the World War II documentary generally, the British Free Cinema (*Every Day Except Christmas*,

IDEOLOGY AND THE IMAGE

1957; *We Are the Lambeth Boys,* 1959), and television news reports like *Selling of the Pentagon* (1971). In these "mainstream" documentaries, each sequence sets in place a block of argumentation that the image track illustrates, with more or less redundancy (shading from unqualified verification to bitter irony—see 6.14–48). If there is a counterpart to the "classical narrative cinema," this form of "classical expository cinema" would seem the most likely candidate.

A recent innovation in classical expository cinema has been developed by Emile de Antonio, whose films include *Point of Order* (1963), *Rush to Judgment* (1967), *In the Year of the Pig* (1969), *Milhouse: A White Comedy* (1971), *Painters Painting* (1973), and *The Weather Underground* (1975). These still amount to "classical expositions," but they avoid the traditional locus for the line of the argument, the narrator. Instead, de Antonio marshals his argument through the relationships established by editing between the comments of various characters. The spectator's responsibility for ferreting out and following the line of reasoning is consequently increased, although the continued use of direct address (via characters) militates against a very radical shift from the place of the spectator in classical exposition.

Newsreel, a political film making group begun in 1968 as part of the New Left, has employed another significant variation. Rather than elimination of the narrator, they favor his or her dispersion: more than one narrator, women as narrators, or narrators and characters both choreographed into a singular line of exposition. *Revolution Until Victory* (1973), *We Demand Freedom* (1973), *Teach Our Children* (1972), *In the Event Anyone Disappears* (1973), *Rompiendo Puertas (Break and Enter)* (1971)—these and other films typify this tendency with varying degrees of success. As a more prismatic, less assertive or dogmatic means of argumentation, this innovation is one of Newsreel's tactical strengths. It correlates well with their concern to have people speak for themselves, to film rank-and-file individuals rather than more rhetorically accomplished leaders, and can be expected to remain a mode to which Newsreel will give priority. We also find it surfacing in historical documentaries such as *Union Maids* (Julia Reichert and Jim Klein, 1977) and *With Babies and Banners* (Lorraine Gray, 1978) where a serious problem emerges. By eliminating the narrator altogether in favor of a restricted range of character-witnesses, the film maker becomes bound to the point of view of the characters (unless she or he reverts to some form of counterpoint or irony, which is probably even more unacceptable in these particular cases than the addition of commentary). The result is an historical fidelity that centers upon the (selective) remembrance of certain key figures at the sacrifice of any broader notion of historical accuracy. (The most glaring lack in these two films, for example, is any reference to, or explanation of, the role of the Communist Party [USA] during the period of union struggle that the films examine, the 1930s.) This raises serious questions which, together with the difficulties that arise when cinéma vérité turns to historical reconstruction, suggest the continuing importance of the narrator as a contextualizing voice capable of introducing a perspective independent of any character's.

Principles of sequence construction in indirect address have been less well elaborated, partly because the techniques of cinéma vérité are more recent and partly because the tradition in most countries has been towards a fusion of direct and indirect address sequences within a composite whole (e.g., *Back Breaking Leaf*, *I Was A Ninety-Pound Weakling*, *Woodstock*, *Dead Birds*, *Mondo Cane*, *Still a Brother*). The American style of cinéma vérité described by Stephen Mamber in *Cinema Verite in America* has been the most rigorous in utilizing indirect address in an unalloyed fashion; and of its practitioners, Frederick Wiseman has been perhaps the most significant.

Full discussion of his work is reserved for the next chapter, but it represents a radical restructuring of the viewing experience (aligning it, ironically, in this abrupt departure from classical exposition, closer to classical narrative). The qualities of the overall organization of Wiseman's films raise questions of considerable theoretical importance at a level somewhat different from the ideologically complicit debates about bias and honesty in documentary, debates which usually endorse in some fashion the dubious definitions of documentary cited earlier. In any case, indirect address poses distinct problems and to a large extent must be considered separately.

Narrators and Characters in Direct Address

Our present concern, however, is the mode of direct address, and, most immediately, a further consideration of the functions of narrators and characters. The narrator in direct address often serves to bridge sequences: to make manifest the logical principle that orders the sequence into larger units, segments, and a textual whole. When direct-address documentaries lack coherence or incisiveness, the commentary often lies at the heart of the problem. Sometimes commentary is minimized in order to avoid an overly rigid or doctrinaire impression as in *Dead Birds* (Robert Gardner, 1963) or the laconic commentary of *The Battle of San Pietro* (6.49–66). Some films, like Emile de Antonio's, run the risk of neglecting the narrator's "coherence function" altogether, although it is also possible that discrete moments of confusion or incoherence may be symptomatic of unresolved tensions or ideological contestations accessible to the kind of

IDEOLOGY AND THE IMAGE

reading suggested by the *Cahiers du Cinéma* study of *Young Mister Lincoln*.

When the line of reasoning of the narrator bridges sequences, threading its way through the entire film, it usually promotes the verbal sound track to a position of dominance, organizes the remaining tracks (location sound, music, image, and graphics), and provides the viewer's point of entry to the expository whole. Hence the criteria for argument developed elsewhere (in formal logic and rhetoric) can to a large degree be applied as tests of the coherence of the narration. Conversely, the actual form of the argument (like the actual form of narrative in fiction films) may be, in part, specifically cinematic. To what degree this calls for new criteria of assessment we cannot know until we have a more complete elaboration of the specifically cinematic codes of exposition (perhaps especially those involving sound/image relationships: verbal statements followed by visual and musical illustration, verbal statement accompanied by confirmation, contradiction, ironic shading, etc.).

However, something more can be said, in two connections:

First, vis-à-vis the relationship between denotative and connotative signification in the verbal sound track. Although the literal signification of spoken words, the denotation, may be the primary organizing component, it may also be subordinate to its own connotative aspects. For example, a monotonous commentary explaining the strategy and tactics of a national-liberation struggle may completely undermine the understanding provided by its denotative aspect, however brilliant. On the other hand, this lackluster quality of the commentary serves as a perfect overtone to the factual recitations in *US Techniques and Genocide in Vietnam*[15] and *Land Without Bread* or *Night and Fog*. It is not the absolute priority of the connotative codes that is in question but their effect in context. Newsreel's domestic films about such issues as housing, day care, or medical services available to working-class people are rich in the tonal inflections and rhythms of characters in direct address. In this regard these films are more exemplary than the national-liberation films Newsreel distributes, where character speech is overshadowed by unpersuasive interpretative commentary.

Second, vis-à-vis the relationship between the verbal sound track and the other sound tracks: Total absence of location sound in sync with the image track tends to make the expository "diegesis" into an argument operating on an abstract plane to which images, operating on another abstract plane, are appended, rather than one where the images concretize or specify the argument. Synchronous sound and images often act to provide specificity as they root the argument in the visual and aural texture of a particular time and place. Sync sound helps anchor the meaning of the images in a manner akin to the anchoring processes discussed in chapter 1. Without it the images may be more free-floating, rootless, and unable to fulfill the function for which the film recruits them.

This is a tactical point, not a claim about the ontological status of sounds and images in the film medium. Given that a film proposes a structure in which such a Bazinian formulation is implicit, the utilization of location sound seems to be a prerequisite for overall integration of sound and image tracks, an integration that may still leave major ideological problems unexamined. That there is no *inherent* necessity for this integration is perhaps made clear by films of the Dziga-Vertov Group such as *Letter to Jane,* in which the narration, by also functioning as a commentary upon itself, locates a specificity at the level of the textual codes rather than in the extra-textual referent, the "real world" "captured" by synchronous sounds and images.

The narrator can also be localized within a sequence, in which case his or her function is usually restricted to either the statement or elaboration of a particular point, and sometimes both. This is the predominant function of the narrators in Newsreel's prison films (*We Demand Freedom, Teach Our Children,* and *In the Event Anyone Disappears*), where intertitles also serve to elaborate aspects of the argument. The risk inherent in systematic localization within sequences is fragmentation, the loss of overall coherence. Great care is required if the coherent bridging that a narrator could provide is to arise from other sources. Newsreel seems to be most successful in achieving this bridging in those films organized around characters, discussed below.

Characters in direct address figure prominently in Newsreel's films, as in many other recent documentaries (de Antonio's work being the extreme case). *The Woman's Film, 38 Families, El Pueblo Se Levante (The People Rising), Rompiendo Puertas (Break and Enter), GI José, Black Power, Redevelopment, Homefront,* and *A Space to Be Me* are among the films where characters primarily or exclusively organize the exposition. Like the dispersion of the narrator, the predominance of direct-address characters seems motivated by Newsreel's desire to document contemporary struggle as it is articulated by the participants themselves, and, as such, it is a highly effective technique.

Organization of the verbal sound track in relation to sequences can once again be of two kinds: characters can serve a bridging function or their commentary can be localized within the sequence.[16] The first case needs clarification, since it can easily lead to a confusion of characters and narrators. Characters cannot serve a bridging function themselves deliberately without foreknowledge of the film's overall

Ideology and the Image

structure, in which case they do in fact occupy a status in between that of character and narrator. John Watson's commentary in *Finally Got the News* is an excellent example: Watson participated in the film's planning but also appears as himself, as a worker-organizer. He is not only the embodiment of an argument whose integrity resides strictly within the film; he also extends integrity by reference to his extra-filmic autonomy as a social actor or real person in the midst of the struggle to which he refers.[17] The films of Michael Rubbo such as *Sad Song of Yellow Skin* or *Waiting for Fidel* also examine this possibility within the context of personal journalism.

Characters who are strictly characters only serve an extra-sequential, bridging function through the manipulation of cinematic codes. In this case their bridging function for the film is implicit, not part of the original design of their commentary. Bridging via character then becomes a function of the editing process. De Antonio's work is the purest example, but *I Was A Ninety-Pound Weakling* offers a lighter, more ironic but equally valid illustration of the same point. *Portrait of Jason,* on the other hand, carries the dominance of characters in direct address to its extreme while also minimizing the effects of editing: bridging, here, simply becomes a function of chronological condensation.

However, in most cases characters in direct address function within sequences rather than between them. If a film stresses the development of such sequences with comparatively slight attention to their overall connection, the result need not be a garbled whole. In fact, the latter is more often produced if exposition is directed toward advancing a specific argument or line of reasoning, and suffers in consequence from any weakness of the connective tissue. A less problematic course is to aim the exposition toward elucidation or description rather than argumentation. It is then possible to flatten the overall argument into a simple assertion or maxim (a commonplace) (e.g., the U.S. Army is an agent of imperialist, racist policies) and emphasize a description or elaboration of this assertion at the personal level of testimony by character witnesses, as in *Only the Beginning, Winter Soldier,* or *GI José.*

This is also the strategy of investigative reportage such as CBS's *60 Minutes* where characters offer testimony in relation to a particular theme introduced by the narrator: Some small record companies prey upon aspiring singers by charging exorbitant fees to record and promote a record and then making very little effort to promote it in fact; or, some construction companies exploit government subsidies for minority-controlled companies by installing token minority-group members in positions of ostensible control. Interviews then provide elaboration. They also contribute emotional and moral proofs—we

The Documentary Film and Principles of Exposition   201

align ourselves for and against characters according to their apparent credibility. By giving us access to "ordinary people," the narrator's own moral status rises: their testimony invariably bears out the narrator's thesis; the viability of our access to knowledge through the locus of He-Who-Knows is reconfirmed.

The development of a typology of character-sequences and their possible relationships must await further elaboration of the codes of exposition. But some general observations can be offered. Characters in direct address (classically, the interview format) have a wide range of modes available to them, from the description of events or situations that were intensely personal experiences to these seen with calm detachment or perhaps indirectly experienced—the range from personal witness to detached authority. They can speak about the effects of events or situations on themselves or about their own level of awareness, their beliefs at the time of the event or situation. Alternatively, this level can be completely suppressed or ignored in favor of comments that belie any direct effect of the situations or events discussed upon the character-authority who speaks. All of these alternatives are combinatory among themselves, and their formal combination in the film, along with other choices (e.g., does each character develop a different point or do several characters elaborate on the same one?) works to realize the textual system in its distinctiveness.

In general, it can be said that interviews have worked particularly well in Newsreel films and women's movement films like *The Woman's Film* (San Francisco Newsreel, 1970), *Rape* (JoAnn Elam, 1977), *Joyce at 34* (Joyce Chopra, 1972), or *Self-Health* (San Francisco Women's Health Collective, 1974) where the emphasis is on the articulation of a change of consciousness by characters, especially insofar as it has been altered by the experience of a specific event, process, or situation. For example, in *Oil Strike* workers describe changes in their attitudes to the company, the police, and the law as a result of their strike; in *In the Event Anyone Disappears* prisoners describe their changing attitudes toward prison on the basis of day-to-day experiences; and in *GI José* Puerto Rican ex-GIs describe changes in their attitude toward machismo, the military, and Vietnam after a tour of duty. The effectiveness of the strategy depends on the congruence between the characters' goal (to describe or explain a change in the values or beliefs that he or she can articulate) and the kind of discourse facilitated by direct address (explicit statements) with characters instead of narrators (an element of personal involvement or witness). But it also correlates with a larger political goal: to provide a focus on, and forum for, changes of consciousness that contribute to a process of radicalization. Interviews of this kind therefore often fit well within a film that may be directed thematically toward questions of education, consciousness-raising, or radicalization.

Sound/image relationships involving characters in direct address appear to break down into four categories. Most common is sync sound accompanying images of the character (the interview). This relationship is virtually indispensable: to hear and never see a character would be highly unusual. Sync sound/image shots or sequences serve to anchor characters within their milieux and to realize (make real) the surface manifestations of their social identity (dress, physique, gestures, etc.). In a film like *Rompiendo Puertas* these sequences are a valuable means of specifying the hazardous physical conditions of the buildings inhabited by the tenants who address us.

Similarly, in a program like *60 Minutes* such sequences help disarm the suspicion that all has been fabricated in a television studio. The narrators go out into the field and take pains to interview characters in situations that can be readily seen as indicative of their milieu. An entire iconography has gradually developed around the use of background space in interviews, normally to provide verification of the role or status of the interviewee. Sometimes, though, it acts in a more subversive or ironic way. For example, an interview with the Roller Derby star who is one of the central characters in *Derby* (Robert Kaylor, 1970) takes place in front of his very typical suburban home as he talks about the material benefits he has derived from roller skating. As he continues in all earnestness, the camera pans to reveal a skyline crowded with virtually identical houses—"ticky-tacky" in Pete Seeger's vocabulary—thereby undercutting the sense of pride and distinction the character obviously attaches to his own material achievement.

Three relationships are possible within the general class of non-sync sound/image combinations:

The first involves images of *illustration* that serve to clarify or specify a speaker's point. Sometimes cutaways used for this purpose maintain the space-time continuum established by a sync interview, but whether the diegesis is maintained or not, the structuring principle remains that of illustration. Unless the shift is made within the shot—by panning or zooming away from the speaker as he or she continues to speak—the assumption that spatio-temporal continuity is being maintained seems to depend upon apparent continuity on the sound track. If spatial continuity is broken—by a cutaway to another location, say—the diegesis does not need careful protection against disintegration as in narrative films, where such breaks are signalled by a change of sequence, point-of-view shots, flashbacks, etc., thereby absorbing potential rupture into a narrative flow. This again suggests that, although the "diegesis" in documentary sometimes depends upon an imaginary spatio-temporal continuum that stands for the

The Documentary Film and Principles of Exposition 203

"real time and space" of social actors, this level operates more intermittently than in narrative, the integrity of the "diegesis" being guaranteed predominantly by the codes of exposition.

Counterpoint, or circumscription, or contradiction of the verbal sound track, is the least common relationship in Newsreel films. Newsreel seldom interviews characters with whom they profoundly disagree and whose integrity or logic they wish to subvert. This is one of the principal differences between Newsreel's use of characters in direct address and that of film makers who have satiric, ironic or iconoclastic intentions, such as Emile de Antonio, Dusan Makavejev, Claude Jutra, Chris Marker, or John Huston in *San Pietro* (6.14–48). Counterpoint might also include the so-called objective approach in which both sides of a question are presented (usually within an overall framework itself left unquestioned): the segment of CBS's *60 Minutes* program called "Point/Counterpoint" illustrates this use in a debating format.

Extension of a character's commentary is most often seen in Newsreel's utilization of metaphor, a subcategory of the topic usually called comparison and contrast. The problems of this method are well known, in particular its tendency to deny historical specificity to particular events and situations. *Teach Our Children* metaphorically identifies prisoners, slaves, and workers in terms of their oppression, for example, which established one common bond at the expense of distinctions between stages of historical development and the forms of exploitation and oppression peculiar to each stage. In Wiseman's *Titicut Follies* the process of force-feeding an asylum inmate is intercut with the preparation of the same man for burial, setting up a metaphorical statement about the quality of institutional care for the insane. (When he's alive, a doctor with a cigarette dangling from his mouth stands over the funnel pouring in liquid food whereas when he is dead, activity proceeds in an apparently far more hygienic manner.) Newsreel films often establish metaphorical links by editing disparate scenes to the rhythms of a single piece of music. In either case, the metaphor reveals an unexpected similarity between usually distinct phenomena. This similarity becomes singled out or emphasized by the act of comparison and the context in which the similar qualities originated becomes displaced. We may lose sight of the specific nature of this context or of its other qualities: the danger of overshadowing nonsimilar but important aspects of the context must be taken into account. The differences between two contexts make a genuine difference, at least to history. Failure to account for these differences may produce an excess that threatens to undercut the drift of the metaphor. Film images lack tense or markers like "like" so that it is exceedingly difficult to identify one scene as the primary diegesis and the other as a scene recruited solely to evoke a resemblance. Each set of images enjoys equal status on the screen; each invites reading at the same level of specificity. Metaphor, though, cuts against the grain of that specificity and can easily seem forced or distortional. Making metaphorical statements therefore comes laden with risks, especially when the goal is to re-present a situation or event in the context of its own historical specificity.

The Place of the Viewer

Expository cinema, especially direct-address documentaries, establishes a temporal relationship stretched, like that of the narrative, between a hope and a memory. With exposition, though, the anticipation of closure centers less around moves carried out by characters in a world of their own and more around propositions made by narrator(s) referring to a world we all know. In fact, exposition usually makes a tacit proposal to the viewer as part of its contract negotiations: the invocation of, and promise to gratify, a desire to know. Its beginning proposes an ending; inauguration signifies closure. The contract, if accepted, is binding, perhaps spellbinding, but only temporarily. Exposition begins; it proposes an ending: the temporal trace of the film will provide the arena within which we are led to believe we can possess the truth. Knowledge can be ours, its acquisition will afford us pleasure; what was promised will be provided, what was invoked will be gratified. And if the succession of sequences and segments, the reflux of the whole back upon the parts, the hierarchy of meta-communicative or self-reflexive devices fail to provide what has been promised, the film may collapse into no more than the sum of its parts. (The rhetorical department of *dispositio*, or arrangement, investigates the sequential or metonymic procedures whereby this invocation and promise to gratify a desire to know can be made to serve a persuasive end.) In either case we enter into the difficult terrain of desire once again, this time as it pivots around the act of knowing and the questions of how knowledge is produced and what kind of knowledge is produced by a succession of sound and images. Is it what we truly need to know or what others need to have us know; where does it leave us, where does it propose we go?

The concluding chapter on ethnographic film pursues these questions somewhat further; in the present context elaboration on two aspects of this invocation of the desire to know can serve as summary and conclusion. The desire to know that is invoked lacks the kind of continuous filmic referent involved in the inculcation of desire by narrative. A diegesis, if present, is not mandatory for the film as a whole.

The Documentary Film and Principles of Exposition

Moreover, insofar as the "diegesis," or rhetorical fiction, can be identified with the plane of the exposition, it has no continuous physical marker, unlike the diegesis of the narrative plane, which has the image track. But when documentary does utilize a diegesis, various cues within the film usually imply that this spatio-temporal continuum should be associated with external reality rather than an imaginary space and time. This only serves to shorten the already slight distance between sign and referent in the narrative cinema: the desire to know invoked by exposition expects to be fulfilled in terms of the real conditions of existence, the pro-filmic event or "real world" apart from the mediation of the system of textual codes. The uncritical adoption and regular deployment of realist techniques in documentary facilitates this slippage between sign and referent, textual system and real conditions, our relation to an expository "diegesis" and our relation to the real conditions of existence.

The second significant aspect of this film/viewer interaction—the invocation of the desire to know—involves the characteristics of direct address itself, the mode of most traditional expository cinema. This mode explicitly invokes the viewer as subject. Its appeal to reason presumes a center for its own discourse, the locus of He-Who-Knows, which reciprocally calls the viewer into being as a comparable center or locus, distinguished by the lack of the knowledge that is promised him or her. Despite differences between the expository system and the classical narrative system, the mode of direct address, at least in its "mainstream" form, offers a fundamentally similar place to the subject. The verbal sound track is used in a manner that preserves, at the level of the desire to know, the place of the subject, which is being challenged in much contemporary writing on the cinema and literature. The films of the Dziga-Vertov Group have explored ways of challenging this invocation of the viewer as subject within the structure of their films, but for most documentary film work the subject remains a completely untheorized category. Both necessary and insufficient, the subject is far too central a concept to remain a simple given. The challenges to it issued by many experimental films certainly help account for some of the theoretical interest in these films, but the necessity remains of developing a critical awareness of the implications of the position of self-as-subject for the expository cinema as well.

It is clear that the manner in which the viewer is addressed, the precise way in which the desire to know is invoked and gratified by the exposition, is a matter of political importance. It is a point of intersection between ideology and text whose parameters and implications need much closer examination, to avoid the risk of overgeneralization about its tyranny, and to specify precisely at what levels ideological operations are in greatest force and how to contest them. The psychical investments we make in our relationship to the film experience—how we are addressed, what promises or propositions are established by exposition or narrative and how they are fulfilled—constitute a repetition of psychical investments in our relationship to the material processes of communication and exchange. The investment we make in a film is a structural investment, promoted by a textual system grounded in style, and dedicated to propositions whose ideology we must carefully consider.

7.

Frederick Wiseman's Documentaries: Theory and Structure

Approaching Observational Cinema

EXAMINING FRED WISEMAN's documentaries can be of value in at least two ways: we can extend our consideration beyond the expository form of direct address to the observational form of cinéma vérité and we can attempt to look at a selected group of documentary films in close critical detail as we did with *Blonde Venus* and *The Birds*. Documentary films seldom receive analysis that attempts to describe their structure rigorously, since their content is taken to be of paramount importance. Attention turns to that content; and structure and, to an even greater extent, style are usually considered only as evidence of the director's attitude toward his subject matter, this usually being posed in terms of categories like honesty/dishonesty, objectivity/subjectivity, neutrality/bias, sensitivity/indifference, respectfulness/manipulativeness, or sympathy/cynicism. Debate arises about how "faithfully" something has been represented. Assumptions prevail that a certain transparency exists between film (text) and referent (reality), the transparency Eisenstein sought to transcend, Bazin to celebrate. To a large extent the possibility of scrutinizing documentary films as textual systems every bit as intricate as those of narrative or experimental becomes subordinated to other approaches. This chapter seeks to establish a priority and rationale for study of the textual system as the site of formal and ideological manifestations of considerable importance in their own right.

As we pursue this study of documentary into the realm of indirect address, the strategies of rhetoric begin to recede into the background. Instead of advancing arguments, films now observe situations and events. A theory or line of reasoning must be inferred since the film maker no longer speaks to us directly. Like the narrative or poetic film maker, the observational film maker is mute. In an interview,

208

Wiseman has said his films provide "a theory about the event, about the subject in the film," but if they do, they do so quite differently than *The Battle of San Pietro* or the television news. Discovering how they succeed in making propositions about the pro-filmic events they refer us to will be a central aspect of our examination.

Wiseman's films form a distinctive grouping in that they are virtually all studies of tax-supported, public institutions: *Titicut Follies* (1967), about a mental institution; *High School* (1969); *Law and Order* (1969), about a city police force; *Hospital* (1971); *Basic Training* (1971), about the U.S. Army; *Juvenile Court* (1973); *Primate* (1974), about federally supported primate research; and *Welfare* (1975).[1] Partly because these kinds of institutions are familiar to most viewers and partly because of the structure of these films, a strong tendency exists to read the films like Rorschach tests in which responses are a function of predispositions toward the institutions or toward Wiseman's distinctive, and subjective, style. Before analyzing this style in detail it may therefore be useful to precipitate some of these predispositions in summary form.

1. Wiseman disavows conventional notions of tact, breaking through what would otherwise be ideological constraints of politeness, respect for privacy, queasiness in the face of the grotesque or taboo, the impulse to accentuate the positive, etc. (A two-minute-long take of a patient vomiting in *Hospital* is one striking example of this aspect of Wiseman's approach.) Wiseman's "tactlessness" allows him not to be taken in by institutional rhetoric; it helps him disclose the gap between rhetoric and practice. But this lack of tact also pulls Wiseman's cinema toward the realm of voyeurism and visual pleasure; a very striking aspect of his films on first viewing, this threatens to block access to those more conceptual or formal strategies discussed here. Tactlessness thus provides a tension that requires further exploration but lies beyond the scope of the present discussion.

2. Wiseman's films are documentary primarily in their cinéma vérité approach to recording the pro-filmic event (discussed further below). They are secondarily documentary in re-presenting a recognizable aspect of social existence in our culture (encounters with tax-supported institutions). This is a distinctive choice of subject among cinéma vérité film makers and challenges assumptions about the individual as the locus of social interaction (and, in the guise of "characters," as the locus of narrative).

3. Wiseman's films fall within the experimental film making tradition in terms of their overall formal organization and within the narrative tradition in their local organization (the level of the sequence). Wiseman achieves a cinematic whole akin to the overall structure of films by Jean-Luc Godard, Michael Snow, Paul Sharits, or David

Rimmer; while at the level of the sequence he devises an editing pattern similar in its effect to the continuity editing of classical narrative. The overall structure of Wiseman's films is decidedly non-narrative (lacking closure, a diachronic trajectory, and the full deployment of the codes of actions and enigmas that usually pose and subsequently resolve puzzles or mysteries by means of the characters' activities.) At the same time the overall structure is built from facets themselves narrative-like (in their construction of a singular diegesis—the imaginary space and time of a narrative).

Wiseman's films fall within the amorphous category of cinéma vérité documentary, but they also belong to a more distinct subcategory, characterized by their almost exclusive use of indirect address (the absence of commentary, interviews with the film maker, and even extra-diegetic music or sound effects), the lack of staged or re-enacted events (acknowledging but minimizing the "staging" provoked by the camera's presence), and the reliance upon social actors (individuals, or "characters," acting their normal social roles). This kind of cinéma vérité adopts a modified form of the continuity editing found in classical narrative films to present an imaginary spatial and temporal universe (the diegesis). The practitioners of this style include Richard Leacock, D.A. Pennebaker, the Maysles brothers, William Jersey, John Marshall, Asen Balicki, David MacDougall, Allan King, and Craig Gilbert; but Wiseman's films stand out as a particularly pure example.

Stephen Mamber claims that this kind of cinéma vérité involves "a faith in unmanipulated reality, a refusal to tamper with life as it presents itself."[2] The ghost of André Bazin notwithstanding, neither Wiseman nor the others mentioned create a neutral or objective style; indeed we often hear charges of manipulation or bias against Wiseman. His choice of "characters," of types of encounter, and his choice of camera angle and distance (especially extreme close-ups) are obviously expressive indicators within Wiseman's stylistic repertoire.[3] From such crucial, ideologically informed aspects of style it is possible to gauge Wiseman's attitude toward his subject. The concern here, however, will be with larger formal questions in the hope of teasing open those ideological implications of style embedded in the organizing principles of the parts, the whole, and the part/whole relationships of Wiseman's films. Let us begin by noting how Wiseman's own style departs from classical narrative.

Documentary Mosaics

First, Wiseman's style is statistically different. Barry Salt analyzed a variety of feature films and found that the average shot

IDEOLOGY AND THE IMAGE

length for classic Hollywood films was around 9–10 seconds.[4] Average shot length for a 30-minute passage from Wiseman's *Hospital* is 32 seconds. Such results (computed by the same method Salt describes), may not be statistically rigorous, but they are highly suggestive. A tabulation of closeness of shot (from extreme close-up to very long shot) for the same passage from *Hospital* also reveals a significant departure from the classical pattern: Wiseman's films rely far more heavily on the closest shots and have fewer medium and long shots than the narrative films analyzed by Salt.

Second, Wiseman's style does not function strictly within a narrative context. The whole is not organized as a narrative but more poetically, as a mosaic; only the parts have a diegetic unity. Between sequences editing seldom establishes a chronological relationship: sequences follow each other consecutively but without a clearly marked temporal relationship. The whole thus tends toward poetry (metaphor, synchronicity, paradigmatic relations)—an all-at-once slice through an institutional matrix re-presented in time—rather than narrative.

Although "mosaic" is a useful term to describe the structure of Wiseman's films, they are mosaics of a distinctive kind. In a conventional mosaic the *tesserae* (facets) merge to yield a coherent whole when seen from a distance, whereas an individual facet conveys little sense of the overall design.[5] The *tesserae* (or sequences) of a Wiseman film are already coherent and do not merge into one impression or one narrative tale so much as supplement each other (with each sequence conveying a recognizable aspect of the overall design). The whole of a mosaic is almost invariably embedded in a larger architectural whole but such a larger whole is absent in Wiseman's case; not only do the films stand on their own, they offer little overt acknowledgment that the institutions under study directly relate to a larger social context. (Though we might, perhaps, think of each Wiseman film as a facet in a mosaic constituted by his overall oeuvre.) Both kinds of mosaic, however, clearly exhibit their facets as facets, a strategy that associates the structure of Wiseman's films with cinematic collage as well as traditional mosaic.

The addition of new facets in Wiseman's films helps complete our picture but also constitutes it in such a way that completion in any absolute sense becomes impossible (each new facet proposes a new lack at the same time as it fills in a previous one). Thus, whereas a narrative can be complete when the ending resolves a lack initiated in the beginning, Wiseman's films lack narrative closure itself. They are associational rather than expository, or poetic rather than assertive or narrative.

Much debate revolves around definitions of narrative structure but, without attempting to resolve this debate, it may still be possible to specify at least one consequence of the difference between Wiseman's mosaic structure and narrative structure. Narrative requires the adoption of assumptions or codes governing the inclusion, exclusion, and arrangement of events. As we have seen, these assumptions amount to an explanation of situations and events: they tell us why subsequent occurrences follow from previous ones. Put differently, narrative accounts for a change between initial and final states by means of "an intervening description of actions or occurrences that account for that change."[6]

Lacking narrative structure, Wiseman's films also lack this kind of linear-causality explanation of events. They do, however, imply a theory of the events they describe—one consonant with a mosaic structure and at variance with a model of linear causality. Eschewing narrative on the one hand and the documentary mode of direct address on the other (where an explanation can be explicitly announced by a narrator), Wiseman adopts an alternative principle of organization with a corresponding basic shift in assumptions about the arrangement of, and relationship between, events. This principle is: mosaic structure of the whole but narrative structure of the parts (the sequences). It assumes that social events have multiple causes and must be analyzed as webs of interconnecting influences and patterns. It is dialectical rather than mechanical.

Though Wiseman's films are not narratives, his sequences tend to be of two types in Metz's classification of the *grande syntagmatique* of classical narrative film: "scenes" and "descriptive syntagmas." The descriptive syntagma, unlike the scene, does not convey a sense of temporal progression; objects shown in successive images enjoy a relationship of spatial coexistence.[7] In Wiseman's films such descriptive sequences are not full-blown: they are more suggestive than wholly assertive. Through their very brevity they acquire a surplus of meaning that takes off from the specificity of each shot and evokes the general milieu (the institution) from which they are taken. Wiseman's scenes represent "a spatio-temporal integrality experienced as being without flaws . . . those brusque effects of appearance or disappearance . . ."[8] but they tend to blur into what Metz calls the "ordinary sequence" where the temporal order is discontinuous and unorganized.[9]

We may also analyze the spatio-temporal flow of scenes and ordinary sequences into what Vladimir Propp calls "functions" (and Barthes, "actions"): "a noun expressing an action" or "an act of a character, defined from the point of view of its significance for the course of the action."[10] Here, however, the difference in overall

212

structure of Wiseman's films compared to narrative films makes itself felt. Wiseman's sequences are like narrative sequences diegetically, and thus can be roughly catalogued in Metz's taxonomy; but they are quite unlike narrative sequences in the nature and arrangement of the functions. Since Wiseman's functions are in fact governed by social interactions in institutions, they differ from Propp's more "mythological" narrative functions in several ways.

If we say that agents carry out functions (such as "the hero leaves home," "the hero is tested," "the villain is defeated," "the hero returns home") and are individuated as characters, then these principles apply to Wiseman's films as well as to narratives. But no longer is the motor for these codes narrative. In Wiseman's films the agents carry out functions determined by the institutional structure in which they are embedded rather than by a narrative structure. The institution imposes certain functions and excludes others; it acts like a code or a *langue* similar to a narrative code. Like a narrative code it is extracinematic but capable of being recruited into a cinematic structure.

One striking characteristic of this institutional code (or the portion Wiseman considers) is that the kinds of agents it requires are very limited in number, In fact only two dominate: the hero and his complement, to which can be added, secondarily, helpers. The hero is roughly analogous to the fictional hero in structural analyses, but the complement is unlike the fictional villain: the complement is the character necessary for the hero to carry out the functions assigned him by the institutional code.

Sociologically, such processes are described under the rubric of role-playing, but what is peculiar to the institutional role-playing studied by Wiseman is that it always involves a complementary relationship in Gregory Bateson's sense: "To this category we may refer all those cases in which the behavior and aspirations of the members of two groups are fundamentally different."[11] In fact, they are usually oppositional as in assertive/submissive or nurturing/dependent behavior and tend toward schismogenic escalation—increased assertiveness begets increased submissiveness—and the breakdown of the system unless moderated by negative feedback (a feature present in institutions but seldom detailed in Wiseman's films). This schismogenic quality also corresponds very closely to Marx's notion of class struggle: the "fundamental differences" alluded to by Bateson are often class differences. Placement of the encounters between institutions and clients in these terms, however, is not attempted by Wiseman even though the encounters themselves cannot be fully understood without reference to class and class struggle.

Additionally, the institutional code governs the interaction of numerous heroes and complements inasmuch as it governs the relationships between existing social groups or classes. It is feasible to isolate a hero and follow the sequence of functions he performs and this is a choice many documentaries make—for example, *A Time for Burning* or *A Married Couple* (Allan King, 1970). But Wiseman opts not to do this. Instead of following one hero through a large set of functions as in narrative, Wiseman follows many heroes through a small set of functions (each hero's performance of a function usually constituting one facet of the overall mosaic). The heroes are often individuated as characters, but a repertoire of characters is picked up, followed, and dropped as they perform a few select functions over and over.

Wiseman's mosaic structure does not establish a fixed series of moves (in Propp's analysis, an invariant succession of functions) that could constitute a narrative whole. Instead functions recur throughout a film, but individual characters do not. Characters, as represented by social actors, carry out functions and thereby give individuality to the agent types; but this relationship is not locked into a single mold: there are many characters, there is no "star." The processes of identification between viewer and hero/actor/star that occur in most narrative films, as well as the ideological consequences of fusing these three distinct realms into one seemingly coherent image, are sidestepped.[12] Wiseman's films move away from this imaginary homogeneity toward what Stephen Heath calls "figure": the character as a "point of dispersion, a kind of disarticulation."[13] This reasserts a dialectical relationship between cinematic structure and social reality by refusing to subsume or conflate the two through imaginary unities like "star," and contrasts with films by other cinéma vérité practitioners where a full-fledged narrative analysis along Proppian lines may prove instructive.

Insofar as Wiseman substitutes characters for one another in variations on the performance of a few functions, it would seem likely that these functions could be isolated and identified. Utilizing the procedures described by Will Wright in *Sixguns and Society* I have attempted this for *Titicut Follies, High School, Law and Order, Hospital, Basic Training,* and *Juvenile Court.* The result is the following eleven functions:

1. The hero is a member of, and acts on behalf of, an institution; he enjoys a special status.

2. The complement is initially a member of society; he lacks special status.

3. The hero determines whether to interact with a social actor as his complement or not. (This involves "fact-finding" in *Juvenile*

IDEOLOGY AND THE IMAGE

Court and *Law and Order* and "diagnosis" in *Hospital* and *Titicut Follies*.)

4. The hero isolates his complement from society at large into a special group under his control.

5. The hero imparts values or knowledge (social or institutional) to his complement. (The complement may contest the hero's actions but usually to little avail; this is discussed further below, since contestation is more generally a key contributor to social change.)

6. The hero accepts his complement as one of his own. (In the graduation and promotion ceremonies in *Basic Training* primarily, though hierarchical rankings are retained.)

7. The hero seeks to control or modify the behavior of his complement. (This may involve long- or short-term modification — sentence terms in *Juvenile Court*, "discipline" in *High School*, arrests in *Law and Order*, and physical or mental modification — medical treatment in *Hospital* or psychiatric treatment in *Titicut Follies*.)

8. The hero seeks to protect society from the harmful acts of his complement. (In which case function 3 takes on added importance.)

9. The hero seeks to aid a complement in distress. (Function 3 may be a precondition, or "a social actor in distress" may define a complement.)

10. Heroes or complements relax among themselves. (In Wiseman's films, though, they are always recognizable in terms of their roles; for example, we may see an Army recruit with his family but he is in uniform at a military base, not at home.)

11. Helpers (janitors, orderlies, receptionists, etc.) maintain the hero's institutional facilities.

These broadly defined functions may seem overly obvious, but sometimes a task of analysis is precisely to point out what may seem obvious. Very often it may be so taken for granted that we fail to see how to organize the obvious into categories that can relate it to the not-so-obvious. In the case of Wiseman's functions it is striking that so disparate a range of institutions and events can be reduced to so few functions. (We should bear in mind that Wiseman studies a particular aspect of institutions, though — their interface or boundary with society at large.)

It is also striking that even though some of the functions can be arranged into narrative sequences in which the middle term explains the difference or change between the first and last terms, this very seldom occurs in the actual arrangement of functions in Wiseman's films. Functions 4, 5, 6, for example, compose such a sequence but do not occur in that order at the level of either facets (sequences) or the whole. (*Basic Training* and *High School* display this arrangement to some degree at the level of the whole: the parts in each case, though, fail to chart a linear progression of intervening functions and instead favor variations on recurrent functions, as in the other films. As such, this gross arrangement is at best a very weak form of narrative.)

Another result of Wiseman's non-narrative organization of functions is the loss of certain predictive possibilities present in a narrative chain of functions. Since the middle function explains the difference between initial and final states we can often predict the final state if we know the initial and middle functions (storytellers often play upon this predictive tendency in a variety of ways). Rather than an anticipatory relationship to the text, Wiseman's mosaic structure and the supplementary nature of the facets frequently demand a retroactive relationship to the text. On first encounter we have no way of even anticipating a sequence's duration (since the characters and functions it introduces bear no necessary relationship to the succeeding sequence). Sequences in *Hospital*, for example, may elaborate on function 9 over a considerable number of shots and minutes or may encompass the same, abbreviated function in one shot lasting a matter of seconds. This kind of "play" within the text is integral to our reading of it and recalls the *Cahiers du Cinéma* editors' distinction between turning a film into a text readable a priori and making the reading itself participate in the film's process of becoming a text.[14] (This is exemplified in the detailed analysis which follows.)

Constraints and Social Change

> . . . *the human essence is no abstraction inherent in each single individual. In its reality it is the ensemble of the social relations.*
> —Karl Marx. *Theses on Feuerbach*

The mosaic structure of Wiseman's films implies a theory or perspective toward the institutions he studies, but due to the utilization of indirect address, it is never explicit. Wiseman's films become unlabelled metaphors (lacking a word or figure for "like") rather than statements, as documentaries in direct address can be. As such his films challenge the convention of causal or deterministic explanation characteristic of narrative and direct-address commentary (which did not earn the name "voice-of-god" by accident). At this level Wiseman's films propose an epistemology with remarkable kinship to some of the premises of systems theory. The supplementary or associational nature of Wiseman's mosaic pattern stresses goal-seeking and constraints more than determinism and causality. A later event does not occur because of a previous event as it does in narrative: rather

IDEOLOGY AND THE IMAGE

any event occurs because of the constraints imposed upon all events (within a given system—in Wiseman's case, the system governed by the institutional code): "In other words, a description of the possible behavior of the 'organism' 'in itself' is inadequate without a description of the constraints exerted on those possibilities by the 'environment.' . . . in this perspective it is not a question of 'why such-and-such happened' but a question of what constraints operated so that 'the same old thing' or 'anything at all' DIDN'T happen.'"[15] The most recurring constraints in Wiseman's films are those of institution and role, especially in terms of how they are manifest at the boundary between an institution and those with whom it interacts.

This is perhaps most evident in the translation processes that occur at the boundary. Messages from numerous codes are translated into the dominant code of the institution, a process which also involves repression. Everything that cannot be translated, even though it may be understood, is repressed. Agents of the institution cannot respond to untranslated material within the constraints of the institutional code. In this respect the facets of Wiseman's mosaics evoke the similarity of encounters, the characteristic profile of typical communication at the interface between an institution and those who encounter it. The power of the process of typification involved in institutions and roles is best demonstrated by recalling that many of these highly structured encounters occur between complete strangers who are nonetheless willing to play their parts before a camera.

Individual social actors, despite the prescriptions of their roles, do struggle to respond to messages they understand on the level they are meant, but they are constrained to respond in relation to the institutional code defining their roles. Significantly, even in the synchronic moment displayed by a Wiseman film, minor acts of subversion, little contestations, take place—exploiting "free play" within the presiding code. The psychiatrist in the scene analyzed below, for example, seeks to obtain welfare aid for his patient long after he is aware that the welfare system ("played" by Miss Hightower) cannot translate his message: his patient is technically ineligible. Likewise, in an earlier scene, Dr. Schwartz, the doctor described below who aids a fellow on a "bum trip," telephones another hospital to complain about their improper transfer of a patient. In *High School* a group of students clearly articulate their school's limitations ("morally, socially, this school is a garbage can"), even though when lunch is over they slip back (or are slipped back) into the roles they criticize.

The dialectic of individual and institution suggested here is a long way from Durkheimian functionalism, or the kind of structural determinism evidenced, for example, in the work of Louis Althusser and some film theorists who have adopted his thought and applied it to the cinema. Only ongoing struggle can yield significant changes in institutional structure or social organization, but even Wiseman's synchronic studies posit a base for this process in their description of role-playing, ploying;[16] or what are called, more politically, "resistance strategies," in Brecher and Costello's *Common Sense for Hard Times* (New York: Two Continents, 1976). Whether the resistance comes from hero (the psychiatrist and Dr. Schwartz in *Hospital*, for example) or complement (some of the students in *High School*, patients in *Titicut Follies*, and recruits in *Basic Training*) much of the subjective "bias" in Wiseman's style suggests Wiseman's own sympathy and support for those whose resistance provides an initiating moment for social change.

Building Sites for Observation

> One of the things that intrigues me in all the films is how to make a
> more abstract, general statement about the issues, not through the
> use of a narrator, but through the relationship of events to each
> other through editing.
> —Frederick Wiseman, interview

In order to examine the relationship of events to each other without recourse to direct-address commentary, Wiseman requires a site upon which to base his examination. This site is the diegetic plane of spatial and temporal unity. As in fiction it provides the arena in which agents carry out functions, albeit functions governed by an institutional code rather than a narrative one. The diegesis supports Wiseman's study not of individuals but of an ensemble of social relations.

As in classical narrative, the construction of the diegesis depends upon continuity editing. Such editing sutures the traces, the cuts or gaps, of its own production to conjure up a plausible but imaginary universe. Wiseman's formal organization relies heavily upon the ability to mask potentially huge gaps in the real time of the pro-filmic event within sequences. A good example is the scene with the psychiatrist in *Hospital* mentioned above. Donald E. McWilliams reports that the scene, uncut, lasted an hour and a half.[17] On screen it lasts approximately ten minutes and yet appears to cover virtually the entire encounter.

Achieving this effect requires the use of some of the tactics of *découpage* derived from classic continuity editing of the image track but without many of its resources: Wiseman never shoots with more than one camera, for example.[18] It also requires skillful manipulation of sound/image relationships. The narrative film maker can plan his shots and their accompanying sound beforehand to yield a sense of

IDEOLOGY AND THE IMAGE

continuity and realism, but Wiseman has minimal control over what his social actors do. Continuity emerges *ex post facto,* as a function of editing. If Wiseman's strategies are at all instructive to political documentarists and theorists alike, as I believe they are, then it will be well worth examining in detail how an imaginary continuity can be constructed in a situation where the film maker controls the pro-filmic event so weakly.

This examination must focus on the joins or articulations between shots rather than between sequences. I propose to adopt several categories of spatial and temporal articulation involving the image and sound tracks. These derive from Noel Burch's categories in *Theory of Film Practice,* modified to accommodate cinéma vérité editing as well as classical narrative.

First, for the image track there are three kinds of spatial articulation. *Spatial continuity* involves overlapping visual fields: if a character reappears it must be against an overlapping background. *Spatial proximity* lacks overlap and is implied by various cues such as matching—reoccurring objects or characters across a cut in which no large spatial displacement has been otherwise suggested, or eyeline matching and its subcategory, the point-of-view figure. *Spatial discontinuity* occurs when there is no overlap and there are no cues to proximity. Reoccurrence of a character may not overcome discontinuity if movement is stated or implied.

We can also identify three kinds of temporal articulation for the image track. *Temporal continuity* is when action appears continuous across a cut. This depends upon such devices as match-cuts (which are rare in Wiseman, who cannot stage his shots to provide the desired overlap of actions), inserts, and shot/reverse-shot figures, which usually depend upon continuous sound as a cue to temporal continuity. Point-of-view figures also imply temporal continuity. Deviations from a clear sense of temporal continuity are possible, though, leading to indefinite ellipses generally rather than flashbacks specifically as Edward Brannigan suggests.[19] Second, a *definite temporal ellipsis* indicates a precise, measurable time gap. Since there is no absolute scale of reference to the diegesis, a temporal baseline must be established before the cut (the velocity of someone walking, for example). This articulation, often dependent on scripted shots, is rare in Wiseman. Finally, unmeasurable time gaps are indicated by *indefinite temporal ellipses.* If the ellipsis involves *abridgment,* the temporal flow continues to originate from a previously established coordinate (the onset of an interview, for example). Gaps in Metz's "ordinary sequence" are of this kind. In Wiseman's films where match-cutting is difficult, such elisions often take the form of jump-cuts. If the elision involves a *shift,* the temporal flow is reset to a new time scale. Such cuts often occur between sequences as a function of the mosaic structure in Wiseman. Also, deviant point-of-view shots may represent abridgments or shifts which can usually be determined only by a retroactive reading of the cut.

As for the sound track, it is more useful to analyze its relationship to articulations of the image track than to examine its own articulations, which are, in fact, often impossible to determine from a film print. (Access to mixing sheets would generally be essential since there may be overlapping articulations of speech, music, and location sound.) Spatial articulations of the sound track play little role in Wiseman and have been deferred (although they are very significant in Robert Altman's films, a director with many striking similarities to Wiseman). Temporal relationships implied by the sound track at points of image-track articulation are crucial, however, since they often resolve or determine how to read the articulation. In Wiseman's films these relationships normally involve the verbal sound track ("presence" or location sound is usually continuous throughout a scene and music absent). *Temporal continuity* involves speech continuing uninterrupted across a visual cut (a sound bridge). *Temporal proximity* involves speech before and after a visual cut that is closely related either logically or analogically (tone of voice, rhythm, or loudness, for example). Slight logical or analogical shifts often serve as cues to temporal elision, the magnitude of which is seldom discernible. *Temporal discontinuity* involves verbal statements bearing no clear relationship to each other. This relationship usually prevails between sequences.

In the analysis that follows, these categories are applied to a representative segment of *Hospital*. In overview, we are dealing with four units, or facets, which comprise a segment dealing with hospital/social-deviant interactions ("deviant" strictly in a descriptive sense): A1-8, B9-16, and C17—three syntagms that constitute an "ordinary sequence" about a psychiatrist/homosexual patient encounter; D1-4 about a hospital staff/alcoholic encounter; E1, a doctor/drug-addict encounter; and F1-9, a doctor/drug-overdose-victim encounter. The letter and number designations indicate articulations; in the parentheses the running time of the second shot is given in minutes and seconds; and the conventional abbreviations of shot type help specify the kind of visual cut involved. Slash-marks indicate cuts. Some of the articulations that repeat previous strategies have been omitted.

A1/A2 (1:20). MS of patient named Mr. Vivas/CU of Mr. Vivas.*

---

*Capital letters designate syntagms, numbers designate shots, lower-case letters designate stills taken from different parts of the same shot. A2A signifies an insert (a shot recorded at one time relative to other shots, but inserted into the text at a different time).

IDEOLOGY AND THE IMAGE

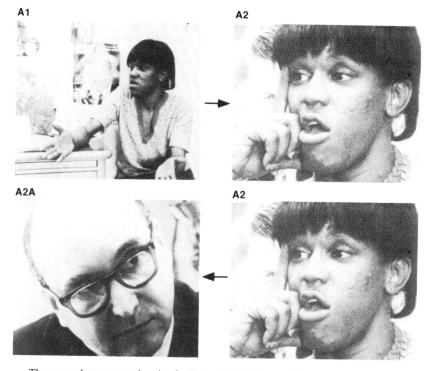

A1

A2

A2A

A2

The arrow between each pair of stills in A1–8 indicates the direction of the cut.

Spatial continuity occurs because of overlap, but the editing lacks match and appears as a jump-cut. We must attend to the sound track to determine whether the articulation involves temporal continuity or proximity. In this case the last statement before the cut is:

Mr. Vivas (before the cut, in shot A1): "There are things that are not normal and this is what I mean."

After the cut we hear:

Doctor (in shot A2): "I want to establish one thing with you." No clear case for continuity exists, but proximity and abridgment are indicated by the word logic of the cut: the doctor's statement appears to continue a line of thought established before the cut.

A2/A2A (:06). CU patient/CU doctor.

The new shot is read as an insert due to visual and aural cues. We hear the doctor begin to interrupt before we cut ("Mr. Vivas . . ."), but the patient continues his previous line of thought as we cut to the doctor whose expression indicates a certain eagerness to speak. The insert also exhibits an eyeline match: Mr. Vivas on the right of the

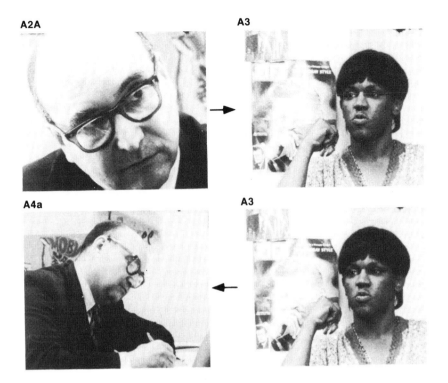

A2A

A3

A4a

A3

screen/the doctor looking screen right. Because Wiseman cuts from CU to CU, spatial continuity is difficult to establish (there is minimal background and no overlap), but the close-ups also establish a graphic match between the two faces, which helps reduce the impression of a jump-cut.

A2A/A3 (:15). CU doctor/MS patient.

This articulation involves a normal point-of-view shot showing whom the doctor sees (Mr. Vivas) and implies temporal continuity. The sound track reinforces this sense of continuity by an articulation based on word logic:

Patient (before the cut, in shot A2A): "I would assure you that it would do me a heck of a lot of good."

Patient (after the cut, A3): " . . . 'cause I'm having somewhat of a difficulty obtaining what is known as social service with, in other words, welfare."

IDEOLOGY AND THE IMAGE

A4b

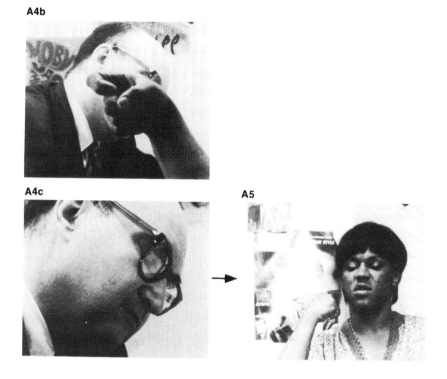

A4c   **A5**

Between A2A and A3, however, there is a slight shift in Mr. Vivas's tone and rhythm. These analogical cues suggest that Wiseman may have omitted an indeterminate amount of dialogue and joined together two statements which still maintain a logical progression. The possibility of abridgment emerges but its actual presence or extent cannot be determined exactly. The image-track articulation implies continuity. The word logic of the sound track reinforces this implication even as it leaves cues to possible abridgment. The ultimate ambiguity of the articulation is characteristic of Wiseman's films and of the *imaginary* continuity of the diegesis generally; it also clearly illustrates the central importance of sound/image relationships in Wiseman's editing style.

A3/A4a-c (:08). MS patient/MS doctor, zooming in to ECU doctor.

A4/A5 (:20). ECU doctor/MCU patient.

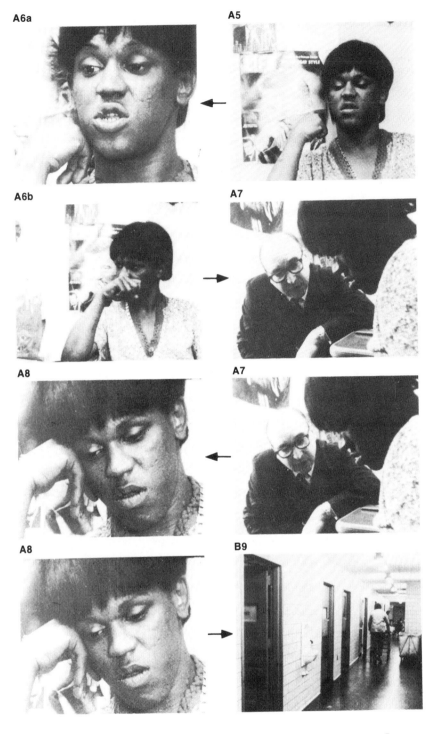

A6a

A5

A6b

A7

A8

A7

A8

B9

224   IDEOLOGY AND THE IMAGE

A5/A6 (:52). MCU patient/CU patient, zooming out to MCU patient.

Spatial continuity is implied by overlapping background and reappearance of the patient. The graphic match reduces the sense of a jump-cut (as does Wiseman's long-take style). The sound track exhibits a slight pause and analog shift which could be a cue to abridgment although word logic gives a sense of a continuing line of thought (some degree of shift in logic and analog values is endemic to normal conversation, a quality Wiseman exploits to full advantage). The very fact that a cut occurs is perhaps the best, though still ambiguous, cue to abridgment since in terms of classical continuity editing it is unmotivated (showing the same character from approximately the same position—a 30° rule violation to boot):

Doctor (before the cut, in shot A5): "Because what?"

Patient (before the cut): "Because I am a minor."

Patient (after the cut, in shot A6): "But you know, when I do go over to the welfare center they tell me, 'And how have you been supporting yourself and eating and doing this and that?' And you know what I've been doing, prostituting . . ."

A6/A7 (:18). MCU Mr. Vivas/MS doctor, over patient's shoulder.

Spatial continuity emerges from the match element, the reappearance of the patient. This is the first two-shot in the sequence (3:20 or so into the encounter) and allows for a retroactive placement of the two characters in relation to each other. A slight logical and analogical shift in the doctor's dialogue before and after the cut is a cue to abridgment but, as elsewhere, its very slightness encourages a reading of temporal continuity:

Patient (before the cut, A6): "I have told them about it."

Doctor (before the cut, A6): "Yeah, I know. Well, don't tell them any more. I'll tell them to forget it."

Doctor (after the cut, A7): "When a person tries as hard as he can to do the best he can and it doesn't work, he gets very upset and confused and he thinks to himself, I must be all mixed up, there must be something wrong with me, I must be bad even though I don't feel it."

A7/A8 (:30). MS doctor, over patient's shoulder/CU Mr. Vivas.

A8/B9 (:10). CU Mr. Vivas/LS hospital corridor.

This articulation signals spatial discontinuity and a temporal shift. A new source of presence appears (general corridor noise and paging messages) and continues throughout B9–B16, which develops as a descriptive syntagma of hospital corridors and people sitting in waiting rooms. The film abandons the doctor and patient as we seek new spatial and temporal coordinates.

B9

B10

B11

B12

B13

B14

B15

B16

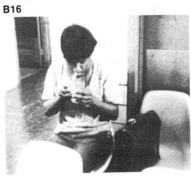

IDEOLOGY AND THE IMAGE

B9–B16. A descriptive syntagma. Note the variations in numbers of people and that we end once again with Mr. Vivas.

B16/C17 (4:55). MS Mr. Vivas, sitting on a waiting room bench/ CU doctor on the telephone.

B16 concludes the descriptive syntagma by returning to the previous patient, Mr. Vivas. This return invites a retrospective analysis of the syntagma (has this description of "waiting" in general actually been a description of Mr. Vivas's waiting?) and implies, though by no means guarantees, that the next sequence may be a very direct supplement to A1–8.

C17 returns to the psychiatrist who interviewed Mr. Vivas, confirming one of the possibilities opened by B16. (In Wiseman's overall pattern, not returning to the psychiatrist is also entirely possible.) Temporal continuity arises from a sound bridge between the shots (we hear the doctor begin a conversation with Miss Hightower, a welfare worker, before we cut away from Mr. Vivas to the doctor). C17 continues for nearly five minutes as the doctor tries to obtain assistance for Mr. Vivas. His last words: "I don't wish for you to tell me that you don't know what you're going to do . . . (looking up). She hung up on me."

During the telephone exchange the doctor's role subtly shifts from hero to complement: his function as agent of the hospital's code becomes subordinated to Miss Hightower's function as agent of the welfare code. Wiseman's long take provides a coherent diegetic base for this transition and also retrospectively stands as the third part of an "ordinary sequence" composed of a scene, descriptive syntagma, and autonomous shot. The three together complete a fairly well elaborated account of functions 3 and 9 in which the descriptive syntagma represents a preparatory interval between "diagnosis" and "seeking to aid a complement."

Discontinuity between C17 and D1 demarcates two facets, although the viewer must remain constantly alert to the possibility of a

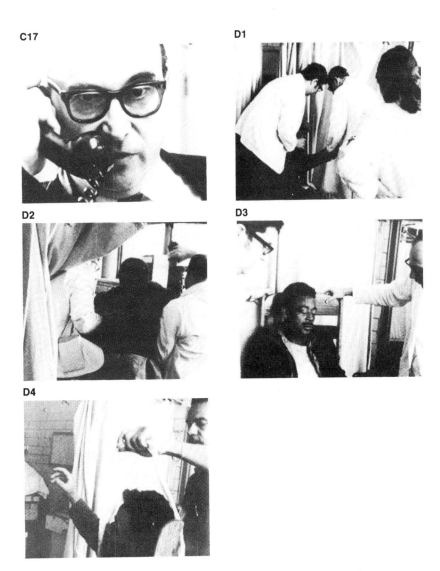

C17

D1

D2

D3

D4

retroactive fusion (that A-F all involve a hospital/deviant interface, for example). D1–4 is much more brief (1:45) and breaks off before any clear-cut course of action is pursued to aid the patient.

D2–D4. This facet has a total running time of 1:45 minutes (D1–4). In it an apparently drunk patient is taped to a wheelchair for his own safety.

E1, a 35-second autonomous shot of another encounter, follows and again breaks off before "diagnosis" seems complete. This lack of

228   IDEOLOGY AND THE IMAGE

E1a

E1b

E1c

E1d

E1e

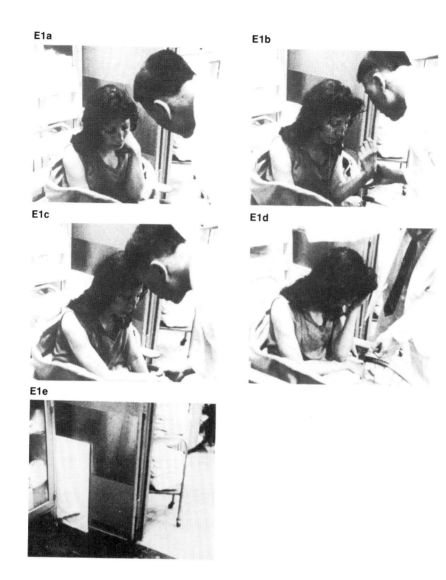

completion is one of the qualities that allows facets to supplement one another and that demands active, and retroactive, engagement by the viewer.

The complete dialogue in shot **E1**:

Doctor (E1): "Do you drink?"
Patient: (mumbles, very garbled, slurred speech, inaudible).
Doctor: "Do you inject the needle?"
Patient (in wheelchair): "Yeah . . ."

F1a

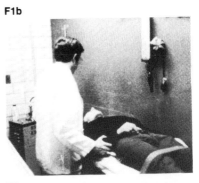

F1b

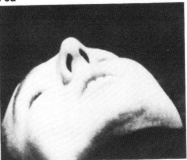

F2

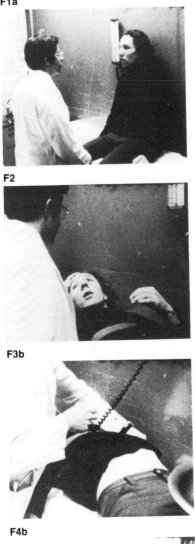

F3a

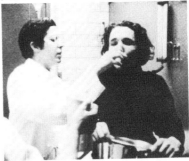

F3b

F4a

F4b

F5a

IDEOLOGY AND THE IMAGE

Doctor: "When did you inject? When did you inject? (pause) What, heroin?"

Patient: (mumbles, inaudible)

Doctor: "Well, you come over to the side, and I'll check . . ."

(Doctor wheels patient out of frame.)

E is a single long take. Near its conclusion the doctor wheels the patient out of frame. The camera lingers on the empty frame before we cut to F1.

E1e/F1 (:47). MS hospital room where doctor and patient had been/MS Doctor (Dr. Schwartz) and patient in an emergency room.

This final sequence involves the administration of an emetic to a patient who has had a bum trip on a psychedelic drug. (F4 is a 2:15 shot of the patient vomiting profusely, an example of "relentless empiricism" at its extreme.) Editing on word logic prevails throughout most of the scene and even introduces it. Dr. Schwartz seems to continue the same line of questioning pursued in E1 but in this case the patient responds far more articulately:

Doctor (beginning of F1): "What do you think they gave you? What did they give you?"

Patient: "They told me it was mescalin, but I was chewing on it and it tasted sort of funny, like soap or something like that."

Doctor: "Uh huh."

Patient: "Shit."

Doctor: "They told you it was mescalin but it tasted . . ."

Patient: "Yeah, I know it was poison."

Doctor: "Lie down."

Patient: "OK, OK. I don't wanna die. I don't wanna die."

Doctor: "You're not going to die . . ."

F1b/F2 (:48). MS doctor and patient/MCU doctor and patient.

F2/F3a (:46). MCU doctor and patient (CU patient zooming out to)/MS (doctor releases strap around patient's chest).

F3b/F4a (2:15). MS doctor and patient/MS doctor and patient (doctor administers an emetic).

F4b Patient vomits.

F4b/F5a (:60). MS patient/CU patient zooming out to MS patient (use of CU helps make possible indefinite temporal ellipsis, i.e., jump-cut).

F5b

F6

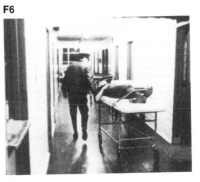

F7

F8a

F8b

F8c

F8d

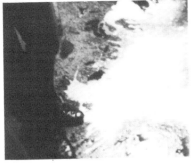

F9

F5b/F6 (:08). MS patient/LS patient wheeled down corridor.

F6/F7 (1.05). LS patient/MS patient and two attendants.

F7/F8a (1:40). ECU patient's face (a zoom in from MS of patient and attendants)/MS patient stumbles and vomits on the floor (F8b).

F8c. Patient looks off-screen, toward the floor.

F8d. Camera pans to the floor at patient's feet.

F8d/F9 (:40).

F8d/F9 (:40). MS patient in profile, camera pans to patient's vomit on the floor/CU patient in profile.

This articulation holds special interest as a deviant point-of-view figure. F8 concludes with a camera movement (pan) from the patient's face to what he sees. F9 returns to the patient, securing what Edward Brannigan calls a "closed point of view." Rather than guaranteeing simultaneity between shots, however, the articulation is a cue to abridgment. It lacks the guarantees found in narrative film such as an expressive reaction to what is seen or subsequent action that would imply simultaneity. Instead the sound track carries a verbal pause followed by a statement with logical and analogical shifts from the previous statement:

Patient (before the cut, F8d): "Anybody know how to sing or play music or something? I don't know. Oh shit."

Patient (after the cut, F9): "I think I should go back with my family."

The strong possibility of abridgment, an indefinite ellipsis, cannot be pinned down. We have no final recourse to an objective or absolute spatial and temporal scale. Continuity and its attendant realism is of an imaginary order and in Wiseman's films the impression of continuity emerges forcefully at the same time as the origins of this impression depends upon an active, and retroactive, reading of cues embedded in shots and their articulations.

Re-viewing Mosaics

A living language is a concrete fact—grammar is its abstract substratum. These substrata lie at the basis of a great many phenomena of life . . .

—V. Propp

The time has come to redefine Wiseman's mosaic structure or abstract substratum a little more precisely by way of conclusion. If a narrative consists of a number of functions arranged in a fixed order, then Wiseman's mosaic favors repetition of a few functions at the expense of the many. It is as though he had removed them from their narrative linkage and then substituted, paradigmatically, different variations of the same function. These substitutions are displayed consecutively but do not constitute a narrative order. The textual system is metaphoric (poetic) more than metonymic (narrative or expository), and supplemental or associative more than strictly additive.

Sequences in a Wiseman film exhibit the diegetic characteristics of narrative sequences although the whole film is not a narrative. Nevertheless, it is still possible for the whole of a Wiseman film to have some characteristics of a narrative sequence. In fact, Wiseman's films, as wholes, or mosaics, are remarkably similar in organization to the narrative sequence type Metz calls a bracket syntagma: "A series of very brief scenes representing occurrences that the film gives as typical samples of a same order of reality, without in any way chronologically locating them in relation to each other. . . . None of these little scenes is treated with the full syntagmatic breadth it might have commanded, it is taken as an element in a system of allusions. . . ."[20] Even in the narrative context of his *grande syntagmatique,* Metz's description aptly conveys the poetic potential of this choice of sequence.

This form of overall organization is distinctly cinematic. It adopts the strategy of organizing the whole in terms of the characteristics of a cinematic part. As such it is akin to Godard's use of band construction (lateral tracking shots) in *Weekend* and *One Plus One.*[21] As a bracket syntagma Wiseman's mosaic also bears comparison with Michael Snow's use of the autonomous segment (long take/zoom) in *Wavelength* or long take/tracking shot in *Breakfast,* or Paul Sharits's use of the single frame in *Ray Gun Virus* as controlling cinematic structures for the whole. It is in this sense that Wiseman's concept of the whole places him in association with the experimental film-making tradition. His films provide a distinctive fusion of extracinematic codes (especially those of existing institutions) with cinematic codes (the mosaic or bracket syntagma structure to the whole).

Wiseman does not seem to have developed this fusion for overtly formal or political ends. Politically, Wiseman's choice of an "ensemble of social relations" is extremely narrow and fails to examine the larger ensemble circumscribing the boundary between institutions and the public or the characteristics of class struggle found at that boundary itself. Nonetheless, the structure of his films carries a set of theoretical and ideological implications with it. Among them, it seems to me, is the political challenge to gauge the significance of his focusing on constraints more than on linear causality and to understand how this focus is related to historical materialism, especially to the constraints of ideology on social role-playing. His films also issue a challenge to examine some of the overly generalized and at least potentially elitist critiques of narrativity and realism that have recently emerged, those which stress contestation against narrative and expository structure per se rather than contestation within and against these structures but in relation to a referent of ongoing historical reality. Although Wiseman's films are not self-reflexive in a formalist or political (Brechtian) sense, neither are they simple transparencies of a bourgeois world that we, as spectators, passively contemplate. They demand an active/retroactive way of seeing, and raise more questions about the political uses of narrative, documentary, and cinematic structure than they answer.

The question of the place of the viewer, referred to here and earlier in relation to Wiseman's "tactlessness," looms as one of the most central questions. It invokes considerations of pragmatics, the effects of communication, and revives debate about the degree to which realist texts operate primarily to install the viewer in the place of the self-as-subject. Films such as Wiseman's that feign invisibility for the observing camera/sound recorder promote an imaginary relationship of opposition-identity with the world of the diegetic representation. Without the pandering sensationalism of a *Mondo Cane* this level of Wiseman's work seems to confront us with questions of the type Can you believe this? Can you take this? Such questions threaten to trap us in a variation of Marcuse's performance principle or Lacan's mirror-phase. A semiotic study of Wiseman's films necessarily deemphasizes this level of effect. Stress falls on the pattern of organization distinctive to the text as a whole and its effect, but lacks explanatory power to account for the effect of transparency, those short-circuits that mis-take sign for referent and mis-recognize the nature of the whole. To account for this level as well and, even more, the interaction of different levels, will require forms of analysis capable of founding themselves upon the untenable terrain of contradiction and paradox, terrain for which we have little more than small-scale aerial survey maps at present.

We might note, though, that the risk of a purely imaginary relationship is but one aspect of Wiseman's films, and the same could perhaps be said of a great many other realist narratives or documentaries. In pursuing the ways in which realist texts constitute us in the place of the self-as-subject, we run the risk of overlooking the fact that we are not only constituted but moved, and not only moved aesthetically or emotionally but also positionally. Narrative, exposition, and poetics provide strategies for containing that movement, for keeping things in place, but they also clearly open up the possibility of exceeding any imaginary or ideological containments. Just as we are experientially bound, not by one explicitly formulated master paradox from beginning to end of a narrative, but by its crystal-like growth through an implicit series of condensations and displacements, so documentary does not suture us into the place of the self-as-subject with absolute finality. Not only placement occurs but displacement, and just as narrative paradox emerges over and over in a metonymic series of structural and stylistic variations, so we pass through and beyond the place of the subject as we negotiate passage into the observational space of Wiseman's films. Our place is constantly put at risk as the film unfolds into the future, jeopardized less by rhetorical variations than structural and stylistic ones similar to those usually associated with narrative. The partiality of the present moment of unfolding—stretched between expectation and memory, with new information demanding continual re-interpretations of what has gone before—corresponds to the instability of our "fix." A sense of imaginary solidity or unity never quite jells. We exceed that mold just as contradictions, if they are real, exceed the molds of the global dominants in ways we can discern and comprehend.

The danger of settling into the imaginary and settling for the pleasures it affords remains real. Some realist texts with their homogeneous diegesis, their perceptible but "self-effacing" style, their claims of access to a higher (idealist) truth where contradictions are apparently resolved constitute a formidable danger to be sure. For this very reason they require the most careful scrutiny. Not all realist texts present this danger equally. Some, like Wiseman's, operate in a multi-leveled manner, remaining within a realist tradition yet moving us in ways that are instructive as well as pleasurable, symbolic as well as imaginary. A more extended look at one of the main subgenres of realist documentary, the ethnographic film, will offer us a chance to consider these dangers and possible ways of counteracting them in greater detail.

8.

Documentary, Criticism, and the Ethnographic Film

Some Basic Considerations

A CENTRAL QUESTION posed by documentary film is what to do with people. Documentary films inform us about historical situations or events and usually depict individuals who are actually involved in those situations or events.[1] How should they be depicted? What investments of desire will be elicited and what position will be marked out for the viewer? To what degree will our recognition of a pro-filmic reality, external to but depicted by the film, be counterbalanced by our knowledge that this reality remains a construct, an approximation and re-presentation, to which we do not gain truly direct, unimpeded access? What understanding of how people organize themselves into collectivities, establish meanings and values, and both conduct and comprehend ongoing social interaction can a documentary afford?

Ethical questions, which cannot be pursued here at length, also arise regarding what the film maker does with people recruited into a documentary film: how responsible to their ongoing life situation is he or she; what level of involvement in their lives does he or she establish; what limits exist on what can or cannot be used of footage shot or sound recorded? *Things I Cannot Change* (NFB of Canada, dir. Tanya Ballantyne, 1967) was one of the first films to pose these questions in the context of cinéma-vérité film making.[2] The working-class family depicted by Ballantyne encountered a series of major problems as a direct result of the film, and the attempt to rectify some of the errors made contributed to the framework within which the NFB's Challenge for Change program developed. Ethical considerations arise in any film making situation involving other people, but they become particularly acute when those people are non-àctors photographed in the course of their ongoing everyday lives. The issues we will take up here bear upon these ethical considerations, but we will approach them less from the perspective of ethics than from the arenas of signification and pragmatics: how people—or, more precisely, the images of people mapped onto and coded by analog and digital systems of signification pertinent to the cinema—are represented in the documentary. Of greatest concern will be not the solitary individual but the collective ensemble, the interrelationships between people and the attempts to explain those interrelationships in film.

Such films form a loosely defined thematic genre. Most often ethnographic films attempt to explain or describe some aspect of another culture to members of the film maker's own culture within a context informed to a varying extent by traditional anthropological and ethnographic concerns and concepts and perpetuating most of their political limitations: ideology is a word seldom used in studies of other cultures, and considerations of who defines culture and how (where do We draw the line around Them?) or, even more, of the ideological implications of representing one culture to another receive scant attention. These limitations contribute, I suspect, to the generally ill-defined nature of this entire enterprise. They certainly help account for much of the difficulty we encounter when trying to place films that only partially place themselves. Even the loose thematic definition adopted here poses a number of problems, some of which we shall examine later, but no better alternative seems possible. Some advocate defining ethnography more loosely so that feature films and most documentaries could be considered ethnographic films so far as they tell us things about the culture in which they are made. In this case, though, ethnography becomes a critical approach similar to structuralism or *auteur* criticism rather than a documentary genre. And although this approach has much to recommend it, the emphasis here will attempt to address that particular sub-genre of the documentary described above.

Ethnographic films have much in common with documentary generally, but their concern with cultural patterns maintained between actual social actors brings several concerns to the fore, principally the question of what to do with people. In particular, such films normally depict individual characters, but they focus their attention upon a level of abstraction beyond the individual. This is not only their strength but also their potential weakness. Individual social actors risk becoming no more than examples, illustrations of ethnographic principles, with their value assessed solely by the quality of their exemplification. A telling indication of the difficulties this question can pose occurs in *Microcultural Incidents in Ten Zoos* (1969) where Ray Birdwhistell demonstrates proxemic patterns of behavior between family members at zoos in different societies. In most instances his footage, taken without the subjects' knowledge, provides clear illustration for his points about how closely the animals are approached, who initiates feeding, parent-child interaction, and so on. But when Birdwhistell attempts to analyze behavior at an Indian zoo he encounters great difficulty: the frame is too crowded with subjects, no one can be singled out for prolonged study. As an aside to his listeners (the direct-address commentary is a recording of his actual remarks during screening of the same footage to an anthropological convention), Birdwhistell blurts out, "This whole India thing needs to be looked at."

This remark, both amusing in the frustration it registers in the face of the difficult task of reducing complex phenomena to discrete items of empirical data and disturbing in the indifference it suggests to the meaning such phenomena might hold for the people actually engaged in them, not only betrays the limitations of a behavioralist approach but also returns us to our central dilemma—what to do with people in the ethnographic film.

This question can also be posed as what to do with the cinematic sign's indexical relation to its referent. Unlike an iconic sign, such as a cartoon drawing, and its relation of resemblance to its referent, or the arbitrary sign, such as a word, and its relation of non-resemblance to the object or quality referred to, the indexical sign—e.g., a photograph, sundial, or medical symptom—enjoys an existential bond between itself and that to which it refers. In some manner and to some degree its appearance is determined via specific correspondences with its referent as the photographic image is via the physics of lenses and light.

Documentary film, and ethnography in particular, depend heavily upon the indexical nature of the cinematic sign. Sometimes it serves as a form of authentication as in the battle footage used to support the commentary in *The Battle of San Pietro*. More generally, it is this indexical relation that motivates the use of film footage as courtroom evidence or, with ethnographic film, as cultural evidence. Whereas in a fictional film we suspect that a character's display of emotions may be fabricated by learned techniques (acting skill, for example), in a documentary we regard a character's display of emotion(s) as direct responses to situations or events we witness. For example, the anger Billy Edwards directs at his wife, Antoinette, when he throws her out of the house in *A Married Couple* is understood to be the result of previous events we have seen occur in their lives with the assumption that their occurrence has very little to do with the film maker's presence or even participation. For it to be otherwise, as it is in *David Holtzman's Diary* (Jim McBride, 1967), would seem a betrayal of a central documentary *convention*—convention because we seldom have the means to determine the actual degree of indexicalness or, conversely, of fabrication, at more complex levels than the mechanical fixing of light patterns on film (and even this is subject to considerable alteration).

This invocation of the cinema's potentially indexical relation to its referent often brings us to the other side of Birdwhistell's frustration: awe. The existential bond between sign and referent makes it seem that a situation or event can exist in more than one time and place at the same time. There is a sense of the magician's *"voila!"* to the documentary: "Here it is! I hold up before you what you thought to be elsewhere." What prompts awe in this case is not our access to the pro-filmic event per se (that which occurred elsewhere but in the presence of a camera), but the sense of replication. Though true of all realist cinema, and therefore the great bulk of documentary, this paradoxical impression of a replicated uniqueness is particularly compelling in the context of a claim to re-present historical occurrences. What we see and hear before us happened in a particular place at a particular time; it is not a fictional fabrication meant to approximate actual events (in which case it is the fabrication—the appearance of Marlon Brando as Kurtz in *Apocalypse Now* for example, which becomes historically documented).

Most documentary film and virtually all ethnographic film aim at reproducing historically specific occurrences for us. Unlike poetry, these films do not aim directly at universal insights. Unlike fiction they do not claim to fabricate an imaginary time and space, peopled by characters, in which insights will be revealed. The world we see on film seems to bear indexical links to another world with autonomy and specificity of its own. That which was historically singular is re-presented for us. It is not real historical process that necessarily prompts wonder when we encounter it in the cinema (unless we choose to posit a Source for such wonder as André Bazin did), but the *apparent* duplication of historical process. This approximates magic—the ability to control nature, to bend it to our bidding. The existential bond establishing the indexical aspect of the cinematic sign system provides a powerful inducement to awe, to the sense of being spellbound, so much so that it is easy to forget completely that we are dealing with a sign system rather than a direct, unmediated duplication of reality.

Remembrance is what gives specificity to the cinematic experience. We sit spellbound amidst oscillations between the duplication of reality and the reality of the duplication, between a two-dimensional image and a three-dimensional world, between a system of signs and an external realm to which we are referred. Taking up a position within the domain of remembrance has been the subject of much of

IDEOLOGY AND THE IMAGE

this study. Here we need to pursue the implications of this unstable, oscillatory situation itself and how it relates to the ethnographic film.

The dynamic of forgetting and remembrance figures into the effect of all representational art. Such art transports us to another realm (the one represented); such art relies on transport mechanisms we can comprehend. This impression of transport tends to overshadow the underlying transport mechanism in some cases, perhaps particularly in those cases where the indexical aspect of the sign predominates. We seem, then, to lack remove. The referential quality that is readily apparent in the arbitrary signs of verbal discourse (though here too, it can be forgotten) becomes effaced.

This quality of remove is highly valued for the flexibility it allows: the possibility of precise statement increases since a choice of words can stress certain things and deemphasize others without the limitations imposed by any existential bond (the same lens cannot operate at more than one f-stop, or focal length, simultaneously). The image generated by it bears more of an "all or nothing" quality with certain constancies of relation between its parts than do the words concatenated into a sentence or paragraph. Remove allows metacommunication and the rise of logical typing as a way of mediating interaction, and although forms of remove are clearly operative in the documentary film (it is, after all, a distinct textual system), the effect of such films very often is to mask what remove there is.

As a result, two impossible identities often propose themselves for our consent in documentary and ethnographic film. (1) What you see is what there was. (2) What there was is what there would have been. The first proposition invites us to believe that our access to the pro-filmic event is complete and unmediated. The diegesis, constructed to minimize the signs of its construction, except those that signify "This is authentic documentation," matches the event like a template; and if there are gaps, the "diegesis"—the plane of rhetorical ordering supporting the exposition—papers them over. The second proposition invites us to believe that what occurred in the presence of the film maker(s) would have occurred in their absence as well; that the process of observation had no significant effect upon the situation or event. This claim is often made apparent in cinéma-vérité forms of documentary or ethnography like *High School* or *Magical Death* (Napoleon Chagnon, 1975) where the camera appears to be an invisible, completely neutral observer. Sometimes both propositions combine: what you see is what there would have been were you not watching. It is an impossible proposition to disprove since it invokes an unverifiable hypothesis—that we could verify what would occur if we were not observing what is occurring. Even without going to this paradoxical extreme we can see how these two propositions tilt the experiential balance toward acceptance of the illusion that we stand before the original situation or event itself without having our own relation to the event called into account. (This is also the illusion that invites, understandably, comparison with the psychoanalytic concepts of voyeurism and fetishism.)

Though, as we shall see, these lacks of remove are not encountered in every film, they do draw upon the indexical aspect of the cinematic sign and therefore pose a continuing risk. Ethnographers, for example, may wish not only to point to visible and audible aspects of culture but also to those aspects that are not visible but have visual signs or correlations, relations of dominance, say (as in *A Joking Relationship*, John Marshall, 1966, which describes how certain Bushman relations permit bawdy joking between a man and woman but only upon the male's initiative), or an attitude of patience (as in *At the Winter Sea Ice Camp*, pt. I in the *Netsilik Eskimo* series, NFB, 1967, where the main character sits at an ice hole for several hours waiting for a seal to take his bait). But this concern to address a level of abstraction that is itself at a remove from the depicted situation or event may still rely upon the propositions sketched out above as a strategy to authenticate its evidence: the indexical bond seems to guarantee that what there is is what there was, even when we address intangibles like "dominance" or "patience." The indexical quality of the image can indeed serve as a powerful source of evidence (though not without difficulty as we shall see). This raises the question of whether the scientific goals of the ethnographer are sometimes complicit with essentially paradoxical propositions advanced by the documentary film form. The ramifications of this possible complicity, in scientific, cinematic, and ideological terms, become another aspect of the controlling question—what to do with people.

Were the documentary or ethnographic film strictly a replication of a unique situation or event it would indeed qualify as a form of magic, but such films are clearly a mode of discourse: by deploying a system of signs, albeit indexical signs in large degree, they operate at a remove, though at a lesser remove than verbal discourse per se. Nonetheless, verbal discourse remains available to such films as narrator or character commentary and in the form of written sub- or inter-titles. As such, verbal discourse is instrumental in the fabrication of the "diegesis," which may remind us of our remove; but there is also the arrangement of the indexical signs themselves on paradigmatic and syntagmatic axes. The resultant, limited degree of remove, though, often favors the impression of magical transport; this is a starting point from which any theoretical consideration of the documentary concerned with the experiential level of such films must begin just as it must be a consideration for any practicing film maker.

For the ethnographer, an overriding question is how to understand this form of discourse in relation to traditional scientific discourse. For the film theorist, a central question is how to understand this form of discourse in relation to ideological effect (for example, the invocation of the self-as-subject through the lure of a desire to know) and the development of alternative strategies that tilt the balance between forgetting and remembrance toward a more even keel.

Criteria: Science and Criticism

Ironically, a great deal of discussion regarding the ethnographic film has a proscriptive coloring. Margaret Mead, Jay Ruby, and others have argued that ethnographic film must conform to criteria derived from the tradition of written anthropology and scientific investigation. The relation of cinematic discourse to social science is unproblematic; the latter dictates the articulation of the former. A few individuals have challenged this assertion, suggesting that ethnographic film may require a new paradigm, another way of seeing, not necessarily incompatible with written anthropology but at least governed by a distinct set of criteria. David MacDougall, for example, writes

> If anthropologists have consistently rejected film as an analytical medium, and if they have themselves often relegated it to subordinate record-making and didactic roles, the reason may not be merely conservative reluctance to employ a new technology but a shrewd judgment that the technology entails a shift in perspective which raises major problems for scientific conceptualization.[3]

For most, though, assimilation to existing criteria remains the norm. As Jay Ruby stipulates, "ethnographic film makers, like ethnographic writers, have a primary obligation to meet the demands and needs of anthropological investigation and presentation."[4]

Some have pushed the process of assimilation still further and argued that the activity of reading an ethnographic film is basically comparable with the kind of reading proposed by post-structuralists like Roland Barthes, in S/Z, for example. Here, the relation between the discourse of ethnographic film and the ideological implications of the production of meaning becomes unproblematic: the former makes the latter transparent. This relationship of similarity between the anthropologist faced with an ethnographic film and the post-structuralist faced with a text has been explored by John W. Adams in a provocative article; he argues that the success of ideology in narrative requires convincing us that characters, their motivations and actions, are "perfectly natural." The sense of justified and coherent activity is what ideology produces in "subjects." Anthropologists, in their turn, study a similar form of production in myth and ritual where events also unfold. Ethnographic films are often about myths or rituals and good examples exhibit disjunctions similar to those which a post-structuralist can find embedded within a narrative. (He alludes to Stephen Heath's study of *Touch of Evil* [*Screen* 16:1, 2 (1975)] as a model.) He concludes

> For, just as "narrative" does not entirely control fictional films, so "ritual" as an organizing principle in peoples' lives does not by any means entirely account for their actions. This enables anthropologists to analyze specific films with regard to their inclusion, or lack, of sufficient context for understanding the communications depicted in them. This is precisely the project of post-structuralist film criticism, as I see it, though posed in different terms.[5]

The congruence Adams seeks to establish founders, though, on the different notions of "lack" and "context" employed. In the analysis of narrative a lack is inevitable, and its resolution is the function of a complex mechanism that enforces closure by masking contradiction. This masking remains incomplete, however, and it becomes possible to read the text symptomatically to tease out what it seeks to hide beneath the "perfectly natural." "Context," here, comes close to meaning the repressed and makes reference to the workings of ideology or the unconscious. It also refers explicitly to formal operations within the chain of signifiers, especially those involved in disguising or naturalizing the saying, the production of meaning. Context does not refer primarily to the pro-filmic situation or event or to questions of adequacy regarding its description.

"Lack" in an ethnographic film, though, is not so much a function of inevitability as deficiency. Its presence demands the importation of supplementary knowledge at the level of the signified, the anthropological content. Context is "out there," in the field. "Lack" and "context" no longer refer to the chain of signifiers, production of meaning, and the mechanism whereby it is masked, but to the meaning produced, the said rather than the saying, and the adequacy with which it is adduced. The indexical sign serves as a guarantee of evidence (with *possible* "lacks") in ethnography and as guarantee of the "perfectly natural" (with an attendant ideology that *systematically* masks "lacks" such as lack of awareness of its own operation) in narrative.

The analogy between the two types of endeavor only holds true if we equate attempts to comprehend signification with attempts to comprehend significance, the production of meaning by a system of signs with the meanings produced by a system of signs. These are radically different activities. Even when an ethnographic film contains "an explicit description of the methodology used to collect, to analyze, to organize the data for presentation,"[6] this need not be at all comparable to those forms of self-reflexiveness, favored by structuralists in avant-garde texts, that operate on the production of meaning and the position for the self-as-subject customarily established. The anthropologist's concern lies with content and tends to take the signifying system for granted; the structuralist's concern lies with the signifying system itself and often tends to regard questions of content as secondary.

If, however, we begin with an acknowledgment of the ways in which documentary and ethnographic films erect themselves directly upon the paradoxical formulations made possible by the indexical sign, then we will need to give greater consideration to analyses that neither assume that form is beside the point nor believe that form is all we need discuss. Ethnographic films may feign neutral access to the real or to truth; they may speak in an academic language that appears authorless; they may consistently ignore questions of how the production of meaning is a function of an institutional apparatus, the representations modes of representation this apparatus favors and the ideology complicit therewith;[7] but these films also provide a form of access to situations and events valuable in its own right. Once again, distinctions must be made. Within the relatively practical, nonpolitical (i.e. naively ideological), pre-modernist, un-self-reflexive realm of ethnographic film, some films will find a better way of dealing with people and positioning us between forgetting and remembrance than others. Finding criteria to elaborate on distinctions of this kind will be one of our principal tasks.

David MacDougall's question whether ethnographic film does not "raise major problems for scientific conceptualization" can help orient us in relation to the contexts in which ethnographic film receives the most consideration—the science of anthropology and, more recently, the science of semiotics (an umbrella beneath which to group psychoanalysis, structuralism, linguistics, narratology, and some variants of Marxism). The status of semiotics as a science remains debated, especially when brought to a focus on the traditional object of aesthetic criticism—the literary or artistic text. For that reason, it is tempting to place the science of semiotics in quotation marks, but that would, I believe, confuse and pre-judge the issue, for what I want to suggest is at stake is an (incorrect) image of science, not semiotics, that informs most commentary whether made by anthropologists or semioticians.

This image of science strongly invokes the principle of precision or exactitude; assumes that logic, knowledge, and justification fall on the side of science whereas rhetoric, belief, and inspiration fall on the side of ideology, or subjective and impressionistic criticism; and thereby places science in an imaginary realm clearly opposed to non-science. This image of a solid, coherent, noncontradictory body of practice is, like all representations in the imaginary (as distinguished from the symbolic), a mis-representation. A look at recent work in the philosophy of science will show us how this mis-representation occurs even in relation to the natural sciences. I suspect that this same mis-representation stands behind most defenses of the scientific status of semiology as well.

What Is Science

Science gives the impression of an intellectual machine that eats its own past, turning it to waste. Its progress is qualitative and old theories prove to be wrong or special cases of more recent ones. Some, for example, argue that Newtonian physics can be made a derivation of relativity theory when velocities are sufficiently low. This notion is itself wrong. Although science may progress in the refinement of its operations, the quality of its theoretical underpinnings remains basically the same, and strikingly close in form and function to other kinds of theory. Thomas Kuhn observes that if Aristotelian dynamics, phlogistic chemistry, or caloric thermodynamics "are to be called myths, then myths can be produced by the same sort of methods and held for the same sort of reasons that now lead to scientific knowledge."[8]

Scientific theories do not succeed one another because they afford a truer explanation of nature in any ontological sense. Instead, "the pragmatic success of a scientific theory seems to guarantee the ultimate success of its associated explanatory mode. Explanatory force, however, may be a long time coming."[9] In Kuhn's view, pragmatic success is intimately associated with problem-solving, the endeavor that characterizes science more than any qualitatively distinct method, theory, or mode of knowledge-production. In normal times this activity proceeds apace, with little debate about fundamentals, a state of affairs quite unlike that in the arts or their criticism. Only in times of crisis does profound disagreement occur. Should an upheaval take place, then there will be a "consequent shift in the problems available for scientific discovery and in the standards by which the profession determines what should count as an admissible problem or as a legitimate problem-solution."[10]

This shift, though, does not occur in a course charted upon a mono-planar, logical map where some instance of faulty reasoning has sent the ship of scientific progress off course. There is no Absolute, no equivalent of a magnetic North, by which to determine when we are on course in the first place. The way we use our logical maps itself changes, irrevocably. And the way this change takes place is also worth close examination.

Paul Feyerabend's detailed study of Galileo's defense of Copernican astronomy offers an extremely instructive demonstration of how major shifts occur in science.[11] After scrutinizing Galileo's writings at length, especially *Dialogue Concerning the Two Chief World Systems*, he summarizes the task confronting Galileo by asking how Galileo could lure people away from a successful system of thought in favor of one that appeared incomplete and absurd. Feyerabend's conclusion, which he demonstrates was Galileo's actual solution, is that allegiance to the new system will require more than logical argument: "It will have to be brought about *by irrational means* such as propaganda, emotion, *ad hoc* hypotheses, and appeals to prejudices of all kinds. . . ." (italics Feyerabend's).[12] "To express it differently: Copernicanism and other 'rational' views exist today only because reason was overturned at some time in their past."[13] It is only after facts and arguments gradually accrue that transform a new faith into sound knowledge that reason will once again appear to reign.

Kuhn adopts a basically similar position in differentiating his understanding of science from Sir Karl Popper's.[14] Popper's criterion of falsifiability as developed in *Conjectures and Refutations* is examined at length (discussed below). Kuhn then refers to Popper's summarizing statements regarding the role of scientific inquiry in which Popper speculates that if we choose to attempt to explain "this unknown world of ours" by means of laws and explanatory theories "*then there is no more rational procedure than the method of . . . conjecture and refutation:* of boldly proposed theories; of trying our best to show that these are erroneous; and of accepting them tentatively if our critical efforts are unsuccessful" (italics Popper's).[15] Kuhn discovers here the same buttressing of reason that Feyerabend found in Galileo. He comments, "We shall not, I suggest, understand the success of science without understanding the full force of rhetorically induced and professionally shared imperatives like these. Institutionalized and articulated further . . . such maxims and values may explain the outcome of choices that could not have been dictated by logic and experiment alone."[16]

This conception of science does not invite a perpetual free-for-all of contending theories. Feyerabend, Kuhn, and others take pains to point out the vast amount of scientific research necessarily done under the sign of a given set of theories or methodological principles. But, though exemplary, such theories, principles, or paradigms do not accede to the status of absolute knowledge, and any assumption that they do so simply becomes an irrational impediment to fundamental change. Feyerabend asks how can we discover the kind of world our assumptions fabricate. His own response is that, "We cannot discover it from the *inside*. We need an *external* standard of criticism, we need a set of alternative assumptions or, as these assumptions will be quite general, constituting, as it were, an entire alternative world, *we need a dream-world in order to discover the features of the real world we think we inhabit*" (his emphases).[17]

One consequence of this is to erase the distinction between contexts of discovery and justification: we can no longer say, "How you arrive at your hypothesis or puzzle solution lies beyond the scope of scientific inquiry; its justification, though, must conform to known criteria such as falsifiability." The attempt to enforce a clear demarcation pivots on a fixed set of criteria governing the context of justification, but basic change can only occur by overruling the existing context of justification. The previous criteria no longer apply and can no longer serve as a standard. In considering these two contexts, "we are dealing with a single uniform domain of procedures all of which are equally important for the growth of science. This disposes of the distinction."[18] Any field, such as ethnography or semiology, seeking to establish itself as a science needs to remain sensitive to this disposal if it is to avoid rigidifying into dogma, or a closed system of thought immunized against change.

A second consequence of this conception of science is to erase any sense of contradiction or antagonism between art and science. The difference becomes one of degree or emphasis. In art technical puzzles are solved to arrive at a text capable of aesthetic effect. In science aesthetic effects enter admissibly, and frequently, into the paramount goal of puzzle-solving. Kuhn notes that "considerations of symmetry, of simplicity and elegance in symbolic expression, and of other forms of mathematical aesthetic play important roles in both disciplines. But in the arts, the aesthetic is itself the goal of the work," whereas in science it is primarily a tool.[19] A non-antagonistic relation of converse priorities together with science's occasional need for rhetorically induced imperatives and the overturn of reason should signal both caution to disciplines (such as semiology) seeking to shape themselves in the image of a purer, more rational science and receptiveness to activities (such as some ethnographic filmmaking) seeking to open up new possibilities for what the comprehension of culture might entail.

The way in which a certain image of science functions as a support for semiology draws heavily upon Louis Althusser's defense of Sigmund Freud and Jacques Lacan as founder and elaborator, re-

IDEOLOGY AND THE IMAGE

spectively, of the science of psychoanalysis.[20] Althusser argues that a science constitutes its object (it is not a given) and that Freud constituted a new object, namely, the unconscious. He goes on to say, "If psychoanalysis is a science because it is the science of a distinct object, it is also a science with the structure of all sciences: it has a *theory* and a *technique* (method) that make possible the knowledge and transformation of its object in a specific practice"[21] (italics his). Yet, if we return to the philosophy of science, we discover that such a conception fails to distinguish adequately between what Karl Popper calls science and pseudo-science. For Popper this is a matter of whether falsifiable propositions lie at the center of the science's activity or not.[22] If not, the resulting pseudo-science may have enormous explanatory power, but this becomes a definite liability: in relation to astrology Popper comments, "by making their interpretations and prophecies sufficiently vague they were able to explain away anything that might have been a refutation of the theory. . . . In order to escape falsifiability they destroyed the testability of their theory."[23]

While agreeing on the validity of a distinction that would preclude astrology or psychoanalysis from the status of science, Kuhn locates it elsewhere. He argues that the modes of explanation adopted in astrology were not different in kind from those of a science; they only seemed to be ways of begging the question (of acting to "explain away," as Popper puts it, rather than explain) after the entire endeavor fell into disrepute. Astrologers were aware of numerous failures and did seek more adequate theories but this search could not justify abandoning what theory they had even if it was "adequate only to establish the plausibility of the discipline [i.e. constitute an object of study—BN] and to provide a rationale for the various craft rules [or technique—BN] which governed practice."[24] In Kuhn's view, falsification may or may not take place before a theory is replaced, but a theory will certainly be replaced if it fails to support a puzzle-solving tradition adequately, the primary activity of any science. And in the case of astrology, or psychoanalysis, "neither the astrologer nor the doctor could do research. Though they had rules to apply, they had no puzzles to solve and therefore no science to practice."[25]

But if psychoanalysis, and perhaps textual criticism as well, do not qualify as sciences in either Kuhn's or Popper's view, obviously they do not of necessity deserve consignment to a dustbin reserved for ill-founded, misguided, or "wrong" practices. We have spoken earlier of the practice of interpretation that textual analysis, the reading of signs, entails, of the difficulties of this practice, and also of its vital importance. If psychoanalysis, semiology, or textual criticism are likened to science, or an incorrect image of science, as a means of justifying their activity and if the errors of this tactic become apparent, this does not discredit the practice so much as demand refutation or refinement of the analogy. If ethnographic film is measured against a context of justification developed in anthropology that these films may, arguably, overthrow by offering, in Feyerabend's terms, a dream world from which we may discover features of the real (scientific) world we think we inhabit, then the possibility that we also need to discover a new context of justification must be entertained. If science itself is an impure or paradoxical mixture of rhetoric and logic, discovery and justification, belief and knowledge, we can scarcely expect other realms of inquiry to be any less impure or paradoxical. We are left, finally and again, with the question of purpose—why these puzzles and these criteria for solution, why these modes of interpretation and these standards for adequacy; do we seek to understand or change the world, for whom, in what direction? And it will always be from the context—from that source of wisdom in the total mind as an integrated network of which consciousness is but a sampling—that purpose must take its direction if we are to avoid the pitfalls of a false epistemology.

Ethnographic Practice: Critical Problems

Recourse to the notions of science that most anthropologists and semiologists have adopted in their discussions of film, then, does not afford firm theoretical footing so much as the impression of such solidity. We are still left with the question of what to do with people, of how the indexical sign splays our attention between discourse and unimpeded referentiality and the paradoxical claims this doubling up of possible meanings has on us. Thinking that what we see is what there was and that what there was is what there would have been creates an impossible (but often pleasurable) place for the viewer similar to the self-contradictory space of an Escher painting or the impossible triangle. This effect also creates an impossible place for the critic, for it can be formulated in the same terms as the narrative paradoxes discussed earlier: "If I am to analyze this film properly, I must not mistake it for reality; but if I do not mistake it for reality, I cannot analyze it properly."[26]

The act of criticism helps dissipate the palpability of the impossible space created for the viewer, and yet this act must also accept the full force of the paradoxical if it is to attempt to understand it. We ignore this dilemma at our own peril. (The discussion of Wiseman's films points to the limits of a critical approach that refuses to acknowledge the necessary mistake.) Speaking from a position to the side of the paradoxical zone in which we actually experience a film certainly does not preclude generating useful results, but in this chapter our goal will be to attempt an understanding more directly linked to the experience of film, especially ethnographic film.

The Nuer (Hilary Harris and George Breidenbach, 1970), for example, presents a highly evocative, if not poetic, view of the Nuer of southern Sudan and Ethiopia. This approach prompted considerable criticism from anthropologists. Karl Heider's remarks are typical, though somewhat harsh: " . . . the film is almost without ethnographic integrity. By this I mean that its principles are cinema aesthetic: its framing, cutting, and juxtaposition of images are done without regard for any ethnographic reality."[27] "It is reminiscent of contemporary 'underground' filmmakers who use footage of childbirth or other real events to create a personal aesthetic pattern. This approach can result in an interesting film, but it makes little sense to judge such a film by the standards of ethnographic reality."[28]

Though Heider would appear guilty of creating an unnecessary antagonism between aesthetics and science and of invoking a reified notion of ethnographic reality, he also points to a crucial problem: at what point and to what degree must we attend to cinematic discourse as the necessary point of access to the pro-filmic event. Also, in what manner does this discourse return us to the historically specific when it is the domain of ethnographic investigation.

Like John Adams, Heider appears to trust in a transparency of cinematic discourse which, once achieved, will allow us to evaluate the adequacy of the ethnographic content by previously established and well-known standards. And although it is true that *The Nuer* departs further from conventions of access (of realism) than a number of other ethnographic films, I suspect that the problems of reading this film are very common, and instructive, ones. In fact, I will attempt to show that it is easier to read *The Nuer* and understand its conception of ethnography than it is to read *The Hunters* (John Marshall, 1956), a work held up by most anthropologists as a classic ethnographic film.

The Nuer does not solve the problem of what to do with people, but it shares this problem and helps illustrate the need for close textual reading if we are to make distinctions of any consequence. Rather than simply dismiss *The Nuer* for its "cinema aesthetic" we should ask how it works and what kind of world it establishes, on the assumption that a comparable activity will be essential for films that disingenuously appear to lack an aesthetic or significant formal organization.

The opening of *The Nuer* clarifies the problem (8.1–47). The sequence precedes the credits and could be dismissed as evocative "noise": the hard information will surely follow, these are only random shots of tribal life. On the contrary, this passage proposes a mode of reading that remains appropriate for the entirety of the film.

Basically, this passage suggests, "Don't ask questions. Don't seek explanations. Experience the present." Cues to the duration of shots are rhythmic, a function of the textual system, rather than referential, a function of actions carried out by characters. Characters fail to emerge in any individuated form. Events do not unfold in a spatio-temporal matrix promoting their legibility. Instead, they are superseded by a primarily poetic system of shot linkage. Though the opening passage does loosely depict an event—the herding of cattle back to the village at dusk—we are not invited to attend to this event as much as to the formal organization of shots, internally and in relation to one another.

The opening passage suggests that enigmas will indeed be posed but not resolved. A surplus of meaning will not be accounted for but allowed to overflow the pattern of organization. Bodies and heads will be offered as forms or shapes, not as the individuated figures of social actors. What we see of characters and their actions remains sub-assertive, only suggestive of some broader pattern, but this larger pattern fails to coalesce as it does in Wiseman's film. We remain at a sub-assertive evocative level as paradigmatically related shots tumble forward along the syntagmatic axis. (Note how cuts between 8.2/8.3a, 8.10/8.11/8.12, 8.23/8.24, and 8.25/8.26 emphasize formal similarities like vertical form, conical huts, or facial resemblance.) This is a classic configuration for poetry.

This strategy, in which poetic imagery gains only minimal specificity from verbal commentary or synchronous location sound (the opening has no commentary, the film as a whole very little, and sound appears to derive from the general location, tribal songs, for example, but not necessarily from the scene depicted), pries the film away from any claim of representing historically specifiable situations or events. There is, however, no sense of the frustration we find behind Birdwhistell's exclamation ("This whole India thing needs to be looked at"); instead there is a meaningful pattern of formal control. Little sense of the chaotic impenetrability of another culture arises such as we find in Louis Malle's *Calcutta,* which also opens with a prolonged passage lacking commentary. Instead, there is the sense that these situations and events may well be knowable in a variety of ways (other points of access are not impossible as Malle's more realist style implies they are: if, in transparent depiction, an event does not yield up its meaning, how can we ever hope to know it?), and that here they are knowable in terms of poetic rendering. Thus, Nuer culture, or our experience of it, can be known through a formal strategy of "making strange" in order that overlooked qualities of the everyday can be rediscovered. *The Nuer* attempts to restore a sense of the poetic to the everyday world of another culture. Though this

Documentary, Criticism, and the Ethnographic Film   253

8.6, 8.8, 8.9b, 8.10   8.7, 8.9a, 8.9c, 8.11

IDEOLOGY AND THE IMAGE

Documentary, Criticism, and the Ethnographic Film   255

IDEOLOGY AND THE IMAGE

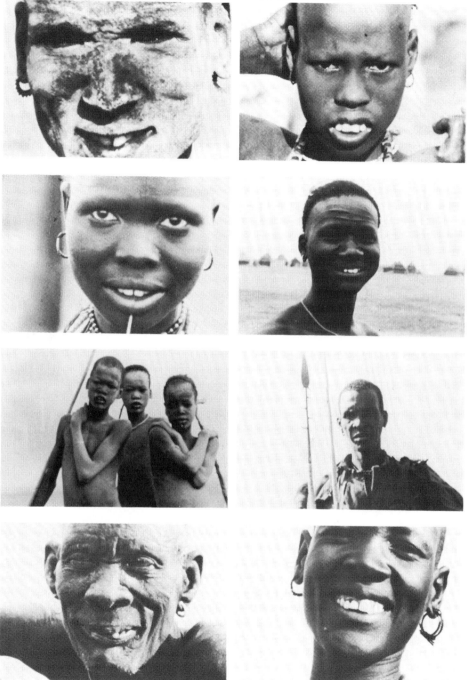

Documentary, Criticism, and the Ethnographic Film   257

IDEOLOGY AND THE IMAGE

Documentary, Criticism, and the Ethnographic Film   259

may push it further toward the art end of a sliding scale between art and science, it also suggests that the balance between these realms may indeed require shifting when we move from written to visual anthropology.

Even the beginnings of a formal analysis indicate some of the ways in which *The Nuer* organizes material drawn from an historical situation into a meaningful, but nonhistorical pattern. When we examine the ethnographic classic, *The Hunters,* we begin to discover some of the ways in which it too diverts us from deriving meaningful patterns from historically specific events, but far less openly.

The cultural historian William Irwin Thompson indicates the extent of the problem when he discovers in *The Hunters* not insight into Bushman culture but "a model of the universal form of conflict in values in human institutions. Hidden in the film, as hidden in a fairy tale, is an archetypal structure, a mandala of the species' specific form of human consciousness."[29] The concrete depiction of Bushman culture is erased to reveal, as in a palimpsest, yet another inscription, which bears the secrets of human consciousness itself. What relationship, though, exists between these levels of inscription, and how does the textual system of *The Hunters* establish it?

The film depicts a prolonged hunt for food by four Bushmen, using footage taken over a period of years and several hunts to fabricate a single event—the tracking and killing of a giraffe. Thompson identifies the four hunters as the Headman, the Beautiful, the Shaman, and the Clown; and from this scheme he derives an elaborate model of human conflict and culture. Although the film itself offers no large-scale theory of culture, there are qualities to its organization that do fail to insist on a clear balance between the specific and the general. Like Jean Rouch's *The Lion Hunters* on Flaherty's *Nanook of the North,* Marshall's film invites the viewer to regard it as a poetic evocation of a basic human response to the exigencies of physical survival. Using in this case Bushman culture as pretext, a more universal story will be told: Men will venture into a dangerous world to being back food for people who might otherwise starve. They will show us knowledge, skill, patience, humor. Their success in the face of adversity commands respect; their qualities are qualities of enduring value. We must celebrate them.

This tone, strongly conveyed by the laconic voice-over commentary, is also found in Robert Gardner's *Dead Birds* and clearly invites a mythopoetic response, being one itself (an interesting study could be made of the continuation in ethnographic film of the commentative style begun by Hemingway himself in *Spanish Earth.* Additionally, the compilation editing of *The Hunters* to give the illusion of a single hunt (rather than a representation of the hunting process generally without being tied to a singular instance) and the lack of synchronous location sound both work to render the images less concrete, less contextually bound to a specific time and place. Just as the poetic qualities of Chaplin and Keaton are partially defeated by the addition of sound effects,[30] so, conversely, the lack of concretizing sound here further invites a generalized reading. Though this invitation could be offset by a long-take shooting style, à la Flaherty, or by commentary dwelling on concrete, visible events, it is not. For example, when Kaow removes baby birds from a nest to feed himself, our attention is not drawn to this act; instead, the commentary attributes a distancing thought to Kaow, "As he removed the birds, he thought of the giraffe."

Although some of these limitations are a function of available technology, their combination is not. As a group, they suggest a particular view of human nature that favors the mythic over the historic, that attempts to transform the prosaic into the poetic, although it is also a view more hidden by the film's style than displayed as it is in *The Nuer*, which may account for the film's higher standing among anthropologists.

It would seem that a primary concern of anthropologists is to distinguish between, on the one hand, historically, culturally specific processes and any extrapolations based on them, and, on the other, deductions derived from timeless first principles (e.g., man hunts because it is his fate to prove himself in the face of death—as ethnocentric a notion as one could ever hope for). To attach to one side of the distinction certain strategies of ethnographic film making (sync sound, long takes, concrete descriptive commentary), however, will not guarantee success. The nuances of technique, and style, are too manifold. As a first approximation, though, it seems safe to say that those strategies that encourage us to understand a situation in the context of its historical specificity will be strategies of particular interest to the ethnographer (though the paradigm here is more likely to be the complex textual system of finished films than techniques in isolation). The search for strategies capable of this is itself historical and ongoing; it cannot be resolved once and for all. *The Hunters* does not address this or other questions of this magnitude explicitly, but the readings it has received certainly prompt some reflection at this level almost as a matter of necessity. For, even if *The Hunters* is not a truly exceptional work of ethnography or cinema, it is exemplary of a problem of film makers and critics alike: how can we re-present the uniquely historical in a form that neither hides the fact that it is a representation (not a magical repetition of the unique) nor uses its status as representation to enter a world of deductive idealism. We can certainly continue to learn from *The Hunters,* but perhaps our examination of this film can teach us as much about the problems of ethnographic film making as about Bushman culture.

Necessary Distinctions: visible/empirical, observation/description/explanation

Another large problem plaguing the ethnographic film centers on the relationship between the visible and the empirical. Once we are aware of how science as much as any other system of explanation constructs its own object, we should also be aware that the world of visual sense impressions does not constitute irrefutable evidence for a given set of statements. The evidence itself must be constituted and, with it, the facts we sometimes think are "out there" in the visible world. Were it otherwise, presumably there would be a finite number of facts that one, and only one, theory would organize with maximum accuracy, consistency, simplicity, and explanatory power. Some no doubt believe this to be the case, making the march of science a trail blazed by progress toward the pinnacle of a single, unified theory. I do not. My own view is much closer to Kuhn's, "We [he and Karl Popper] do not believe that there are rules for inducing correct theories from fact, or even that theories, correct or incorrect, are induced at all. Instead we view them as imaginative posits, invented in one piece for application to nature."[31]

The visible and aural world recorded by a camera and sound recorder, then, serves as a source for empirical statements but does not yield singular, or even necessarily obvious ones. A grid or matrix must be applied, differentiating appearances into conceptual bins of significance. (The medical doctor, for example, needs to distinguish the rotund belly of a well-fed child from the bloated abdomen of a victim of kwashiorkor.) That these conceptual bins are not readily apparent is exemplified by Margaret Mead and Gregory Bateson's film, *The First Days in the Life of a New Guinea Baby* from the *Character Formation in Different Cultures* series (shot in 1936–38, edited and released in 1952). (See 8.48–50.) During the course of the film we depend upon Mead's verbal commentary to define relationships within a meaningful conceptual context. What we see is an Iatmul woman and a baby in a shady grove. The woman holds the baby up, tosses it, then puts it on a grass skirt while another woman pours water over her. Another woman arrives and flicks at flies near the baby. In another location a two-year-old throws a cloth across the baby as this other woman gathers the child up.

Without verbal commentary the sequence is impossible to

IDEOLOGY AND THE IMAGE

understand. We are told, though, that the first woman has just given birth, that the events in the grove are birth rituals (including such acts as severing the cord and placing the placenta in a coconut shell— because of the poor quality of the image, these are recognizable only with the aid of verbal description), that the second woman is a wet nurse and the two-year-old her own, jealous child. Without this commentary we might easily mistake the first woman for a midwife and the second for the mother.

A visual field can be the source for more than one set of empirical statements. (The one in *First Days* could serve to illustrate proxemic relations or attitudinal ones, for example.) The danger exists of assuming that only one set is obvious and natural and that the visible furnishes absolute proof rather than confirmatory evidence in the form of facts that are themselves constituted by the theory in question. Similarly, the danger exists of thinking that a film transparently discloses the real rather than producing, through a set of discourses, a particular reality. And although an ethnographer may be more likely to acknowledge the first danger than the second, there are numerous films that suggest their maker has forgotten both.

The question of the relation between the visible and the empirical can be put in even broader terms: we can ask about the relation between observation and explanation. Observation, first of all, is not the same as description, the usual accompaniment to explanation. Cinematic observation circles around re-presentations still in need of description (such as Margaret Mead's commentary in *First Days* or John Marshall's in *The Hunters*). Observation involves taking a particular stance vis-à-vis a situation or event, a stance that defers, and differs from, description. "It is description which labels events with words and sentences; these create images of the events in the minds of those who use the descriptions,"[32] as William Skidmore puts it; or as he says in another passage, "a description has the ability to call forth images or understanding of [an] event."[33]

Image, as a term of descriptive or explanatory power, supplements discrete representations or images.[34] In this usage it is of a different (higher) logical type. Images involve linking parts to whole by an organizing principle that may be descriptive or explanatory, though the boundary between the two is not always entirely clear-cut in practice. (Elements of explanatory assumptions often slip into descriptions.) Explanation, though, usually involves explicitly relating "a conceptual problem or set of observations to a theoretical construction of reality which fits it."[35] Explanation, too, is of a different logical type from observation, it is a higher logical type than description. It is more than simply making something clear: "It is an exercise contained by a more or less formal structure of concepts with specific relationships. These arrays of concepts have, to some degree, the power to bring our curiosity to rest, to do it logically and coherently, and to pertain to reality" (or "observable phenomena").[36]

Usually in ethnographic film, description and explanation depend on verbal commentary but they need not necessarily. Fred Wiseman's films, for example, propose explanations through the arrangement of sequences at a second-order level without recourse to direct verbal statement. Explanation can take the form of literal statement but may also appear in the form of what is said metaphorically or even in the form of what is exemplified or expressed, as we saw with narrative.[37] But the general association of the literal with the favored form of scientific explanation directs us toward some of the distinctive problems of ethnographic film, beginning with the characteristics of cinematic observation.

In order to obtain the coherence and plausibility of a written explanation, observation requires some semblance of unity, some kind of observation platform. On a cinematic level, this guarantor of unity and, frequently, pertinence to reality, to "observable phenomena," is the diegesis. Even though more intermittent than its counterpart in most fictional narrative, the imaginary time and space fabricated as the diegesis serves to peg the film down to discrete, historical phenomena rather than allowing it to skitter off into a more purely formal poetics (as *The Nuer* threatens to do). It is, of course, assisted by the "diegesis," the rhetorical fiction or "logical" ordering that supports verbal exposition, though a variety of relationships are possible between the two levels (see pp. 184–207).

On an extracinematic level, the guarantor of unity and pertinence is the representation of situations or events. Ill-defined as these terms generally are, they stand as recognizable units of social punctuation. They depend heavily on time, the time necessary to "read" a situation and determine the complexities at work within it, actually or potentially, the time necessary for an event to unfold. This also tends to be the time needed for representations to produce an "image" in the sense of a recognizable, conceptual "picture" of the situation. This guarantor, then, provides cues to the duration of a shot or sequence: once representation of a situation or event commences to generate an "image" of it, we expect it to continue instead of being displaced by some new representation before the process is complete. (This latter course is what we find in *The Nuer*, where cuts like 8.25/8.26 depend on formal correspondences that bear little relation to social situations or events.)

The construction of a diegetic space that affords the viewer a unified place from which to observe situations and events acts as a necessary but not sufficient condition for an ethnographic film. Alone, it fails to offer a distinction between a film and footage. The anthropologist may be entirely satisfied with footage recording a particular event such as proxemic behavior in the face of an overly aggressive stranger. *Invisible Walls* (Richard Cowan and Lucy Turner, 1969) is an example of such footage—long takes of encounters between an interviewer trained to violate "personal space" and unwitting subjects at a shopping plaza. By adding verbal commentary, a "diegetic" plane, the footage in *Invisible Walls* begins to shift toward a film; it exhibits some higher level of organization that links parts to whole.) Though "mere film" may be quite adequate for the researcher's purposes, concern here will be limited to that footage which bears the mark of an organizing principle capable of producing a textual system and, therefore, film.

The construction of a place for the viewer via diegetic space offers the possibility of containing more than a description or explanation; it may also contain the viewer in the position of self-as-subject. In ethnographic film this general risk condenses around particular forms of fetishism: (1) a fetishism of the visible, inviting the voyeuristic desire to see and not be seen, especially in relation to the exotic; and (2) a fetishism of the word (in the guise of scientific discourse eliciting the desire to know and not be known in relation to the subject-who-knows, that is, the one who speaks the commentary). Each fetishism masks a lack—a lack of presence for both viewer (as subject) and film maker, who observe without being seen and with effect that can be fully contained (as either disavowal—what there was is what there would have been, or avowal—my effect is what you see, nothing more and nothing less). Each fetishism also masks another lack, that of the production of meaning and position, place. Observation bears the innocence of scientific neutrality or, if acknowledged, the innocence of the neutral but participatory observer. Not all ethnographic films turn observation to fetishism along with knowledge, but many do. The strength of this tendency prompted David MacDougall to argue that

> [the ethnographic film maker] reaffirms the colonial origins of anthropology. It was once the European who decided what was worth knowing about "primitive" peoples and what they in turn should be taught. The shadow of that attitude falls across the observational film, giving it a distinctively Western parochialism. The traditions of science and narrative art combine in this instance to dehumanize the study of man. It is a form in which the observer and observed exist in separate worlds, and it produces films that are monologues.[38]

It is difficult to pursue this point much further since there are virtually no ethnographic films that confront this indictment head on. Only a few film makers come to mind: Jean Rouch for one, the film-making team of Judith and David MacDougall for another, and the team of David MacDougall and James Blue, who made *Kenya Boran*,[39] and even in these cases, problems abound. For the time being we will continue our general examination of the ethnographic film and turn to the question of the relation between observation and explanation.

In order to explain a situation or event, concepts and context become necessary. Explanation operates at a remove, at a different level of logical typing. Hence explanation, like a map, is not the territory. There is a gap between it and the observable phenomena, the pro-filmic event it sets out to explain, a gap that can act as a fissure in the indexical sign, removing us from the place of paradox at the same as it arises from that very place. This gap involves recognition of the sense in which there is more to understanding a situation or event than meets the eye (either in terms of the cinematic apparatus and the production of meaning or the event and its attendant explanation).

We read observations, or have them read to us, in relation to a theoretical matrix distinct from any specific observation. Particular observations and their bits of information can readily fit more than one matrix. As Gregory Bateson discovered during his research in

Bali, even observations or facts were "labels for points of view voluntarily adopted by the investigator," and a given item could be explained by several theories simultaneously.[40] The fit is governed by the principle of tautology when scrutinized formally,[41] and by the principle of purpose when examined contextually. And although the principle of tautology may establish relatively fixed criteria for judging the validity of a fit, purpose remains subject to considerable social, historical, and ideological variation.

Modes of Explanation

In ethnographic film we find that two modes of explanation predominate, along with at least one broad type of explanation. The modes are familiar ones: narrative and exposition. And even though science tends to favor literal truth and thus exposition, ethnographic films, like documentary films generally, make use of narrative principles of explanation to a surprising degree (beginning with the fabrication of a diegesis). Narrative and exposition are two large envelopes containing explanations that come addressed to, and address, us, the viewers. Exposition, the more common mode, also poses the more distinctive problems and therefore invites the greater scrutiny.

The greatest problem lies in the consignment of explanation to the verbal sound track, usually in the form of direct address by a narrator. Like the poetic, associative editing of *The Nuer*, voice-over commentary tends to render the image track subassertive. It becomes a set of illustrations for conceptual points, presenting that information of which the explanation can most readily dispose. In films like *Dead Birds*, *The Hunters*, the Mead-Bateson films (*Character Formation in Different Cultures*, 1952), *Les Maîtres Fous* (Jean Rouch, 1953), and some of the Yanomamö and Bushman series (*The Feast* or *Meat Fight*, for example), the fully assertive presence of the image track portends an embarrassment of riches that the verbal explanation, because of its difference in logical type and the uncontrolled abundance of the visual information, cannot contain. As observation, the image track (and location sound) remains prior to description, offering itself to numerous descriptive terms and explanatory theories. We see more than we are told to look at.

In the course of a film, observations are filed, and portions of these filings arrange themselves along the magnetic lines of force of the verbal commentary. The portions that do not so arrange themselves then appear as noise or excess and may even support contradictory readings. In *Dead Birds*, for example, we are told about the risks and seriousness of warfare among the Dani of New Guinea, but we see a method of (ritual) warfare that follows rules clearly designed to minimize casualties and escalatory repercussions: basically, no overall strategy unfolds—attacks are uncoordinated; warriors act largely as individuals without any noticeable recourse to military tactics; battles take place on an open plain and neither flanking movements nor ambush are employed; battle stops if a death occurs and may even waver if the weather looks threatening. Yet all this is barely acknowledged, just as both *The Hunters* and *The Lion Hunters* build up a dramatic image of brave warriors confronting the dangerous beasts of the jungle with no more than poison-tipped arrows, only to spring on us, well into the films, the sight of these warriors setting steel traps, their principal and preferred weapon. The commentary acknowledges the use of traps, but begrudgingly, as though this evidence resisted induction into the film's chosen theory and must therefore be treated as noise or an excess to be contained as unobtrusively as possible.

Another variation on the alignment of observation with verbal description occurs in two of the Mead-Bateson films. *First Days in the Life of a New Guinea Baby* and *Childhood Rivalry in Bali and New Guinea* both use the same footage of a wet nurse with a newborn child (see 8.51–55 on pp. 270–72). In *First Days* Margaret Mead observes how the Iatmul wet nurse's own baby displays jealousy toward the newborn child by throwing a cloth, but in *Childhood Rivalry* (where the point being demonstrated is that New Guinea Iatmul mothers do not provoke jealousy, but Balinese mothers do) no attitudinal significance is attached to this action. In each case the commentary guides us along the line most advantageous to its own thesis.

Another problematic aspect of voice-over commentary occurs along the margin between exposition and narrative and demonstrates how noise or excess can be contained with either minimal acknowledgment or none. If a commentator highlights actions that we see occur, the simultaneous emergence of enigmas, which would normally occur in narrative, becomes dramatically reduced. This can lead to a flattening of the film experience as questions of the "what will happen next" or "why did that happen" sort become ceded to the verbal commentary. Some enigmas will still arise since a commentary is selective, stressing those points pertinent to its own explanatory frame of reference. But enigmas that arise at the boundaries of commentary lack a referential matrix within the film. They remain unauthorized, a lure offering little or no promise of gratification. We may well choose to attend to them but in doing so we also must choose to read against the grain of the text. Our motivation is frequently that the description or explanation advanced is omitting significant information that can be organized beneath an explanatory principle. In *Dead Birds*, for example, we may begin to seek out those behavioral puzzles ignored by the commentator that provide evidence for the ritualistic aspect of the warfare we see. Even though Walter Benjamin no doubt correctly stressed the importance of pinning down a single image's meaning with words or other images,[42] we should bear in mind that such supplementations pin down possible meanings and perhaps not the most important meanings at all. Unresolved enigmas on the margins of expository commentary act as a vital cue to such a possibility.[43]

Narrative, as a dominant form of explanation, is relatively rare in ethnographic film. Many films use a weak narrative, similar to the weak sense of narrative closure produced in several of Wiseman's films (the long shot of the hospital building at the end of *Hospital,* for example) as an element of their overall structure. Examples include *The Lion Hunters, Dead Birds, The Netsilik Eskimo* series, and several of the *Navajo Film Themselves, Yanomamö* and *Bushman* series. These films share with narrative a sense of closure pertaining to a beginning, a middle, and an end; the fabrication of a diegesis; and a focus on characters around whom actions and enigmas unfold. Some like *Les Maîtres Fous* have recourse to the short story structure of a surprise ending, an O. Henry twist that re-interprets what has gone before. But perhaps the most interesting film to discuss in some detail is *The Ax Fight* (1975) from the Yanomamö series.[44]

The film has five parts. First we see a fight break out in a Yanomamö village. This is shot in long takes with sync sound. As the fight breaks up, the sequence concludes with a woman hurling extremely derogatory epithets at visitors from another village— presumably she and they were antagonists in the conflict. Next, the screen goes black as we hear the voices of Chagnon and Asch (the anthropologist and the film maker, respectively) speculate on the cause, apparently at or very near the time when the fight subsides and the first part ends. Chagnon attributes the fight to incest, on the basis of what an informant tells him. Third, a set of written comments crawl across the screen explaining that this speculation was incorrect and that the actual cause involved a three-way lineage conflict in which a visitor demanded food from one of the village women and hit her when she refused. Her return to the village, wailing, prompted two of her relatives to begin a fight with the visitor. This part turns to graphic diagrams of the three lineages and points out how the various combatants are related. Fourth, the original footage is replayed with direct-address commentary and superimposed pointers highlighting aspects that correspond to the correct explanation. Finally, the film

Childhood Rivalry in Bali and New Guinea

[The child] plays with his own hand, plays with the baby's foot, plays with his lips, lays his head down lovingly on the little new baby, and the mother's whole attitude is both protective towards the baby and unprovocative towards her own child. The mother and wet nurse are coming back to the village,

and the wet nurse is getting ready to nurse the newborn.

The wet nurse's older child throws a cloth over to his sister who is taking care of their baby while the wet nurse picks up the newborn, only a few minutes old, and settles it on her lap for its first nursing.

Once the newborn is safely nursing. (to 8.55)

8.51–55. Commentary from two films using the same shots.

First Days in the Life of a New Guinea Baby

8.51. Seen in *Childhood Rivalry* only: a New Guinea wet nurse.

8.52. Seen in both films.

While the wet nurse gathers up the new baby,

8.53. Seen in both films.

her slightly jealous two-year-old throws a cloth across to

8.54. Pan from 8.53. Seen only in *First Days*.

his older sister, who is holding the wet nurse's baby.

she takes back her own child and performs a very difficult feat of keeping her breast steady for the newborn and, at the same time, amusing her own child by bouncing it up and down on her shoulder. What a contrast this is to the way in which the Balinese mother borrows a baby to provoke her own child!

Here the wet nurse is performing a difficult function and still has time to make certain that her own baby is not made jealous.

makers present an edited version of the original footage with sync sound but without commentary. This part begins and ends with the woman who hurls epithets at the visitors.

Several points can be made about this attempt to demonstrate the relationship between observation and explanation, and the film's use of both exposition and narrative. First, commentary in the fourth part stresses conflict between lineages; and the ways in which the conflict is moderated by specific kinds of actions, such as the use of the blunt side of an axe rather than its edge. Alternative sources of moderation, such as the hierarchy of authority represented by the village chief, receive only passing mention, possibly because they are not as visually manifest in the footage. In fact, brief mention of the chief poses one of those marginal enigmas that silently question the adequacy of the explanation adduced.

Part 3 also raises the question of the relation between written and visual ethnography, since the most precise anthropological explanation (the lineage diagrams and voice-over commentary) is also at the greatest remove from the indexical representation of the pro-filmic event (the long take, sync footage). What becomes of the excess represented by that footage? Does part three contain the scientific explanation or contain the pro-filmic event within an insufficient explanation? How adequate is such an explanation to visual observation, can an alternative, more exhaustive one be found? Is it even possible to explain the structure and function of the social codes an individual internalizes (of combat or lineage relations here, for example) without recourse to explanatory models that evacuate moving pictures of their full indexicality? Can the emotional, affective dimensions of internalization emerge alongside explanations of their social consequence, or must they inevitably be an excess in need of containment? *The Ax Fight* raises these questions indirectly; few films confront them directly; no paradigmatic solutions are at hand. The most exemplary ethno-

8.55. Seen in *Childhood Rivalry* only.

graphic films mainly exemplify problems still in need of resolution. That these problems recur across much of documentary, if not the cinema, is part of what makes the challenge of confronting them so urgent.

Finally, part 5 of *The Ax Fight* offers an explanation of the event independent of the anthropological explanations developed in parts 2–4. Part 5 explains primarily because it is a narrative with a beginning, a middle, and an end, in which the change between beginning and end is accounted for by the middle. Narrative structure itself has become an explanation of the event: a woman provokes visitors, a fight breaks out, the woman gloats over vanquished visitors. Narrative structure, then, contains the original footage, but at a considerable price. Part 5 reinforces parts 2–4 in the suggestion that the visible is not self-explanatory, and poses, implicitly, the question whether narrative or exposition provides the more adequate explanation.

This narrative explanation, on which the film does not comment, presents at least two major inadequacies. First, relations between social actors are not identified: we see the same woman at the beginning and end of the fight, but neither her relation to the combatants nor the combatants' relations among themselves receive clarification. Lineage conflict (or incest for that matter) does not appear as an evident explanation, nor even as a possibility. Second, this part leaves us with an (unidentified) image of a woman as provocateur of physical violence between men, a violence moderated only by their obedience to social rules of conflict resolution. This flirts with an ethnocentric essentialism—an assumption about the "given" nature of women that is peculiar to our culture, namely, the notion of the eternally feminine as bitch (reserving whore, mother, goddess for other occasions). The narrative sequence requires no further explanation: that's the way women are (as we all know, it seems to say in its complicity of silence).

The Ax Fight vividly demonstrates the lack of any one-to-one correlation between the visible and the empirical or between observation and explanation, yet it does not make this demonstration openly. (No discussion of these questions occurs: the film seems to trust to an unproblematic transparency between part 1 and parts 2–4 and a non-contradictory alternative transparency in part 5.) *The Ax Fight* demonstrates the need to pose the question of what to do with people in terms of organizing sounds and images to give an account of, and to account for, an "ensemble of social relations" without lapsing into essentialism at the level of "science," or the "ontology" of the image, or the "nature" of mankind.

A Common Type of Explanation

One type of explanation that recurs frequently and problematically involves recourse to some form of essentialism. We have already seen an example of this in *The Ax Fight* and in *The Hunters* where universalized meaning cloaks depicted actions in a transcendent idealism. Essentialism posits an ontology to things and, in drawing on observation, proposes transparency between what is seen and the knowable: things are what they can be seen to be. What they are seen to be in ethnography, most frequently, is some version of the family-of-man myth.[45]

Not only is there an underlying commonality to human experience, it bears a one-to-one correlation to the visible. In indirect address, images are allowed to speak "for themselves," with all their ideological associations passed on as a natural coefficient of meaning: in direct address, commentary ascribes to visual manifestations singular motives and feelings that leave little or no room for the multi-leveled meanings of manifest/latent, literal/metaphoric, or of the symbolically expressive generally. Thought attributions distill the ambiguity from mute images to give us the living essence. Even the introduction of subtitles to translate synchronous speech in unfamiliar languages, one of the most welcome innovations in ethnographic film making, runs the risk of naturalizing the exotic by corraling human communication within the perimeter of our own written language's syntax and semantics. (At least the nontranslatable still remains behind the subtitles, like those enigmas on the margins of a verbal commentary, rather than being wholly expunged.)

Conversely, indirect-address ethnography (films like *The Nuer,* the *Netsilik Eskimo* series, perhaps *Calcutta*) may propose an ultimate impenetrability to human experience (from which the textual system or contextual materials—study guides for the Netsilik films, for example—attempt to salvage some knowable dimension). This is simply the other side of the same coin: whether one-dimensional cor-

Ideology and the Image

relations exist between the visible and the knowable or whether such correlations fail to be exhaustive, leaving an uncontained and uncontainable excess of meaning, the correlation resides "out there," in the nature of things. A "full relation between word and thing, a mysterious unity of sign and referent"[46] is at work, exhausting meaning in its fullness or re-presenting an essential mysteriousness in all its grandeur. What remains lacking is a consideration of how these correlations are constructed, what ends they serve, what relations they sustain with ideology, or, in ethnographic documentary, with the dynamic of forgetting and remembrance, with the paradoxes of the indexical and the place we occupy within them.

One particularly prevalent form of essentialist reading evoking the mysteries of man's ways while also elaborating one-to-one correlations between the visible and the knowable can be called, for lack of a better term, the "bullfight syndrome." Found in *The Hunters, Dead Birds, The Lion Hunters*, in fact, in much of Flaherty and Rouch generally, and in parts of the Yanomamö series, this syndrome exhibits the following characteristics: recourse to a narrative telling of stories revolving around rituals or actions that present a manifest challenge or crisis; a tendency to speak mythopoetically about observed situations or events; depiction of central (invariably male) characters as heroes with similar relations to the environment as romantic or mimetic heroes in Northrop Frye's classification of literature;[47] the suggestion that heroes are motivated by impulses with a stoic cast and a masculine aura that possess an alignment with the unfathomable and an affinity for the exotic. Actions and enigmas often pose the question of how well one acquits oneself in the face of crisis as though the act of acquitting oneself offered testimony from some timeless region of human essence. It is a strange form of explanation for a branch of anthropology otherwise eager to uphold a differentiation between itself as science and the realm of myth. And although I have suggested these realms may not be so separate after all, the problem here revolves around the degree to which the lack of separation is itself explained, the absence of theoretical justification, the constant risk of ideological mis-representation that once again recalls the colonial enterprise in its enlightened phase: if We and They share an essential commonality, why should They not be willing to become more like Us (i.e., abandon what impedes Our progress, preserve what does not threaten it)?

The Search for a Model

Models, specific forms of puzzle-solution which Kuhn calls paradigms, imperfect though they are, can be found among existing ethnographic films. Seeking a couple of them out by way of conclusion seems preferable to advancing proscriptive rules or general theories when the actual practice of ethnographic film making remains in a relatively rudimentary state. It can no doubt continue to profit from experimentation or trial and error. If we ask, then, which ethnographic films have succeeded best in resolving the difficulties that circulate around the representation of people, the balance between observation and explanation, and between the historically specific and the culturally general, at least two come to mind: *Magical Death* (the Yanomamö series, 1973) and *Kenya Boran* (David MacDougall and James Blue, 1974).

Magical Death attempts to address a problem that frequently confronts the ethnographer: how to describe or explain a second-order system, a meta-system, of communication or behavior. These are systems of interaction based on a first-order system of signs, or conventionalized behavior that no longer mean what they would otherwise mean. Rituals and activities involving altered states of consciousness are often of this type. The emergence of a second-order system depends on the rules of logical typing and the presence of levels of referentiality in communication. Consider, for example, the difference between "Here he is" and "The sentence you just read is in English." The second statement is of a higher logical type; it metacommunicates about utterances made in English. In discussing the emergence of play as a form of communicative behavior among animals, and as a precursor to language, Gregory Bateson distinguishes the meaning of a nip from the meaning of the bite to which it refers in the following formulation, "'These actions, in which we now engage, do not denote what would be denoted by those actions which these actions denote.' The playful nip denotes the bite, but it does not denote what would be denoted by the bite."[48]

In some suggestive ways introduction of a second-order system doubles up on the paradoxical status of the film-as-experienced, its status a transparent index and organized discourse, simultaneously. Things are not what they appear to be. Their meaning cannot be finally pegged down as one thing or the other since meaning lies precisely in the space between, in both referentiality *and* self-referentiality. By referring to another level of significance, an activity can be both similar to, and different from, it. Rather than a "full relation" between word and thing, there emerges a clearly partial relation, a play of presence and absence, similarity and difference that approximates the symbolic far more than the imaginary.

Magical Death attempts to describe and explain the ceremonial activities of Dedeheiwä, a Yanomamö shaman, and several of his peers over the course of several days as he manipulates spirits hostile to another village with which his own village seeks alliance. Chag-

IDEOLOGY AND THE IMAGE

non's voice-over commentary orients us toward the ritual meaning of Dedeheiwä and the other shamans' acts. These begin with blowing an hallucinogenic powder into each other's nostrils which results in unusual behavior: rolling on the ground, making strange sounds, imitating the movements of children and animals. The commentary does not highlight aspects of what we do see, then, but describes and explains it in terms of what we cannot see, telling us, for example, that the powder is hallucinogenic or that as the shamans roll on the ground with green mucus pouring from their nostrils, the *hekura* (spirits) who will aid them in their work are taking up residence in their chests. At such a moment the shaman is like the bread and wine of the Eucharist, neither one thing nor another, or, more accurately, both things at once. As Chagnon puts it, "they were no longer just men but *hekura*."

Magical Death necessarily refutes any one-to-one bond between the visible and the empirical or between observation and explanation. It acknowledges the work of signifying systems as constructs of the analyst and, for the participants, as algorithms of the unconscious (see pp. 26–29). These unconscious rules or codes generate the visual or aural (material) signs of communication and exchange. Though manifest, these signs do not announce the invisible, conceptual system to which they belong or the first-order system(s) to which they refer other than through their sheer activity: they do not arrive with meta-communicative labels pinned to them. For someone who does not know the code, to understand what kind of message such a message is, labels of the "This is play" or "This is shamanism" type must be applied. This is what Chagnon's voice-over commentary does.

The task is distinctly different from other attempts to organize observations into descriptive or explanatory frames. Thought-attribution, for example, fills in an absence rather than identifying a second level of meaning supplementary to one already present. When Robert Gardner, in *Dead Birds,* comments on a shot of a young Dani Boy, Pua, observing male adults cultivate some land by saying, "He watches, thinking of the day when he himself will be a farmer," the attribution diverts attention from the visually manifest to disclose another level of meaning essentially autonomous from the visible. Likewise, commentary that highlights aspects of the visible, leaving an excess to contend with, or emphasizes actions so as to resolve some enigmas and suppress others, also fails to establish a precise relation between manifest/latent, presence/absence, similarity/difference. These other forms of direct-address commentary, like indirect address itself in many cases, simply appear insufficient: they leave things unsaid; they do not contain what they describe.

By contrast, "This is X" type commentary about a second-order system of communication contains without pretending to exhaust. No claim emerges that such statements contain the meaning of what we see and hear: that continues to reside in the play of difference between seen and unseen, in the doubled meaning of symbolic interaction. Instead, the statements alert us to what kind of context, what signifying systems, must be invoked in order to understand the full meaning of the visible, which continues to exist with all its paradoxical force intact rather than being deflated by attempts to fit communication and exchange to a Procrustean bed of one-dimensional signification.

Explanatory statements, then, with all their generalizing power are necessarily pegged to discrete, observable situations or events, since a second-order system like shamanistic cures or sorcery has no manifestation apart from these concrete signs it uses as the vehicle for a new system of meaning. Specific, observable acts of communication or exchange provide the essential surface.

A statement like, "This is the sacrament of communion," for example, has nothing to pin itself to except the taking of bread and wine even though for the celebrants of communion the bread and wine are no longer simply physical nourishment or a token of He who no longer lives in the flesh but *both* bread and wine *and* the flesh and blood of Christ. This paradox remains intact and exhausts (if paradox can be said to exhaust anything other than its analyst) the visibly observable, regardless of the labelling statement. Other forms of commentary establish hierarchies that attempt to flatten paradox inside a singular frame of reference. This is no more possible than the resolution of genuine contradictions through recourse to myth or narrative. (Though finally impossible, the effort may still be of value. All systems generate paradox; questions of purpose remain. But as a model proposed to encourage further exploration, *Magical Death* remains of a distinctly different type worth considerably more attention than it has received.)

Although a model, *Magical Death* is not perfect. As with Wiseman's films, some elements tend to undercut others. Specifically, Dedeheiwä's actions prompt an elaborate analogy to the country doctor of our own culture. At one point, for example, Chagnon says, "When there is sickness, Dedeheiwä is called any time of day or night to drive away spirits." This naturalizing effort raises all the familiar problems of ethnocentrism though Chagnon may have judged it an acceptable risk if the analogy helped explain Yanomamö practices to those with the political power to alter them: in this light Chagnon's analogy helps defend use of an hallucinogen in Yanomamö culture—despite pressure to prohibit it—by placing it in an understandable

IDEOLOGY AND THE IMAGE

medical context. This strategy, though, is not explicit in the film but can be inferred from the final chapter of Chagnon's book, *Yanomamö The Fierce People*, 2d edition (New York: Holt, Rinehart, Winston, 1977). Similar motivation, in this case to demonstrate the social value of an apparently bloody and senseless ritual, may have led Jean Rouch to introduce his O. Henry twist at the end of *Les Maîtres Fous*. But neither film, despite its virtues, shows any particular awareness that its subject raises significant questions and possibilities for ethnographic film generally.

Kenya Boran, by comparison, does not treat second-order systems of signification. Instead, it attempts to elicit "This is X" type meta-statements from its participants directly but in a cinematic form that departs from the normal (direct-address) means of doing so. This film, too, poses a relation between observation and explanation that allows it to remain pegged to discrete, historical events and to avoid the dangers of an essentialism. It does so, interestingly, within the mode of indirect address and by recourse to a weak narrative structure that begins to propose points of possible contact between ethnographic film and modernist texts like *Two or Three Things I Know About Her* (Jean-Luc Godard, 1966) or *Film about a woman who . . .* (Yvonne Rainer, 1974). (The most glaring deficiency in this regard, however, is the failure to take account of the saying, the production of meaning, a particularly acute deficiency for reasons discussed below.)

Kenya Boran confronts the seldom-posed problem of acculturation directly. With most ethnographic films it is as if the film makers took deliberate pains to preserve the pristine integrity of "untouched" cultures, ignoring not only their own presence as film makers but the ongoing process of cross-cultural contact as well. David MacDougall, in his article "Beyond Observational Cinema" states the problem vividly:

> What is finally disappointing in the ideal of filming "as if the camera were not there" is not that observation in itself is unimportant, but that as a governing approach it remains far less interesting than exploring the situation that actually exists. The camera *is* there, and it is held by a representative of one culture encountering another. Beside such an extraordinary event, the search for isolation and invisibility seems a curiously irrelevant ambition.[49]

Kenya Boran attempts to pose the problems of acculturation by straddling the space between generations of Boran, a pastoral tribe in northern Kenya. The film focuses on a particular village and within it on two pairs of father-son relationships. Since one son has gone off to school while the other has remained to work as a herdsman, interactions between the two youths also take on considerable importance as do discussions amongst the elders when they talk about issues such as the effect of formal education or government birth-control policies on their traditional way of life.

Lacking direct-address commentary, *Kenya Boran* cannot enunciate a theory or give a closely reasoned explanation of the issues it indirectly raises. Instead, as with Wiseman, the structure of the film as a whole provides a level of organization that itself serves as theory or explanation, though it does not do so overtly. The structure is not a theory, strictly speaking, but the manifestation or consequences of one somewhat as the shape of a bird is not a theory of aerodynamics but a manifestation or consequence of such a theory carried at the tacit level of genetic information. In fact, what the structure of the film allows us to understand about acculturation is probably closer to an interpretation offered from a perspective than an explanation informed by a rigorous theory.[50] As a weak narrative, however, the film offers the same form of explanation as part five of *The Ax Fight* or some of Wiseman's documentaries.

The mechanisms of lack, resolution of lack, and codes of actions and enigmas revolving around a hero or set of highly individuated characters are strongly attenuated. Instead, narrative closure remains at a more formal level of organization, uncoupled from the movement of particular characters. Compare figure 8.56, from the opening part of the film, with 8.57, from the closing sequence. Foreground-background relationships have been reversed. At the outset a modern road, in the process of construction, occupies the background while a herdsboy drives his cattle across the proximate terrain. At the end of the film the road, and its construction equipment, dominate the image in a vista reminiscent of the final shot from *My Darling Clementine* (John Ford, 1946). The examination of acculturation in the film attempts to account for the difference, the change between beginning and end. The large middle of the film addresses the question of change itself within an historical context, and demonstrates as well as any documentary done in indirect address the possible strategies by which history, change, and memory can become the focus of a film that does not attempt reconstruction, does not use historical footage or photographs, and does not rely on direct-address commentary to establish a context or perspective.

Yet this is not entirely true: the film does utilize direct-address commentary but in a way we are not likely to recognize correctly. This, in fact, is one of the more innovative aspects of the film. Films in indirect address like *Kenya Boran* often invoke the claim that what you see is what there would have been were you not watching, with

all the attendant problems discussed earlier. Recourse to direct address, such as the interview, abolishes the putative dimension to such a claim: what you see would never have happened were you not watching. The event (interview) took place expressly for the film.

Kenya Boran steps beyond observation, but surreptitiously, and produces the effect of interviews without the appearance of them. On several occasions, for example, when the village men gather to drink and discuss population control policies or when the two younger boys have a debate about the merits of education, these situations develop partly at the behest of the film makers. MacDougall and Blue learned what the typical routine of village life was like, when and where certain kinds of conversation were likely to occur, and then asked one of the tribespeople to raise a particular issue appropriate both to the occasion and the needs of the film makers. The resulting situations or events then unfolded without any further overt prompting and were

Documentary, Criticism and the Ethnographic Film 281

filmed in a typical observational style (long takes, unobtrusive camera, sync sound, etc.).

By recruiting one of the social actors to the catalytic function of the interviewer, *Kenya Boran* eases away from the direct-address mode of the documentary interview and toward the indirect address of observation or fiction. The result, though, actually approaches both alternatives at once: closer to fiction in the creation of situations and perhaps even of the *mise-en-scène* (along with a weak form of overall narrative structure), closer to exposition and direct address in prompting characters to speak about issues or problems that might otherwise be lived out but not articulated, or at least not so concisely articulated.

Such an approach seems to dovetail effectively with the concerns of symbolic interactionism, that branch of sociology initiated by George Herbert Mead and continued by people like Herbert Blumer or Erving Goffmann, where a primary goal is to make available the articulated perceptions or, by empathetic techniques, to gain access to the felt perceptions of social actors involved in certain situations or events. These insights then form a vital part of any subsequent theorizing. This goal joins up with a notion of self that attempts to avoid any reductive essentialism: "The person has not so much a given 'nature' from which all his activities spring and by which they can be explained, but a capability for adjusting and defining his world, taking on features of it as needed for action and gaining his 'content' from the surrounding constellation of group definitions of objects, including himself."[51] Without presenting explicit theoretical statements of this sort, *Kenya Boran*'s overall focus on acculturation and its discernible effects across and within generations provides an interpretation of change compatible with this view.

Concern to record the articulated perceptions of social actors themselves, articulations in which larger issues emerge because of their relation to the difficulties encountered in everyday life also corresponds to a dominant concern of feminist film makers who have regarded such activity, usually recorded in interview format, as an essential part of consciousness-raising around questions of women's oppression.[52] But although *Kenya Boran* shares this concern for how an articulated consciousness of patterns embedded in everyday life can lead to larger levels of understanding, it fails to locate itself in relation to this process. The "masked interview" method remains effectively masked for the viewer so that when and to what degree the film makers have opted for participation over observation, for modified interviews rather than the claim that what there is is what there would have been, remains unclear. The film makers' own position as

IDEOLOGY AND THE IMAGE

active participants in shaping the "extraordinary event" of cross-cultural communication stays tucked inside the apparent invisibility of an observational shooting style. The film makes no statement explaining its method, and those scenes that were "set up" are not marked or labelled so we can tell them apart from those that are not (except for those slight variations in speech pattern and body language that suggest a slightly more formal situation, but those are extremely difficult to identify accurately: some discussions, for example, are formal occasions in tribal culture and might easily be mistaken for occasions "set up" for the film). We must resort to extra-textual information such as discussions with the film makers or their written accounts to know how to read the film correctly.

This represents a serious deficiency, since the film can be read as purely observational and the engagement of the film makers in eliminating the putative in favor of the constructed overlooked. This leaves the place of the film makers in their own theoretical perspective unclear, and that, it seems, represents a grave methodological error. Clearly, though, this kind of error is readily surmountable, and with all its flaws, *Kenya Boran* represents as provocative and satisfactory an answer to the question of what to do with people as the ethnographic film has yet discovered.

Questions remain, but perhaps we have at least established a general sense of orientation from which to proceed. Despite *Kenya Boran*'s tentative efforts, the question of ideology, for example, continues to stand outside the domain of the ethnographic film for the most part. The awesome authority of science warrants this overt exclusion only to allow a clandestine trade in forms, assumptions, and claims that reinsert ideology in its most effective guise—as the natural and obvious (epitomized, perhaps, by a largely unwritten faith in neutral, observational camera styles and factual but also poetic voice-over commentary). Most importantly, though, ethnographic film allows us to confront certain key questions head on: what to do with people and how to erect both a film form and a film theory within the paradoxical space of the relationship between indexical sign and referent. Approaches disavowing this space and the places it tends to mark out for the viewer certainly exist, but they will almost certainly continue to exist within the marginal space of a formalistic avant-garde. (Any political avant-garde, though it may learn from formalists, will have to ground itself in representational, referential space if it is to close the distance between sign and referent to the point where the one is always on the horizon of the other.) Ethnographic film making remains fraught with risks stemming from the ease with which people can be made use of to their own detriment, and the ease with which ideology can make use of images, representations, the power and paradoxes of the indexical to keep us fixed within an imaginary, oppressive space. Yet, direct confrontation with these risks provides the greatest challenge and the most urgent task—largely because across wide swaths of the documentary and ethnographic film, it has scarcely begun.

Conclusion:
Pitching Camp on a Journey
Not Yet Ended

NO ONE HAS yet determined that, like cigarettes, the cinema is harmful to your health. Probably no one will. But the analogy does warrant a moment's pause. Not only do we develop perceptual habits of a general kind, we also develop image-viewing habits of a more specific kind. Societies manifest themselves to their members through representations, views produced to be consumed within a cycle whereby consumption grooves or scores those concrete patterns of communication and exchange through which needs are gratified. Representations are produced to satisfy wants. Wants are satisfied in the consumption of the representations produced.

In our society, representations are also produced to make profits. Behind the psychic investments established and satisfied lie economic investments made and multiplied. Visual speculations reflect economic ones. If, as Marx argued, these economic investments depend on the extraction of surplus value from individuals who sell their labor-power, then our investments in the representations offered for the gratification of wants serve to guarantee our own exploitation. Psychic investments, grounded in the sexual economy charted by Freud, flow through the conduits of production/consumption, the channels of material economics charted by Marx. Seeing is believing, they say, and so it is. The representations in which we invest constitute the nexus of ideology: our own desire seeks to gratify and replenish itself through representations that fix us in an imaginary relationship to the material conditions of existence. Speculation divests knowledge of its power: who can challenge investments that make us what we are when those very investments teach us that what we are is all there is to be?

But if we are less than we might be, then there is more to desire and speculation than meets the eye. The habits we are so accustomed to hide as much or more than they reveal. They hide the possibilities

285

of what might be in the reification of what is. These habits hide the price we pay to recognize ourselves in representations fabricated with surplus-value. We must examine our repertoire of habits carefully if we are ever to escape the fate of seeing through a glass darkly.

This challenge is an oft-repeated one.

Northrop Frye: "One who possesses such a standard [of detachment from contemporary social values] is in a state of intellectual freedom. One who does not possess it is a creature of whatever social values get to him first: he has only the compulsions of habit, indoctrination, and prejudice."[1]

Henri Bergson: "Thus, even in our own individual, individuality escapes our ken. We move amidst generalities and symbols as within a tilt-yard in which our force is effectively pitted against other forces; and fascinated by action, tempted by it, for our own good, on to the field it has selected, we live in a zone midway between things and ourselves, externally to things, externally also to ourselves."[2]

Peter Berger: "Society provides us with warm, reasonably comfortable caves, in which we can huddle with our fellows, beating on the drums that drown out the howling hyenas of the surrounding darkness. 'Ecstasy' is the act of stepping outside the caves, alone, to face the night."[3]

The response posed by Berger is also familiar. Traditionally it is delegated to liberal education and art—those forms of experience that unveil what habits, investments, regulated desires have hidden and which, for myself, combine with others to make possible change in the historical world itself.

Northrop Frye: "The ethical purpose of a liberal education is to liberate, which can only mean to make one capable of conceiving society as free, classless, and urbane. No such society exists, which is one reason why a liberal education must be deeply concerned with works of imagination."[4]

Henri Bergson: "So art, whether it be painting or sculpture, poetry or music, has no other object than to brush aside the utilitarian symbols, the conventional and socially accepted generalities, in short, everything that veils reality from us, in order to bring us face to face with reality itself."[5]

Ernst Fischer: "[The artist's] sensibility breaks through the crust of conditioning, of that which is accepted as 'normal' and sanctioned by an unchallengeable 'order'; in 'being-thus' he senses the possibility of 'being-otherwise'; in the daily occurrence he discovers the exceptional, in the inconspicuous detail he finds access to the essential, to the hitherto obscured connection."[6]

This line of reasoning, though, leads to an apparent contradiction. Art frees us from the conventional. Art falls prey to the conventions of production and consumption that guarantee through ideology the economic base of a given society. The cinema may be harmful to our health/The cinema will make us free. This contradiction has traditionally marked the geological fault between culture and popular culture, art and the mass media, the genuinely new and the formulaic. While not wishing to erase this distinction altogether, I do wish to suggest that it is inadequate. If the central concern is *ostranenie*, defamiliarizing or renewing perception, the central question is *why* this concern and not others. The question of where this concern is registered appears to become secondary, although once we have answered why, I believe we will have also suggested why the high art/popular culture division is a spurious one in this context.

The desire to see things afresh has a simple motivation: habit, routine, the usual—they deaden; they snuff out the spark of inspiration. Nothing new can come from strict adherence to what is customary. Arthur Koestler's *The Act of Creation* takes as its central premise that humor, discovery, and art all involve the unveiling of hidden similarities. This requires the bisociation of "two self-consistent but habitually incompatible frames of reference," a moment of "creative instability." At this level the work of art enjoys a privileged status in relation to any social context: it is a reminder of an instant when things were seen afresh; it is an inducement to the beholder to sacrifice the comforts of the customary for the excitement of the creative, the false serenity of logic for the untenable space of paradox.

This break with the habitual takes on additional importance if we suspect that habits are bound to an exploitative social order. In this case "creative instability" has survival value for the individual inasmuch as it allows him or her to perceive the relationship between the habitual and the exploitative that the very nature of habituation tends to veil. What becomes of paramount importance in this case is not a rendezvous with a seemingly ahistorical aesthetic experience but a moment of discovery that reflects back on the very nature of a given historical situation.

The work of art helps us see what habit hides. The discoveries made can be measured in terms of what they reveal about a given historical situation (which, of course, in no way privileges any one style, such as realism, or any one content, such as historical materialism; there are many ways to unveil and many levels on which to do it). But the contradiction posed earlier still remains to some degree: art will make us free/art is produced within the relations of production–consumption that deny us freedom, that alienate, enslave, and exploit (by our psychic investments in what is denied). What more can be said to clarify the relationship of these two sides of the work of art? We need to consider the nature of work itself momentarily.

Labor is normally considered an economic category. In Marx's analysis a worker sells his capacity to work for a price called a wage which, like other costs, is determined by the cost of production— what it takes to produce an individual who will return to work day after day. The value of the worker's labor-power is measured by what he adds to the material he works with. He helps produce commodities that have exchange value (an abstract quality related to the information borne by the commodity) as well as use value (a more concrete quality related to the materiality of the commodity, its properties as matter-energy). Workers collectively create social value in this way. They are part of the productive forces in a capitalist economy. Some of the value the worker produces is returned to him in the form of a wage so that he may purchase the commodities he himself needs. But in capitalism not all of the value contributed is returned. Some, called surplus-value, is retained by the capitalist, the owner of the means of production. The retention of a socially produced value by an individual means that the overall cost of production is less than the final value of the commodity. In short, the worker has been robbed. From this theft arise profits and from profits the growth of capitalism.

Labor-power generates a social value realized in exchange, but this value is retained by a specific class of individuals. As such, surplus-value is privatized and transformed into a thing that can be possessed—property or, more specifically, capital. Capital then becomes the measure of all things. As money it stands as the general equivalent of exchange. Exchange in these terms falls into the realm of the imaginary where the information borne by commodities is reduced to a monetary equivalent. A thing, money, becomes the determinant of all value, and exchange under the sign of money is exchange governed by the sign of a thing.

But the worker's labor-power has been employed precisely to transform things into signs (matter-energy into information). The exchange of information that is not reduced to a general equivalent, that does not occur under the sign of a thing, is symbolic exchange and stands as the sign of a relation. Symbolic exchange marks a relationship between relata; imaginary exchange reduces a relationship to a thing, a general equivalent. In our culture this general equivalent tends to be either money or the phallus.

Commodities bear information. They belong to systems of signification, as Roland Barthes' *Mythologies* so eloquently demonstrates. Their exchange testifies to their status as signs, especially in advanced industrial capitalism where the purchase of commodities is so often surrounded by promises far in excess of what the commodity

IDEOLOGY AND THE IMAGE

can deliver. Their use-value recedes as their function and status as signs inflate. Labor-power fabricates signs (commodities) whose meaning or signification speaks less to relations than to a thing (money). The possibility of symbolic exchange fades as imaginary exchange predominates.

Because economics involves the production of commodities that function as signs signifying their value in relation to a general equivalent of exchange, economics is a semiotic activity. It involves the production and exchange of signs organized into systems (for example, dress, architecture, transportation, entertainment) and governed by codes (those largely unconscious rules determining how production/consumption, one form of communication and exchange is carried out). The overall system or the dominant form of social order is itself produced by the circulation of signs (commodities) in systems through which the society represents itself. The task of ideology is to perpetuate the system as a whole, that is, to reproduce the existing relations of production, even when these relations of production establish a contradiction with the productive forces as they do through the extraction of surplus-value under capitalism.

Ideology is itself an effect of communication and exchange carried out through the material practice of existing institutions. Its purpose is to inculcate an acceptance of the existing relations of production as a given beneficial to both the working class and the ruling class. This acceptance is only sometimes won by conscious acquiescence to reasoned argument. More often it derives from the psychic investments we learn to make, perhaps above all the desire for recognition mediated by those very signs (commodities) that are themselves measured by the general equivalent of exchange (money).

Ideology assigns us a place in the relation of production, the place carved out by Descartes' cogito—the self as ego, consciousness, or, in recent terminology, the subject. The subject is produced as a discrete unit, a clear and distinct individual, so that it may individually sell its labor-power within a nexus of cash relations. The negative side of the ledger, the theft of labor-power as surplus-value (which leads to profit), is masked over. Instead, the positive side gains stress: individuality, freedom and responsibility, choice, initiative. Our sense of self-as-subject becomes obvious, natural. *It becomes a habit.* And within the habitual reside those mechanisms spurring us on to invest in the very relations of production that call us forth at the same time as they exploit us. Under capitalism we exist, in the most fundamental sense, to be exploited. (Of course many of us are exploited rather painlessly—the surplus-value extracted from others [from women, minority groups, most Third World people, the lowest paid, etc.] allows advanced capitalism to reward many individuals handsomely. Whether any reward under such a set of conditions can be, finally, reward enough is something each of us must struggle to answer in his/her own way.)

Ideology seeks to mask contradictions and paradox inherent in a given historical situation. Capitalist ideology seeks to legitimize the accumulation of capital (social property) in the hands of the few (as private property) for the "benefit" of all. The task is impossible. To hide this impossibility, ideology must disavow the existence of class antagonism and struggle. It must do so with the signs and systems of signification at its disposal. Ideology seeks to resolve or hide contradictions (namely, that between the relations of production and the productive forces) with what is on hand—namely, things, things worked into the shape of signifiers by labor. In other words, ideology has to hide contradictions using those things that in their function as signs bear the trace of the very same contradictions ideology seeks to hide!

Ideology operates like Lévi-Strauss's *bricoleur*: it makes do with what's on hand—with the systems of signs produced and circulating at any given historical moment—in order to mask those contradictions that emerge in the production of these very signs. A society shall be known by its works. Its works provide the representations by which a society gives witness to its own existence. Representations provide the material with which ideology proposes an imaginary relationship to the real conditions of existence. But these representations are a product of the real conditions of existence.

To serve ideology, representations must be made to appear to be other than what they are. Above all, they must appear to lack these very contradictions that informed their production. They must appear as signs of eternal values—harmony, wholeness, radiance, a natural and ideal world spun from the representations of an existing social order. Existing social relations and values are confirmed as the souce of a fabricated ideality. By means of such a confirmation, we are led to believe (like the subjects in Plato's cave) that an imaginary relationship to the real conditions of existence provides us with everything there is to be had, including our-selves.

The two sides of a work of art—its potential to liberate/its threat to habituate—stem from its paradoxical relationship to ideology and the relations of production. Like ideology, art must function as does a *bricoleur*, making do with the systems of representation on hand. Unlike ideology, art need not function to confirm what is as all there need be. Instead, art preserves the possibility that what is differs radically from what might be or ought to be. Art can put ideology on display; in its liberating mode it helps us see afresh the pure contingency of what otherwise appears as necessity. The veils hiding the tactics and purpose of ideology are lifted.

Yet the function of ideology is, among other things, to mask or attenuate the threat posed by art. The circulation of art within channels designed for commodity exchange is one such mechanism. The mechanical reproduction of art is another. Film, for example, depends absolutely on mechanical reproduction. This dependence absorbs films within the existing relations of production more thoroughly than those art forms still dependent on artisanal production in the first instance, which only enter into mass production and commodity exchange secondarily (novels, paintings, sculpture, etc.).

Consequently, another paradox emerges: film inevitably bears within it the trace of the existing relations of production at the same time as it is more fully subject to the capacity of those relations of production to cover their own trace through ideology. The balance between training for liberation and routinization seems to shift with the creation of works of art in the age of mechanical reproduction. (Even whether to call them art, or whether art itself has not been fundamentally changed becomes a central question.) In Walter Benjamin's terms, the work of art seems to lose its "aura."

Although the balance may shift, I do not believe the basic tension is lost. It does mean that much art is produced precisely to fulfill an ideological role. Under these circumstances the moment of liberation or discovery may be displaced from the initial encounter with the work of art to a more prolonged struggle of critical engagement directed toward revealing what ideology seeks to deny but which art, and ideology, cannot help but display.

The display may be carefully hidden, however. Like the Indian of yesterday we must become adept at reading signs not left or arranged to facilitate our tracking them to their source. We need to learn how to recognize what Freud termed secondary revision (as well as condensation and displacement)—those arrangements of signs fabricated to mislead, to throw us off the trail. We must know how to recognize and order signs where there appear to be none; the naive traveller may only see a "natural" order where we can learn to find the signs of work, traversal.

This form of reading, a kind of work, and play, seems not only possible but essential. In a situation where so many signs (commodities) are produced specifically to mislead, to throw us off the trail, knowing how to find our way amongst the most numerous and commonplace of signs becomes a matter of survival. On this score I must disagree with James Roy MacBean when he argues that "it is a *secondary* task . . . to apply the Marxist analysis to some of the multitude of films that serve to reinforce the dominant bourgeois capitalist ideology."[7] In MacBean the word "multitude" seems heavy with condescension. For me it is amidst the multitude that our lives are shaped and the possibility *and* necessity for struggle is strongest. Radical films, precisely because they themselves help lift the veil of ideology, need far less critical explication than those that help weave it all the more densely. Films and other art made under the sign of the dominant ideology are part of the series of representations by which our society hopes to maintain our investment in its perpetuation. If, as I've suggested, that perpetuation depends on the extraction of surplus value, then it is essential we gain use of those tools that will enable us to find the trace, however faint, of the real conditions of existence wherein such works of art were in fact produced. In following the signs of the cinema along such a trail we can hope to come upon those very contradictions and paradox that various forms of camouflage attempt to conceal. I hope that my studies of Sternberg, Hitchcock, Wiseman, and ethnographic film have demonstrated the viability of such an approach.

As with ideology, there is more to art than meets the eye. Critical inquiry, materialist praxis, seeks to reveal a hidden dimension within the surfaces of representation. The recognition of a basic eccentricity—that there is more to see and do than meets the eye—is the recognition of all that ideology seeks to deny. A falsely stable, falsely centered set of imaginary relations is overturned. The recognition that "we" is the sign of a relationship—that we are more than I can ever be, that what is is far less than what ought to be—is a pleasurable recognition that threatens to outweigh the pleasure of imaginary recognition. The discovery of how art covers over the signs of contradiction it must bear within it yields an aesthetic pleasure that is none the worse for being historically situated. Rather than the aesthetics of timeless reverie, it is an aesthetics guided by the materialist premise that to change your life you must also change the world.

Appendix A

Flicker and Motion in Film
by Susan J. Lederman and Bill Nichols

IF THE CINEMA differs from still photography in its ability to create the impression of motion, how is this effect achieved? A simple question to which most film books give a simple answer—"persistence of vision."

The catechism runs like this:

> According to the principle of persistence of vision, the eye retains the static image during the period of darkness, so that one image, in effect, is dissolved into the next to provide either a continuous view of a static image, or, more importantly, an illusion of continuous motion. (Lincoln F. Johnson, *Film: Space, Time, Light and Sound*, p. 3.)

> The key to the success of this system of recording and projecting a series of still images that give the appearance of continuous movement lies in what Ingmar Bergman calls a certain "defect" in human sight: persistence of vision. The brain holds an image for a short period of time after it has disappeared, so it is possible to construct a machine that can project a series of still images quickly enough so that they merge psychologically and the illusion of motion is maintained. (James Monaco, *How to Read a Film*, p. 73.)

The catechism is not limited to introductory texts either:

> The meaning effect produced (by projection) does not depend only on the content of the images but also on the material procedures by which an illusion of continuity, dependent on the persistence of vision, is restored from discontinuous elements. (Jean-Louis Baudry, "Ideological Effects of the Basic Cinematographic Apparatus," *Film Quarterly* 38, no. 2 [Winter 1974–75]:42.)

Dr. Susan J. Lederman teaches in the Department of Psychology, Queen's University, Kingston, Ontario.

. . . we must here explain, on the other hand, how it was that the invention took so long to emerge, since all the prerequisites had been assembled and the persistence of the image on the retina had been known for a long time. (André Bazin, "The Myth of Total Cinema," in *What Is Cinema*, I, p. 19.)

It is time to set the record straight. The sheer embarrassment of watching some film scholars repeat what remains for them accepted fact when that information has been discredited by perceptual psychologists since the early part of this century would be reason enough. An added impetus stems from attempts, like Baudry's, to posit ideological effects to the basic cinematic apparatus, including the projection and perception of a series of still images upon a screen. This work depends heavily on analogies with psychoanalytic concepts like the mirror-phase, the imaginary, fetishism, and voyeurism; and while we believe much of it may be of value, it is also important that arguments advanced here not be based upon incorrect concepts at the level of perceptual psychology.

The impression of movement is not due to the persistence of vision. To begin with, "persistence of vision" is itself an imprecise term. We can only guess that film writers are referring to what psychologists call "positive afterimages."[1] When a person stares at a light, he can still see it after the light has been turned off. Positive afterimages retain the color and brightness relations of the original stimulus. Common sense would suggest that the positive afterimage is a plausible explanation for motion perception in film since it allows one image-frame* to "bleed" into another, despite the fact that the beam of light projecting the film-frame is itself intermittent. *But this fusion occurs regardless of whether motion is perceived or not.* The appearance of a continuously visible series of images, in other words, is a phenomenon distinct from the appearance of motion.

Can "persistence of vision" (which we now assume means positive afterimages) explain either one of these phenomena? Not according to research by psychologists. If this is so, we are then presented with a situation involving two distinct perceptual phenomena: *flicker* and *apparent motion.* We shall examine each in turn, bearing in mind that the perceptual mechanisms supporting these phenomena remain areas of active research in psychology today.

The first phenomenon is known as *visual flicker.* Flicker was a discernible problem in the early days of cinema when the frequency of light flashes was between 16 and 24 frames/sec. Psychologists[2] have studied the nature of visual flicker by rotating a sectored disk with a light source directly behind it so that light passes through intermit-

---

Image-frame refers to the image perceived when a single frame of film is projected onto a screen; *film-frame* refers to the actual frame of film itself.

APPENDIX A

tently during the disk's rotation. This will yield different perceptual experiences at different speeds: "As the frequency of intermittence is increased to about 8 to 10^{Hz}, the light part of the cycle becomes brighter, and, to some, peculiarly unpleasant with a hypnotic quality. At higher frequencies, the alternation becomes less and less marked until only a faint tremulous appearance remains. Finally (above a certain threshold), the subject reports seeing a perfectly steady light which he is unable to distinguish from a stimulus that is steadily illuminated and matched in color and brightness to the physically intermittent light."[3]

Fusion only occurs above a certain threshold frequency (called CFF—critical fusion frequency), which is dependent upon variables such as illuminance.[4] The typical relationship between these two variables is shown in the accompanying graph:

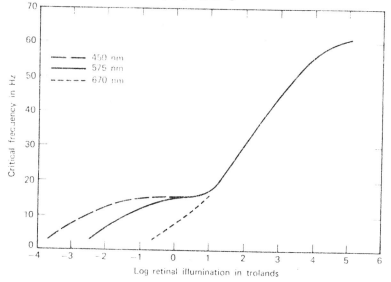

CFF as a function of intensity for several wavelengths

(Source: H. R. Schiffman, *Sensation and Perception: An Integrated Approach*, reprinted with permission of J. Wiley & Sons, Inc. The graph is modified from Hecht and Shlaer, *Journal of General Physiology* 19 (1936):965–77.)

CFF increases as the level of illuminance is increased. The relationship obtained suggests two important ideas that are relevant to our discussion of flicker in film.

First, the low rates of projection originally used in motion pictures were likely below fusion threshold. The flicker perceived might thus have been the result of the visual system's ability to differentiate the on/off periods of successive image-frame presentations. The obvious solution to the problem was to pick a rate which the visual system could *not* resolve, i.e. some frequency above which fusion occurs:

> In the early days of motion pictures, it was discovered that this 24-frames/second rate was not pleasant to watch (due to flicker). By designing the (projector) shutter with two equally spaced blades, it is possible to project each frame twice, thereby increasing the field to 48 times/second.[5]

And where the level of illuminance is relatively high (where we would expect from the graph a higher CFF) as in most 16mm projection, three blades can be used. This increases the rate to 72 "flicks" per second, and further ensures a smooth, continuously fused image.

The relationship between CFF and illuminance also makes it clear that "visual persistence," i.e. positive afterimages, *cannot* underlie the experience of fusion in motion pictures. Graham puts it succinctly:

> The early idea that fusion is the result of "persistence" of vision and that it can be explained in relation to the duration of a positive after-image is obviously untenable. With an increase in the stimulation luminance, although the positive after-image lasts longer, CFF is elevated, that is, the value of "persistence" based on fusion frequency *decreases*.[6]

Other work also challenges the role of positive afterimages in film perception. When a relatively intense stimulus is briefly presented to a person placed in a dark room, as many as seven successive afterimages are frequently observed.[7] This series involves alternating positive and negative afterimages,* an experience never to our knowledge reported during a film presentation. Furthermore, the first afterimage, which is positive, does not occur until some 50 msec. after the cessation of the initial stimulus. During an equivalent period of time in the projection of a motion picture, however, not one but three successive image-frames would be presented. For this reason it is very unlikely that afterimages contribute to the fusion of successive image presentations in film.

The result of the eye's summing successive image-frames over time is fusion, the elimination of flicker, and not necessarily any impression of movement. Fusion masks the work of the cinematic apparatus, the intermittent mechanism of the projector that blocks the projection of light during the interval when one frame replaces another in the projector gate. Fusion operates even in the projection of a shot of an absolutely stationary scene. It creates the impression of a solid, stable world of successive images *but does not yield the impression of movement.*

---

*See note 1 of this appendix.

It seems safe to conclude that explanatory recourse to the term "persistence of vision" is incorrect and outdated. It does not explain the absence of flicker from successive image-frames nor, as we will see next, does it explain apparent motion within those frames. It is to be hoped that we've seen the last of film writing that ignores scholarship in other disciplines. This closed-mindedness provides an artificial life-support system, keeping alive concepts that ought to have died long ago.

Let us now turn to the second phenomenon, *apparent motion*. Clearly, apparent motion, "the perception of movement when the stimulus is not moving physically,"[8] is at work in film rather than the perception of real movement.[9] Each frame, a static image, is held absolutely stationary while light passes through it from the projector to the screen. Any impression of movement from one frame to the next must be apparent under these conditions.

Many kinds of apparent movement have been observed; J.O. Robinson's *The Psychology of Visual Illusion* catalogues most of them.[10] Of these the category pertinent to film perception is stroboscopic movement—"the rapid and successive presentation of stationary stimuli"[11]—first investigated by Max Wertheimer.[12] Wertheimer, a founder of Gestalt psychology, seized on the phenomenon of apparent movement to argue that the perception of movement was "as direct an experience as . . . brightness or hue, an experience mediated by its own physiological mechanism rather than by experiences of change in position."[13] (His point was in contradistinction to older structuralist theories of perception; these theories argued that complex perceptions like movement were the result of a summation of more basic sensations arising from the successive stimulation of points on the retina.)[14]

Wertheimer's own experiments involved two short vertical lines separated by a short distance. They were presented sequentially with a brief interval between the two exposures. With very brief intervals, simultaneity was reported; with longer intervals, successiveness. At intermediate values, however, subjects reported different kinds of apparent movement. Since then, other forms of apparent movement have been discovered. A full description of the various forms of apparent motion (sometimes collectively referred to as the "phi phenomenon") is of some interest:[15]

a. with a very short interstimulus interval, the stimuli appeared simultaneously.
b. over a mid-range of intervals (from 30–200 msec), various forms of apparent movement were reported.
   1. alpha: apparent expansion and contraction seen when two physically or perceptually different stimuli are presented.

2. beta: apparent motion of the stimulus object from point 1 to point 2 (occurred at interval values around 60 msec, but due to the considerable differences in the perception of film, we should not anticipate that the same values will hold true.)
3. gamma: apparent expansion and contraction of the stimulus as the luminance is increased or decreased.
4. delta: apparently reversed motion when the second stimulus is brighter.
5. phi: "pure" or disembodied movement without an attendant stimulus-object.
6. bow: apparent movement follows an arc around an obstruction between the lines in the third dimension rather than the shortest route.
c. with longer exposure intervals, the stimuli appeared successively without the appearance of movement.

Of these the one most prevalent in cinema is beta movement (called "optimal" movement by Wertheimer). The technological apparatus for recording and projecting motion pictures works to produce this phenomenon under a wide range of circumstances.[16]

Although the work of perceptual psychologists makes it very clear that the appearance of smooth, continuous movement in film is dependent on exceeding the CFF and establishing the conditions necessary for beta movement, there is no experimental work we know of that explores the parameters within which the apparent movement of recognizable visually complex objects like people remains possible in film. Even under restricted experimental conditions such as Wertheimer's, where only two simple stimuli are utilized, there is an appreciable range of limits (some of which have been semi-formalized as Korte's Laws[17]).

These limits, however, pertain to carefully controlled conditions and can be stretched. Continued practice or learning leads to increased reports of beta movement, even under controlled conditions,[18] and "the more nearly two stimuli presented in sequence connote a familiar moving object, the greater will be the range of other stimulus variables (such as exposure duration, the interstimulus spatial separation, and the interstimulus temporal separation) giving rise to the perception of good apparent movement."[19] Even when forms of apparent movement other than beta movement are present and discernible, most filmgoers do not perceive them.[20]

Today, scientific research in this area aims primarily at determining the nature of the mechanisms involved in the perception of apparent movement. At this point two hypotheses are under investigation, although they are not mutually exclusive. Both hypotheses are well

APPENDIX A

summarized in a recent paper by Jacob Beck and Albert Steven:

> The results (of the reported experiments) are interpreted to support the hypotheses that the perception of apparent movement involves the excitation of specific neural mechanisms selectively responsive to sequential changes in stimulus position. An alternative hypothesis is that the perception of apparent movement involves an inference based on the separate registrations of the position of that stimulus at an earlier point in time.[21]

This alternative hypothesis is pursued in a study by Sigman and Rock. They suggest that stroboscopic movement perception may be considered " . . . as the solution on the part of the perceptual system to the problem posed by the alternating appearance and disappearance of the stimulus objects. Under typical conditions there is no information provided which could account for such unexplainable stimulus change, so that movement is the plausible solution."[22] Sigman and Rock set up conditions in which the alternating appearance and disappearance of two lights could be explained as continuously present lights that were progressively covered and uncovered by an object passing in front of them. Under such conditions, the subjects did not perceive apparent motion. "These findings are interpreted as supporting the theory that perception results from a process analogous to intelligent problem solving."[23] Although it remains quite likely that both movement-detection cells and a higher-order process of inference or "filling in" are involved, the only qualification about their possible relationship that can be advanced with certainty is that the work of a feature detector "needs to be consistent with contextual stimulus information which indicates that motion is a plausible explanation of the alternating appearance and disappearance of the stimuli."[24]

Further, in keeping with previous attempts in recent film theory to relate socially significant phenomena to ideology, we may speculate that the perception of apparent movement, the impression of movement in the cinema, holds more than psycho-physiological interest. Certainly innumerable commentators have cited the impression of movement as a fundamental part of any cinematic appeal based on realism. It so closely approximates our perception of real movement that Bazin's sense of film as a decal or imprint is easy to understand even though he fails to see that it is the approximation of the codes of normal perception at work rather than a literal transfer of the stimulus-object.

We might just note that once it was possible to project film above the Critical Flicker Frequency a potential point of contact was made with ideology (independent of the appearance of motion). Jean-Louis

Baudry, for example, argues that this masking of difference (by projecting "flicks" at a rate greater than CFF) yields an illusion of continuity central to setting the viewer-as-subject into place: "continuity is an attribute of the subject. It appears in the cinema in the two complementary aspects of a 'formal' continuity established through a system of negated differences and narrative continuity in the filmic space."[25] By guaranteeing that under normal conditions perception always occurs above the CFF, the cinema appears to present difference as unity, absence and presence as continuous presence, a stable, coherent fullness that guarantees the reciprocal unity of the (imaginary) subject in a manner similar to the still photographic image or Renaissance painting.

The development of cinematic technology has served to guarantee the sense of animated unity and coherence to a series of immobile, flickering images in such a way that we are tempted to recall Lacan's theory of a mirror-phase. We may even speculate whether the cinema does not propose a place for us similar to that of the mirror-phase, namely incorporation as subjects, the fixation of self-as-subject. There can be no simple repetition, however; for better or worse the mirror-phase has been left behind in childhood. What recurs are situations reinforcing or based on our initiation into the imaginary realm, situations of considerable ideological significance:

> And if the eye which moves is no longer fettered by a body, by the laws of matter and time, if there are no more assignable limits to its displacement—conditions fulfilled by the possibilities of shooting and of film—the world will not only be constituted by this eye but for it.[26]

Created in our own image, as an image of an omnipotent I (eye), the cinematic universe exists to be beheld, an act leaving us beholden to occupy our place as subjects: . . . of the people, by the people, for the people—the very cornerstone of an ideology based upon the proclamation of emancipation for subjects thereby beholden to it.

This line of argument requires something of a proviso, however. It is too easy. The cinema is ideologically tainted from square one—by the work of the technological apparatus. An ideology is embedded so deeply that no discourse, no text is conceivable that would not fall prey to it (even films reflecting upon, say, fusion like Sharits's "T, O, U, C, H, I, N, G" must do so with the same "dirty" apparatus as the films that simply transmit the "taint" unquestioningly). Besides, as we have noted earlier, the imaginary realm and the constitution of the self-as-subject are not wholly ideological in a negative sense. The constitution of the subject or ego is a necessary stage toward the child's initiation into the symbolic realm as it is mediated by language. The ideological risk, in our society, comes from the irruption or return of the imaginary within the symbolic—the reduction of language to empty speech between reified subjects rather than a sign of relationship, the reduction of exchange generally to imaginary exchange between subjects measured in terms of a reifying general equivalent, most often, in our case, money. It is here that the imaginary realm joins with and supports ideology.

Care must be taken not to throw out the baby with the bathwater. The concept of self-as-subject is not ideological through and through. What is at stake is how this subject is placed within a larger, and, ideally, controlling context of symbolic exchange. Politically revolutionary cinema need not necessarily denounce its own technological base and refuse to present a coherent, stable world of successive images in apparent movement. The self-as-subject can be the locus of social change as well as the anchor point of ideology. Brecht, for example, envisioned an art that would call forth conscious subjects desirous of realizing their capability to change the way things are for how they might be. Conceptions of ideology like Baudry's run the risk of eliminating any site from which contestation and change might issue. There is a danger of fetishizing the materiality of the cinema, of valorizing critiques of the technological apparatus above and beyond questions of the use of the apparatus so that the possibility of a thorough deconstruction or critique of the cinema as a social institution becomes remote:

> This difficulty may . . . spring from a nondialectical notion of ideology. Dominant ideology is dominant, not total, and the technology, as well as the signifying practice, of the cinema is created in the field of ideology and is subject to the stresses and contradictions of that field. [without being utterly identical to that field; a text is not only subject to contradictions, contradictions may also be subjected to the work of the text—BN] Baudry assigned to the cinema instruments a single ideological effect. . . . this required him to refrain from questioning why discontinuity was present in the linking of shots, a discontinuity necessitating the "violence" of the codes of continuity.[27]

In other words, discontinuity may be a necessary step toward continuity where a dialectical relationship of continuity/discontinuity is upheld. Calling forth the self-as-subject does not necessarily place us under the heel of a total ideology. In our society the risk is always that the imaginary relations sustained between subject and other will be dominant, but it is as much as subjects as anything else that we must contest this dominance if we are to avoid lapsing into a romantic vision of pre-imaginary, pre-verbal one-ness with the world. It is one thing to argue that practice occurs within an ideological field, another to argue that it is wholly determined thereby. It is the first assertion that guides the present study.

Flicker and Motion in Film

The dichotomies summarized below are based on Metz's description in *Film Language*, pp. 119–46.

1. Autonomous Shot (a segment with only one shot; includes four types of inserts: extradiegetic, subjective, displaced diegetic, explanatory)

Autonomous Segments (parts of the whole film; not parts of parts)

Syntagmas (segments of more than one shot)

Achronological Syntagmas

2. Parallel Syntagma (2 or more alternating motifs, no temporal or spatial relationship specified)

3. Bracket Syntagma (no temporal or spatial relationship, nonserial [not alternating], typical samples of a given order of reality, a conceptual mode)

Chronological Syntagmas

4. Descriptive Syntagma (succession of shots but no temporal progression, denotes simultaneity)

Narrative Syntagmas (nonsimultaneous; exhibit temporal progression)

APPENDIX B

Appendix B   Christian Metz's
Grande Syntagmatique

5. Alternate Syntagma ("parallel montage," alternating series of
shots—each occurring simultaneously, but each series
progressing temporally as well)

{

Linear
Narrative
Syntagmas
(images
displaying
a single
temporal
succession)

{

6. Scene (experienced as a
spatio-temporal continuum despite
editing)

Sequences
(exhibit
spatio-
temporal
disconti-
nuities)

{

7. Ordinary Sequence (omits
insignificant time
periods, spatial
transitions; omissions
carry no special
significance)

8. Episodic Sequence
(organized omissions;
each shot becomes
representative of a
longer frame of reference
which is therefore
presented in a distilled
form)

Selected Sources

Adams, John W. "Viewing Practices/Ethnographic Films." Manuscript. Published as "Representation and Context in Ethnographic Film." *Film Criticism* 4,1 (Fall 1979).

Alberti, Leon Battista. *Della Pittura*. Ed. G.C. Sansoni. Florence: n.p., 1950.

Allen, Jeanne. "Self-Reflexivity in Documentary." *Ciné-Tracts* 1,2 (1977).

Althusser, Louis. *For Marx*. Trans. Ben Brewster. New York: Vintage-Random House, 1969.

———. *Lenin and Philosophy and Other Essays*. Trans. Ben Brewster. New York and London: Monthly Review Press, 1971.

Altman, Charles F. "Psychoanalysis and Cinema: The Imaginary Discourse." *Quarterly Review of Film Studies* 2,3 (1977).

Anderson, Joseph, and Barbara Fischer. "The Myth of Persistence of Vision." *Journal of the University Film Association* 30,4 (1978).

Anderson, Lindsay. "The Films of Alfred Hitchcock." *Sequence* No. 9 (1949).

Andrew, Dudley. "The Neglected Tradition of Phenomenology in Film Theory." *Wide Angle* 2,2 (1978).

Appel, Alfred, Jr. "The Eyehole of Knowledge: Voyeuristic Games in Film and Literature." *Film Comment* 9,3 (1973).

Aristotle. *The Rhetoric of Aristotle*. Trans. J.E.C. Welldon. London: Macmillan, 1886.

Arnheim, Rudolf. *Art and Visual Perception*. Berkeley and Los Angeles: University of California Press, 1971.

Arnold, Gary H. "Birds and Gulls." Review of *The Birds*. *Moviegoer* No. 1 (1964).

Atkins, Thomas R., ed. *Frederick Wiseman*. New York: Simon and Schuster, 1976.

Balickci Asen. *The Netsilik Eskimo*. Garden City, New York: The Natural History Press, 1970.

Barnouw, Eric. *Documentary: A History of the Non-Fiction Film*. New York and London: Oxford University Press, 1975.

Barsam, Richard, ed. *Nonfiction Film: Theory and Criticism*. New York: E.P. Dutton, 1976.

Barthes, Roland. "Science vs. Literature." *Times Literary Supplement*. 28 September 1967.

———. "Rhetoric of the Image." *Working Papers in Cultural Studies* No. 1 (1971).

304

——. "Style and Its Image." In *Literary Style: A Symposium.* Ed. Seymour Chatman. London and New York: Oxford University Press, 1971.

——. *Mythologies.* Trans. Annette Lavers. London: Jonathan Cape, 1972.

——. *S/Z: An Essay.* Trans. Richard Miller. New York: Hill and Wang, 1974.

——. *The Pleasure of the Text.* Trans. Richard Miller. New York: Hill and Wang, 1975.

Bate, W.J., ed. *Criticism: The Major Texts.* New York: Harcourt Brace Jovanovich, 1970.

Bateson, Gregory. *Naven.* 2d ed. 1936. Reprint. Stanford: Stanford University Press, 1958.

——. *Steps to an Ecology of Mind.* New York: Ballantine Books, 1972.

——. *Mind and Nature.* New York: E.P. Dutton, 1979.

Bateson, Gregory, and Margaret Mead. "'For God's Sake, Margaret.' Conversation with Gregory Bateson and Margaret Mead." *The CoEvolution Quarterly* 10, 21 (1976).

Baudrillard, Jean. *The Mirror of Production.* Trans. Mark Poster. St. Louis: Telos Press, 1975.

Baudry, Jean-Louis. "Ideological Effects of the Basic Cinematographic Apparatus." *Film Quarterly* 28, 2 (1974–75).

——. "The Apparatus." *Camera Obscura* No. 1 (1976).

Baxter, John. *The Cinema of Josef von Sternberg.* London: A. Zwemmer, 1971.

Baxter, Peter. "On the Naked Thighs of Miss Dietrich." *Wide Angle* 2, 2 (1978).

Bazin, André. *What Is Cinema?* 2 vols. Berkeley and Los Angeles: University of California Press, 1967.

Beck, Jacob, and Albert Steven. "An After Effect to Discrete Stimuli: Producing Apparent Movement and Succession." *Perception and Psychophysics* 12, 6 (1972).

Beck, Jacob, A. Elsner, and C. Silverstein. "Position Uncertainty and the Perception of Apparent Movement." *Perception and Psychophysics* 21, 1 (1977).

Becker, Howard S., ed. *Perspectives in Deviance.* New York: Collier-Macmillan, 1964.

Bellert, Drena. "On a Condition of the Coherence of Texts." *Semiotica* No. 2 (1970).

Belz, Carl. Review of *The Birds. Film Culture* No. 31 (1963–64).

Benjamin, Walter. *Illuminations.* Trans. Harry Zohn. Ed. Hannah Arendt. New York: Harcourt, Brace and World, 1968.

——. "A Short History of Photography." Trans. Stanley Mitchell. *Screen.* 13, 1 (1972).

Benoist, Jean-Marie. "The Fictional Subject." *Twentieth Century Studies* No. 6 (1971).

Benveniste, Emile. *Problèmes de linguistique générale.* Paris: Gallimard, 1966.

——. *Problems in General Linguistics.* Trans. Mary Elizabeth Meek. Coral Gables, Florida: University of Miami Press, 1971.

Berger, John, et al. *Ways of Seeing.* London: BBC and Penguin-Allen Lane, 1972.

Berger, Peter L. *Invitation to Sociology: A Humanistic Perspective.* Garden City, New York: Doubleday, 1963.

Selected Sources

Berger, Peter L., and Thomas Luckman. *The Social Construction of Reality.* Garden City, New York: Doubleday, 1966.

Bogdanovich, Peter. Review of *The Birds. Film Culture* No. 28 (1963).

———. *The Cinema of Alfred Hitchcock.* New York: Museum of Modern Art, 1962.

Booth, Wayne C. *The Rhetoric of Fiction.* Chicago: University of Chicago Press, 1966.

Bordwell, David. *"Notorious." Film Heritage* 4, 3 (1969).

Brannigan, Edward. "Formal Permutations of the Point-of-View Shot." *Screen* 16, 3 (1975).

Brecht, Bertolt. "Against Georg Lukács." *New Left Review* No. 84 (1974).

Breen, Myles P. "The Rhetoric of the Short Film." *Journal of the University Film Association* 30, 2 (1978).

Britton, Andrew. "The Ideology of *Screen." Movie* No. 26 (1978/79).

Brown, Bruce. *Marx, Freud, and the Critique of Everyday Life: Toward a Permanent Cultural Revolution.* New York and London: Monthly Review Press, 1973.

Brown, Harold I. *Perception, Theory, and Commitment: The New Philosophy of Science.* Chicago: Precedent Publishing, 1977.

Browne, Nick. *"Cahiers du Cinéma's* Rereading of Hollywood Cinema: An Analysis of Method." *Quarterly Review of Film Studies* 3, 3 (1978).

Burch, Noël, and Jorge Dana. "Propositions." *Afterimage* No. 5 (1974).

———. *Theory of Film Practice.* Trans. Helen R. Lane. New York: Praeger Publishers, 1973.

Burgin, Victor. "Looking at Photographs." *Screen Education* No. 24 (1977).

Burke, Kenneth. *A Grammar of Motives.* 1945. Reprint. Berkeley and Los Angeles: University of California Press, 1969.

———. *A Rhetoric of Motives.* Berkeley and Los Angeles: University of California Press, 1969.

Burnett, Ron. "Film/Technology/Ideology." *Ciné-Tracts* 1, 1 (1977).

Butterfield, Hubert, *The Origins of Modern Science.* London: G. Bell and Sons, 1957.

Callenbach, Ernest. Review of *The Birds. Film Quarterly* 16, 4 (1963).

Calvino, Italo. "Notes Toward a Definition of Narrative Form as Combinative Process." *Twentieth Century Studies* No. 3 (1970).

Cameron, Ian, and V.F. Perkins. "Hitchcock." *Movie* No. 6 (1963).

Campbell, Russell, ed. "Radical Cinema in the 30's: Film and Photo League." *Jump Cut* No. 14 (1977).

Caughie, John, ed. *Television: Ideology and Exchange.* London: British Film Institute, 1978.

Cavell, Stanley. *Must We Mean What We Say? A Book of Essays.* New York: Charles Scribner's Sons, 1969.

Chagnon, Napoleon A. *Yanomamö: The Fierce People.* 1968. Reprint. New York: Holt, Rinehart and Winston, 1977.

Chatman, Seymour. *Story and Discourse: Narrative Structure in Fiction and Film.* Ithaca: Cornell University Press, 1978.

"Cinéthique on *Langage et Cinéma." Screen* 14, 1/2 (1973).

Cohen, Hart. "Ethno-Hermeneutics: Ethnography as Anomaly." *Ciné-Tracts* 1, 1 (1977).

———. "Mapping Anthropology on Film." *Ciné-Tracts* 2, 2 (1979).

Collins, Richard. *Television News.* London: British Film Institute, 1976.

Cooley, Charles Horton. *Human Nature and the Social Order.* New York: Charles Scribner's, 1902.

Coward, Rosalind, and John Ellis. *Language and Materialism: Developments in Semiology and the Theory of the Subject.* London: Routledge and Kegan Paul, 1977.

Cowie, Elizabeth. "Women, Representation, and the Image." *Screen Education* No. 23 (1977).

Culler, Jonathan. "Paradox and the Language of Morals in La Rochefoucauld." *Modern Language Review* 68, 1 (1973).

———. *Structuralist Poetics.* Ithaca: Cornell University Press, 1975.

———. "Structure of Ideology and Ideology of Structure." *New Literary History* 4, 3 (1973).

De George, Richard, and Fernande De George, ed. *The Structuralists from Marx to Lévi-Strauss.* New York: Doubleday, 1972.

Dijk, Teun A. Van. "Foundation for a Typology of Texts." *Semiotica* No. 4 (1972).

Dilthey, Wilhelm. *Pattern and Meaning in History.* Ed. H.P. Rickman. New York: Harper and Row, 1961.

Donato, Eugene. "Of Structuralism and Literature." *Modern Language Notes* No. 82 (1967).

Douchet, Jean. *Hitchcock.* Paris: Cahier de l'Herne, 1965.

Durgnat, Raymond. *The Strange Case of Alfred Hitchcock or The Plain Man's Hitchcock.* Cambridge, Massachusetts: MIT Press, 1974.

Eagleton, Terry. *Criticism and Ideology; A Study in Marxist Literary Theory.* London: New Left Books, 1976.

———. *Marxism and Literary Criticism.* London: Methuen, 1976.

Eckert, Charles. "The Anatomy of a Proletarian Film: Warner's *Marked Woman.*" *Film Quarterly* 27, 2 (1973–74).

Eco, Umberto. "James Bond: une combinatoire narrative." *Communications* No. 8 (1966).

———. "On the Contribution of Film to Semiotics." *Quarterly Review of Film Studies* 2, 1 (1977).

———. *A Theory of Semiotics.* Bloomington: Indiana University Press, 1976.

Eisenstein, Sergei. *Film Form and the Film Sense.* Trans. and ed. Jay Leyda. New York: World Publishing, 1957.

Ellis, John. "Art, Culture, and Quality—Terms for a Cinema in the Forties and Seventies." *Screen* 19, 3 (1978).

Evans-Pritchard, E.E. *The Nuer.* New York: Oxford University Press, 1940.

Fargier, Jean-Paul. "Parenthesis or Indirect Route." *Screen* 12, 2 (1971).

Feldman, Seth, and Joyce Nelson. *Canadian Film Reader.* Toronto: Peter Martin Associates, 1977.

Fischer, Ernst. *Art Against Ideology.* Trans. Anna Bostock. London: Penguin-Allen Lane, 1969.

Fischer, Lucy. "The Image of Woman as Image: The Optical Politics of *Dames.*" *Film Quarterly* 30, 1 (1976).

Foucault, Michel. *The Order of Things.* New York: Vintage-Random House, 1970.

French Freud: Structural Studies in Psychoanalysis. Yale French Studies No. 48 (1972).

Freud, Sigmund. *The Standard Edition of the Complete Psychological Works of Sigmund Freud.* 24 vols. Trans. James Strachey. London: Hogarth Press, 1953.

Frye, Northrop. *The Anatomy of Criticism.* Princeton, New Jersey: Princeton University Press, 1957.

Ganz, Leo. "Vision." In *Experimental Sensory Psychology.* Ed. Bertram

Selected Sources

Scharf. Glenview, Illinois: Scott Foresman, 1975.

Garnham, Nicholas. *Structures of Television*. London: British Film Institute, 1978.

Garroni, Emilio. "The Heterogeneity of the Aesthetic Object and Problems of Art Criticism." *Afterimage* No. 5 (1974).

Gavron, Laurence. "Jean Rouch 'Revisited.'" *On Film* No. 8 (1978).

Girard, René. *Deceit, Desire, and the Novel*. Trans. Yvonne Freccero. Baltimore: Johns Hopkins University Press, 1965.

Gledhill, Christine. "Recent Developments in Feminist Criticism." *Quarterly Review of Film Studies* 3, 4 (1978).

Godard, Jean-Luc, and Jean-Pierre Gorin. "Excerpts from the Transcript of Godard-Gorin's *Letter to Jane*." *Women and Film* 1, 3/4 (1973).

Goffman, Erving. "Gender Advertisements." *Studies in the Anthropology of Visual Communication* 3, 2 (1976).

———. *The Presentation of Self in Everyday Life*. Garden City, New York: Doubleday, 1959.

Goldman, Lucien. "Ideology and Writing." *Times Literary Supplement*, 28 September 1967.

Gombrich, E.H., *Art and Illusion*. Revised ed. Princeton, New Jersey: Princeton University Press, 1961.

Gombrich, E.H., Julian Hochberg, and Max Black. *Art, Perception, and Reality*. Baltimore: Johns Hopkins University Press, 1972.

Goodman, Nelson. *Languages of Art*. Indianapolis and New York: Bobbs-Merrill, 1968.

———. *Ways of Worldmaking*. Indianapolis and Cambridge: Hackett Publishing, 1978.

Graham, Clarence H., ed. *Vision and Visual Perception*. New York and London: John Wiley and Sons, 1965.

Gregory, R.L. *Eye and Brain*. London: World University Library, 1966.

———. *The Intelligent Eye*. New York: McGraw-Hill, 1970.

Halbertstadt, Ira. "An Interview with Frederick Wiseman." *Filmmakers Newsletter* 7, 4 (1974).

Hall, Stuart. "The Determinations of News Photographs." *Working Papers in Cultural Studies* No. 3 (1972).

Halliburton, David. "The Hermeneutics of Belief and the Hermeneutics of Suspicion." *Diacritics* 6, 4 (1976).

Handelman, Janet. "An Interview with Frederick Wiseman." *Film Library Quarterly* 3, 3 (1970).

Hanson, Norwood. *Patterns of Discovery*. Cambridge: Cambridge University Press, 1961.

———. *Perception and Discovery*. Ed. Williard C. Humphreys. San Francisco: Freeman Cooper, 1969.

Harris, Marvin. *The Rise of Anthropological Theory*. New York: Thomas Y. Crowell, 1968.

Hartman, Geoffrey H. *Beyond Formalism*. New Haven: Yale University Press, 1970.

Harvey, Sylvia. *May '68 and Film Culture*. London: British Film Institute, 1978.

Heath, Stephen. "Lessons From Brecht." *Screen* 15, 2 (1974).

———. "From Brecht to Film—Theses, Problems." *Screen* 16, 4 (1975–76).

———. "Narrative Space." *Screen* 17, 3 (1976).

———. "On Screen, in Frame: Film and Ideology." *Quarterly Review of Film Studies* 1, 3 (1976).

————, ed. *Signs of the Times*. Cambridge: Granta, 1971.

Hebdige, Dick, and Geoff Hurd. "Reading and Realism." *Screen Education* No. 28 (1978).

Heider, Karl G. *Ethnographic Film*. Austin: University of Texas Press, 1977.

Hendricks, W.O. "The Structural Study of Narration." *Poetics* No. 3 (1972).

Hesse, Mary B. *Models and Analogies in Science*. London: Steed and Ward, 1963.

Hochberg, Julian. *Perception*. Englewood Cliffs, N.J.: Prentice-Hall, 1964.

Hockings, Paul, ed. *Principles of Visual Anthropology*. The Hague: Mouton, 1975.

Hogg, James, ed. *Psychology and the Visual Arts*. London: Penguin-Allen Lane, 1969.

Holenstein, E. "Structure of Understanding: Structuralism vs. Hermeneutics." *Poetics of Theory and Literature* No. 1 (1976).

Horkheimer, Max, and Theodor W. Adorno. *Dialectic of Enlightenment*. Trans. John Cumming. New York: Herder and Herder, 1972.

Jacoby, Russell. *Social Amnesia: A Critique of Conformist Psychology from Adler to Laing*. Boston: Beacon Press, 1975.

Jameson, Fredric. *Marxism and Form: Twentieth-Century Dialectical Theories of Literature*. Princeton, New Jersey: Princeton University Press, 1971.

————. "Metacommentary." *PMLA* No. 86 (1971).

————. *The Prison-House of Language*. Princeton, New Jersey: Princeton University Press, 1972.

Johnston, Claire. "Myths of Women in the Cinema." In *Women and the Cinema: A Critical Anthology*. Ed. Karyn Kay and Gerald Peary. New York: E.P. Dutton, 1977.

————, ed. *Notes on Women's Cinema*. London: Society for Education in Film and Television, n.d.

Julesz, Bela. *Foundations of Cyclopean Perception*. Chicago: University of Chicago Press, 1971.

Kaplan, E. Ann, ed. *Women in Film Noir*. London: British Film Institute, 1978.

Katz, John Stuart, ed. *Autobiography: Film/Video/Photography*. Toronto: Art Gallery of Ontario, 1978.

Kaufman, Lloyd. *Sight and Mind: An Introduction to Visual Perception*. New York: Oxford University Press, 1974.

Kay, Karyn, and Gerald Peary. *Women in the Cinema*. New York: E.P. Dutton, 1977.

Kermode, Frank. *The Genesis of Secrecy: On the Interpretation of Narrative*. Cambridge: Harvard University Press, 1979.

Kling, J.W., and Lorrin A. Riggs, ed. *Experimental Psychology*. 2 vols. 3d ed. New York: Holt, Rinehart and Winston, 1972.

Kloeptel, Don V. *Motion-Picture Projection and Theatre Presentation Manual*. New York: Society of Motion Picture and Television Engineers, 1969.

Koestler, Arthur. *The Act of Creation*. 1964. Reprint. London: Picador-Pan Books, 1975.

Koffka, K. *Principles of Gestalt Psychology*. New York: Harcourt, Brace and World, 1935.

Kolers, Paul A. *Aspects of Motion Perception*. Oxford: Pergamon Press, 1972.

———. "The Illusion of Movement." *Scientific American,* October 1964.
Kuhn, Annette. "The Camera I—Observations on Documentary." *Screen* 19, 2 (1978).
———. "Ideology, Structure, and Knowledge." *Screen Education* No. 29 (1978).
Kuhn, Thomas. *The Copernician Revolution: Planetary Astronomy in the Development of Western Thought.* Cambridge: Harvard University Press, 1957.
———. *The Essential Tension.* Chicago: University of Chicago Press, 1977.
———. *The Structure of Scientific Revolutions.* 2d ed. Chicago: University of Chicago Press, 1970.
La Barre, Weston. "Ethology and Ethnology." *Semiotica* 6, 1 (1972).
Lacan, Jacques. *The Language of the Self.* Trans. Anthony Wilden. Baltimore: Johns Hopkins University Press, 1968.
———. "The Mirror-Phase as Formative of the Function of the I." *New Left Review* No. 51 (1968).
de Lauretis, Teresa. "Semiotics, Theory, and Social Practice: A Critical History of Italian Semiotics." *Ciné-Tracts* 2, 1 (1978).
La Valley, Albert J., ed. *Focus on Hitchcock.* Englewood Cliffs, N.J.: Prentice-Hall, 1972.
Leahy, James. "Notes on the Navajo Films." *Film Form* 1, 2 (1977).
Lefebvre, Henri. *The Sociology of Marx.* Trans. Norbert Guterman. New York: Vintage-Random House, 1968.
Leibfried, Erwin. *Kristische Wissenschaft vom Text. Manipulation, Reflektion, transparente Poetologie.* Stuttgart: J.B. Metzerlersche Verlagsbuchhandlung, 1970.
Lemon, Lee T., and Marion J. Reis, trans. and ed. *Russian Formalist Criticism: Four Essays.* Lincoln: University of Nebraska Press, 1965.
Lesage, Julia. "Feminist Film Criticism: Theory and Practice." *Women and Film* No. 5/6, 1974.
———. "The Political Aesthetics of the Feminist Documentary Film." *Quarterly Review of·Film Studies* 3, 4 (1978).
Levin, G. Roy. *Documentary Explorations.* New York: Doubleday, 1971.
Levonian, Edward. "Perceptual Threshold of Discrete Movement in Motion Pictures." *Journal of the Society of Motion Picture Engineers,* No. 71 (1962).
Linton, James. "The Moral Dimension in Documentary." *Journal of the University Film Association* 28, 2 (1976).
Lukács, Georg. *History and Class Consciousness.* Trans. Rodney Livingstone. Cambridge, Massachusetts: MIT Press, 1971.
———. *Realism in Our Time: Literature and the Class Struggle.* Trans. John and Necke Mander. New York: Harper and Row, 1964.
———. *Writer and Critic.* Trans. Arthur D. Kahn. New York: Grosset and Dunlap, 1971.
MacBean, James Roy. *Film and Revolution.* Bloomington: Indiana University Press, 1975.
MacCabe, Colin. "The Politics of Separation." *Screen* 16, 4 (1975/6).
———. "Realism and the Cinema: Notes on Some Brechtian Theses." *Screen* 15, 2 (1974).
———. "Theory and Film: Principles of Realism and Pleasure." *Screen* 17, 3 (1976).
MacDougall, David. "Ethnographic Film: Failure and Promise." *Annual Review of Anthropology* No. 7 (1978).

SELECTED SOURCES

Macksey, Richard, and Eugenio Donato, ed. *The Structuralist Controversy: The Language of Criticism and the Sciences of Man.* Baltimore: Johns Hopkins University Press, 1970.

Mamber, Stephen. *Cinema Verite in America.* Cambridge, Massachusetts: MIT Press, 1974.

Mannheim, Karl. *Ideology and Utopia.* Trans. Louis Wirth and Edward Shils. New York: Harcourt, Brace and World, 1936.

Manz, Hans-Peter. *Alfred Hitchcock.* Zürich: Sanssouci Verlag, 1962.

Marcorelles, Louis. *Living Cinema.* Trans. Isabel Quigly. New York: Praeger Publishers, 1973.

Marx, Karl. *Grundrisse: Foundations of the Critique of Political Economy.* Trans. Martin Nicolaus. Harmondsworth: Penguin-Allen Lane, 1973.

Marx, Karl, and Frederick Engels. *Collected Works.* 3 vols. Moscow: Progress Publishers, 1969.

———. *The German Ideology.* New York: International Publishers, 1970.

McGarry, Eileen. "Documentary, Realism and Women's Cinema." *Women and Film* 2, 7 (1975).

McWilliams, Donald E. "Frederick Wiseman." *Film Quarterly* 24, 1 (1970).

Mead, George H. *Mind, Self and Society.* Ed. Charles M. Morris. Chicago: University of Chicago Press, 1934.

Mead, Margaret. *Growing Up in New Guinea.* 1930. Reprint. New York: William Morrow, 1975.

Metz, Christian. *Film Language.* New York: Oxford University Press, 1974.

———. *Language and Cinema.* The Hague: Mouton, 1974.

Millum, Trevor. "The Study of the Image." *Screen Education* No. 23 (1977).

Mitchell, Juliet. *Psychoanalysis and Feminism.* New York: Random House, 1974.

Mulvey, Laura. "Douglas Sirk and Melodrama." *Australian Journal of Screen Theory* No. 3 (1977).

———. "Visual Pleasure and Narrative Cinema." *Screen* 16, 3 (1975).

Münsterberg, Hugo. *The Film: A Psychological Study.* 1916. Reprint. New York: Dover, 1970.

Naremore, James. *Filmguide to Psycho.* Bloomington: Indiana University Press, 1973.

Nestrick, William. "Primitivism and Film." *University Publishing* No. 6 (1979).

Neuhaus, W. "Experimentelle Untersuchung der Scheinbewegung." *Archiv für gesamte Psychologie* 75 (1930).

Nichols, Bill, ed. *Movies and Methods.* Berkeley and Los Angeles: University of California Press, 1976.

———. *Newsreel: Documentary Filmmaking on the American Left (1971– 75).* New York: Arno Press, 1980.

Nowell-Smith, Geoffrey. "Six Authors in Pursuit of *The Searchers*." *Screen* 17, 1 (1976).

Peritore, N. Patrick. "Descriptive Phenomenology and Film: An Introduction." *Journal of the University Film Association* 29, 1 (1977).

Perkins, David. "A Definition of Caricature and Caricature and Recognition." *Studies in the Anthropology in Visual Communication* 2, 1 (1975).

Perry, George. *The Films of Alfred Hitchcock.* New York: E.P. Dutton, 1965.

Place, Janey, and Julianne Burton. "Feminist Film Criticism." *Movie* No. 22 (1976).

Plamentz, John. *Ideology.* London: Macmillan, 1971.

Selected Sources

Plato. *The Republic*. 2 vols. Trans. Paul Shorey. London: William Heineman, 1930.

Polan, Dana. "Brecht and the Politics of Self-Reflexive Cinema." *Jump Cut* No. 17 (1978).

Popper, Karl. *Conjectures and Refutations: The Growth of Scientific Knowledge*. London: Routledge and Kegan Paul, 1963.

Propp, Vladimir. *Morphology of the Folktale*. Trans. Laurence Scott. Austin: University of Texas Press, 1968.

Pryluck, Calvin. *Sources of Meaning in Motion Pictures and Television*. New York: Arno Press, 1976.

Reisz, Karel. *The Technique of Film Editing*. London and New York: Focal Press, 1958.

Ricoeur, Paul. *Freud and Philosophy: An Essay on Interpretation*. Trans. Denis Savage. New Haven: Yale University Press, 1970.

Roberge, Gaston. *Films for an Ecology of Mind*. Calcutta: Firma KLM, 1977.

Robinson, J.O. *The Psychology of Visual Illusion*. London: Hutchinson, 1972.

Robinson, W.R. *Man and the Movies*. Baton Rouge: Louisiana State University Press, 1967.

Rohmer, Eric, and Claude Chabrol. *Hitchcock*. Paris: Editions Universitaires, 1957.

Rose, Jacqueline. "Paranoia and the Film System." *Screen* 17, 4 (1976/77).

Rosen, Philip, "*Screen* and the Marxist Project in Film Criticism." *Quarterly Review of Film Studies* 2, 3 (1977).

Rosenthal, Alan. *The New Documentary in Action*. Berkeley and Los Angeles: University of California Press, 1972.

Rouch, Jean. "On the Vicissitudes of the Self: The Possessed Dancer, the Magician, the Sorcerer, the Filmmaker, and the Ethnographer." *Studies in the Anthropology of Visual Communication* 5, 1 (1978).

Ruby, Jay. "Anthropology and Film: The Social Science Implications of Regarding Film as Communication." *Quarterly Review of Film Studies* 1, 4 (1976).

———. "The Image Mirrored: Reflexivity and the Documentary Film." *Journal of the University Film Association* 29, 4 (1977).

———. "Is an Ethnographic Film a Filmic Ethnography?" *Studies in the Anthropology of Visual Communication* 2, 2 (1975).

Salt, Barry. "Statistical Style Analysis of Motion Pictures." *Film Quarterly* 28, 1 (1974).

Sarris, Andrew. *The Films of Josef von Sternberg*. New York: The Museum of Modern Art, 1966.

Sartre, Jean-Paul. *Anti-Semite and Jew*. Trans. George J. Becker. New York: Schocken Books, 1948.

———. *Search for a Method*. Trans. Hazel E. Barnes. New York: Vintage-Random House, 1968.

Scholes, Robert. *Structuralism in Literature*. New Haven: Yale University Press, 1974.

Sennett, Richard, and Jonathan Cobb. *The Hidden Injuries of Class*. New York: Random House, 1972.

Sharits, Paul. "Words Per Page." *Afterimage* No. 4 (1972).

Sigman, E., and I. Rock. "Stroboscopic Movement Based on Perceptual Intelligence." *Perception* 3, 1 (1974).

Skidmore, William. *Theoretical Thinking in Sociology*. Cambridge: Cambridge University Press, 1975.

Sontag, Susan. *On Photography*. New York: Farrar, Straus and Giroux, 1977.
Spellerberg, James. "Technology and Ideology in the Cinema." *Quarterly Review of Film Studies* 2, 3 (1977).
Spence, Jo. "What Do People Do All Day?" *Screen Education* No. 29 (1978/79).
Spoto, Donald. *The Art of Alfred Hitchcock*. New York: Hopkins and Blake, 1976.
von Sternberg, Josef. *Fun in a Chinese Laundry*. London: Secker and Warburg, 1965.
Strand, Chick. "Notes on Ethnographic Film by a Film Artist." *Wide Angle* 2, 3 (1978).
Sullivan, Patrick J. "What's All the Crying About? The Films of Frederick Wiseman." *Massachusetts Review* 13, 3 (1972).
Thompson, William Irwin. *At the Edge of History*. New York and Evanston: Harper and Row, 1971.
Todorov, Tzvetan. "The Structural Analysis of Narrative." *Novel* No. 3 (1968).
Truffaut, François. *Hitchcock/Truffaut*. New York: Simon and Schuster, 1968.
Tuchman, Gaye. "Television News and the Metaphor of Myth." *Studies in the Visual Anthropology of Culture* 5, 1 (1978).
Vaughan, Dai. *Television Documentary Usage*. London: British Film Institute, 1976.
Vernon, M.D. *The Psychology of Perception*. London: Penguin-Allen Lane, 1962.
Warshow, Paul. "More Is Less: Comedy and Sound." *Film Quarterly* 31, 1 (1977).
Watzlawick, Paul. *How Real Is Real?: Confusion, Disinformation, Communication*. New York: Random House, 1976.
Watzlawick, Paul, Janet Helmick Beavin, and Don D. Jackson. *Pragmatics of Human Communication: A Study of Interactional Patterns, Pathologies and Paradoxes*. New York: W.W. Norton, 1967.
Waugh, Thomas. "Emile de Antonio and the New Documentary of the Seventies." *Jump Cut* No. 10/11 (1976).
Wertheimer, M. "Experimentelle Studien über das Sehen von Bewegung." *Zeitschrift für Psychologie* No. 61 (1912).
Wilden, Anthony. *System and Structure: Essays in Communication and Exchange*. London: Tavistock, 1972.
Williams, Raymond. *Communications*. London: Penguin-Allen Lane, 1962.
―――. "A Lecture on Realism." *Screen* 18, 1 (1977).
―――. *Marxism and Literature*. Oxford: Oxford University Press, 1977.
Wittgenstein, Ludwig. *Philosophical Investigations*. Trans. G.E.M. Anscombe. Oxford: Basil Blackwell, 1953.
Wollen, Peter. "Counter Cinema: Vent d'Est." *Afterimage* No. 4 (1972).
―――. "Photography and Aesthetics." *Screen* 19, 4 (1978/79).
―――. "*North by North-West*: A Morphological Analysis." *Film Form* 1, 1 (1976).
―――. "'Ontology' and 'Materialism' in Film." *Screen* 17, 1 (1976).
Wollheim, Richard. "The Cabinet of Dr. Lacan." *New York Review of Books*, 25 January 1979.
Wood, Robin. *Hitchcock's Films*. New York: A.S. Barnes, 1969.
―――. *Personal Views: Exploration in Film*. London: Gordon Fraser, 1976.
―――. "Venus de Marlene." *Film Comment* 14, 2 (1978).
Wright, Will. *Sixguns and Society*. Berkeley and Los Angeles: University of California Press, 1975.

Selected Sources   313

Notes

Introduction

1. Peter L. Berger, *Invitation to Sociology: A Humanistic Perspective* (Garden City: Anchor Books, 1963), p. 41.
2. Bertolt Brecht, "Against Georg Lukács," *New Left Review* 84 (March-April 1974):42.
3. Christian Metz, *Language and Cinema,* trans. Donna Jean Umiker-Sebeok (The Hague: Mouton, 1974).
4. "Cinéthique on *Langage et Cinéma,*" *Screen* 14, 1/2 (Spring-Summer 1973):198.

1. Art and the Perceptual Process

1. Fred Camper, "Disputed Passage," in *Movies and Methods,* ed. Bill Nichols (Berkeley and Los Angeles: University of California Press, 1976), p. 341.
2. Julian Hochberg, "The Representation of Things and People," in *Art, Perception, and Reality,* ed. Maurice Mandelbaum (Baltimore: Johns Hopkins University Press, 1972), p. 63.
3. Gregory Bateson, "Style, Grammar, and Information in Primitive Art," in his *Steps to an Ecology of Mind* (New York: Ballantine Books, 1972), p. 139.
4. Berger, *Invitation to Sociology,* p. 35.
5. Charles Horton Cooley, *Human Nature and the Social Order* (New York: Charles Scribner's, 1902), p. 147.
6. Jacques Lacan, "The Mirror-Phase as Formative of the Function of the I," *New Left Review* 51 (Sept.-Oct. 1968):71–77.
7. Bateson, *Steps,* p. 145.
8. George H. Mead, *Mind, Self, and Society,* ed. Charles M. Morris (Chicago: University of Chicago Press, 1934), p. 223n.
9. These "Absolutes" represent a modified version of those listed on p. 321 of James Roy MacBean's *Film and Revolution.* His choice of "Proper Behavior" as the Absolute upheld by the institution of the family, for example, has been changed to the Father to emphasize the central importance of the family in perpetuating sexist ideology.
10. Bateson, "The Logical Categories of Learning and Communication," *Steps,* p. 301.

11. Louis Althusser, "Ideology and Ideological State Apparatuses," in his *Lenin and Philosophy and Other Essays,* trans. Ben Brewster (New York: Monthly Review Press, 1971), p. 172.

12. Sigmund Freud, *Jokes and Their Relation to the Unconscious,* trans. James Stachey (New York: W.W. Norton, 1960), p. 120.

13. Freud, *Jokes,* p. 121.

14. Quoted and translated in Anthony Wilden, *System and Structure: Essays in Communication and Exchange* (London: Tavistock, 1972), p. 66.

2. The Analysis of Representational Images

1. Ferdinand de Saussure, "From *Course in General Linguistics,*" in *The Structuralists: From Marx to Lévi-Strauss,* ed. Richard and Fernande De George (Garden City: Anchor Books, 1972), pp. 71–72.

2. *Metonymy* as it is used in semiotics still refers to part/whole relationships, but the part does not excise the whole from the signifying chain. Instead it follows. Metonymy refers to this sequentiality where the part prepares for what will follow. It involves relationships between materialized presences though they may be temporally or spatially separated, whereas metaphor refers to those relationships between materialized presences (a visible part of the text) and those unmaterialized absences that are alluded to (the invisible aura of a text; those images or associations evoked but not materialized). In the temporal arts metonymy plays with our expectations, metaphor with our associations.

3. Even with written language the case for the primacy of denotation may be open to serious question. Roland Barthes, for example, observes that "the raw material of denotation, with its dictionary and its syntax, is a system like any other; there is no reason to make this system the privileged one, to make it the locus and the norm of a primary, original meaning. . . . [To do so] is to return to the closure of Western discourse (scientific, critical, or philosophical), to its centralized organization, to arrange all the meanings of a text in a circle around the hearth of denotation (the hearth: center, guardian, refuge, light of truth)." Roland Barthes, *S/Z: An Essay,* trans. Richard Miller (New York: Hill and Wang, 1974), p. 7.

4. Whole realms of signification may be entirely overlooked, or only noted impressionistically when their significance reaches fever pitch. The studies in proxemics and kinesics cited in "Selected Sources" provide vivid examples of fully operative codes that are seldom acknowledged for their systematic organization of space and movement into signifying patterns.

5. This point is a central theme in *Ways of Seeing,* parts I and III; each of these 30-minute films is available from the BBC.

6. See Michel Foucault, "Las Meninas," in his *The Order of Things* (New York: Vintage Books, 1970); Daniel Dayan, "The Tutor-Code of Classical Cinema," and William Rothman, "Against the System of the Suture," (a rebuttal), both in *Movies and Methods.*

7. To a large extent this "place" belongs to the masculine gender in our culture. The ease and assurance with which we occupy this place may be very different for women than it is for men. The tradition of the female nude in classic oil painting as an image of availability directed toward the male owner/beholder represents a specific instance of gender as a problem to theories of placement. Many recent theoretical texts in film study and elsewhere ignore this problem and assume that men and women are "placed"

with equal facility by illusionist art. This assumption may be itself symptomatic of uncontested sexist aspects of an ideology otherwise sharply con-
tested.

8. These three possibilities correspond fascinatingly to the interpretations Freud offers for the statement "A child is being beaten": (1) "I am
being beaten by my father," (2) "My father is beating the child I hate," (3) "A
child is being beaten." Each proposes a different relationship involving the
agent, the victim, the placement of the subject, the sado-masochistic content,
and pleasure. And yet all exist within a single, metaphorical utterance.
Analyses along these lines may open up additional understandings of the
viewer's placement in relation to the image, especially the narrative flow of
film images. I am indebted to Steve Fagin for suggesting the possible use of
Freud's paper, "A Child is Being Beaten," to study subject relations in film.

9. "Excerpts from the Transcript of Godard-Gorin's *Letter to Jane*,"
Women and Film 1, 3/4 (1973):48.

10. Bertolt Brecht, "Against Georg Lukács," p. 50.

11. Dana B. Polan, "A Brechtian Cinema? Towards a Politics of Self-
Reflexive Film," *Society for Cinema Studies*, Northwestern University, 25
March 1977.

3. The Cinema: Movement, Narrative, and Paradox

1. Metz, *Language and Cinema*, p. 242.

2. This sense of unity is, of course, a fabrication. There is no solid core,
no kernel of content within the pulpy surround of form, only the meanings
fabricated by this play of differences itself. Roland Barthes makes a similar
point in a discussion of the relation of style to text: "It would be better to see
(the text) as an onion, a construction of layers (or levels, or systems) whose
body contains, finally, no heart, no kernel, no secret, no irreducible principle,
nothing except the infinity of its own envelopes—which envelops nothing
other than the unity of its own surfaces." "Style and Its Image" in *Literary
Style: A Symposium*, ed. Seymour Chatman (London & New York: Oxford
University Press, 1971), p. 10.

3. Bateson's essay "The Logical Categories of Learning and Communication" in *Steps to an Ecology of Mind* offers a vivid example of how "discrimination" as a category of behavior can be made to persist despite failure
or even the impossibility of discrimination in a given context. In this case a
double bind results: "Discriminate even though you cannot possibly discriminate in this context," a situation analogous to that of the schizophrenic.

4. An extended attempt to examine the significance of logical typing for
interaction between characters can be found in Judy M. Miles, "The Semiotic
Self: Ideological Aspects of Communication and Characterization in Films,"
M.A. thesis, Simon Fraser Universtiy, 1979. A more exploratory effort appears in my "Style, Grammar, and the Movies," *Movies and Methods*.

5. See Bateson, *Steps*, especially part 3: "Form and Pathology in Relationship."

6. Paul Ricoeur, *Freud and Philosophy: An Essay on Interpretation*,
trans. Denis Savage (New Haven: Yale University Press, 1970), p. 39.

7. All quotes from Thomas S. Kuhn, "The Relations Between the History and Philosophy of Science," in *The Essential Tension* (Chicago: University of Chicago Press, 1977), pp. 1–20. Will Wright makes a very similar point
regarding narrative as a vital aspect of myth: "The form stories take can be

seen as a paradigm for making sense of life. Not only do stories demonstrate that experience *can* make sense, they also demonstrate *how* it makes sense, by showing that one important event causes another and by ignoring the unimportant events. Narrative *form*—the thing that makes a story a story and not a list of events—is also the form which human consciousness imposes on real experience to give it meaning." *Sixguns and Society* (Berkeley: University of California Press, 1975), p. 193.

8. Wright, *Sixguns,* p. 125.

9. Ibid., p. 129.

10. Bateson, "Style, Grace, and Information in Primitive Art," in *Steps,* p. 129.

11. Bateson, "Form, Substance, and Difference," in *Steps,* p. 461.

12. Reynolds Price, *A Palpable God: Thirty Stories Translated from the Bible with an Essay on the Origins and Life of Narrative* (New York: Atheneum, 1978), p. 34.

13. Stephen Heath, "On Screen, In Frame: Film and Ideology," *Quarterly Review of Film Studies* 1, 3 (August 1976):262.

14. Some, but by no means all, of the articles developing these analogies include: Charles Altman, "Psychoanalysis and Cinema: The Imaginary Discourse," *Quarterly Review of Film Studies* 2, 3 (August 1977):257–72 (This article is largely critical of the use of these analogies. It is included because it discusses problems of analogy specifically. A list of other articles critical of the analogies developed in the articles cited here would be too long for inclusion.); Jean-Louis Baudry, "Ideological Effects of the Basic Cinematographic Apparatus," *Film Quarterly* 28, 2 (Winter 1974–75); Jean-Louis Baudry, "The Apparatus," *Camera Obscura* (Fall 1976): 104–26; Daniel Dayan, "The Tutor-Code of Classical Cinema," *Film Quarterly* 28, 1 (Fall 1974), reprinted in *Movies and Methods;* Stephen Heath, "On Screen, In Frame: Film and Ideology," *Quarterly Review of Film Studies* 1, 3 (August 1976); Stephen Heath, "Narrative Space," *Screen* 17, 3 (Autumn 1976); Colin MacCabe, "Realism and the Cinema: Notes on Some Brechtian Theses," *Screen* 15, 2 (Summer 1974); Colin MacCabe, "The Politics of Separation," *Screen* 16, 4 (Winter 1975–76); Colin MacCabe, "Theory and Film, Principles of Realism and Pleasure," *Screen* 17, 3 (Autumn 1976); Christian Metz, "The Imaginary Signifier," *Screen* 16, 2 (Summer 1975); Laura Mulvey, "Visual Pleasure and Narrative Cinema," *Screen* 16, 3 (Autumn 1975).

15. The emphasis falls on direct address here since indirect address (which lacks interviews and commentary) straddles the boundary between narrative and exposition and presents a more difficult task for analysis. This problem is taken up in detail in the discussion of Frederick Wiseman's documentaries in chapter 7.

16. As early as 1916 much was made of this relationship in a slender book by Hugo Münsterberg (*The Film: A Pyschological Study.* Reprint. New York: Dover, 1970). Münsterberg stressed not the representationalism of the film but its externalization of the mind's "own" (i.e., ideologically informed) processes of thought: "It is as if reality has lost its own continuous connection and become shaped by the demands of our soul" (p. 41). "Events which are far distant from one another so that we could not be physically present at all of them at the same time are fusing in our field of vision, just as they are brought together in our own consciousness" (p. 46). "The photoplay cannot only 'cut back' in the service of memories, but it can cut off in the service of suggestion" (p. 47).

17. *Diegesis* derives from the Greek word for narrative. Using it allows

us to designate the imaginary world of the fiction without building in a bias toward realism or even illusionism, as the word *mimesis* does. The concept of a diegesis emphasizes the fabrication of this imaginary realm, its lack of immediate (unmediated) transparency with any external reality, and guards against the danger of short-circuit leaps between reality and realism.

18. The *grande syntagmatique* is a catalogue of all possible sequence types in the classical narrative film on the basis of how each type of sequence treats the disposition of time. Metz describes the catalogue in detail in chapters 5 and 6 of *Film Language*.

19. Daniel Dayan, "The Tutor-Code of Classical Cinema," and William Rothman, "Against the System of the Suture," in *Movies and Methods*.

20. Articles include: Richard Abel, "Paradigmatic Structures in *Young Mr. Lincoln*," *Wide Angle* 2, 4 (1978); Ron Abramson and Rick Thompson, "*Young Mr. Lincoln* Reconsidered: An Essay on the Theory and Practice of Film Criticism," *Ciné-Tracts* 2, 1 (Fall 1978); Ben Brewster, "Notes on the Text, *Young Mr. Lincoln*, by the Editors of *Cahiers du Cinéma*," *Screen* 14, 3 (Autumn 1973); Nick Browne, "*Cahiers du Cinéma*'s Rereading of Hollywood Cinema: An Analysis of Method," *Quarterly Review of Film Studies* 3, 3 (Summer 1978); Nick Browne, "The Spectator of American Symbolic Forms: Re-Reading John Ford's *Young Mr. Lincoln*," *Film Reader* 4 (1979); *Cahiers du Cinéma* editors, "John Ford's *Young Mr. Lincoln*," *Screen* 13, 3 (Autumn 1972); Brian Henderson, "Critique of Cine-Structuralism, Part II," *Film Quarterly* 27, 2 (Winter 1973–74); Bill Nichols, "Style, Grammar, and the Movies," *Film Quarterly* 28, 3 (Spring 1975); J. A. Place, "*Young Mr. Lincoln*, 1939," *Wide Angle* 2, 4 (1978); Peter Wollen, "Afterword," *Screen* 13, 3 (Autumn 1972).

21. For additional elaboration of these qualities see Peter Wollen, "Counter-Cinema: *Vent d'Est*," *Afterimage* 4 (Autumn 1972):7–16.

22. Raymond Durgnat, *The Strange Case of Alfred Hitchcock or The Plain Man's Hitchcock* (Cambridge, Mass.: MIT Press, 1974), p. 80.

23. Roland Barthes, *S/Z*, p. 19.

24. Contrariwise, this very play across boundaries (actor/character/actor-star—and the "image" thereby fixed in place) allows for an ambiguity, a hide-and-seek play of referrals from one level to another, what Stephen Heath terms "figure," illustrated by the play between Orson Welles and his character-role, Quinlan, and Marlene Dietrich and her character-role, Tanya, in *Touch of Evil* (Stephen Heath, "Film and System: Terms of Analysis, Part II," *Screen* 16, 2 [Summer 1975]:105–6).

25. Vladimir Propp, *Morphology of The Folktale*, trans. Laurence Scott (Austin: University of Texas Press, 1968), pp. 21–24.

26. Claude Bremond, *Logique du recit* (Paris: Seuil, 1973).

27. Paul Watzlawick, Janet Helmick Beavin, and Don D. Jackson, *Pragmatics of Human Communication: A Study of Interactional Patterns, Pathologies, and Paradoxes* (New York: W.W. Norton, 1967), pp. 21–22.

28. Watzlawick, *Pragmatics*, pp. 51–52.

29. Fred Davis, "Deviance Disavowal," in *The Other Side: Perspectives in Deviance*, ed. Howard S. Becker (New York: Collier-Macmillan, 1964), pp. 120–21.

30. Wilden, *System and Structure*, p. 103.

31. Gregory Bateson, *Mind and Nature: A Necessary Unity* (New York: E.P. Dutton, 1979), pp. 116–17.

32. Wilden, *System and Structure*, p. 103.

33. Watzlawick et al., *Pragmatics*, p. 194.

34. Ibid., p. 195.

35. Arthur Koestler, *The Act of Creation* (1964. Reprint. London: Pan Books, 1975).

36. Ibid., p. 35.

37. Ibid., p. 88.

38. Charles Eckert, "The Anatomy of a Proletarian Film: Warner's *Marked Woman*," *Film Quarterly* 27, 2 (Winter 1973–74):18.

39. Claude Lévi-Strauss, "The Structural Study of Myth," in *The Structuralists*, p. 193.

40. Nichols, "Style, Grammar, and the Movies," *Movies and Methods*.

41. Bateson, *Steps*, p. 217.

42. Ibid., p. 218.

43. Koestler makes an intriguing observation on some of the qualities of logical opposition:

> The so-called law of contradiction in logic—that a thing is either A or not-A but cannot be both—is a late acquisition in the growth of individuals and cultures. The unconsious mind, the mind of the child and the primitive, are indifferent to it. So are the Eastern philosophies which teach the unity of opposites, as well as Western theologians and quantum physicists. The addicts (of a television drama) who insist on believing in the reality of (one of the characters) have merely carried one step further the momentary split-mindedness experienced by a sophisticated movie-audience at the climax of a Hitchcock thriller; they live in a more or less permanently bisociated world."—*The Act of Creation*, p. 303.

44. Sigmund Freud's *Interpretation of Dreams* is the key work, but in *Jokes and Their Relationship to the Unconscious* he extends many of the same concepts of dream-work to explain joke-work. He notes, "The psychogenesis of jokes has taught us that the pleasure in a joke is derived from play with words or from the liberation of nonsense, and that the meaning of the joke is merely intended to protect that pleasure from being done away with by criticism" (Norton edition, 1963, p. 131). Likewise, narrative creates pleasure and, through its form, shields it from criticism. Narrative operates like jokes and myth to disarm a rigorous logic capable of scoffing at its embroilment in contradiction.

45. Ricoeur, *Freud and Philosophy*, p. 400.

46. Emile Benveniste, *Problèmes de linguistique générale* (Paris: Gallimard, 1966), p. 86. Benveniste also notes, "the unconscious uses a veritable 'rhetoric' which, like style, has its 'figures' . . ." (p. 86).

47. Jacques Derrida, "Structure, Sign, and Play in the Discourse of the Human Sciences," in *The Structuralist Controversy: The Language of Criticism and the Sciences of Man*, ed. Richard Macksey and Eugenio Donato (Baltimore: Johns Hopkins University Press, 1970), p. 248.

48. Bateson in *Steps* and Watzlawick et al. in *Pragmatics of Human Communication* discuss this possibility in relation to the use of "therapeutic double binds" during psychotherapy; and in *The Essential Tension*, Thomas S. Kuhn points out that Galileo's thought-experiments created puzzles involving the difficulties in Aristotle's ideas of motion that appeared to have mutually contradictory solutions: "Galileo's thought-experiments brought the difficulty to the fore by confronting readers with the paradox implicit in their mode of thought. As a result, it helped them to modify their conceptual apparatus" (p. 251).

4. *Blonde Venus:* Playing with Performance

1. Wilhelm Dilthey, *Pattern and Meaning in History,* ed. H.P. Rickman (New York: Harper & Row, 1961), p. 25.

2. See Paul Ricoeur's discussion of intentionality and the unconscious, especially in relation to Merleau-Ponty's notion of flesh: when meaning exists without being conscious, its mode of being is that of the body. In *Freud and Philosophy,* pp. 378–83.

3. Ibid., p. 34.

4. Quoted and translated in Ricoeur, *Freud and Philosophy,* p. 394n.

5. In *Perception, Theory, and Commitment: The New Philosophy of Science* (Chicago: Precedent Publishing, 1977), Harold I. Brown argues the need for a dialectical logic in the understanding of scientific research. Such a logic, he says, "does not provide a set of formal rules for analyzing the relationships between statements, as does deductive logic, but let us recall that the reason why formal rules are of central importance for deductive logic is that deduction is concerned only with formal relations, not content. A dialectic logic, however, is a content logic, not a formal logic. . . . What the concept of a dialectic logic provides, then, is a tool for examining the structure of research in terms of the historical context" (p. 134).

6. Andrew Sarris, *The John Ford Movie Mystery* (Bloomington: Indiana University Press, 1975), p. 183.

7. See Jean-Luc Commolli and Jean Narboni, "Cinema/Ideology/Criticism," *Screen* 12, 1 (Spring 1971), reprinted in *Movies and Methods.*

8. *Cahiers du Cinéma* editors, "John Ford's *Young Mr. Lincoln.*"

9. Louis Gianetti, *Understanding Movies,* 2d ed., (Englewood Cliffs, New Jersey: Prentice-Hall, 1976), p. 15.

10. James Monaco, *How to Read a Film* (New York: Oxford University Press, 1977), p. 169.

11. Calvin Pryluck, *Sources of Meaning in Motion Pictures and Television* (New York: Arno Press, 1976), pp. 76–77.

12. Jonathan Culler, "Structure of Ideology and Ideology of Structure," *New Literary History* 4, 3 (Spring 1973), p. 477. Strictly speaking, Culler's recourse to relativism is incorrect. Attempts to generate logical proofs for any system do indeed lead to paradox and hence inconclusiveness but, nonetheless, there is an ultimate and absolute justification for a system: namely, the long-range survival of both a system and its environment. Any system that destroys its environment must also destroy itself; any system that fails to contribute to long-range survival, that fails to yield wisdom, will be discarded, or, as a contribution to false epistemology, aid and abet the kinds of destruction that we see around us at every turn. A game theory of critical relativism can only legitimate itself as a closed system isolated from any larger social or historical context.

13. Ibid.

14. Kristen Thompson and David Bordwell, "Space and Narrative in the Films of Ozu," *Screen* 17, 2 (Summer 1976):73.

15. Ben Brewster, "Editorial," *Screen* 17, 2 (Summer 1976):7.

16. Thompson and Bordwell, "Ozu," p. 63.

17. Richard Griffith, "The Film Since Then," an additional section to Paul Rotha, *The Film Till Now* (1930, revised 1949. Reprint. London: Spring Books, 1967), p. 474.

18. Andrew Sarris, *The Films of Josef von Sternberg* (New York: The Museum of Modern Art, 1966), p. 36.

19. Laura Mulvey, "Visual Pleasure and Narrative Cinema," p. 11.

20. Roland Barthes, *The Pleasure of the Text*, trans. Richard Miller (New York: Hill and Wang, 1975), p. 9.

21. Laura Mulvey dissects this act of disavowal with great precision:

in psychoanalytic terms, the female figure poses a deeper problem (than being a simple object for visual pleasure). She also connotes something that the look continually circles around but disavows: her lack of a penis, implying a threat of castration and hence unpleasure. Ultimately, the meaning of woman is sexual difference, the absence of the penis as visually ascertainable, the material evidence on which is based the castration complex essential for the organization of entrance to the symbolic order and the law of the father. Thus the woman as icon, displayed for the gaze and enjoyment of men, the active controllers of the look, always threatens to evoke the anxiety it originally signified. The male unconscious has two avenues of escape from this castration anxiety: preoccupation with the re-enactment of the original trauma (investigating the woman, demystifying her mystery), counterbalanced by the devaluation, punishment or saving of the guilty object . . . or else complete disavowal of castration by the substitution of a fetish object or turning the represented figure itself into a fetish so that it becomes reassuring rather than dangerous (hence overvaluation, the cult of the female star). [Mulvey, "Visual Pleasure," pp. 13–14.]

22. Ibid.

23. Wilden, *System and Structure*, p. 287. See pp. 283–89 generally for a lucid account of the general question of "The Phallus as the Instrument of Exploitation."

24. *Cahiers* editors, "Young Mr. Lincoln," *Movies and Methods*, p. 522. *Cahiers*, though, fails to note how common the suppression of labor, actual work, is to the Hollywood cinema, considering it instead to be an effect peculiar to John Ford's idiolect or style.

5. For *The Birds*

1. Peter Wollen, "Counter Cinema: *Vent d'Est*," p. 7.

2. Laura Mulvey, "Visual Pleasure."

3. Raymond Durgnat, for example, writes, "The birds, like the blitz, force people back on to their bedrock qualities, and, although shocking and humiliating them, bring out the extent to which humanity, in a tight corner, is 'all right'" (*The Strange Case of Alfred Hitchcock*, p. 339). By contrast, Donald Spoto extols the physical courage of Tippi Hedren for enduring real bird attacks as much as Hitchcock's moral vision, *The Art of Alfred Hitchcock* (New York: Hopkinson and Blake, 1976), pp. 392–93.

4. Robin Wood exemplifies this approach in his book, *Hitchcock's Films* (New York: Paperback Library, 1969).

5. See note 8 of chapter 2 for a suggested link between this triangulated gaze of camera/character/viewer and Freud's analysis of a single, equally complex utterance, "A child is being beaten."

6. The Documentary Film and Principles of Exposition

1. Elizabeth Sussex, "Grierson on Documentary," *Film Quarterly* 26, 1 (Fall 1972):24.
2. Henry Breitrose, review of *Documentary* by Eric Barnouw, *Film Quarterly* 28, 4 (Summer 1975):38.
3. Jean-Paul Fargier, "Parenthesis or Indirect Route," *Screen* 12, 2 (Summer 1971):137.
4. Metz, *Film Language*, pp. 94–95.
5. William Sloan, "The Documentary Film and the Negro," in *The Documentary Tradition*, ed. Lewis Jacobs (New York: Hopkinson and Blake, 1971), p. 425.
6. These proofs are discussed in Book I, Chapter II of Aristotle's *Rhetoric.*
7. I am indebted to Maaret Koskinen for this analysis of television advertising in the CBS News. She originally prepared and delivered this material as part of a program recorded on videotape for our first-year film course at Queen's University.
8. Dai Vaughan makes a similar point in *Television Documentary Usage*, p. 16.
9. Kenneth Burke, *A Rhetoric of Motives* (Berkeley and Los Angeles: University of California Press, 1969), p. 41.
10. Ibid., p. 55.
11. By cinéma vérité I mean that kind of film making represented by the work of Leacock-Pennebaker, Wiseman, the Maysles brothers, and others, where the entire film is built around characters in sync and indirect address. Other forms of cinéma vérité such as Rouch's work, film from the Canadian National Film Board, Allan King, etc., tend to mix modes more freely and represent less clearly a pole or extreme possibility. This does not represent any kind of judgment about the films; it simply seems useful as a descriptive or taxonomic procedure.
12. Brian Henderson, "Two Types of Film Theory," *Film Quarterly* 24, 3 (Spring 1971):33–42, reprinted in *Movies and Methods.*
13. Metz, *Film Language*, p. 115.
14. Metz, *Language and Cinema*, p. 201.
15. Third World Newsreel distributes the film under this name. I believe this is the same film as the one called *Some Evidence (Vai Toibac Cua de Quoc My*, 1969) in Erik Barnouw: *Documentary: A History of the Non-Fiction Film* (New York and London: Oxford University Press, 1975), p. 274.
16. Sequence-localized commentary by characters in *Attica* (Firestone, 1972) supports the call to redefine diegesis in documentary. Sequences are intercut or alternate, but rather than proposing any kind of temporal matching (in fact a temporal disparity is made evident by various cues) as such cross-cutting may do in Metz's *grande syntagmatique*, the editing establishes a continuity of logical argument. The editing relationship between sequences replaces bridging devices, which rely on a narrator, missing here, but serve the same purpose. Firestone's tactic is carried to an even greater extreme in John Lowenthal's *The Trial of Alger Hiss* (1979).
17. For additional discussion of this film see Dan Georgakis, "Finally Got the News," *Cineaste* 5, 4 (1973):2–6.

7. Frederick Wiseman's Documentaries: Theory and Structure

1. Other Wiseman films include: *The Cool World* (1963), Fred Wiseman, producer, Shirley Clarke, director; *Essene* (1972), about a Benedictine monastery; *Meat* (1976), about a slaughterhouse/packing plant; *Canal Zone* (1977); and *Maneuvers* (1979), about a NATO combat exercise in West Germany. This paper is based on an analysis of all Wiseman-directed films except *Welfare, Primate, Meat, Canal Zone,* and *Maneuver.* Except for *Welfare,* which I have not seen, these other films seem to pose significantly different problems of analysis and may require different hypotheses about their structure.

2. Stephen Mamber, *Cinema Verite in America* (Cambridge, Mass.: MIT Press, 1974), p. 4.

3. This argument is further elaborated in Eileen McGarry's "Documentary, Realism, and Women's Cinema," *Women and Film* 2, 7 (Summer 1975):50–58.

4. Barry Salt, "Statistical Style Analysis of Motion Pictures," *Film Quarterly* 28, 1 (Fall 1974):21.

5. See, for example, Peter Fischer, *Mosaic: History and Technique* (London: Thames and Hudson, 1971).

6. Will Wright, *Sixguns and Society,* p. 126.

7. Christian Metz, *Film Language,* pp. 127–28.

8. Ibid., p. 129.

9. Ibid., p. 130.

10. Propp, *Morphology of the Folktale,* p. 21.

11. Bateson, *Steps,* p. 68. This concept is discussed on several occasions in the selection of articles on "Form and Pattern in Anthropology."

12. See Stephen Heath, "Film and System: Terms of Analysis, Part II," *Screen* 16, 2 (Summer 1975):102–6.

13. Ibid., p. 105.

14. The editors of *Cahiers du Cinéma,* "John Ford's *Young Mr. Lincoln,*" *Screen* 13, 3, reprinted in *Movies and Methods.*

15. Wilden, *System and Structure,* p. 356.

16. The notion of role playing is best developed by Erving Goffman. Stephen Potter originally explored the idea of ploying, and Peter L. Berger applies Potter's ideas to sociological theory in *Invitation to Sociology* (New York: Doubleday, 1963), pp. 131–34.

17. Donald E. McWilliams, "Frederick Wiseman," *Film Quarterly* 24, 1:25.

18. Personal communication with Fred Wiseman, 4 November 1977.

19. A comprehensive taxonomy of point-of-view figures appears in Edward Brannigan's "Formal Permutations of the Point-of-View Shot," *Screen* 16, 3 (Autumn 1975):54–64.

20. Metz, *Film Language,* p. 126.

21. These Godardian strategies are discussed in Brian Henderson's "Towards a Non-Bourgeoise Camera Style," *Movies and Methods,* pp. 422–38.

8. Documentary, Criticism, and the Ethnographic Film

1. Historical reconstructions like *Nanook of the North* or the *Netsilik Eskimo* series pose special problems since that which was is re-presented as that which is. History is not recorded but reconstructed to a much greater

degree than when a unique situation or event occurs in front of a camera for the first time. But the historical reconstruction trails into the reconstructed history *(Triumph of the Will)* and the documentary into the fiction film *(Battleship Potemkin, The Rise to Power of Louis XIV)*. Sorting through these questions of degree and kinship must be reserved for another occasion.

2. See Patrick Watson, "Challenge for Change," in *Canadian Film Reader*, ed. Seth Feldman and Joyce Nelson (Toronto: Peter Martin Associates, 1977), pp. 112–19 and Marie Kurchak, "What Challenge? What Change?" in *Canadian Film Reader*, pp. 120–28.

3. David MacDougall, "Ethnographic Film: Failure and Promise," *Annual Review of Anthropology* 7 (1978):419.

4. Jay Ruby, "Is an Ethnographic Film a Filmic Ethnography?" *Studies in the Anthropology of Visual Communication* 2, 2 (1975):105.

5. John W. Adams, "Viewing Practices/Ethnographic Films," typescript made available courtesy of the author, p. 4. Published as "Representation and Context in Ethnographic Film," *Film Criticism* 4, no. 1 (Fall 1979):89–100.

6. Ruby, "Is an Ethnographic Film a Filmic Ethnography?" p. 107.

7. These problems and others are well analyzed in Annette Kuhn's "The Camera I: Observations on Documentary," *Screen* 19, 2 (1978):71–83.

8. Thomas S. Kuhn, *The Structure of Scientific Revolutions*, 2d. ed., (Chicago: University of Chicago Press, 1962), p. 2.

9. Thomas S. Kuhn, "Concepts of Cause in the Development of Physics," in *The Essential Tension: Selected Studies in Scientific Tradition and Change* (Chicago: University of Chicago Press, 1977), p. 29.

10. Kuhn, *Scientific Revolutions*, p. 6.

11. Paul Feyerabend, *Against Method: Outline of an Anarchistic Theory of Knowledge* (London: New Left Books, 1975).

12. Ibid., pp. 153–54.

13. Ibid., p. 155.

14. See "Logic of Discovery or Psychology of Research," in *The Essential Tension*, pp. 266–92.

15. Ibid., p. 292.

16. Ibid.

17. Feyerabend, *Against Method*, p. 32.

18. Ibid., p. 167.

19. Kuhn, "Comment on the Relations of Science and Art," in *The Essential Tension*, p. 342.

20. See "Freud and Lacan," in *Lenin and Philosophy and Other Essays*, trans. Ben Brewster (New York: Monthly Review Press, 1971), pp. 189–219.

21. Ibid., p. 198.

22. See Karl Popper, *Conjectures and Refutations: The Growth of Scientific Knowledge* (London: Routledge and Kegan Paul, 1963), especially chapter 1.

23. Ibid., p. 37.

24. Kuhn, "Logic of Discovery," p. 275.

25. Ibid., pp. 275–76.

26. Dai Vaughn approaches this formulation in his monograph on British television documentary. He describes documentary as "a movement toward mystical union between putative and pro-filmic events and between pro-filmic event and diegesis—unions which, though they may be approached, may never be consummated. It is a quest for a medium wholly transparent to the world yet still able to function as discourse" *Television Documentary Usage*, p. 26.

27. Karl G. Heider, *Ethnographic Film* (Austin: University of Texas Press, 1976), p. 35.

28. Ibid., p. 79.

29. William Irwin Thompson, *At the Edge of History* (New York and Evanston: Harper & Row, 1971), p. 75.

30. See Paul Warshow, "More is Less: Comedy and Sound," *Film Quarterly* 31, 1 (Fall 1977):38–45.

31. Kuhn, "Logic of Discovery," p. 279.

32. William Skidmore, *Theoretical Thinking in Sociology* (Cambridge: Cambridge University Press, 1975), p. 54.

33. Ibid., p. 43.

34. This formulation approximates Eisenstein's distinction between representation and image although the particular representations need not be made as devoid of information, or at least meaning, as Eisenstein's montage theories made them. He writes, " . . . each montage piece exists no longer as something unrelated, but as a given *particular representation* of a general theme that in equal measure penetrates *all* the shot-pieces. The juxtaposition of these partial details in a given montage construction calls to life and forces into the light that *general* quality in which every detail has participated and which binds together all the details into a *whole,* namely, into that generalized *image,* wherein the creator, followed by the spectator, experiences the theme. . . . A work of art, understood dynamically, is just this process of arranging images in the feelings and mind of the spectator" [italics his] Sergei Eisenstein, "Word and Image," in *Film Form and The Film Sense,* ed. and trans. Jay Leyda (New York: World Publishing Co., 1957), pp. 11, 17.

35. Skidmore, *Theoretical Thinking,* p. 15.

36. Ibid., p. 71.

37. Nelson Goodman advances the notion that truth can appear in several forms and that no one form is privileged absolutely. (Interestingly, these forms seem to correspond roughly to the three linchpins: exposition, narrative, and poetics.) "Truth, moreover, pertains solely to what is said, and literal truth to what is said literally. We have seen, though, that worlds are made not only by what is said literally but also by what is said metaphorically, and not only by what is said either literally or metaphorically, but also by what is exemplified or expressed—by what is shown as well as by what is said. In a scientific treatise, literal truth counts most, but in a poem or novel, metaphorical or allegorical truth may matter more. . . ." Nelson Goodman, *Ways of Worldmaking* (Indianapolis, Cambridge: Hackett Publishing Co., 1978), p. 18.

38. David MacDougall, "Beyond Observational Cinema," in *Principles of Visual Anthropology,* ed. Paul Hockings (The Hague: Mouton, 1975), pp. 118–19.

39. Jean Rouch's films include: *Les Maîtres Fous* (1953), *Jaguar* (1953), *Moi un Noir* (1957), *La Pyramide Humaine* (1959), *Chronicle of a Summer* (1960), *The Lion Hunters* (1965), *Tourou and Bitti* (1971), *Cocorico, Monsieur Poulet* (1974), *Babtou* (1976).

David and Judith MacDougall's films include: *Indians and Chiefs* (1972), *Nawi* (1970), *To Live with Herds* (1973), *Under the Men's Tree* (1974), *Kenya Boran* (1974, made by David MacDougall and James Blue), *Good-bye, Old Man* (1977), *The Wedding Camels* (1978), *Lorang's Way* (1978), *To Get That Country* (1978), *Takeover* (1979).

40. Gregory Bateson, "Experiments in Thinking about Observed Ethnological Material," in *Steps,* pp. 73–87.

41. In *Mind and Nature* (E.P. Dutton, 1979), Bateson offers a succinct

account of the relation between description and explanation. He says that tautology involves making valid connections between propositions, then adds, "Tautology contains no information whatsoever, and explanation (the mapping of description onto tautology) contains only the information that was present in the description. The 'mapping' asserts implications that the links which hold the tautology together correspond to relations which obtain in the description. Description, on the other hand, contains information but no logic and no explanation. For some reason, human beings enormously value this combining of ways of organizing information or material," p. 82.

42. Walter Benjamin, "A Short History of Photography," trans. Stanley Mitchell, *Screen* 13, 1 (Spring 1972):5–26.

43. See, for example, the detailed analysis of a photograph and its caption of Jane Fonda in Vietnam conducted by Jean-Luc Godard and Jean-Pierre Gorin in *Letter to Jane* (1972).

44. A comprehensive discussion of *The Ax Fight*, to which I am indebted, occurs in Hart Cohen's "Mapping Anthropology on Film," *Ciné-Tracts* 2, 2 (Spring 1979):62–73.

45. Roland Barthes dissects this myth in *Mythologies* (London: Jonathan Cape, 1972).

46. Colin MacCabe, "Theory and Film: Principles of Realism and Pleasure," *Screen* 17, 3 (Autumn 1976):13.

47. See Northrop Frye, *Anatomy of Criticism* (New York: Atheneum, 1969).

48. Bateson, "A Theory of Play and Fantasy," *Steps*, p. 180.

49. MacDougall, in *Principles of Visual Anthropology*, p. 119.

50. William Skidmore develops this distinction in *Theoretical Thinking about Sociology*. He states at one point that "perspectives are collections of concepts which are important basically as 'sensitizing agents'," and then adds, "Perspectives are separated from pattern and deductive theories not by matters of kind so much as matters of degree. . . . They point out important aspects of reality. But perspectives are relatively less coherent and developed internally" (p. 65). Interpretation is the application of the descriptive or explanatory content of a theory to a real situation (p. 70).

51. Skidmore, *Theoretical Thinking*, p. 210.

52. See, for example, Julia Lesage, "The Political Aesthetics of the Feminist Documentary Film," *Quarterly Review of Film Studies* 3, 4 (Fall 1978):507–23.

Conclusion

1. Northrop Frye, *Anatomy of Criticism* (New York: Atheneum, 1969), p. 348.

2. Henri Bergson, "Laughter," in *Comedy*, introduction and appendix by Wylie Sypher (Garden City: Anchor-Doubleday, 1956), p. 160.

3. Peter L. Berger, *Invitation to Sociology: A Humanistic Perspective* (Garden City: Anchor-Doubleday, 1963), p. 150.

4. Frye, *Anatomy*, p. 347.

5. Bergson, "Laughter," p. 162.

6. Ernst Fischer, *Art against Ideology*, trans. Anna Bostock (London: Penguin, 1969), p. 57.

7. James Roy MacBean, *Film and Revolution* (Bloomington: Indiana University Press, 1975), p. 3.

Appendix A

1. Positive afterimages are usually followed, perceptually, by negative afterimages. These reverse brightness and color relations: for example, bright becomes dark, colors become their complement (e.g., red shifts to blue-green). Such a phenomenon is only rarely observed in film: it is clearly not central to the perception of movement. For a treatment of these and other visual phenomena, see Clarence H. Graham, ed., *Vision and Visual Perception* (New York: John Wiley & Sons, 1965).

2. Clarence H. Graham, ed., *Vision and Visual Perception* (New York: John Wiley & Sons, 1965), pp. 69–70. Also see Lloyd Kaufman, *Sight and Mind: An Introduction to Visual Perception* (New York: Oxford University Press, 1974) for an explanation of visual flicker utilizing linear systems analysis.

3. Leo Ganz, "Vision," in *Experimental Sensory Psychology*, ed. Bertram Scharf (Glenview, Illinois: Scott, Foresman and Co., 1975), p. 240.

4. In dim light the different wavelengths of light have separate thresholds, but as illuminance increases the threshold becomes independent of wavelength.

5. Don V. Kloeptel, ed., *Motion-Picture Projection and Theatre Presentation Manual* (New York: Society of Motion Picture and Television Engineers, 1969), p. 28.

6. Graham, *Vision*, p. 291.

7. Graham, *Vision*, pp. 480–81.

8. Kaufman, *Sight and Mind*, p. 392.

9. In the perception of real movement, for instance, a moving object stimulates all the intermediate points on the retina during its passage from point a to point b. The perception of apparent movement occurs even though the intermediate points on the retina are not stimulated. Also, apparent movement occurs only within certain rates of stimulation across the retina far more limited in range than those under which real movement is perceived. Real movement produces a blur at very rapid speeds whereas apparent movement produces the blurry effect called "phi" at speeds lower than those that yield optimal movement ("beta"). Other marked differences have also been reported, for example, "A line in real movement affects the perceptibility of objects in its path; a line in illusory movement does not" (Paul A. Kolers, "The Illusion of Movement," *Scientific American,* October 1964, p. 6).

10. J.O. Robinson, *The Psychology of Visual Illusion* (London: Hutchinson and Co., 1972).

11. E. Sigman and I. Rock, "Stroboscopic Movement Based on Perceptual Intelligence," *Perception* 3, 1 (1974):9.

12. M. Wertheimer, "Experimentelle Studien über das Sehen von Bewegung," *Zeitschrift für Psychologie* 61 (1912):161–265.

13. J.W. Kling and Lorrin A. Riggs, eds., *Experimental Psychology* (2 vols.; 3d ed.; New York: Holt, Rinehart, Winston, 1972), vol. I: *Sensation and Perception*, p. 527.

14. A summary of Wertheimer's experiment can be found in Kaufman, *Sight and Mind*, pp. 393–94. The debate between structural and Gestalt theories is treated in Julian Hochberg, *Perception* (Englewood Cliffs, N.J.: Prentice-Hall, 1964).

15. This summary is adapted from Kling and Riggs, *Experimental Psy-*

chology, pp. 525–26, and Graham, *Vision*, p. 581.

16. Other effects can be achieved, though in most films they are considered an annoyance. Certain image sequences involving overly large gaps between the successive locations of the stimulus can produce apparently discrete or saltatory movement—abrupt or jumpy movement of the object. Sometimes rapid movements in a shot or jump cuts produce this effect, the result of crossing a perceptual threshold (partly dependent upon the visual angle subtended by the successive stimulus locations at the spectator's eye). For further treatment, see Edward Levonian, "Perceptual Threshold of Discrete Movement in Motion Pictures," *Journal of the Society of Motion Picture Engineers* 71 (April 1962):278–81.

Some filmmakers have deliberately explored questions of apparent movement. *Ray Gun Virus* by Paul Sharits, for example, produces gamma movement of the entire frame, one aspect of its investigation of the flicker phenomenon, while David Rimmer's *Surfacing on the Thames* sets out to eliminate the possibility of beta movement by an elaborate process of freeze-frame printing and lap dissolves.

17. Summarized in Graham, *Vision*, pp. 581–82.

18. W. Neuhaus, "Experimentelle Untersuchung der Scheinbewegung," *Archiv für gesamte Psychologie* 75 (1930):315–458, summarized in Graham, *Vision*, p. 582.

19. J. Beck, A. Elsner, and C. Silverstein, "Position Uncertainty and the Perception of Apparent Movement," *Perception and Psychophysics* 21, 1 (January 1977):33.

20. Levonian, "Perceptual Threshold," p. 280.

21. Jacob Beck and Albert Steven, "An After Effect to Discrete Stimuli Producing Apparent Movement and Succession," *Perception and Psychophysics* 12, 6 (1972):482.

22. Sigman and Rock, "Stroboscopic Movement," p. 9.

23. Sigman and Rock, "Stroboscopic Movement," p. 9.

24. Beck, Elsner, and Silverstein, "Position Uncertainty," p. 37.

25. Jean-Louis Baudry, "Ideological Effects," p. 44.

26. Baudry, "Ideological Effects," p. 43.

27. James Spellerberg, "Technology and Ideology in the Cinema," *Quarterly Review of Film Studies* 2, 3 (August 1977):295.

Index

Note: The small letter "c" refers to captions.

Acculturation, 279, 282
Actions, 82, 87, 90, 92, 93, 181, 212–13, 275, 280
Act of Creation, The, 287
Adams, John W., 243–44, 251
Advertising, and television news, 175
Advertising image, 54c, 57c, 58–62
Aesthetics: 81, 103; of the film, 6; and logical typing, 73; and bisociation, 97; and documentary, 171; in art and science, 248
Afterimages: positive, 294, 296; negative and positive, 327
Agents, 213, 218
Aggression: in *The Birds*, 147c, 148c, 152c, 154, 156, 159
All That Heaven Allows, 86c, 88c, 92, 98, 101
Althusser, Louis, 34, 35, 39, 217–18, 248–49
Ambiguity: 15c, 223, 225, 318; in perception, 22c; in still images, 54–64 passim; in advertising images, 62c, 63; in narrative, 78. *See also* Paradox
Analog, 18c, 32, 78, 238
Analog codes, 47, 48, 56c, 61, 70, 93, 108
Analogical sign. *See* Iconic sign
Analogy, 79, 250
Apparent movement in film, 69, 69n, 70, 293, 293-99 passim, 327
Arbitrary sign: definition of, 11, 239, 241
Art: 77, 266, 287, 290–91; and recognition, 39; and pleasure, 41; and bisociation, 97; and science, 248
Articulations, spatial and temporal, 219–33
Assumptions: in rhetorical proofs, 179
Auteur criticism, 107–8, 110
The Ax Fight, 269, 272–74, 280

Barsam, Richard Meran, 173
Barthes, Roland, 87, 90, 123, 180, 212, 243, 288, 315, 316

Basic Training, 209, 215, 216, 218
Bateson, Gregory, 29, 39, 77, 96, 98, 213, 262, 276, 319
Battle of San Pietro, The, 81, 185–95, 239
Baudry, Jean-Louis, 293, 294, 300, 301
Bazin, André, 10, 84, 172, 196, 200, 208, 210, 240, 294, 299
Benjamin, Walter, 269, 291
Benveniste, Emile, 101, 182
Berger, John, 28, 52, 70
Berger, Peter, 29, 30, 286
Bergson, Henri, 286
Birds, The, 23c, 77, 91, 99, 105
Birdwhistell, Ray, 238–39, 240, 252
Bisociation, 97, 319
Blonde Venus, 16c, 94, 99, 103, 134, 136, 154
Bologna: in textual system, 71
Boundary, 14, 15, 22c, 31–34 passim, 40–49 passim, 53, 61, 215, 217, 234, 318
Bracketed perception: 19, 21, 25, 26, 28, 41; definition of, 12–13
Bracket syntagma, 234
Brannigan, Edward, 89c, 219, 233
Brecht, Bertolt, 6, 57, 64, 67, 68, 101, 110, 126, 301
Breitrose, Henry, 171
Burch, Noel, 219
Burke, Kenneth, 178, 179

Cahiers du Cinéma, 107, 216
Calcutta, 185, 252
Camera angle, 108, 151c
Camera lens, 19–20
Camouflage, 16c, 119
Caricature, 17c
Catharsis, 97
Causality, linear, 212, 216, 234
CBS Evening News, 174–78
CFF (Critical Flicker Frequency), 295, 296, 298, 299
Chagnon, Napoleon, 269, 276–77, 278, 279

Index

Labor-power, 288, 289
Lacan, Jacques, 30, 31, 34, 68, 165, 235, 248, 300
Lack, 74, 90, 211, 244, 266, 280
Law and Order, 209, 215
Letter to Jane, 55c, 63, 81, 200
Lévi-Strauss, Claude, 91, 97, 290
Lighting: low-key, 112, 118–19; high-key, 113
Linear perspective, 19c, 20, 50c, 52c, 159
Lion Hunters, The, 260, 268, 269
Location sound: in documentary, 199–200
Logic: 81, 178, 246; dialectical, 107, 320
Logical typing, 72–73, 93–96 passim, 102, 105, 106, 241, 264, 266, 267, 276, 316

MacBean, James Roy, 291
MacDougall, David: 243, 245, 266, 279, 281; films of Judith and, 325
Magazines, 60–62
Magical Death, 276–79
Magritte, René, 23c, 44c, 50c, 51c
Maids of Honor, The, 88c
Maîtres Fous, Les, 267, 269, 279
Malinowski, Bronislaw, 33
Marcuse, Herbert, 165, 235
Marked Woman, 100, 102, 103
Married Couple, A, 214, 239
Marx, Karl, 9, 34, 106, 133, 213, 216, 285, 288
Marxism, 5, 6, 108, 133-34, 170, 291
Match cuts. *See* Editing
Mead, George H., 34, 282
Mead, Margaret, 243, 262, 264, 268
Meaning: and base/superstructure, 2; and still image, 21, 24, 32, 35; and the sign, 44c, 46; and codes, 47; and narrative, 87, 106–8; and rhetoric, 181; in ethnographic film, 244; as surplus, 252; and the visible, 262–67; essentialist, 274–75; and meta-communication, 276–78; and form, 316; and the flesh, 320. *See also* Textual system
Meta-communication, 93, 95, 96
Metaphor, 29, 123, 216, 234, 315
Metaphor/metonymy, 70–71, 100
Metonymy, 69, 234, 315
Metz, Christian, 6, 70, 81, 82, 112, 172, 173, 179–84 passim, 196, 212, 213
Microcultural Incidents in Ten Zoos, 238–39
Mirror-phase, 30, 31, 75, 300
Mis-recognition, 42
Modernism, 64, 110
Moirê pattern, 48, 48n, 57, 70, 104
Monaco, James, 108, 293
Money, 32, 165–66, 288

Motif, 85, 86c, 119
Movies and Methods, 5
Motivated sign. *See* Iconic sign.
Mulvey, Laura, 113, 134, 321
Munch, Edward, 22c
Münsterberg, Hugo, 317
Myth, 76, 77, 91, 97–98, 246, 275, 278 316–17

Nachträglichkeit, 75. *See also* Forgetting and remembrance, Feedback
Nanook of the North, 260, 323
Narrative: 7, 74, 102, 105, 106, 184, 216, 319; in observational cinema, 209–16, 223–36; as explanation, 267, 269, 273–74, 279, 280. *See also* Classical narrative
Narrative closure, 96, 103, 160–66, 211
Narrative discourse, 82, 91
Narrative-work, 100–103
Netsilik Eskimo series, 242, 269, 274
Newsreel (film-making group), 197–98, 199, 200, 202
Night and the City, 55c, 92
Nodal point, 46, 59, 108, 128
Non-representational images, 49–50
Normal perception: 20, 21, 25, 41, 43, 50c, 85, 87; defined, 12–13; purpose of, 25c, 26
Nuer, The, 251–60, 261, 265, 267

Oil painting, 52, 315
180° rule, 88c
Opposition, 14, 31, 213
Ordinary sequence, 219, 220, 227
Other, the, 34, 35
"Other scene," 83, 88c, 106
Ozu, Yasujiro, 109, 125

Palm Beach Story, The, 99, 103
Paradox: x, 16c, 34, 107, 136n, 138, 140–41, 167, 169, 182, 235, 236, 291, 292, 319, 320; and sense of self, 31; and the imaginary, 33; and pragmatics, 94, 96, 97–103; in documentary, 240–50 passim, 266, 275–84 passim; and art, 287
Paradoxical injunction, 98–103
Paranoia, 31, 135, 159
Perception, 30–33, 36. *See also* Bracketed, Depth, Normal perception
Persistence of vision, 293–97 passim
Perspective. *See* Linear perspective
Phallocentrism, 127, 129, 165–66
Phallus, 129, 288
Phi phenomenon, 297–98
Photograph, 11, 20, 21, 57. *See also* Still image
Photography, 4, 293, 300

Index